Cracking the Kubernetes Interview

Discover expert tips and best practices to ace your Kubernetes technical interviews

Viktor Vedmich

Alexander Dovnar

Cracking the Kubernetes Interview

Portfolio Director: Kartikey Pandey
Relationship Lead: Preet Ahuja
Project Manager: Sonam Pandey
Content Engineer: Apramit Bhattacharya
Technical Editor: Simran Ali
Copy Editor: Safis Editing
Indexer: Tejal Soni
Proofreader: Apramit Bhattacharya
Production Designer: Deepak Chavan
Growth Lead: Amit Ramadas

First published: October 2025

Production reference: 1131025

Published by Packt Publishing Ltd.
Grosvenor House
11 St Paul's Square
Birmingham
B3 1RB, UK.

ISBN 978-1-83546-003-0
www.packtpub.com

To all the curious minds out there, always striving to learn and grow.

This book is the result of years of real-world experience, late-night debugging sessions, and countless conversations about how to make Kubernetes more approachable for everyone.

We dedicate it to the engineers, learners, and builders who believe that knowledge should be shared, not hoarded.

And personally, to my friend and colleague, Viktor Vedmich, with whom I had the privilege of building this work side by side.

— Alexander Dovnar

Foreword

Kubernetes knowledge is everywhere. The real challenge, especially in an interview, is turning what you know into clear, confident answers under pressure. Many strong engineers stumble not because they lack fundamentals, but because they haven't organized their knowledge or practiced how to communicate it effectively. This book is designed to close that gap.

Cracking the Kubernetes Interview book is more than a reference; it's a structured way to organize what you know and make it count when it matters. It combines fundamentals with real-world production context and includes more than 200 practical, interview-style questions, complete with follow-ups, gotchas, and short command or YAML examples. The goal is to give readers a concise, reliable resource they can turn to when preparing for interviews, design reviews, or technical discussions.

What stands out is the balance: thorough coverage of critical areas such as networking, storage, security, deployment strategies, GitOps, observability, and recovery, alongside the common mistakes that often derail strong answers. The troubleshooting frameworks and answer-shaping tips are designed to help you think out loud, demonstrate sound judgment, and move beyond facts to trade-offs—skills that distinguish good candidates from great ones.

So how do you actually get the most out of this guide? Start by systematizing what you know. Use the sections and checklists to organize each area so you can see the bigger picture. Then, practice with intent. Go through the questions out loud, but don't just memorize; focus on the trade-offs and how you'd explain your reasoning. Finally, turn your own experience into stories. Use the patterns in the book to shape real incidents you've faced into clear, outcome-driven answers. That's what makes your knowledge stick, and what makes it shine in an interview.

If you're preparing for an interview where Kubernetes is on the agenda, or you need a reliable reference between meetings, this book will help you organize your knowledge, steer clear of common traps, and communicate with the confidence of someone who runs these systems in production. It does not offer shortcuts; it offers something more valuable: a clear mental model, practical examples, and repeatable ways to reason under pressure.

I recommend it without hesitation.

Viktoria Semaan

Principal Technical Evangelist, Databricks

Contributors

About the authors

Viktor Vedmich is a senior solutions architect at Amazon Web Services (AWS), who helps engineering teams across Central and Eastern Europe design resilient, scalable cloud-native platforms. A hands-on DevOps/SRE leader since 2011, Viktor blends real production experience with clear, practical teaching.

Viktor has conducted 1,000+ technical interviews for DevOps, SRE, and platform roles—designing hiring loops, writing rubrics, and training panels to evaluate real-world Kubernetes skills. On the delivery side, he has built and operated Kubernetes platforms and advised dozens of customers on migrations, multi-tenant clusters, security hardening, cost-aware autoscaling, and GitOps— across both managed services and self-managed clusters.

He holds a master's degree in computer science and certifications in AWS and Kubernetes (CKA and CKS). A frequent conference speaker and community mentor, Viktor focuses on turning complex topics into simple, repeatable patterns you can use on the job and in the interview room.

Alexander Dovnar is a technical leader at Naviteq Ltd., with over a decade of hands-on experience designing, building, and scaling cloud-native infrastructure. His work bridges deep technical expertise in Kubernetes, CI/CD, and cloud automation with a passion for knowledge sharing and mentoring.

Alexander's career has taken him through key roles at companies such as EPAM Systems, where he led DevOps initiatives and shaped deployment strategies for complex systems under tight security and performance constraints. While most of his work is under NDA, his impact spans large-scale platform delivery and team leadership across multiple industries.

He holds a bachelor's degree and maintains AWS Certified Solutions Architect and AWS Certified Security – Specialty certifications. An AWS Community Builder in the containers track, he co-hosts a blog and YouTube channel with Viktor Vedmich, where he shares actionable DevOps practices.

About the reviewers

Kirill Kazakov is a DevOps engineer who began his career as a JavaScript and PHP developer before moving into infrastructure to eliminate deployment pain—much like the fixes in Docker in Practice. He designs Kubernetes platforms, architects cloud-native projects, and guides provider migrations. His work also includes building CI/CD pipelines, enabling GitOps workflows, and implementing observability systems. Kirill actively shares his expertise through conference talks, DevOps courses, and technical articles. Holding CKA and AWS SA certifications, he focuses on creating resilient, efficient, and developer-friendly systems.

Siri Varma Vegiraju is a senior software engineer at Microsoft Azure, where he leads the Network Isolation team, securing over 20 global Azure data centers. With deep, hands-on expertise in cloud infrastructure, security, and developer tooling, Siri builds mission-critical systems that protect some of the world's most sensitive commercial and government workloads. An influential voice in the cloud-native ecosystem, Siri is a core contributor and reviewer for Dapr, a CNCF project used by 40,000 organizations worldwide to build resilient distributed applications. His contributions span both the Java and .NET SDKs, helping shape developer experiences at scale. Siri regularly publishes on DZone, IBM Developer, CNCF, and Cloud Native Now, bringing practical insight to topics such as API security, DevSecOps, and agentic infrastructure. He is also a sought-after speaker, delivering technical sessions at global conferences including DeveloperWeek, IEEE Cloud Summit, and Cloud Security Summit.

Table of Contents

Part 2: Schedulers, Workloads, and Scaling 51

Chapter 3: Exploring Kubernetes Basics 53

Chapter 4: Principles of Scaling: Horizontal vs Vertical   87

Chapter 5: Autoscaling in Action   107

Part 3: Networking, Services, and Security   139

Chapter 6: Essentials of Kubernetes Networking   141

Chapter 11: Understanding GitOps: Principles and Practices — 273

Chapter 14: Monitoring Best Practices   357

Part 6: Troubleshooting and Best Practices   411

Chapter 16: Real-World Troubleshooting Scenarios   413

Chapter 17: Common Mistakes and How to Avoid Them   461

Preface

Kubernetes is the backbone of modern cloud-native systems—but the engineers who stand out are the ones who can explain it under pressure and fix it when it breaks.

This book is built for exactly that. You'll learn about the way Kubernetes is used in the real world, with production-style scenarios, more than 100 interview-ready questions with model answers, and dozens of clear diagrams that make tough topics click. We draw on years of hands-on work to show how Kubernetes behaves in production, how to troubleshoot it systematically, and how to talk through your approach with confidence.

Whether you're new to Kubernetes or sharpening for a senior interview, you'll get practical depth—and the language to communicate it.

This is what you'll get in this book:

- 100+ practical, interview-style questions with model answers that you can rehearse
- Clear, plain-English explanations that go beyond surface definitions
- Dozens of visual diagrams that simplify networking, scaling, storage, and security
- Hands-on mini-labs and checklists to turn concepts into muscle memory
- Guidance that's useful for developers, DevOps engineers, SREs, and ML engineers who run workloads on Kubernetes

By the end of this book, you will be able to do the following:

- Explain how Kubernetes works "from the inside out"
- Answer Kubernetes questions confidently in interviews and design reviews
- Troubleshoot, scale, and secure real clusters using modern best practices
- Operate with GitOps and automation to manage applications at scale
- Recognize and resolve common production pain points
- Communicate your decisions clearly to teammates and interviewers

Who this book is for

This book is for people who want to use Kubernetes with confidence—in real projects or technical interviews. It's written for software developers running services on Kubernetes, DevOps and SRE practitioners operating clusters, and ML engineers deploying training/serving workloads.

To get the most out of this book, you should already know some basics—such as how Linux works, what containers are, and have a general understanding of networking and IT concepts.

Many people learning Kubernetes find it hard to move beyond the basics. They can follow tutorials, but still struggle when asked real-world questions or face problems in production. This book helps close that gap. It explains complex topics in a way that's practical and easy to understand, so you can go from theory to hands-on confidence. It also helps you stay current with the fast-moving Kubernetes ecosystem and gives you the tools to succeed in both interviews and real DevOps work.

To effectively use this book, work through the diagrams first, then try the mini-labs. For each section, answer the included questions out loud using **STAR (Situation–Task–Action–Result)**. Keep a short log of pitfalls you hit and how you fixed them; these become great interview stories. If you're preparing for a panel, practice explaining trade-offs in plain English before you touch YAML.

What this book covers

Chapter 1, Understanding Kubernetes from Containers to Orchestration, introduces containers and shows why Kubernetes became the standard for running applications at scale.

Chapter 2, Kubernetes Key Components and Their Functions, covers the control plane (API server, scheduler, controller manager, and etcd) and how these parts work together.

Chapter 3, Exploring Kubernetes Basics, explains Pods, Namespaces, and workload primitives (Deployments, Jobs, CronJobs, DaemonSets, and static Pods), including labels/selectors and lifecycle.

Chapter 4, Principles of Scaling: Horizontal vs. Vertical, compares HPA and VPA, when to use each, and how to avoid common scaling pitfalls.

Chapter 5, Autoscaling in Action, goes deeper with Cluster Autoscaler and Karpenter for node-level scaling, with real guidance on cost and performance.

Chapter 6, Essentials of Kubernetes Networking, breaks down CNI, kube-proxy, DNS, and Pod/Service communication so you can reason about traffic paths.

Chapter 7, Kubernetes Network Architecture: Services and Ingresses, explores Service types, ingress controllers, and introduces the Gateway API. It also covers the basics of service mesh.

Chapter 8, Storage: Persistence and CSI Drivers, covers PVs, PVCs, StatefulSets, snapshots, and CSI drivers to design reliable stateful workloads.

Chapter 9, Security Best Practices in Kubernetes and RBAC, focuses on RBAC, secrets management, network policies, and building secure container images.

Chapter 10, Real-World Deployment Scenarios and Continuous Deployment, walks through rolling, blue/green, and canary strategies; it also introduces Helm and Kustomize for day-to-day delivery.

Chapter 11, Understanding GitOps: Principles and Practices, explains GitOps fundamentals with Argo CD and shows how to run pull-based, auditable deployments.

Chapter 12, Custom Resource Definitions and Operators , shows how to extend the Kubernetes API with custom resources, what operators are, and includes a small, hands-on operator example to demonstrate its functions.

Chapter 13, Ensuring High Availability and Reliability, teaches patterns for resilient clusters and applications: redundancy, failover, and reliability design.

Chapter 14, Monitoring Best Practices, covers metrics, logs, tracing, and alerting with tools such as Prometheus and Grafana.

Chapter 15, Backup, Maintenance, and Disaster Recovery in Kubernetes, builds backup strategies, plans safe maintenance, and designs recovery procedures for real failures.

Chapter 16, Real-world Troubleshooting Scenarios, works through production-style incidents in deployment, scaling, storage, and networking—with step-by-step diagnosis.

Chapter 17, Common Mistakes and How to Avoid Them, focuses on communication under pressure, structured problem-solving, and avoiding frequent Kubernetes pitfalls.

Chapter 18, Interview Stories from Authors, shares real interview stories, lessons learned, and practical preparation tips to sharpen your edge.

To get the most out of this book

You should have some basic Linux experience, understand concepts of containers, and be familiar with networking basics.

Be attentive and read the special "Interview tips" sections.

Download the example code files

The code bundle for the book is hosted on GitHub at https://github.com/PacktPublishing/ Cracking-the-Kubernetes-Interview. We also have other code bundles from our rich catalog of books and videos available at https://github.com/PacktPublishing. Check them out!

Conventions used

There are a number of text conventions used throughout this book.

CodeInText: Indicates code words in text, database table names, folder names, filenames, file extensions, pathnames, dummy URLs, user input, and X/Twitter handles. For example: "The restartPolicy parameter is set to Never, so if the container exits, the Job will not restart it unless the Pod fails."

A block of code is set as follows:

```
---
apiVersion: v1
kind: Service
metadata:
  name: hello-sample-ext
  namespace: default
spec:
  type: ExternalName
  externalName: google.com
```

Any command-line input or output is written as follows:

```
Kubectl get pods
```

Bold: Indicates a new term, an important word, or words that you see on the screen. For instance, words in menus or dialog boxes appear in the text like this. For example: "Automatic recovery process, often called a **reconciliation loop**, is a cornerstone of Kubernetes' resilience."

> Warnings or important notes appear like this.

Tips and tricks appear like this.

Get in touch

Feedback from our readers is always welcome.

General feedback: If you have questions about any aspect of this book or have any general feedback, please email us at customercare@packt.com and mention the book's title in the subject of your message.

Errata: Although we have taken every care to ensure the accuracy of our content, mistakes do happen. If you have found a mistake in this book, we would be grateful if you reported this to us. Please visit http://www.packt.com/submit-errata, click **Submit Errata**, and fill in the form.

Piracy: If you come across any illegal copies of our works in any form on the internet, we would be grateful if you would provide us with the location address or website name. Please contact us at copyright@packt.com with a link to the material.

If you are interested in becoming an author: If there is a topic that you have expertise in and you are interested in either writing or contributing to a book, please visit http://authors.packt.com/. Your Book Comes with Exclusive Perks - Here's How to Unlock Them

Unlock this book's exclusive benefits now

UNLOCK NOW

Scan this QR code or go to https://packtpub.com/unlock, then search this book by name. Ensure it's the correct edition.

Note: Keep your purchase invoice ready before you start.

Enhanced reading experience with our Next-gen Reader:

- **Multi-device progress sync**: Learn from any device with seamless progress sync.

- **Highlighting and notetaking**: Turn your reading into lasting knowledge.

- **Bookmarking**: Revisit your most important learnings anytime.

- **Dark mode**: Focus with minimal eye strain by switching to dark or sepia mode.

Learn smarter using our AI assistant (Beta):

- **Summarize it**: Summarize key sections or an entire chapter.

- **AI code explainers**: In the next-gen Packt Reader, click the **Explain** button above each code block for AI-powered code explanations.

> **Note**: The AI assistant is part of next-gen Packt Reader and is still in beta.

Learn anytime, anywhere:

- Access your content offline with DRM-free PDF and ePub versions—compatible with your favorite e-readers.

Unlock Your Book's Exclusive Benefits

Your copy of this book comes with the following exclusive benefits:

- Next-gen Packt Reader
- AI assistant (beta)
- DRM-free PDF/ePub downloads

Use the following guide to unlock them if you haven't already. The process takes just a few minutes and needs to be done only once.

How to unlock these benefits in three easy steps

Step 1

Keep your purchase invoice for this book ready, as you'll need it in *Step 3*. If you received a physical invoice, scan it on your phone and have it ready as either a PDF, JPG, or PNG.

For more help on finding your invoice, visit https://www.packtpub.com/unlock-benefits/help.

> **Note**: Did you buy this book directly from Packt? You don't need an invoice. After completing Step 2, you can jump straight to your exclusive content.

Step 2

Scan this QR code or go to https://packtpub.com/unlock.

On the page that opens (which will look similar to Figure 0.1 if you're on desktop), search for this book by name. Make sure you select the correct edition.

Figure 0.1: Packt unlock landing page on desktop

Step 3

Sign in to your Packt account or create a new one for free. Once you're logged in, upload your invoice. It can be in PDF, PNG, or JPG format and must be no larger than 10 MB. Follow the rest of the instructions on the screen to complete the process.

Need help?

If you get stuck and need help, visit `https://www.packtpub.com/unlock-benefits/help` for a detailed FAQ on how to find your invoices and more. The following QR code will take you to the help page directly:

Note: If you are still facing issues, reach out to customercare@packt.com.

Share your thoughts

Once you've read *Cracking the Kubernetes Interview*, we'd love to hear your thoughts! Scan the QR code below to go straight to the Amazon review page for this book and share your feedback.

https://packt.link/r/1835460038

Your review is important to us and the tech community and will help us make sure we're delivering excellent quality content.

Part 1

Introduction to Kubernetes

This part opens with a quick dive into container technology before introducing you to Kubernetes, the industry's go-to platform for orchestrating containers at scale. But Kubernetes isn't just another DevOps tool—it's a full ecosystem that's transformed how teams build, ship, and manage applications in the cloud. Whether you're just starting out in DevOps, eyeing a role in cloud engineering, or simply curious about how today's software infrastructure really works, this part will give you the foundational knowledge you need to move confidently into the world of containerized applications.

This part of the book includes the following chapters:

- *Chapter 1, Understanding Kubernetes from Containers to Orchestration*
- *Chapter 2, Kubernetes Key Components and Their Functions*

1
Understanding Kubernetes from Containers to Orchestration

In today's world, having strong engineering skills is crucial to career advancement. For DevOps professionals, architects, and developers, understanding complex systems orchestration tools such as Kubernetes is essential. To get the most out of this book, you should be comfortable using a **command-line interface (CLI)** and understand fundamental software development concepts such as applications and dependencies. Kubernetes is the foundation of modern container orchestration, where system agility and scalability are key. As microservices and distributed systems become the norm, mastering Kubernetes is an essential part of modern-day systems engineering and DevOps practices.

That's where this book comes in. Rather than just providing answers, it delves into the reasoning behind those answers to help you build a strong understanding of Kubernetes. From the basics to complex orchestrated scenarios, this book ensures a smooth learning curve. It's not just about preparing you for interviews, but also ensuring you're competent to handle real-world challenges on the job.

The narrative of this book is crafted to be engaging and reader-friendly. Best practices and common pitfalls will be discussed, debated, and pondered. Each chapter is meticulously organized, starting with a clear statement of purpose, followed by a deep dive into core concepts, interspersed with real-world examples, common interview questions, and their comprehensive answers.

This first chapter serves as a springboard for the journey. Here, we will explore the essence of containers and Kubernetes and build a strong foundation to help you become an asset to your organization.

So, let's dive into the fascinating world of containers and Kubernetes together.

In this chapter, we're going to answer basic questions about the nature of containers in general and will start talking about Kubernetes basics (what it is and what components it consists of).

We will cover the following main headings:

- What are containers?
- What is Kubernetes?
- What components does Kubernetes consist of?

What are containers?

Today, **containers** are the core part of every modern software application development. There's a constant need to deploy applications quickly, consistently, and scalably. Here's where containers come into play. But before we delve into the world of containers, let's start by understanding why we need them.

Think of a scenario where developers work on an application on their local machines, and everything seems to be running smoothly. However, when the application is deployed to a testing or production environment, they don't work as expected. The common phrase, *"but it works on my machine!"* echoes. This is where containers come to the rescue, which is the key reason why companies today are eager to adopt them.

You can think about a container like a lightweight, standalone, and executable **software package** that includes everything needed to run a piece of software, including the code, runtime, system tools, system libraries, and settings. This is typically called a **container image**. Container images are built using a layered filesystem. Each instruction in a Dockerfile creates a new layer, making images efficient to build and distribute, as only the changed layers need to be updated. The container itself is just an instance of this image, which runs a single process (a.k.a. the entry-point) of this image in an isolated environment (from other containers and the host system). They run the same regardless of the environment, ensuring that the *"but it works on my machine"* scenario doesn't occur. The main goal of containers is to create a consistent environment for applications from development to production. They encapsulate the application and its environment, ensuring it runs the same everywhere.

Containers versus virtual machines

When diving into the world of development and deployment, it's easy to mistake containers for **virtual machines (VMs)**. At a glance, they might appear to serve similar purposes, but their core functionalities and structures differ significantly.

VMs can be visualized as minicomputers within a larger computer. They rely on physical hardware abstraction, essentially transforming a single server into multiple virtual servers. These VMs operate under a hypervisor, which lets them coexist on one machine. However, there's a catch: each VM carries its own full-fledged operating system, not to mention the application, necessary binaries, and libraries. This comprehensive setup causes VMs to be quite resource-intensive.

Interview tip

Question: *Can you elaborate on the specific architectural differences that lead to this efficiency?*

Answer: The core difference lies in their level of abstraction. A VM abstracts the hardware layer. It uses a hypervisor to create virtual hardware, upon which a full, independent guest **operating system (OS)** runs. This means every VM carries the overhead of a complete OS kernel, its libraries, and binaries, making them large and slow to boot. Containers, on the other hand, abstract the operating system layer. They run on a shared host OS kernel and package just the application code with its specific libraries and dependencies. They don't need to boot an entire OS. This sharing of the host kernel is what makes them so lightweight, resource-efficient, and fast to create and deploy—often in seconds.

In contrast, containers take a more streamlined approach. Instead of replicating the entire operating system, they focus on the application layer. Despite running on the same OS kernel, each container operates in its own isolated environment, ensuring that application processes don't overlap or interfere. The result? Containers are nimble and efficient, a stark contrast to the bulkier VMs.

To get a clearer picture of how these two differ, refer to the following figure. This visualization will underscore the unique architecture and efficiency of containers in comparison to VMs.

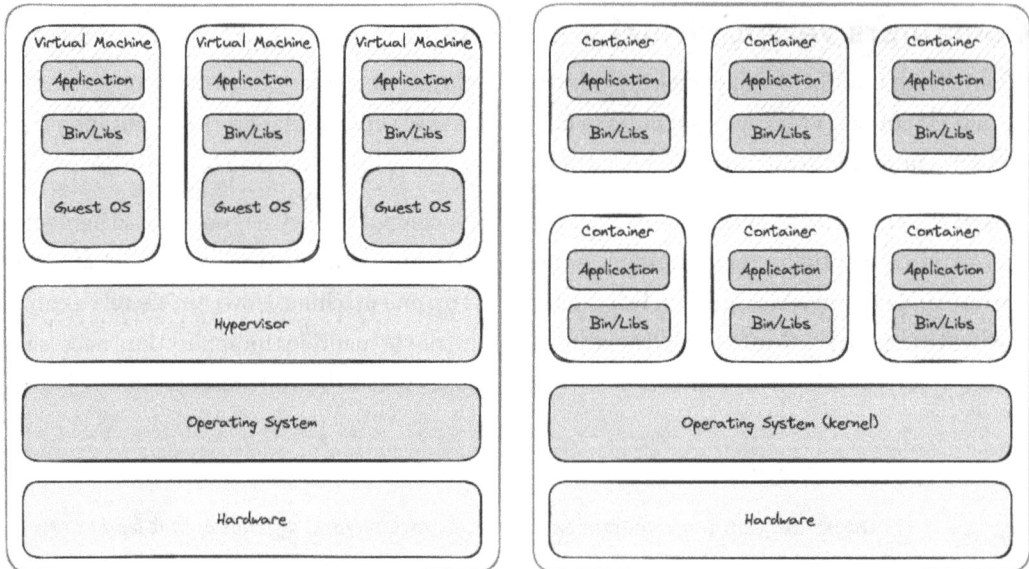

Figure 1.1 – VMs vs. containers

When to use containers and when to use VMs

Use containers when you need the following:

- Fast, consistent deployments
- Scalability
- Isolation for microservices
- Efficient use of system resources

Use VMs when the following apply:

- You need to run multiple applications on different OS types
- Complete OS isolation is required
- Running applications that need all the resources and functionalities of an entire OS

Understanding these use cases helps you decide whether a container is the right tool for your specific needs. Once you've determined that containers are the best fit, the next logical step is to understand how to package your application into one. This process, known as **containerizing**, involves a few key steps to create a portable and efficient unit for your software.

Containerizing an application

Containerizing an application involves packaging your application and its dependencies into a container image. The steps usually include the following:

1. Creating a **Dockerfile**, which is a text document that contains all the necessary commands that you would normally run manually on the command line to build an image
2. Building the image using a containerization tool such as Docker
3. Running the container from the created image

This three-step process forms the core workflow of containerization. The following diagram provides a visual representation of this journey, illustrating how a Dockerfile, your application code, and its dependencies are combined on a developer's machine to create a portable container image. This single image can then be deployed consistently across any environment—from development to production—to run as an identical container.

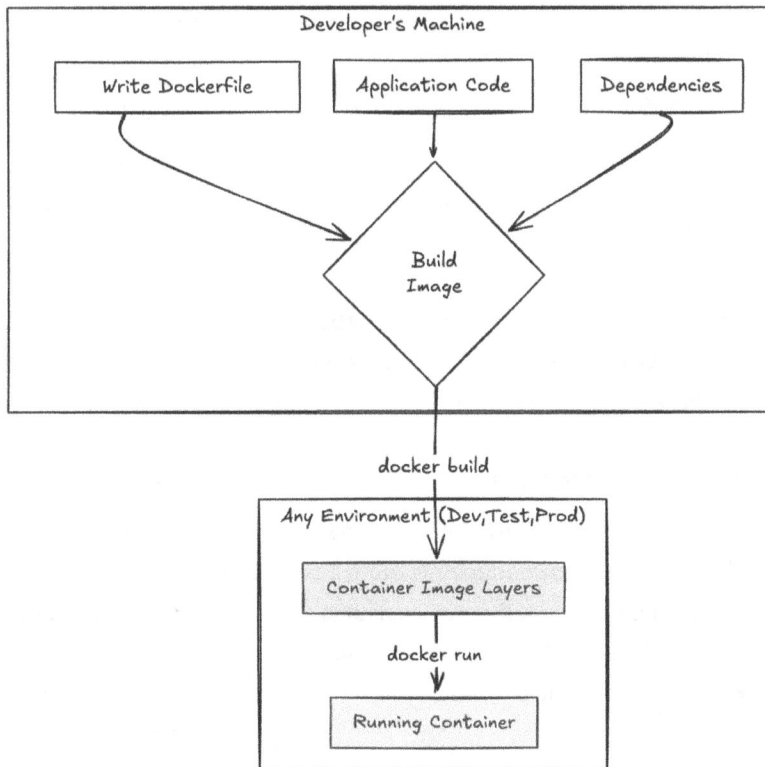

Figure 1.2 – The containerization workflow

Advantages of using containers

Compared to VMs and other deployment options, containers offer the following:

- **Consistency**: They run the same everywhere—from a developer's local machine to production (VMs have a much bigger size and the dependency on the hypervisor type and configuration).
- **Efficiency**: Containers share the same OS kernel, making them lightweight.
- **Isolation**: Each container runs in its isolated environment, ensuring that it doesn't interfere with other containers (for VMs, you can separate them using virtual networks, but anyway, it's still a high security risk you need to take care of).
- **Scalability**: They easily scale up or down as per the application demand (mostly because of the size).
- **Fast deployment**: You can create and deploy containers in seconds (the same reasons).

> **Interview tip**
>
> **Question**: *Describe three Linux kernel features that make containers possible.*
>
> **Answer**: (1) Namespaces (`pid`, `net`, `mnt`, `ipc`, `uts`, and `user`) for isolation; (2) cgroups for resource limits; (3) union filesystems (`overlayfs`) enabling copy-on-write images

There you have it! An introduction to containers that covers the basics and provides clarity on the concepts. As we move forward in this book, we'll explore Kubernetes, the orchestration platform that manages these containers, ensuring that applications run smoothly and efficiently.

What is Kubernetes?

Kubernetes, often called **k8s**, is an open source system that helps manage containerized applications. It can be compared to a conductor leading an orchestra. Just as a conductor ensures every instrument plays in harmony, Kubernetes ensures all your containers work together smoothly. If something goes off-key, such as a container misbehaving, Kubernetes steps in to fix it, just like a conductor keeping the music on track.

Now, what does Kubernetes actually do for you?

- **Diverse deployment**: Want to deploy an application to multiple locations while keeping it in sync? Kubernetes has you covered.

- **Mass updates:** Need to roll out changes to hundreds of containers? Kubernetes ensures seamless updates across the board.

- **Scale on demand**: Experiencing a traffic spike? Kubernetes can scale. During off-peak hours? It scales down.

Let's dive into a few scenarios to understand the true potential of Kubernetes:

- **Multi-location deployment:** Imagine an application that must run in containers in different locations. With Kubernetes, you can ensure that changes are synchronized across all instances, regardless of where they're hosted.

- **Bulk updates:** When your application spans hundreds of containers, making updates or changes manually can be tedious. Kubernetes simplifies this by enabling consistent updates across all containers.

- **Adaptive scaling:** In some scenarios, demand can spike, requiring more resources. Conversely, there may be times when demand is low. Kubernetes can automatically scale resources up or down based on the current load.

When or why not to use Kubernetes

Kubernetes, while powerful, is *not always* the go-to solution for every scenario. Just as it has its strengths, there are situations where its capabilities might be more than what's required or perhaps not entirely aligned with specific needs. Here are reasons to reconsider diving into Kubernetes:

- **Complexity and learning curve:** Kubernetes is a robust system with many features and configurations. Getting it up and running, understanding its components, and maintaining it requires significant time and expertise. For teams unfamiliar with container orchestration, the learning curve can be steep.

- **Limited resources:** If your organization is running on a tight budget or needs the infrastructure to support a Kubernetes cluster, it might be challenging to justify its setup and maintenance costs.

- **Team size and project scope**: Kubernetes can be overkill for smaller engineering teams (e.g., less than 20 members) that don't anticipate massive scaling needs. More straightforward projects with fewer containers might not require Kubernetes's expansive orchestration capabilities.

- **Application characteristics**: If your application is straightforward, doesn't demand high availability, or isn't performance-intensive, diving into Kubernetes might be an unnecessary complication. Traditional monolithic applications that are stable and don't require frequent updates might not benefit significantly from Kubernetes' features.

- **Nature of the application**: Transitioning a traditional monolithic application to Kubernetes can be challenging. If the application is stable and doesn't need updates or scaling, let it run in its current environment.

However, it's essential to highlight that managed solutions have emerged as the cloud ecosystem has evolved to alleviate some of Kubernetes' complexities. Cloud providers such as AWS offer services such as **Elastic Kubernetes Service (EKS)**. Using such offerings, you remove administrative complexities from your organization, particularly concerning the control plane. This allows teams to focus on deploying applications without the added overhead of cluster management.

In conclusion, while Kubernetes offers many advantages, it's crucial to assess whether its features align with your team's needs and the nature of your project. Sometimes, a more straightforward solution might be more efficient and cost-effective.

Key features of Kubernetes

Kubernetes is more than just a platform for deploying applications. It's a comprehensive ecosystem designed to manage containerized workloads with a range of features that simplify and automate various aspects of container management:

- **Self-healing capabilities**: One of the standout features of Kubernetes is its proactive approach to maintaining the health of containers. It consistently monitors each container's health, and it doesn't wait for human intervention if it identifies any failures. Instead, it automatically restarts the problematic container to ensure uninterrupted service.

- **Load balancing**: Kubernetes is savvy when it comes to traffic distribution. Depending on the condition of the Pods, it ensures incoming requests are effectively distributed among the available application instances, guaranteeing optimal resource utilization and enhanced user experience.

- **Operators**: These specialized applications are tailored for Kubernetes. They interface directly with the cluster's API and can modify its state. Additionally, they can execute specific actions in response to particular events, offering a dynamic response mechanism.

- **Automated rollouts and rollbacks**: The power of Kubernetes lies in its automation. It supports phased updates to applications and provides a safety net. If an update doesn't go as planned, Kubernetes can automatically revert the application to its previous stable state.

- **Auto-scaling**: Kubernetes shines in its ability to adapt. It can dynamically scale applications and their associated resources based on the current demand. This ensures that applications remain responsive even during peak loads.

- **Lifecycle management**: Kubernetes takes the hassle out of deployments and updates. It offers functionalities such as rolling back to a previous version, pausing ongoing deployments, and even resuming them, providing granular control over the application lifecycle.

- **Declarative model**: Instead of constantly monitoring and tweaking, with Kubernetes, you can declare your desired state for the application. Kubernetes then tirelessly works in the background to maintain this state, recovering from disruptions if they occur.

- **Resilience and self-healing**: Beyond just monitoring, Kubernetes actively ensures applications are running optimally. Features such as automatic placement, restarts, replications, and scaling ensure applications are resilient and recover quickly from potential issues.

- **Persistent storage**: Data persistence is crucial for many applications. Kubernetes provides the flexibility to attach storage dynamically, ensuring data remains intact even if the container goes down.

With these features and more, Kubernetes stands out as a powerhouse in container orchestration. Whether you're a developer looking to streamline deployments or an organization aiming for high availability, Kubernetes offers tools and functionalities to meet and exceed those needs.

Automatic recovery process, often called a **reconciliation loop,** is a cornerstone of Kubernetes' resilience. The following sequence diagram illustrates this concept in action. It shows how the controller manager detects a discrepancy between the desired state (three replicas) and the actual state after a Pod crashes, and then automatically launches a new Pod to restore the desired state—all without any human intervention.

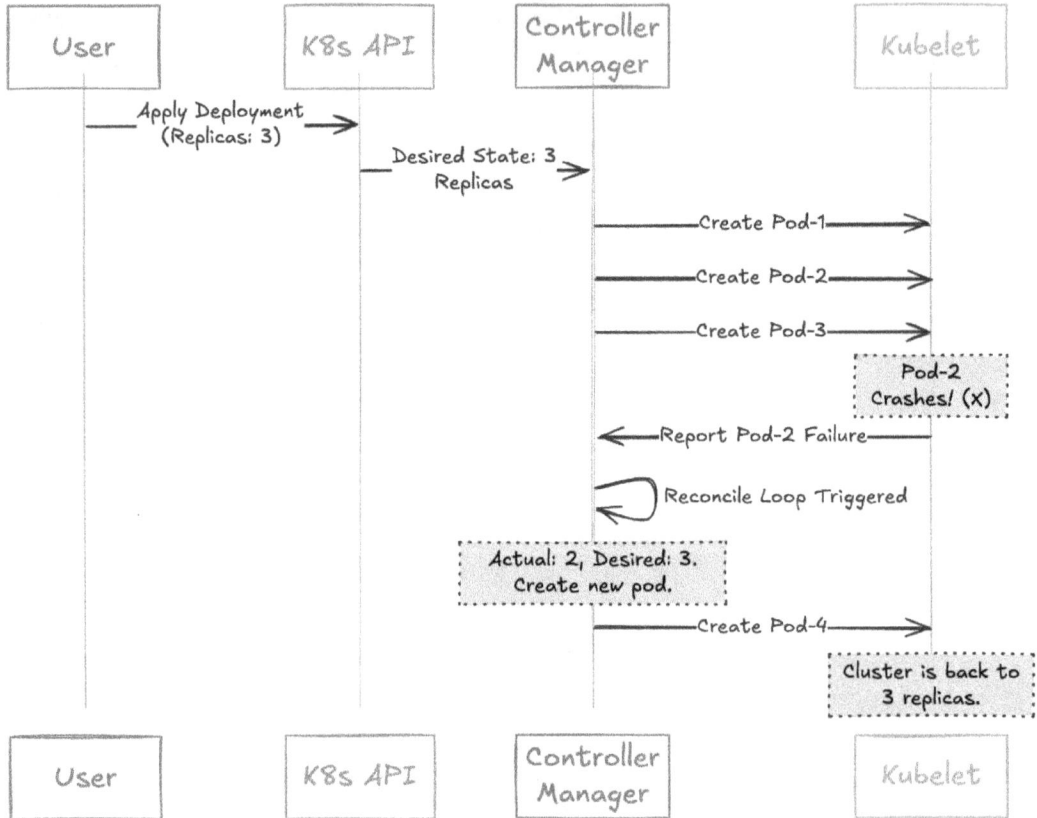

Figure 1.3 – Kubernetes self-healing in action

Now that we know what Kubernetes is, let's look at its differences in comparison with another orchestration tool called **Docker Swarm**—you can receive this question right after explaining what Kubernetes is.

Docker Swarm vs. Kubernetes: A quick comparison

In container orchestration, two names often emerge as frontrunners: Kubernetes and Docker Swarm. Both have their unique strengths, and choosing between them depends mainly on specific needs and the scale of operations.

Before diving into a direct comparison, it's crucial to assess whether there are some fundamental differences between the two. Docker Swarm is part of the Docker ecosystem, making it easy to install with a single command and quick to set up. In contrast, Kubernetes is a more complex system that requires additional steps, such as installing add-ons and plugins, such as ingress controllers and networking plugins (CNI), to fully function.

Another key difference is in their container runtimes. While Docker Swarm is tightly integrated with Docker and requires Docker Engine, Kubernetes offers more flexibility and does not rely solely on Docker. Kubernetes can work with various container runtimes, with containerd being a popular option.

With these key distinctions in mind, here's a side-by-side comparison to help you make an informed decision:

Property	Docker Swarm	Kubernetes
Setup and configuration	Known for its simplicity, it allows users to set up and manage a cluster quickly. Its straightforward commands and fewer components make the initialization process relatively smooth.	Though it offers a more comprehensive environment with a robust cluster setup, Kubernetes can be more challenging to configure due to its complexity. However, this complexity brings versatility.
Scalability	While Docker Swarm may not have automatic scaling like Kubernetes, it boasts rapid scaling capabilities, allowing containers to scale in seconds.	It offers auto-scaling based on CPU usage and other select metrics. However, it might scale slower than Docker Swarm; its scalability is more intricate and versatile.
Load balancing	It provides automatic load balancing, routing traffic to containers based on the standard configuration.	While it offers more advanced load-balancing features, it might require additional manual configuration and setup.
Monitoring and logging	It doesn't come with built-in monitoring tools. Instead, it often relies on external tools, with the ELK stack being a popular choice.	It offers integrated tools for both monitoring and logging, providing insights into cluster health and performance without additional dependencies.
Service discovery	It uses DNS to provide service discovery. It assigns a unique DNS name to a service and load balances it in a round-robin manner.	It utilizes a more intricate system, combining Pods IP, Service IP, and DNS to provide service discovery.

Property	Docker Swarm	Kubernetes
Updates and rollbacks	It supports rolling updates but lacks the feature of automatic rollbacks.	Not only does it provide phased rolling updates, but it also comes with the safety net of automatic rollbacks in case of issues.
Networking	It offers a node-level embedded DNS server, ensuring that containers can communicate easily.	It provides a flat network model, enabling all Pods to interact with each other seamlessly, even if they are on different nodes.

Table 1.1 – Difference between Docker Swarm and Kubernetes

To visualize the contrasting architectures and functionalities of Docker Swarm and Kubernetes, please refer to the accompanying diagram:

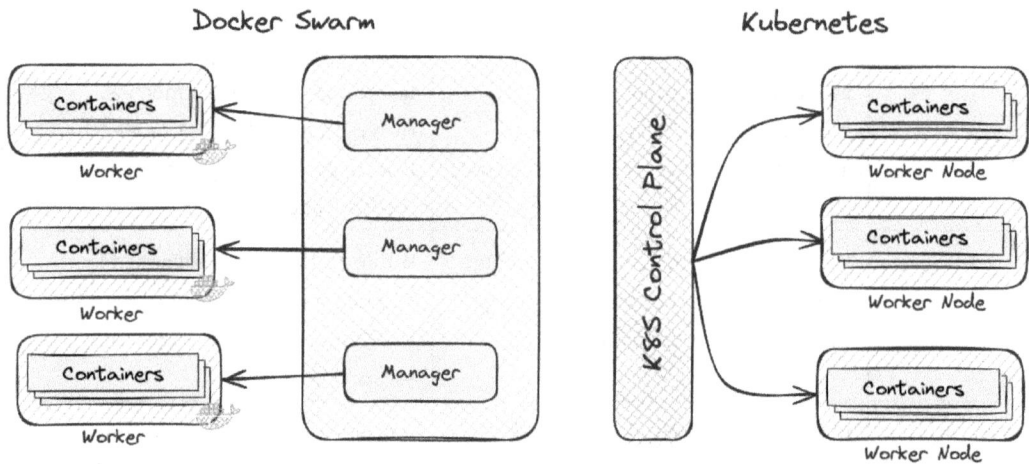

Figure 1.4 – Docker Swarm vs. Kubernetes

As shown in the diagram, Docker Swarm can manage multiple nodes but relies on a manager to coordinate the worker nodes. While it's possible to configure a single manager to oversee all the workers, if that manager fails, it disrupts the cluster's control, though your services will continue running. However, to restore full functionality, you'll need to recreate the cluster. Another important point is that Docker Swarm requires Docker Engine as the container runtime on every worker node. On the other hand, Kubernetes offers more flexibility by supporting various container runtimes, with containerd being the most common choice.

This fundamental difference in architecture—a resilient, distributed control plane versus a simpler manager model—is a primary reason why Kubernetes has become the industry standard for large-scale deployments. The flexibility to use different container runtimes, such as containerd, further underscores its modular design.

Having now positioned Kubernetes against a key alternative, we will shift our focus inward for the remainder of the chapter. To truly understand its power, we must dissect the system into its core functional parts.

What components does Kubernetes consist of?

Uncovering the architectural anatomy of Kubernetes reveals a meticulously orchestrated system that automates the deployment, scaling, and management of containerized applications. This chapter gives you an aerial view of the core components forming a Kubernetes cluster, focusing on the control and worker nodes (data planes) and their integral parts.

A Kubernetes cluster primarily consists of two main components: the control plane and the worker nodes (data plane). Let's explore these components and their roles in ensuring your Kubernetes cluster's smooth operation. And remember, we'll explore each component in *Chapter 2*.

Control plane

The control plane acts as the brain of the Kubernetes cluster, ensuring the maintenance of the cluster's desired state. There are some important components of the control plane (we will dive deeper into their details in the next chapter):

- **API server**: This hub facilitates all communication within the cluster, processing and validating REST requests to update the cluster's state accordingly.
- **Scheduler**: This allocates a worker node to every new Pod, considering factors such as resource availability.
- **Controller manager**: This works tirelessly to maintain the cluster's desired state. If a node goes down or someone deletes a pod, the controller manager jumps into action to restore the intended state.
- **etcd**: This highly available key-value store holds all cluster data, ensuring consistency in the cluster configuration and state.

Worker node (data plane)

Worker nodes host the applications and workloads, maintaining the runtime environments these applications require. Here are some of the worker nodes' components (we will dive deeper into their details in the next chapter):

- **Kubelet:** This acts as a liaison between the control plane and the worker nodes, ensuring not only that the containers run within a Pod but also managing the Pods themselves. This includes overseeing the entire lifecycle of Pods, from creation to deletion, and ensuring that their desired state is maintained.

- **Kube-proxy:** This manages network rules, allowing network communication to your Pods from network sessions inside or outside your cluster.

- **Container Runtime Interface (CRI):** This engine runs the containers; examples include containerd, CRI-O, and Docker Engine, among others.

- **Cloud controller manager:** This component integrates Kubernetes with cloud provider APIs, allowing the cluster to interact with external resources, such as load balancers or storage volumes, provided by the cloud platform. It ensures that cloud-specific operations, such as managing cloud-based resources, are handled properly within the cluster.

- **Containerd:** On the worker node, containerd acts as the container runtime, responsible for managing the lifecycle of containers. It pulls container images, creates and manages containers, and ensures that the containers are running as defined by Kubernetes. While Docker Swarm relies on Docker Engine, Kubernetes communicates with the container runtime using the CRI. This standard API allows Kubernetes to use various runtimes, such as containerd or CRI-O, without being tightly coupled to a single one like Docker Engine. This decoupling was a key driver for the deprecation of the dockershim.

> **Note**
>
> **Addressing a common query:** A Kubernetes cluster requires at least one control plane to manage the cluster. While it can technically operate with zero worker nodes, this setup won't host any applications.

The following architecture diagram visually encapsulates the components discussed in this chapter, providing a more intuitive understanding of the Kubernetes architecture:

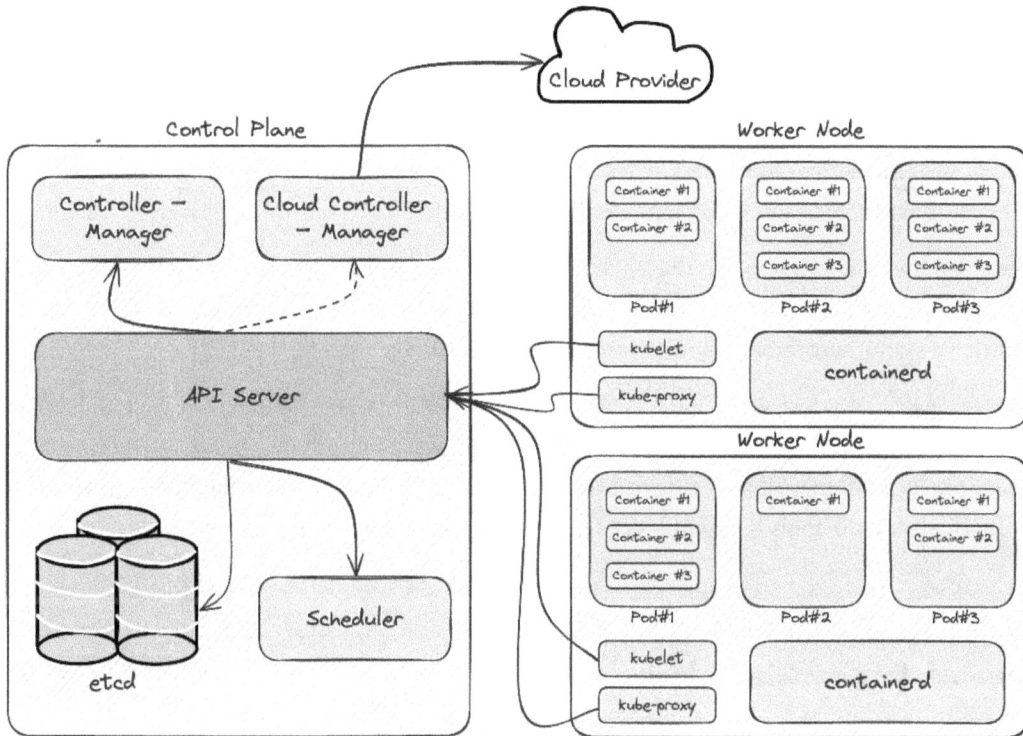

Figure 1.5 – Kubernetes architecture

In the Kubernetes architecture diagram, each component plays a vital role in ensuring the smooth operation of the cluster.

Interview tip

Question: *Why did Kubernetes deprecate Docker Engine as a runtime, and what replaced it?*

Answer: The kubelet now talks to container runtimes via CRI. Docker Engine lacked a stable CRI shim, so Kubernetes adopted containerd/CRI-O for lower overhead and direct OCI compliance.

These components, along with the core control plane elements such as the kubelet, API server, and scheduler, all work together to manage and maintain the desired state of your applications.

As a precursor to the more detailed exploration in the next chapter, understanding these core components lays a solid foundation for mastering Kubernetes knowledge.

Summary

In this chapter, we unraveled the essence of containers—self-contained units that revolutionize software management. We delved into the comparison of containers and VMs, highlighting the agility and efficiency of containers in deploying applications, and smoothly started to dive deeper into the main topic of this book, in the Kubernetes world.

We compared Kubernetes with the Docker Swarm and understood why Kubernetes emerges as a robust orchestrator, offering scalability, resilience, and automation capabilities that surpass alternative solutions for managing containerized workloads at scale.

As we transition to the next chapter, expect a closer look at the core elements shaping the Kubernetes landscape. We'll dissect nodes, controllers, and more, demystifying the orchestration magic that propels containers into the heart of modern software deployment. The journey continues with a focus on the tools that empower seamless container orchestration.

Unlock this book's exclusive benefits now

UNLOCK NOW

Scan this QR code or go to `https://packtpub.com/unlock`, then search for this book by name.

Note: Keep your purchase invoice ready before you start.

2

Kubernetes Key Components and Their Functions

By now, you should know that Kubernetes is not just another application; it's a container orchestration tool designed to automate the deployment, scaling, and management of containerized applications. But beyond that, it's a thriving ecosystem of microservices that power this revolutionary platform. If you're aiming to master Kubernetes or preparing for technical interviews, this chapter is your essential guide to navigating the intricate web of its components.

We will delve into some of the most frequently asked questions that may arise during interviews in this chapter, and you'll gain detailed insights into critical Kubernetes concepts, starting with a deep dive into the core of the system—understanding what the control plane is and the components that make it function. We'll explore the API server and its central role in orchestrating Kubernetes resources, followed by an examination of the **scheduler** to understand how it enables Kubernetes to be an efficient and powerful orchestrator. Finally, we'll look at how companies typically set up clusters and why managed Kubernetes solutions are often the preferred choice.

Understanding these fundamentals will give you a strong foundation, not just for conducting interviews, but for working confidently with Kubernetes in real-world projects. It's the kind of knowledge that will help you make smarter decisions as you grow in your DevOps or cloud-native career.

We will cover the following topics:

- The core architecture: Control plane and worker nodes
- The muscle: The worker node
- Essential cluster services
- Managing and deploying a cluster

Technical requirements

For scripts execution (optional):

- Any PC/Laptop with modern OS (requires Python being installed)

The core architecture: Control plane and worker nodes

In technical interviews, questions about the Kubernetes control plane and the components it holds can be answered with the expected responses in almost any technical interview. Why? Because this, and only this, can give the interviewer an understanding of how you have prepared theoretically, and what other questions should follow based on your answers.

In this section, you'll be able to answer (without going into deep technical details) how the Kubernetes cluster works, what its internals do, and how to troubleshoot core component failures.

A high-level overview of the manager—worker relationship

We mentioned the basic functionality of these components in the previous chapter. With this question, we want you to answer what components make up a cluster.

When asking this question, the interviewer usually expects you to describe the core components responsible for the cluster's functionality.

You can start by simply listing all the components that can be part of the control plane:

- **API server**: The frontend of the Kubernetes control plane, acting as the cluster's gateway. It exposes the Kubernetes API, serving as the entry point for various administrative tasks. By validating and processing REST requests, it acts as an essential communication hub, linking all other control plane components together.
- **etcd**: This is a distributed key-value store that stores the entire cluster's configuration data, including cluster state and configuration. It's the cluster's single source of truth, ensuring consistency.
- **Controller manager**: This runs controller processes that manage the system's state. These controllers are responsible for node and Pod replication, endpoints, and service accounts.
- **Scheduler**: This is responsible for assigning work to nodes. It evaluates Pod resource requirements, quality of service requirements, and policies to make decisions about where to place Pods.

- **Cloud controller manager:** This is responsible for interacting with the cloud provider's APIs and services. It integrates with cloud-specific resources such as load balancers, block storage, and virtual networks, allowing Kubernetes clusters to take advantage of the cloud's native capabilities.

Let's go through what these components do one by one.

The brains of the operation: The control plane

The control plane is the command center that makes all global decisions for the cluster. It's composed of several core components, each with a distinct job: the **API Server**, **etcd**, the **Scheduler**, and the **controller Manager**. Let's break down each one, starting with the central gateway that everything communicates through.

API Server: The front door

When asked this question, you are expected to expand upon your knowledge about the API models that Kubernetes operates under the hood. First of all, you need to highlight that this component is not just *an entry point* for all internal and external requests to the Cluster API. It also does the following:

- Exposes the Kubernetes API to users, operators, and components
- Validates and processes REST requests from clients
- Serves as the entry point for administrative tasks
- Serves as a central communication hub for other control plane components
- Authenticates and authorizes requests, ensuring that only authorized users and components can access and manipulate the cluster

> **Interview Tip**
>
> **Question:** *What are the four core components of the Kubernetes control plane?*
>
> **Answer:** The control plane is composed of four core components: the **API Server**, etcd, the **Scheduler**, and the **Controller Manager**. The API Server acts as the cluster's gateway, etcd is the distributed key-value store that acts as the single source of truth, the Scheduler assigns work to nodes, and the Controller Manager runs the processes that manage the system's state.

This diagram shows the step-by-step process that occurs when a user creates a new Pod. The request flows from kubectl to the API Server, which writes the initial "Pending" state to **etcd**.

The **Scheduler** sees this new Pod, assigns it to a node, and updates its status in etcd. Finally, the **Kubelet** on the assigned node sees the Pod, instructs the **Container Runtime** to start the container, and reports the final "Running" status back to the API Server.

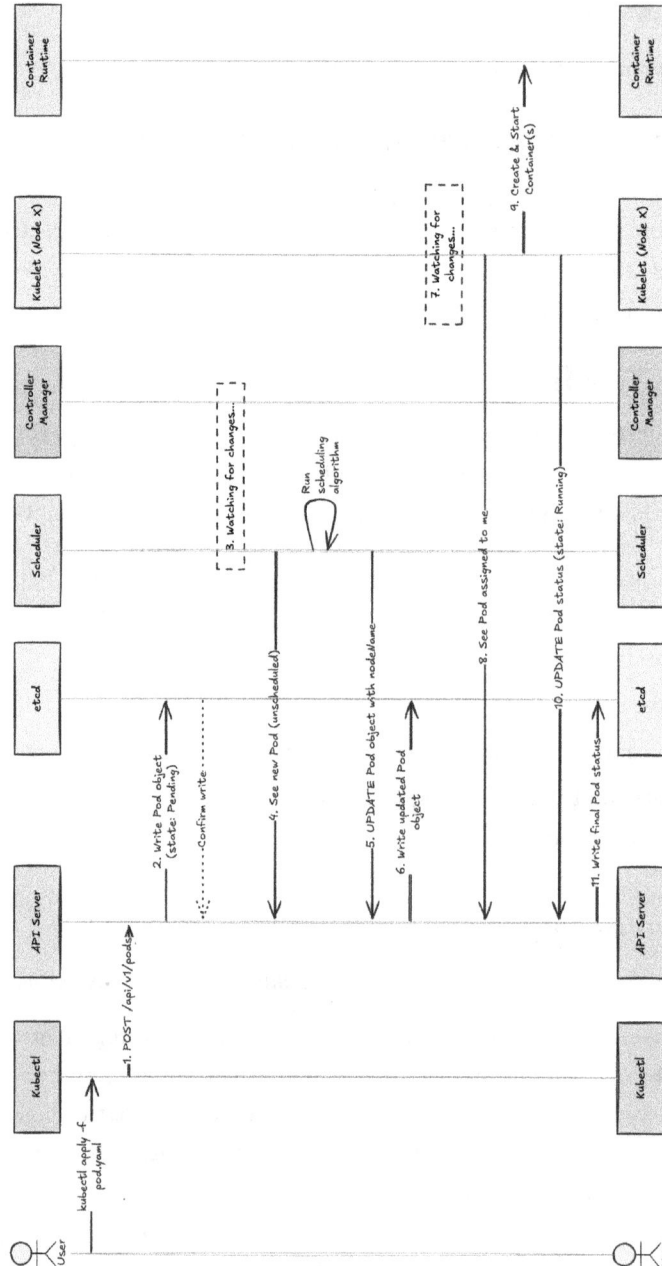

Figure 2.1 – A sequence diagram illustrating the Pod creation flow

Note

Authentication is the process of verifying the identity of a user, system, or entity trying to access a resource or system. It ensures that the entity is who it claims to be. **Authorization** determines what actions or resources an authenticated user, system, or entity can access or perform. It establishes the permissions or privileges of the entity after successful authentication.

etcd: The single Source of truth

First, understand that etcd is a separate, open-source project that Kubernetes uses for storage. Kubernetes, like any other complex solution, requires some form of persistent storage to keep data for the long term.

While Kubernetes itself is a highly scalable and available platform by design, almost all of its components are stateless. Here, etcd plays the critical role of being a durable and safe place to keep all desired states of everything that's deployed and configured in the cluster.

Interview Tip

Question: Wha*t is etcd's role, and what happens if the etcd cluster loses quorum?*

Answer: etcd's role is to serve as a strongly consistent, distributed key-value store that holds all of a Kubernetes cluster's configuration and state data. It is the cluster's single source of truth, using a consensus algorithm like **Raft** to ensure data consistency across all nodes. The text does not specify what happens upon losing quorum.

etcd is a strongly consistent, distributed key-value store that provides a reliable way to store data that needs to be accessed by a distributed system or cluster of machines.

etcd takes care of the following aspects:

- **Cluster state storage**: etcd is the central repository for all configuration data and the current state of a Kubernetes cluster. This includes information about Pods, services, nodes, configurations, and more. The cluster's desired state, as defined by the configuration, is stored in etcd.
- **Data consistency**: etcd provides strong data consistency and consistency guarantees. It uses a distributed consensus algorithm (usually Raft) to ensure that the data stored in the key-value store is consistent across all nodes. This consistency is crucial for maintaining the integrity of the cluster's state.

- **Configuration management**: All changes to the cluster's state, such as creating, updating, or deleting resources, are recorded in etcd. This makes it possible to roll back to a previous state and track changes over time, which is essential for troubleshooting and auditing.

Storing a resource's configuration in etcd is only the first step. The cluster must now act on this information to make the desired state a reality. The first component to spring into action for a new Pod is the **Scheduler**, whose critical job is to find the perfect node for it to run on.

Scheduler: The matchmaker

The scheduler, also known as **kube-scheduler**, is one of the core components of the entire cluster because its primary responsibility is scheduling Pods on nodes available in the cluster. Expanding your answer, you can name the following functions of this component:

- **Node selection**: The scheduler's primary task is to select an appropriate node for a Pod to run on. It evaluates several factors to make this decision, including resource availability, affinity/anti-affinity rules, taints and tolerations, and node locality.

- **Resource requirements**: The scheduler ensures that the selected node has the necessary resources available by considering the resource requirements specified in the Pod's definition, such as CPU and memory requests and limits.

- **Quality of service**: Pods in Kubernetes can have different quality of service classes, such as Guaranteed, Burstable, or BestEffort. The scheduler takes these classes into account when making scheduling decisions.

- **Affinity and anti-affinity rules**: Pods can define affinity and anti-affinity rules to specify their preferred or avoided co-location with other Pods. The scheduler respects these rules when making placement decisions.

- **Node locality**: Some workloads may benefit from being placed on nodes with specific attributes or conditions, such as being close to certain data sources or hardware devices. The scheduler can consider these requirements when placing Pods.

- **Inter-Pod spreading**: The scheduler can spread Pods from the same service or application across different nodes to ensure high availability and fault tolerance, reducing the risk of all Pods being affected by a node failure.

- **Load balancing**: The scheduler helps distribute workloads evenly across nodes to optimize resource utilization and application performance.

All of these settings are controlled by the developers or operations engineers who are responsible for Kubernetes manifest preparation. By leveraging these scheduler features effectively, you can build production-ready, highly available systems that take full advantage of the Kubernetes platform.

Controller Manager: The reconciliation loop

If the API Server is the cluster's front door and the Scheduler is the matchmaker, the **Controller Manager** is the tireless operator working behind the scenes to ensure the cluster's state matches your intent. It is the driving force behind Kubernetes' famous self-healing and declarative nature, operating on a simple but powerful principle: the reconciliation loop. Essentially, each controller watches a specific resource, compares its actual state to the desired state stored in etcd, and then takes action to reconcile any differences.

The term 'controller manager' is a bit misleading; it's not one thing. Think of it as a bundle of automated operators running in a single process. Each controller has one job: watch for changes and make the cluster's actual state match the desired state you define. For example, the **Node controller** watches node health, while the **Replication controller** ensures the correct number of Pod replicas are running. Together, these control loops are the engine that drives Kubernetes' self-healing and declarative nature.

These individual controllers include (but are not limited to) the following:

- **Replication controller**: Ensures the desired number of Pod replicas are running within a ReplicaSet or deployment.

- **Node controller**: Manages nodes in the cluster, monitoring their health and making decisions related to node addition and removal.

- **Endpoints controller**: Populates the Endpoints object (a list of IP addresses and ports for a service) based on service and Pod selection.

- **Service account and token controller**: Manages service accounts, which are used for authentication and authorization within the cluster.

- **Namespace controller**: Ensures that each namespace is initialized correctly and maintains the resource quota.

- **Persistent volume controller**: Manages the life cycle of PersistentVolumes and PersistentVolumeClaims using the **Container Storage Interface (CSI)**. We will discuss these in more detail later in this book.

- **Job controller**: Ensures that batch jobs are completed successfully.

- **DaemonSet controller**: Maintains the desired number of Pods on each node in a DaemonSet.

All the controllers we've just discussed are considered "core" because they are cloud-agnostic and manage resources inside the cluster. However, when Kubernetes needs to interact with external, cloud-specific resources like a load balancer or block storage, it uses a separate, specialized set of controllers. This deliberate separation keeps the main Kubernetes code base clean and vendor-neutral.

Cloud Controller Manager: The cloud whisperer

In Kubernetes clusters, this component extends the functionality of the core control plane components by integrating with cloud-specific services and resources. It is designed to manage and automate interactions with cloud providers, making it easier to deploy and manage Kubernetes clusters on various cloud platforms, such as AWS, GCP, Azure, and others. Today, more and more companies want to use cloud installations of Kubernetes because it can simplify the efforts of the operations team to maintain and support this big platform.

You can mention the following key features in your answers to cover the expected knowledge:

- **Cloud provider integration**: This controller interacts with the cloud provider's APIs and services. It integrates with cloud-specific resources such as load balancers, block storage, and virtual networks, which allow Kubernetes clusters to use the cloud's native capabilities.

- **Resource provisioning**: It automates the provisioning and management of cloud resources that Kubernetes clusters require. For example, when a LoadBalancer service type is created, the cloud controller manager can create a cloud-specific load balancer and configure it to route traffic to the appropriate Kubernetes Pods.

- **Resource cleanup**: Besides resource provisioning, the cloud controller manager also manages resource cleanup. When a Kubernetes resource (e.g., a Node or LoadBalancer service) is no longer needed, it ensures that the associated cloud resources are deprovisioned to avoid unnecessary costs.

- **Isolation from the core control plane**: The cloud controller manager is designed to be an optional component. It allows cloud-specific controller code to be isolated from the core Kubernetes control plane, making the Kubernetes project more modular and allowing cloud providers to maintain their integrations independently.

By using cloud controller managers, companies can take full advantage of their cloud provider's features and resources while managing Kubernetes clusters. It simplifies the process of deploying and maintaining clusters in a cloud-native way, ensuring that Kubernetes workloads can seamlessly interact with cloud services without requiring extensive manual configuration.

The control plane makes all the critical decisions, but it doesn't run your application containers. That is the job of the worker nodes. If the control plane is the brain, the worker nodes are the muscle, responsible for executing the workloads and providing the necessary compute, memory, and storage resources. Now, let's examine the essential components that run on every worker node to bring your applications to life.

The worker node: The muscle

Kubernetes worker nodes are a fundamental part of a Kubernetes cluster as they are responsible for running and managing Pods, the smallest deployable units of a Kubernetes application. Worker nodes execute containers, communicate with the control plane, and collectively form the infrastructure on which applications run. While the control plane infrastructure components take care of the cluster itself and all internals, the worker nodes execute application containers running inside the cluster.

This is why it's also important to understand what Kubernetes component worker nodes consist of and how they function.

Figure 2.2 shows the components of a worker node.

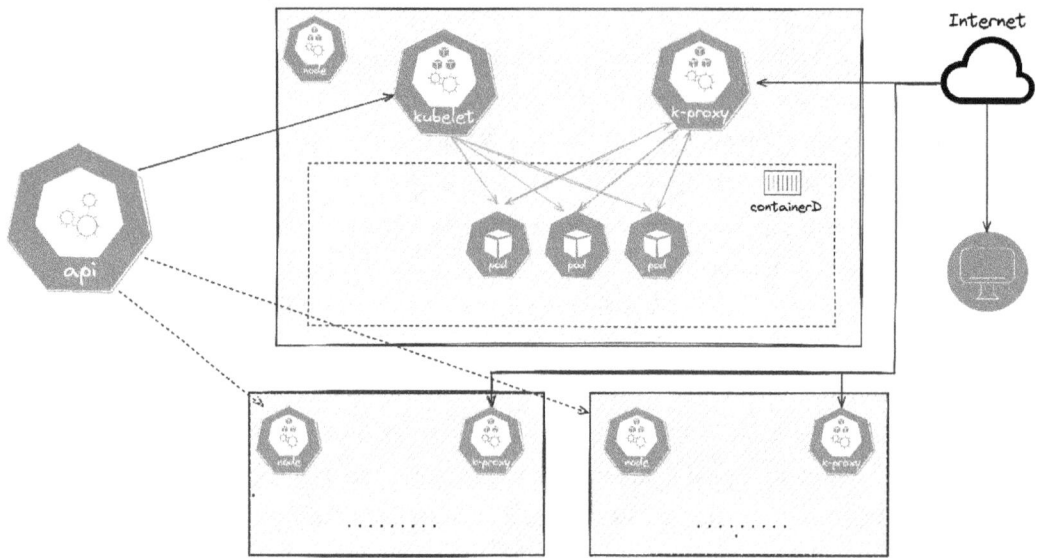

Figure 2.2 – Kubernetes worker node at a high level

Q **Quick tip**: Need to see a high-resolution version of this image? Open this book in the next-gen Packt Reader or view it in the PDF/ePub copy.

🔒 **The next-gen Packt Reader** and a **free PDF/ePub copy** of this book are included with your purchase. Scan the QR code OR visit https://packtpub.com/unlock, then use the search bar to find this book by name. Double-check the edition shown to make sure you get the right one.

This diagram shows the main components that run on a Kubernetes worker node. kubelet communicates with the API server to manage the Pod life cycle, while kube-proxy handles network routing between Pods and services. Pods run inside the node using a container runtime such as containerd, and traffic can flow in and out of the cluster via the internet.

Now, let's dive deeper into the internals of worker nodes and how exactly they interact with the cluster, with each other, and with the container workloads on them.

> **Interview Tip**
>
> **Question:** *What are the three key components that run on every Kubernetes worker node?*
>
> **Answer:** Every worker node runs three key components: the **kubelet**, which ensures containers are running in Pods; the **container runtime** (like Docker or containerd), which is responsible for pulling images and running the containers; and the **kube-proxy**, which handles network routing and load balancing for services.

An interviewer may ask what components comprise the worker node to gauge your basic knowledge of Kubernetes. While you should be brief in your answer, it is essential to cover the key components:

- **kubelet**: This component is responsible for ensuring that containers are running in Pods, as specified in the manifest. It communicates with the control plane to receive Pod definitions and report the health and status of the Pods on the node.
- **Container runtime**: The container runtime, such as Docker or containerd, is responsible for pulling container images and running them as containers in Pods.
- **kube-proxy**: This component is responsible for network routing, load balancing, and service proxying. It maintains network rules to ensure that communication to and from Pods works as expected. Remember, Pods are the smallest deployable units in Kubernetes, and they run one or more containers that share the same network namespace. Each worker node hosts multiple Pods, each with its own set of containers.
- **Container Runtime Interface (CRI)**: This interface standardizes communication between the kubelet and the container runtime, allowing Kubernetes to work with various container runtimes seamlessly. It's not something you can call a "component," but it's important to mention it as well.

Now, let's explore every component in greater detail.

Kubelet: The node agent

The kubelet is a critical component in a Kubernetes cluster that's responsible for managing the containers on individual nodes. It plays a key role in ensuring that containers are running in a Pod as specified by the Kubernetes API server. Here's how the kubelet works:

- **Pod specification**: The kubelet takes its instructions from the Kubernetes API server, which, in turn, provides it with a Pod specification. This specification includes details about the containers that should be running in the Pod, such as container images, resource requirements, and more.

- **Container management**: The kubelet's primary responsibility is to ensure that the containers described in the Pod specification are running and healthy on the node where the kubelet is running. If the containers are not running or are in an unhealthy state, the kubelet takes corrective actions to reconcile the actual state with the desired state.

- **Container life cycle**: The kubelet manages the entire life cycle of containers in a Pod. This includes container creation, startup, monitoring, and automatic restart if a container fails or exits.

- **Resource allocation**: The kubelet monitors the node's resource utilization (CPU, memory, etc.) and ensures that the containers running on that node do not exceed their resource limits. If a container consumes too many resources, the kubelet can take actions to terminate or evict the offending container.

- **Health checks**: The kubelet periodically performs health checks on containers by executing readiness and liveness probes. If a container fails these probes, the kubelet performs certain actions, such as restarting the container or marking it as failed.

- **Reporting node status**: The kubelet regularly reports the node's status and the status of the containers it manages to the Kubernetes API server. This information is used by the API server for scheduling decisions, monitoring, and resource allocation.

- **Pulling container images**: When the kubelet detects that a container specified in a Pod specification is not present on the node, it will contact the container runtime (e.g., Docker) to pull the required container image from a container registry. Once the image is available locally, the kubelet will create and start the container.

- **Pod life cycle management**: The kubelet ensures that the overall Pod life cycle is managed appropriately. This means that all containers in a Pod are started and stopped together, and if the entire Pod fails, the kubelet takes appropriate actions, such as restarting it.

- **Eviction and node cleanup**: In the case of resource shortages or other node-related issues, the kubelet can take actions to evict Pods or containers to free up resources for different critical workloads. It also cleans up containers and resources when a Pod is deleted.

- **Syncing with etcd:** The kubelet communicates with etcd, the cluster's distributed key-value store, to ensure that it has the latest information about the desired state of the Pods running on the node.

> **Interview Tip**
>
> **Question:** *What is the kubelet and why is it so important?*
>
> **Answer:** The **kubelet** is the critical agent that runs on each worker node and is responsible for managing the containers on that node as specified by the API server. It's important because it acts as the bridge between the control plane and the worker node, taking instructions from the API server and translating them into actions for the container runtime, as well as reporting the health and status of Pods back to the control plane.

In summary, the kubelet is the node agent responsible for ensuring containers run as expected on a Kubernetes node. It monitors, manages, and reports on the state of containers and the node itself, ensuring that the cluster's desired state is maintained. The kubelet is a critical part of Kubernetes as it directly interfaces with the necessary hardware and the container runtime to maintain the health and reliability of applications in the cluster.

Kube-proxy: The network plumber

Kubernetes Proxy, also known as kube-proxy, is an essential component of a Kubernetes cluster that facilitates network communication between Pods and services within the cluster. Its main function is to provide network connectivity and load balancing for services, ensuring seamless communication between applications.

kube-proxy provides the following functionality feature sets:

- **Service abstraction and service types:** In Kubernetes, services are abstractions that allow you to expose a set of Pods as a network service with a stable IP address and DNS name. Other Pods can use these services within the cluster. Kubernetes supports various service types, including ClusterIP, NodePort, LoadBalancer, and ExternalName. kube-proxy works with different service types to provide various networking features.
- **ClusterIP service:** When a service of the ClusterIP type is created, kube-proxy ensures that an internal virtual IP address is assigned to the service. This virtual IP is used to route traffic to the service, and it is not directly accessible from outside the cluster.

- **NodePort service:** For NodePort services, kube-proxy opens a port on each node in the cluster. This port listens for traffic that matches the service, and when such traffic is received, it is forwarded to the appropriate service in the cluster. NodePort services can be accessed from outside the cluster by connecting to any node's IP address on the specified port.

- **LoadBalancer service:** When a LoadBalancer service is created, Kubernetes interacts with an external load balancer to distribute incoming traffic to the service's Pods. In cloud environments, kube-proxy interacts with the cloud provider's load balancer service through the cloud controller manager to handle this traffic. However, in on-premises environments, a similar setup can be achieved using solutions such as **MetalLB**, which provides load balancer functionality for bare-metal or non-cloud Kubernetes clusters. This type of service is typically used to expose services externally, regardless of whether the cluster is running in the cloud or on-premises.

- **iptables or userspace proxy mode:** kube-proxy typically operates in one of two modes: iptables mode (default) or userspace mode. In iptables mode, kube-proxy uses IP table rules to redirect traffic to the correct destination Pod. In userspace mode, it relies on userspace programs to manage network traffic. Sometimes (for specific CNI plugin usage, such as Cilium), it can use another kernel feature, such as eBPF, to implement communication within and with containers.

- **Service discovery and health checks:** kube-proxy watches the Kubernetes API server to monitor for changes in service and endpoint resources. When a new service is created or an endpoint is updated, kube-proxy updates its routing rules to ensure traffic is directed to the correct set of Pods. kube-proxy also performs health checks on the backends (Pods) associated with a service to ensure that traffic is only routed to healthy Pods. If a Pod becomes unhealthy, kube-proxy stops sending traffic to it.

> **Interview Tip**
>
> **Question:** *How does kube-proxy enable service networking?*
>
> **Answer: kube-proxy** runs on each node to facilitate network communication for services. When a Service is created, kube-proxy maintains network rules on the node (typically using **iptables**) to route traffic destined for a Service's stable IP address to the correct backing Pods. It watches the API server for changes to Services and Endpoints to keep these rules up to date.

As we've seen, kube-proxy is a key Kubernetes component that's responsible for routing traffic between services and Pods within a cluster. It supports various service types, such as ClusterIP,

NodePort, and LoadBalancer, and uses IP tables or userspace proxies (or even eBPF with some CNIs) to manage traffic flow. kube-proxy also tracks service and endpoint changes via the API server and ensures traffic is only routed to healthy Pods.

Container runtime: The engine

In Kubernetes, the container runtime is the software component responsible for running and managing containers. Containers are lightweight, standalone, and executable packages that contain an application and all its dependencies, and they can be deployed and executed in a consistent and isolated environment efficiently.

Kubernetes itself does not manage containers directly and instead relies on a container runtime to perform this task. The container runtime interacts with the host operating system's kernel to create and manage containers. The two most commonly used container runtimes in Kubernetes are as follows:

- **Docker**: This was one of the first and most popular container runtimes, and it played a significant role in popularizing containerization technology. Kubernetes has excellent support for Docker containers. Docker provides a user-friendly interface and a wide range of tools for building, sharing, and running containers.
- **Containerd**: This is an industry-standard container runtime that Kubernetes can use as an alternative to Docker. It provides core container runtime functionality, allowing Kubernetes to manage containers without some of the additional features and overhead that Docker brings. Containerd is more lightweight and designed to be embedded in Kubernetes distributions.

Container runtimes are pluggable in Kubernetes, meaning that you can choose the runtime that best suits your needs. Alternatively, your organization's Kubernetes distribution may have a preferred runtime. This flexibility allows Kubernetes to adapt to different runtime environments.

> **Interview Tip**
>
> **Question:** *What is the difference between a Container Runtime and the CRI?*
>
> **Answer:** The **Container Runtime** (like containerd) is the software that is responsible for the core task of running and managing containers. The **Container Runtime Interface (CRI)** is a Kubernetes project that acts as a standardized API bridge, defining the communication interface between the kubelet and the container runtime. The CRI allows Kubernetes to be pluggable, supporting various runtimes without changing its core code.

Why do modern versions of Kubernetes use Containerd as the default runtime?

In January 2022, Kubernetes decided to deprecate and eventually remove Docker as the default container runtime, primarily due to changes in the container ecosystem and the Kubernetes community's desire to standardize container runtimes. Here are some of the key reasons for this decision:

- **Containerd as a standard interface**: Kubernetes aims to provide a standard interface for container runtimes. Containerd emerged as an industry-standard runtime, and its development is driven by the **Cloud Native Computing Foundation (CNCF)**. By adopting Containerd as the default runtime, Kubernetes aligns itself with this standard, promoting interoperability and consistency across various container runtimes.

- **Docker complexity and overhead**: Docker is known for providing a comprehensive containerization solution that includes a daemon, image management, network management, and more. However, many Kubernetes users found that the full Docker stack brought unnecessary complexity and overhead when Kubernetes itself could handle many of these tasks. Using a more straightforward runtime such as Containerd, Kubernetes could streamline the container management process.

- **Reducing the attack surface**: A more minimal container runtime, such as Containerd, reduces the attack surface on a Kubernetes node. The Docker daemon often has more functionalities than needed for running containers in a Kubernetes environment. Reducing the attack surface improves security.

- **Ecosystem evolution**: The container ecosystem evolves continually, and Kubernetes aims to adapt to these changes. Kubernetes maintainers want to ensure that the project remains current with the latest developments and best practices in containerization. By shifting toward a more modular approach, Kubernetes can better accommodate changes in container runtimes and related technologies.

- **Compliance with the CRI**: The CRI is a Kubernetes project that defines the interface between Kubernetes and container runtimes. By adopting the CRI, Kubernetes can maintain a clear and standardized separation between the container runtime and the Kubernetes control plane, making it easier for different runtimes to be used.

The following diagram shows the difference between **Docker** and **Containerd** at a high level:

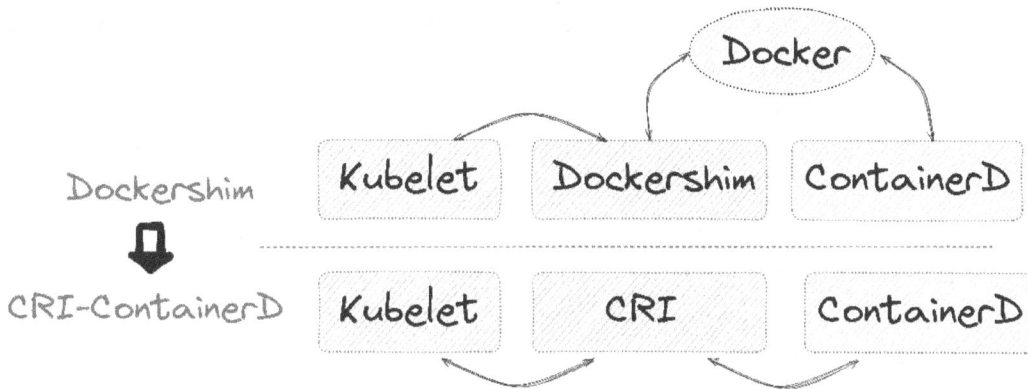

Figure 2.3 – Dockershim versus CRI

This diagram compares the older Dockershim-based architecture with the modern CRI approach. Previously, Kubernetes used Dockershim to connect the kubelet with Docker, which used Containerd internally. With Dockershim deprecated, Kubernetes now talks directly to runtimes such as Containerd via the CRI, simplifying the stack and improving maintainability.

What is Dockershim?

Dockershim was a component in Kubernetes that acted as an intermediary between Kubernetes and the Docker container runtime. It was used to enable Docker as a container runtime for Kubernetes when Docker was the default runtime. The primary purpose of Dockershim was to translate Kubernetes container runtime requests into Docker-specific commands and actions.

To summarize, Dockershim was introduced to maintain compatibility with Docker while Kubernetes transitioned away from Docker as the default container runtime. Its role was to translate CRI requests made by Kubernetes components (e.g., the kubelet) into equivalent Docker commands and operations. Let's take a closer look:

- **Background:** The need for Dockershim arose when Kubernetes decided to deprecate Docker as the default runtime. At this time, Kubernetes shifted toward using Containerd as the standard container runtime. Dockershim provided a temporary solution to continue using Docker while ensuring compatibility with Kubernetes.

- **Functionality**: Dockershim could create, start, stop, and manage containers using Docker commands based on requests from the Kubernetes control plane. It was responsible for translating Kubernetes Pod specifications into Docker containers and managing networking, volumes, and other container-related tasks.

- **Deprecation**: Dockershim was deprecated in Kubernetes version 1.20, when Containerd started to be used as the default runtime (see previous question), and its removal was scheduled for a later release (usually within one or two release cycles). Kubernetes maintainers encouraged users to transition to other container runtimes (e.g., Containerd) to ensure long-term support and compatibility.

- **Impact**: The removal of Dockershim meant that Kubernetes would no longer support Docker as a runtime by default. Users who were still dependent on Docker as a container runtime needed to switch to an alternative runtime, such as Containerd, to continue using Kubernetes effectively.

The deprecation and eventual removal of Dockershim was a significant development in the Kubernetes ecosystem. It reflected Kubernetes' commitment to standardization, security, and modularity while acknowledging the evolving landscape of container runtimes and the need to adapt to industry best practices. Users who had been using Docker with Kubernetes needed to be aware of this change and plan accordingly to ensure a smooth transition to a different container runtime.

What is the difference between the container runtime and the CRI?

The container runtime and the CRI serve different purposes within the Kubernetes ecosystem, but they are closely related. This section provides a breakdown of their differences and their roles.

Container runtime

The container runtime is the software component responsible for the core task of running and managing containers. To understand its role, consider its main characteristics:

- **Purpose**: The container runtime software is responsible for running and managing containers. It is the component that interacts directly with the host operating system's kernel to create, start, stop, and manage containers.

- **Example runtimes**: Docker, Containerd, rkt, and others. The choice of runtime can vary as it affects how containers are created and managed on a node.

- **Features**: Container runtimes may have various features, such as image management, network management, and container storage. Some runtimes are more comprehensive, while others are more minimalistic.

- **Independence**: Container runtimes are not specific to Kubernetes and can be used independently to run containers outside of Kubernetes environments.

- **Flexibility**: Kubernetes can be configured to use different container runtimes based on user preferences or specific use cases. This flexibility allows Kubernetes to adapt to different runtime environments.

The CRI

The **Container Runtime Interface (CRI)** is a Kubernetes project that acts as a standardized bridge, defining the communication interface between Kubernetes components (like the kubelet) and the various container runtimes. Its key aspects are as follows:

- **Purpose**: The CRI is a Kubernetes project that defines an interface between Kubernetes and container runtimes. It serves as an intermediary layer between Kubernetes components (e.g., the kubelet) and container runtimes.

- **Standardization**: The primary goal of the CRI is to standardize the interaction between Kubernetes and container runtimes, making it easier to integrate new runtimes and maintain compatibility. It defines the API for the control plane so that it can communicate with container runtimes.

- **Components**: The CRI consists of two main components: the kubelet container runtime service (the kubelet CRI) and the container runtime (e.g., Containerd). These components work together to create and manage containers within Kubernetes.

- **Security and isolation**: The CRI helps ensure the security and isolation of containers within the Kubernetes environment. It allows Kubernetes to interact with container runtimes securely.

- **Pluggable runtimes**: With the CRI, Kubernetes can support different container runtimes that adhere to the CRI specifications. This pluggable architecture enables users to choose their preferred runtime, such as Docker or Containerd, while keeping Kubernetes in control of container orchestration.

In summary, the container runtime is the software responsible for executing containers, while the CRI defines a standardized interface for Kubernetes to communicate with container runtimes. The CRI is a critical component for Kubernetes because it allows Kubernetes to work with various container runtimes seamlessly, enhancing flexibility and compatibility. By using the CRI, Kubernetes maintains a clear separation between the container runtime and the Kubernetes control plane, making it easier to integrate new runtimes and ensure that containers are managed securely and effectively within the cluster. Please see the following figure and commit it to memory; this will help you give the correct answer to this question.

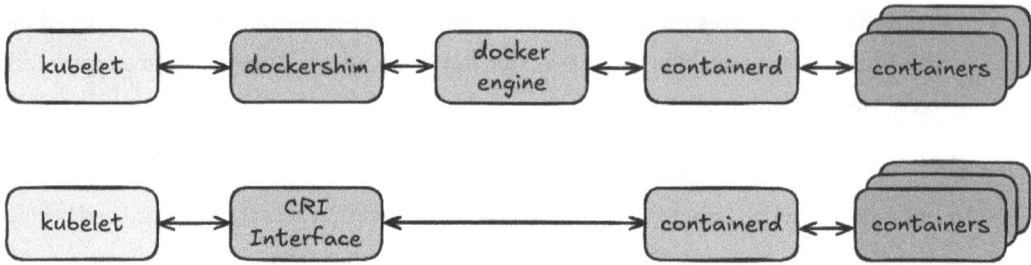

Figure 2.4 – The Shift from Dockershim to the Container Runtime Interface (CRI)

Static Pods: A special case for node-level services

This question can be unexpected at this stage of the interview; we will cover container deployment options in later chapters. According to our experience, interviewers ask these questions right after touching on Kubernetes node components. The reason is obvious—using static Pods, you can maintain more Kubernetes node components if you need them. In Kubernetes, a **static Pod** refers to a type of Pod that is managed directly by the kubelet running on a node, as opposed to being handled by the Kubernetes control plane. Static Pods are typically used for running essential system-level or node-specific services on a Kubernetes node. They are defined as configuration files on the node itself and do not appear in the Kubernetes API server. Here are some key characteristics and use cases for static Pods:

- **Managed by the kubelet**: The kubelet, which runs on each node in the cluster, is responsible for managing static Pods. It watches a specific directory for static Pod configuration files and ensures that the Pods specified are created and maintained.

- **Configuration location**: Static Pod configuration files are typically located in a directory specific to the kubelet. The exact location can vary, depending on the Kubernetes distribution and configuration, but a common location is `/etc/kubernetes/manifests` or `/etc/kubernetes/kubelet.d/`.

- **Node-specific**: Static Pods are usually used to run node-specific services or components that are required for the proper functioning of the node, such as the container runtime (e.g., Docker or containerd), kube-proxy, CNI, or monitoring agents.

- **No API server control**: Unlike regular Pods in Kubernetes, static Pods are not defined or controlled by the Kubernetes API server. They do not have associated PodSpecs in the API server, and therefore, they are not managed through Kubernetes manifests such as Deployments or StatefulSets.

- **Kubelet restart:** When the kubelet starts or restarts, it reads the static Pod's configuration files, creates the Pods, and monitors their life cycle. If a static Pod goes down for any reason, the kubelet attempts to restart it.

Static Pods are useful for deploying essential components on each node in a Kubernetes cluster. They are commonly used for bootstrapping node-specific services and ensuring that critical system components are always running. However, because they are separate from the Kubernetes API, they are not portable and can't be managed through higher-level Kubernetes constructs such as Deployments or ReplicationControllers. They are typically used for components that must be tightly coupled with a specific node's operation.

> **Interview Tip**
>
> **Question:** *What is a Static Pod and when is it used?*
>
> **Answer:** A **Static Pod** is a Pod that is managed directly by the kubelet on a node, without being controlled by the API Server. They are defined by configuration files in a local directory on the node (like `/etc/kubernetes/manifests`). Static Pods are typically used for bootstrapping essential system components on a node, such as kube-proxy, CNI plugins, or even the control plane components themselves.

Essential cluster services

Now that we've covered the architecture of both the control plane and the worker nodes, we need to explore the services that allow them—and the applications they run—to function as a cohesive system. These essential services handle critical tasks like networking and service discovery, tying all the individual components together.

Service discovery with DNS

For services to find each other within a Kubernetes cluster, they need a reliable discovery mechanism. This is the critical role of DNS. While not a core compiled component of the control plane itself, DNS is an essential cluster service, typically running as Pods (like CoreDNS), that enables reliable communication between applications.

Here's how the DNS service fits within the Kubernetes control plane:

- **Kubernetes control plane components:** The Kubernetes control plane comprises several critical components, such as the API server, etcd, the controller manager, and the scheduler, among others.

- **DNS service:** The DNS service is integrated with the control plane. This service provides DNS resolution and service discovery capabilities to Pods and services within the cluster.

- **Service discovery:** Kubernetes applications and services rely on the DNS service to discover other services within the cluster. They use DNS names to communicate with other Pods and services, abstracting the underlying IP addresses.

- **Load balancing:** The DNS service also manages load balancing for services. When a service is created, it automatically sets up DNS records that distribute traffic to the appropriate Pods behind it. This helps ensure an even distribution of traffic and high availability.

- **Custom configuration:** The DNS service can be customized to suit the specific needs of the cluster. Administrators can define custom DNS names and adapt the DNS configuration as required. It plays a vital role in service discovery, load balancing, and DNS resolution, making it easier for applications to interact and communicate seamlessly within the cluster.

The following figure shows how it works:

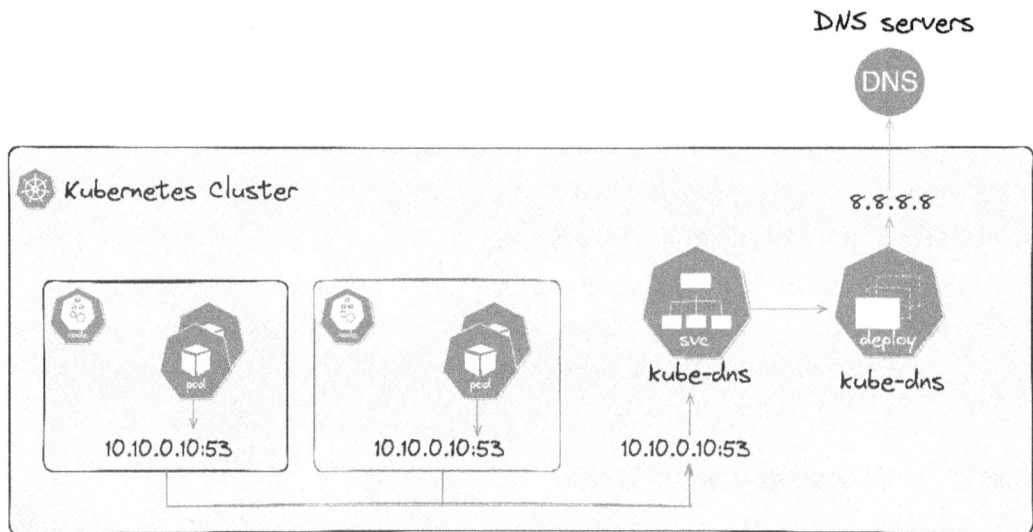

Figure 2.5 – kube-dns in action

This diagram shows how DNS resolution works inside a Kubernetes cluster using the kube-dns service. All Pods send DNS queries to a central kube-dns endpoint (10.10.0.10:53), which resolves internal service names or forwards external queries to public DNS servers, such as 8.8.8.8. This setup enables seamless service discovery and external name resolution within the cluster.

> **Interview Tip**
>
> **Question:** *How does DNS enable service discovery in Kubernetes?*
>
> **Answer:** The cluster DNS service, typically provided by CoreDNS, enables a reliable discovery mechanism for services to find each other. Applications can use stable DNS names to communicate with other services, abstracting away the underlying, ephemeral IP addresses of Pods. When a Service is created, DNS records are automatically set up to distribute traffic to the appropriate backing Pods.

In summary, the DNS service is a critical component of the Kubernetes control plane that plays a vital role in service discovery, load balancing, and DNS resolution. It helps applications interact and communicate seamlessly within the cluster.

CoreDNS vs. kube-dns

When it comes to providing DNS resolution and service discovery within a Kubernetes cluster, there are two DNS server options available: kube-dns and CoreDNS. Both have their advantages, but choosing between them depends on specific requirements and preferences.

For new Kubernetes clusters, especially those running more recent versions of Kubernetes, CoreDNS is often the preferred option. This is because CoreDNS is more extensible and Kubernetes-native, and it has become the default DNS server in most Kubernetes distributions.

For existing clusters still using kube-dns, transitioning to CoreDNS may be beneficial. CoreDNS not only aligns with Kubernetes' future direction but also provides greater flexibility. However, both kube-dns and CoreDNS can adequately handle DNS services within your Kubernetes cluster. The choice ultimately depends on your specific needs, level of familiarity, and the version of Kubernetes you're using. For most cases, CoreDNS is recommended due to its extensibility and community support.

While DNS answers the question *"What is the IP address for this service name?"*, it relies on a fundamental assumption: that every Pod already has an IP address and can send traffic over a network. Providing this underlying network connectivity is the job of the **Container Network Interface (CNI)**.

Pod networking with CNI

We will cover this question in more detail in *Part 3*, but here, it's always beneficial to understand the core aspects of CNI. Kubernetes doesn't handle networking itself. Instead, it uses the **Container Network Interface (CNI)**, a standard plug-in system. Think of CNI as a contract: Kubernetes tells the kubelet to create a Pod, and the kubelet then delegates all network setup—like assigning an IP address and configuring routes—to whichever CNI plugin you've installed (like Calico or Flannel). This modular design makes Kubernetes incredibly flexible, allowing you to choose the networking solution that best fits your security and performance needs.

> **Interview Tip**
>
> **Question:** *What is the role of the Container Network Interface (CNI)?*
>
> **Answer:** The role of the CNI is to provide a standard, plug-in system for networking in Kubernetes. Kubernetes delegates all network setup—such as assigning IP addresses to Pods and configuring routes—to a CNI plugin like Calico or Flannel. This modular design makes Kubernetes incredibly flexible, allowing users to choose a networking solution that fits their needs.

The following are some of the key aspects of CNI:

- **Modularity:** CNI is designed to be modular and extensible. This means that various networking solutions can implement the CNI interface, making it easy to swap or choose different network plugins based on your requirements.

- **Plug-and-play:** CNI plugins can be used to configure container networking as containers are created and destroyed. This allows for dynamic and automatic network setup for Pods and containers.

- **Network isolation:** CNI enables network isolation between containers and Pods, ensuring that they can communicate with each other and external networks while maintaining security boundaries.

- **Common interface:** CNI provides a common interface for different network plugins to help with configuring network interfaces, IP address assignment, routing, and more. It helps ensure that network configurations are consistent and standardized.

Here's how CNI works in the context of Kubernetes:

- **kubelet integration**: The Kubernetes kubelet, which runs on each node in a cluster, interacts with CNI plugins to configure networking for Pods. When a Pod is created, the kubelet calls a CNI plugin to set up the networking environment for the Pod's containers.

- **CNI plugin execution**: The kubelet runs CNI plugins specified in the Pod's network configuration. This typically involves calling the CNI plugin binary and passing it the necessary configuration parameters.

- **Network configuration**: The CNI plugin performs network configuration tasks, such as assigning IP addresses, setting up routing, and establishing network policies based on the specified network configuration.

- **Container networking**: After the CNI plugin has configured the network for the Pod, containers within the Pod can communicate with each other and with external services through the defined network setup.

CNI allows for a wide range of network plugins to be used in Kubernetes, depending on specific use cases and requirements. Examples of CNI plugins include Flannel, Calico, and Weave. These plugins offer different features and capabilities, such as network policy enforcement, overlay networking, and direct routing, making it possible for you to tailor network configurations to the needs of your Kubernetes workloads.

Understanding the components of a Kubernetes cluster is the first step. The next is learning how to interact with and operate it. In this final section, we'll shift from architecture to practice, covering how you communicate with the cluster and the fundamental models for deploying one in the real world.

Managing and deploying a cluster

Understanding the components of a Kubernetes cluster is the first step. The next is learning how to interact with and operate it. In this final section, we'll shift from architecture to practice, covering how you communicate with the cluster and the fundamental models for deploying one in the real world.

Interacting with the Kubernetes API

You can interact with the Kubernetes API in three primary ways. There are different methods to interact with the Kubernetes API, such as using the `kubectl` command-line tool, client libraries, or making HTTP requests directly to the API server. Here's a breakdown of how you can interact with the Kubernetes API using these methods:

- kubectl command-line tool:

  - kubectl is the primary command-line tool for interacting with Kubernetes clusters. You can use it to perform various operations on the cluster, including creating, updating, and deleting resources, as well as inspecting the cluster's state.

  - To interact with the Kubernetes API using kubectl, you typically must set up its configuration by either copying the kubeconfig file generated during cluster initialization or using the kubectl config commands to switch between contexts if you're managing multiple clusters.

The following are some example commands:

```
# List all pods in the default namespace:
>kubectl get pods
# Delete pod
> kubectl delete pod pod-name
# Get Cluster version
>kubectl version
```

- Kubernetes client libraries:

  - Kubernetes provides client libraries for various programming languages (e.g., Python, Go, Java) that allow you to interact with the API programmatically. You can use these libraries to build custom applications or automation scripts that communicate with the API server.

  - Depending on the programming language, you'll need to import the client library and create objects to interact with Kubernetes resources. You'll also need to set up authentication and configure the API client.

The following is an example of using the Kubernetes library in Python:

```
from kubernetes import client, config
config.load_kube_config()
v1 = client.CoreV1Api()
print("Listing pods with their IPs and labels:")
ret = v1.list_pod_for_all_namespaces(watch=False)
for pod in ret.items:
    print(
        f"{pod.status.pod_ip}\t"
```

```python
        f"{pod.metadata.namespace}\t"
        f"{pod.metadata.name}"
    )
    # Print labels
    print("Labels:")
    labels = pod.metadata.labels
    if labels:
        for k, v in labels.items():
            print(f"  {k}: {v}")
    else:
        print("  No labels")
    print("-" * 30)
```

💡 **Quick tip**: Enhance your coding experience with the **AI Code Explainer** and **Quick Copy** features. Open this book in the next-gen Packt Reader. Click the **Copy** button

(1) to quickly copy code into your coding environment, or click the **Explain** button

(2) to get the AI assistant to explain a block of code to you.

Copy   Explain

①   ②

```javascript
function calculate(a, b) {
    return {sum: a + b};
};
```

🔒 **The next-gen Packt Reader** is included for free with the purchase of this book. Scan the QR code OR go to https://packtpub.com/unlock, then use the search bar to find this book by name. Double-check the edition shown to make sure you get the right one.

- Direct HTTP requests:

  - The Kubernetes API is RESTful, and you can make HTTP requests directly to interact with it. This method is typically used when you need to build custom integrations or tools that don't have dedicated client libraries.

  - To interact with the API directly, you'll need to authenticate and authorize your requests using client certificates or tokens. You'll also need to know the API endpoint (usually `https://<cluster-ip>:<port>`) and the API paths for different resources.

Here's an example of listing Pods using a direct HTTP request:

```
# List all pods in the default namespace using curl utility
> curl https://<cluster-ip>:<port>/api/v1/namespaces/default/pods -H
"Authorization: Bearer <token>"
```

When working with Kubernetes, using the API allows you to have precise control over your cluster. You can perform basic operations using kubectl, create your own applications, and integrate with other systems. To ensure safety, it's important to have a clear understanding of the authentication and authorization mechanisms that govern your interactions with the API.

Using `kubectl` or client libraries is how you manage a cluster day-to-day. But before you can manage a cluster, you need to have one. This brings up one of the most critical decisions an organization has to make: how to provision and maintain the cluster itself.

Deployment models: Self-hosted vs managed services

When you need maximum control over your cluster's configuration and underlying infrastructure, a self-hosted deployment is the common approach. This involves provisioning your own servers (cloud VMs or bare metal) and installing the control plane and worker node components yourself. While complex, tools like `kubeadm` can streamline the process. An interviewer will expect you to know the high-level steps involved.

We recommend starting your answer by listing the following items:

1. Mention prerequisites:

   a. Servers or cloud instances with a supported operating system (e.g., Ubuntu, CentOS).

   b. Each server should have containerd or a compatible container runtime installed.

   c. Ensure that the servers can communicate with each other over the network.

2. Describe the control plane initialization process:

   a. Install the necessary software components on the controller node from the binaries or by using the Linux package manager.

   b. Initiate cluster creation using the kubeadm tool.

   c. Configure access to the newly configured cluster using kube-config.

3. Join worker nodes:

   a. For clusters deployed using **kubeadm**, join the worker nodes using the kubeadm join command.

   b. For other deployment tools, such as **kubespray** or **RKE**, the process may vary slightly. It's a good idea to confirm whether there are any specific constraints or preferred tools for the cluster.

4. Configure inter-cluster networking:

   a. Use a **Container Network Interface (CNI)** solution, such as Flannel or Calico, to enable networking between the nodes.

5. Verify nodes and resources:

   a. Use the kubectl tool to check the status of the nodes and other resources.

As you can see, even with tools like kubeadm, the self-hosted approach requires significant effort and expertise in areas like networking, security, and lifecycle management. For many teams, the operational burden of managing the control plane itself is a distraction from their primary goal of deploying applications. This challenge leads to the second major deployment model: using a managed service.

The managed option: The cloud advantage

All the control plane components mentioned previously are significant to any Kubernetes cluster. Supporting and maintaining these components demands substantial effort and a deep understanding of the Kubernetes ecosystem as a whole. Operations teams must manage how these components are monitored, maintained, and upgraded with diligence while ensuring services remain uninterrupted for running workloads.

> **Interview Tip**
>
> **Question:** *What are the main trade-offs between a self-hosted and a managed Kubernetes service?*
>
> **Answer:** The choice between a self-hosted and managed Kubernetes cluster is a trade-off between control and convenience. A **self-hosted** deployment provides maximum control over the cluster's configuration and infrastructure but requires significant effort and expertise to manage. A **managed service** simplifies operations and reduces operational overhead by having a cloud provider manage the control plane but offers less customization.

Public and private cloud providers offer various deployment options for Kubernetes workloads within their environments. In some rare and specialized scenarios, companies may establish their private clouds with custom methods for deploying and maintaining the control plane. However, it's important to note that choosing a managed service from a cloud provider offers several distinct advantages. The following are the most noticeable:

- **Simplified operations**: Managed Kubernetes services abstract away much of the complexity involved in provisioning, configuring, and maintaining a Kubernetes cluster. One of the most significant benefits of managed Kubernetes services is that they simplify operations, making them more accessible to teams with varying levels of Kubernetes expertise.

- **Reduced operational overhead**: Companies can offload the operational burden of managing Kubernetes infrastructure, including patching, upgrades, and scaling, to the cloud provider. This reduces the need for in-house expertise and operational overhead.

- **Cost efficiency**: Managed Kubernetes services often follow a pay-as-you-go model, which can be cost-effective for companies. You pay for the resources you use and avoid the costs associated with maintaining physical hardware or managing a dedicated Kubernetes cluster.

- **Scalability**: Cloud-based managed Kubernetes services make it easy to scale clusters up or down based on changing workloads. This elasticity ensures that resources are available as needed without over-provisioning occurring.

- **High availability**: Many managed Kubernetes offerings provide built-in high availability features, ensuring that clusters and applications remain accessible and resilient to failures. Cloud providers often have redundant infrastructure across multiple data centers.

- **Security features**: Managed Kubernetes services incorporate security best practices and may offer features such as automated security patches, network policies, and integrated identity and access management, enhancing cluster security.

- **Integration**: Cloud providers offer seamless integration with their other services, enabling companies to leverage a broader ecosystem of tools and services for tasks such as logging, monitoring, and CI/CD pipelines.

- **Rapid deployment**: Managed Kubernetes services allow quick cluster deployment, enabling teams to focus on deploying and managing applications rather than dealing with cluster setup.

- **Global reach**: Cloud providers have data centers and regions worldwide, making it easy to deploy Kubernetes clusters close to end users and take advantage of low-latency global access.

- **Vendor support**: Companies receive support directly from the cloud provider, which can be advantageous in case of issues, and they often have access to dedicated support teams.

- **Compliance and certification**: Cloud providers may offer certified Kubernetes distributions that meet specific compliance standards, which is crucial for companies in regulated industries.

- **Community and ecosystem**: Kubernetes is a rapidly evolving open source project. Cloud providers stay updated with the latest Kubernetes releases and contribute to the Kubernetes community, ensuring that companies have access to new features and best practices.

Ultimately, the choice between a self-hosted and a managed Kubernetes cluster is a trade-off between control and convenience. Understanding the responsibilities and benefits of each model is crucial for making informed architectural decisions.

Summary

In this chapter, we reviewed the key components and functions that form the foundation of a Kubernetes cluster. We dissected the architecture into its two main parts: the control plane and the worker nodes. You learned that the control plane acts as the brain of the cluster, with essential components like the API Server, etcd, the Scheduler, and various Controller Managers working together to maintain the desired state.

We then explored the worker nodes, the machinery where your applications run. We covered the roles of the kubelet, kube-proxy, and the container runtime. A key takeaway was understanding the modern shift from Docker to CRI-compliant runtimes like Containerd, and the deprecation of Dockershim, which simplifies the cluster's architecture.

With this solid architectural foundation in place, we are now ready to move from the components of the cluster to running applications on the cluster. In the next chapter, we will explore the fundamental building block of any Kubernetes application: the Pod. You will learn how to create and manage Pods and discover the powerful controllers—such as Deployments, ReplicaSets, StatefulSets, and Jobs—that Kubernetes provides to orchestrate, scale, and manage the life-cycle of your workloads.

Unlock this book's exclusive benefits now

UNLOCK NOW

Scan this QR code or go to https://packtpub.com/unlock, then search for this book by name.

Note: Keep your purchase invoice ready before you start.

Part 2

Schedulers, Workloads, and Scaling

In this part, you'll learn how the scheduler makes placement decisions, the differences between key workload types such as Deployments, StatefulSets, and Jobs, and how to choose the right one for the task at hand. It also covers smart scaling strategies—both manual and automatic—to help you make the most of your resources and ensure your applications stay responsive as demand grows.

This part of the book includes the following chapters:

- *Chapter 3, Exploring Kubernetes Basics*
- *Chapter 4, Principles of Scaling: Horizontal vs. Vertical*
- *Chapter 5, Autoscaling in Action*

3

Exploring Kubernetes Basics

In *Chapter 2*, we explored vital parts of the Kubernetes control plane. Now, this chapter will not only offer hands-on guidance but also prepare you to tackle any questions related to running applications in Kubernetes. This chapter is about connecting the dots between theory and practice and anticipating questions you'll face in real-world scenarios or interviews.

We'll kick things off with Kubernetes Pods, the atomic units of our Kubernetes universe. You'll learn what a Pod is, delve into its operational dynamics, and master its lifecycle and deployment strategies. Understanding Pods is fundamental to any Kubernetes practitioner's toolkit.

As we progress, we'll explore the spectrum of pod orchestration mechanisms—from jobs for one-off executions to CronJobs for scheduled operations; from ReplicaSets for consistent state-keeping to Deployments for smooth updates and scaling. DaemonSets for specialized node tasks and static Pods for node-direct scheduling will also be featured, providing you with a full-circle understanding of workload management.

Equally important are Labels and Selectors, the Kubernetes equivalent of organization and retrieval tools. We'll dissect their importance in managing resources, ensuring you're ready to answer any question about resource organization.

We then transition to namespaces. Beyond hands-on practice, we'll consider the *whys* and *hows*, equipping you with the knowledge to answer questions about the strategic use of namespaces for resource isolation and management.

We will be covering these topics under the following main headings:

- The atomic unit – The Pod
- Managing stateless applications
- Managing specialized workloads

By the end of this chapter, you will have mastered the following:

- **The essence of Pods in Kubernetes**: You'll clearly understand what Pods are and their role in a Kubernetes environment
- **The seven pathways to Pod orchestration**: We'll navigate through the seven methods to run Pods in Kubernetes
- **The significance of Labels**: You'll comprehend why Labels are the linchpins of Kubernetes, crucial for the efficient management and selection of resources
- **The art of resource organization**: We'll tie it all together with namespaces, showing you how to neatly package and isolate resources, which is key to maintaining a well-organized and secure Kubernetes cluster

With these insights, you'll not only be able to perform Kubernetes tasks with confidence but also be prepared to answer any question on these topics with clarity and depth.

The atomic unit — The Pod

Before you can run a complex, scaled-out application, you must first understand the single smallest unit Kubernetes can manage: the **Pod**. Think of the Pod as the atom of the Kubernetes universe; everything else—from scaling to self-healing—is built on top of it. In this first section, we will dissect this fundamental concept. We'll explore why Pods can hold more than one container, how those containers share resources such as networking and storage, and how specialized Init Container and Sidecar Container enhance their power. Finally, we'll dive into the Pod's lifecycle and the health probes that keep it running, which is a critical topic for any troubleshooting interview. Master the Pod, and you've mastered the foundation of all Kubernetes workloads.

What is a Pod? (Core concept: multi-container pattern)

In Kubernetes, a Pod is more than just a wrapper for a container. It's the smallest unit you can create and manage in a Kubernetes environment.

Think of a Pod as a wrapper or a small package for one or more containers. These containers in a Pod share resources and are scheduled together on the same host machine.

Interview tip

Question: *Why do containers within a Pod share storage and network resources?*

Answer: Sharing storage and networking makes inter-container communication faster and more efficient, allowing tightly coupled processes to collaborate seamlessly within the same Pod environment.

This shared context allows for efficient communication and data sharing.

You can also liken a Pod to a process in an operating system. Just as a process can contain multiple threads that communicate quickly and share resources, a Pod encapsulates containers that work in a similar fashion. The containers in a Pod are like threads in a process, offering rapid communication and shared resources. This analogy is particularly useful because it highlights how containers within a Pod can operate with high efficiency and low latency, much like threads within a process.

But why Pods? Why not just use containers directly? Pods allow Kubernetes to manage containers effectively. They provide a layer of abstraction over containerized applications, which is key for deploying, scaling, and managing applications in a Kubernetes cluster. By grouping containers in Pods, Kubernetes can keep your applications running smoothly, even as it moves them around in the cluster for various reasons, such as load balancing or hardware failures, as shown in *Figure 3.1*:

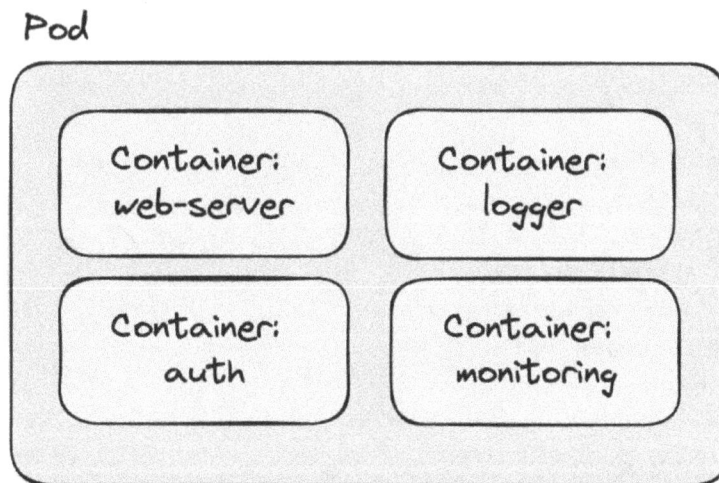

Figure 3.1 – Multi-container Kubernetes pod layout

Inside a Pod: Shared network and storage

Now, let's look inside a Pod. What will you find? Primarily, there are containers. These are the same containers you might run with Docker, but in Kubernetes, they're wrapped in a Pod.

Each Pod can contain one or more containers. When there's more than one container in a Pod, these containers can communicate with each other, and they share a few things:

- **Shared networking**: All containers in a Pod share an IP address and port space. This means they can find and talk to each other easily using localhost. They also share the same network namespace, which is crucial for communication.
- **Shared storage**: Pods can specify a set of shared storage volumes. These volumes can be accessed by all the containers in the Pod, allowing data to be shared between them. This shared storage is key for applications that need to share files, data, or persistent storage.

Having discussed shared storage in Pods, let's see a practical example of how this can work in Kubernetes. Consider the following YAML configuration for a Pod:

```
apiVersion: v1
kind: Pod
metadata:
  name: shared-volume-pod
spec:
  volumes:
  - name: shared-data
    emptyDir: {}
  containers:
  - name: web-server
    image: nginx
    volumeMounts:
    - name: shared-data
      mountPath: /usr/share/nginx/html
  - name: data-updater
    image: debian
    volumeMounts:
    - name: shared-data
      mountPath: /shared
    command: ["/bin/sh", "-c"]
    args:
```

```
- while true; do
    date >> /shared/index.html;
    sleep 1;
  done
```

In this example, we're defining a Pod named shared-volume-pod. The Pod contains two containers: web-server and data-updater. Let's look at this in more detail:

- **Volume setup**: We've defined a volume named shared-data, and its type is emptyDir. This volume is created when the Pod starts on a node and exists as long as the Pod runs on that node. Initially, the volume is empty.

- **Web server container**: The first container, named web-server, uses the nginx image. It mounts the shared volume at /usr/share/nginx/html. This is where nginx expects to find its HTML content to serve.

- **Data updater container**: The second container, data-updater, uses the Debian image. It mounts the same shared volume at /shared. This container has a simple script running in a loop: it writes the current date and time to a file named index.html in the shared volume every second.

- **Working together**: Both containers mount the same emptyDir volume, allowing one to write data that the other can immediately read. The nginx server serves whatever content is in its web directory. Meanwhile, the data-updater container is constantly updating this content. Anyone accessing the nginx server will see the updated date and time with each refresh.

Interview tip

Question: *What is the purpose of* emptyDir *in a Pod volume definition?*

Answer: The emptyDir volume type creates a temporary shared directory accessible by all containers in a Pod, which exists only for the life of the Pod and is useful for transient data sharing.

This example is a simple demonstration of how containers within a Pod can share data using volumes. We'll dive deeper into the concepts of volumes and their types in *Chapter 8*, where you'll get a comprehensive understanding of Kubernetes storage solutions.

In the following diagram, you'll see a visualization of this setup – how the `shared-volume` pod orchestrates interaction between the nginx server and the data updater, utilizing the shared volume for real-time data synchronization.

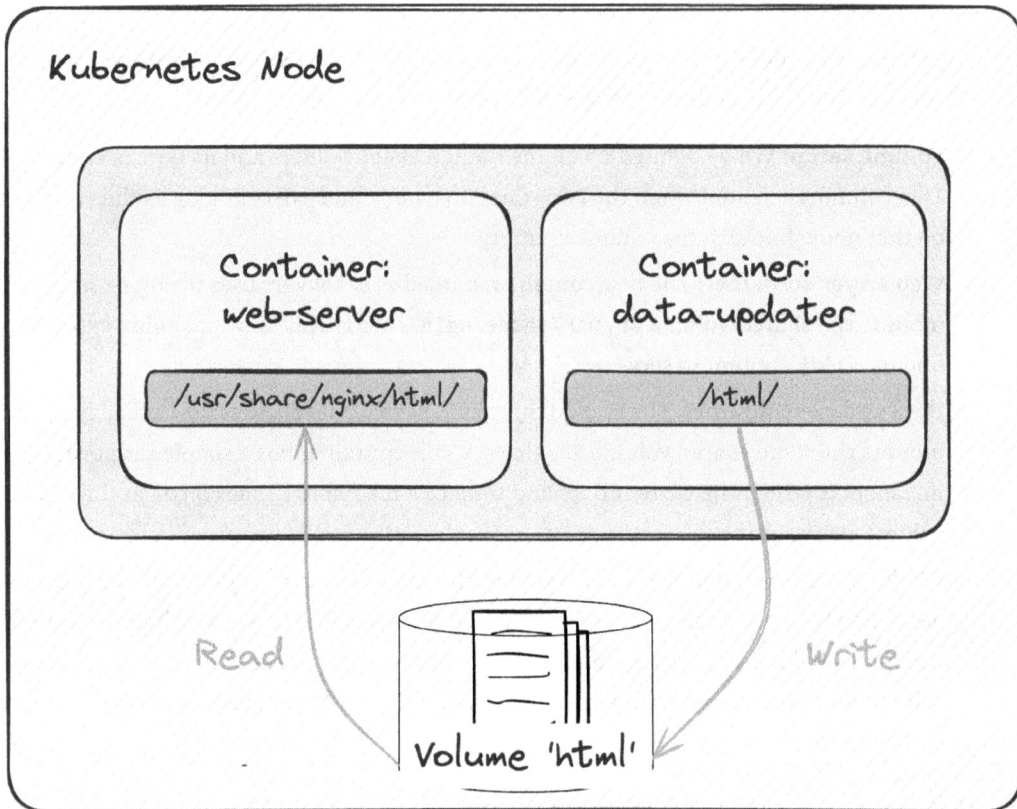

Figure 3.2 – Data sharing between containers using a shared volume within a Pod

So, a Pod is like a small, self-contained environment for your containers. Inside this environment, your containers can run and interact closely, as if they were on the same physical machine, but with the benefits of being in a distributed cloud-native environment. Understanding this will be crucial as you move forward in Kubernetes, whether you're deploying simple web apps or complex distributed systems.

After understanding that a Pod can hold more than one container, you might wonder why this is useful. This brings us to our next topic – Init Containers and Sidecar Containers.

Specialized containers: Init Container and Sidecar Container

As we delve deeper into the Kubernetes ecosystem, two specialized container types, **Init Containers** and **Sidecar Containers**, can enhance your Pod's functionality and reliability. Init Containers and Sidecar Containers are two such enhancements that play unique roles in the lifecycle and operation of pods in Kubernetes.

Init Containers — Preparing the ground

Init Containers are the first to run and complete before any application containers are started. They are designed to perform setup tasks that need to happen before the application container can successfully run. This could involve waiting for a service to be ready, performing system checks, or setting up the environment that the application depends on.

Interview tip

Question: *What is the main difference between an Init Container and a regular container in a Pod?*

Answer: Init Containers run once and must complete successfully before regular containers start. They're ideal for setup tasks, such as preparing environments or checking dependencies.

Unlike regular containers, Init Containers do not support probes such as livenessProbe, readinessProbe, or startupProbe (we will speak about the pod lifecycle shortly), because these are designed for containers that continue running, not those that exit upon completion of their tasks. If an Init Container fails, the Kubernetes cluster will restart it until it succeeds, unless the pod's restart policy is set to Never.

Sidecar Containers — Running alongside your application

Sidecar Containers are used to extend the functionality of the main container without bundling additional capabilities into the main application image. They run in parallel with the main container and are often used for tasks such as logging, monitoring, data synchronization, or other utilities that support the main application.

Interview tip

Question: *When should you use a Sidecar Container in your Pod design?*

Answer: Sidecars are great when you want to add modular support services to your main application—such as logging, monitoring, or proxying—without modifying the core application logic.

Sidecar Containers can also use probes to manage their lifecycle, unlike Init Containers. They continue to run as long as the pod is running, providing ongoing support services to the main application.

Code examples and configuration

In practice, you would define Init Containers in your pod specification under `initContainers`. Here, you can specify multiple Init Containers, which will execute sequentially:

```
apiVersion: v1
kind: Pod
metadata:
  name: example-pod
spec:
  initContainers:
  - name: init-mydb
    image: busybox
    command: ['sh', '-c', "echo Initializing DB"]
  containers:
  - name: mydb
    image: mydb:1.0
    command: ['sh', '-c', "echo Starting DB"]
```

This configuration snippet defines a simple Init Container that runs a command to initialize a database, followed by the main application container that starts the database service.

For a Sidecar Container, you would simply define it as another container within the `containers` section of the pod specification, alongside your main application container:

```
apiVersion: v1
kind: Pod
metadata:
```

```
    name: example-pod
  spec:
    containers:
    - name: myapp
      image: myapp:1.0
      command: ['sh', '-c', "echo Running App"]
    - name: myapp-logger
      image: logger:1.0
      command: ['sh', '-c', "echo Logging App Activity"]
```

Here, a Sidecar Container named myapp-logger is defined alongside the main application container, myapp. It's responsible for logging application activity.

Understanding and utilizing Init and Sidecar Containers will allow you to structure your Kubernetes applications more effectively. Init Containers offer a secure, transient environment for setup tasks, while Sidecar Containers provide a modular approach to enhancing your application's functionality. These container types are fundamental in creating a robust and scalable Kubernetes architecture.

By incorporating these containers into your Kubernetes strategy, you'll ensure that each component of your application is optimized for its specific role, leading to cleaner and more maintainable deployments.

With our exploration of Init Containers and Sidecar Containers, we've seen how they contribute to the setup and extended functionality of a Pod. These containers can influence the status of a Pod, but they don't encompass the whole picture of what's happening under the hood. Now is the perfect moment to pivot to the Pod Lifecycle, where we'll dissect the different phases a Pod can go through, from its inception to its termination.

Understanding the Pod Lifecycle will give you insight into the inner workings of a Pod's existence in a Kubernetes cluster. While the specific phases of Init and Sidecar Containers aren't explicitly labeled in this lifecycle, they are crucial steps in the journey of a Pod. Knowing the phases—Running, Failed, Succeeded, Unknown, and Pending—will equip you with the know-how to pinpoint exactly what's going on with your Pod at any given moment.

So, let's move forward, keeping in mind the groundwork laid by our specialized containers, and delve into the lifecycle of a Pod to understand the stages it goes through within a Kubernetes environment.

Managing Pod health: The Pod lifecycle and container probes

Every Pod in Kubernetes progresses through a lifecycle, a series of distinct phases from creation to termination. Understanding this lifecycle is not just theory; it's the key to debugging your applications. When a Pod gets stuck, its current phase tells you exactly where to start looking—whether the problem is scheduling, image pulling, or a crashing container.

Understanding Pod phases

Pods in Kubernetes go through several stages:

- **Pending**: When a Pod's status is Pending, it means the cluster has accepted the Pod's configuration, but it's not yet operational on a node. This is a transitional state that usually points to one of two common scenarios: the scheduler is still identifying the right node for placement, or the designated node is in the process of downloading the necessary container images.

- **Running**: The Pod has been scheduled on a node, and all of its containers have been created. At least one container is running, in the process of starting, or restarting.

- **Succeeded**: All containers in the Pod have terminated successfully and will not be restarted.

- **Failed**: All containers in the Pod have terminated, and at least one container has terminated in failure—that is, the container either exited with a nonzero status or was terminated by the system.

- **Unknown**: The status of the Pod is unknown. This typically happens due to a failure in communication with the node assigned to host the Pod.

A deeper understanding of these phases is critical for diagnosing and resolving issues with Pod deployment and operation.

> **Interview tip**
>
> **Question:** *Why is understanding the Pod lifecycle important for Kubernetes troubleshooting?*
>
> **Answer:** Knowing the lifecycle phases helps you diagnose and fix issues such as pending Pods, failed containers, or unreachable nodes more effectively during cluster operations or interviews.

How to troubleshoot and fix the CrashLoopBackoff status?

In the journey of a Pod from its creation to a stable state, sometimes things don't go as planned. One common issue that can occur is when a Pod can't reach the cherished Running state and instead falls into a CrashLoopBackOff state or remains in a Pending state indefinitely. This usually happens when the application within the Pod's container fails to start properly or keeps crashing. This situation is a common topic in Kubernetes interviews, where one might be asked how to troubleshoot such issues.

When you encounter CrashLoopBackOff, it's an indication that your Pod is trying to start its container, but the container keeps crashing during startup. Kubernetes will try to restart the container, but after repeated failures, it will back off for longer periods before trying again. A Pod stuck in Pending may indicate scheduling issues or problems with resource availability.

> **Interview tip**
>
> **Question:** *What does the* CrashLoopBackOff *status indicate in a Kubernetes Pod?*
>
> **Answer:** It means the container inside the Pod repeatedly crashes shortly after starting. Kubernetes backs off from restarting it and logs the error to help with debugging.

To troubleshoot these issues, Kubernetes provides several commands to get detailed information about resources and their current states:

- kubectl describe deployment: Use this command to check the status of a deployment. It can provide insights into whether the deployment can create desired replicas and whether there are any errors or issues with the deployment.

- kubectl describe pod: This command provides detailed information about the Pod's state, including events and conditions that can help you understand why a Pod is in a CrashLoopBackOff or Pending state.

- kubectl logs: With this command, you can view the logs from a container in a Pod. If a container is crashing, the logs often include the output from the container up to the point of failure, which can be invaluable in diagnosing the problem.

- kubectl get events: This command lists events in the cluster, which can provide a timeline of what has happened, helping to pinpoint issues.

Let's consider an example where you would use these commands to debug a Pod in a `CrashLoopBackOff` state:

```
kubectl describe deployment my-deployment
kubectl describe pod my-pod-1234
kubectl logs my-pod-1234 -c my-container
kubectl get events --sort-by='.metadata.creationTimestamp'
```

These commands should be run in sequence to gather comprehensive information about the deployment, the problematic Pod, the logs from the failing container within that Pod, and events in the cluster related to this Pod. By examining the output of these commands, you can often find the root cause of the issue.

If the Pod is in `CrashLoopBackOff`, the logs might show application errors, missing configuration files, or other issues that prevent the application from starting. If the Pod is stuck in `Pending`, the `describe` commands can show whether it's due to insufficient resources on the nodes or other scheduling constraints.

For Pods stuck in `CrashLoopBackOff`, it's also essential to look at the application code and its dependencies, as the issue often lies within the container. It could be a misconfigured environment variable, a missing file that the application expects, or a bug in the code itself.

Interview tip

Question: *Why are container probes critical for Pod health management in Kubernetes?*

Answer: Probes allow Kubernetes to detect whether a container is healthy, ready to serve traffic, or still starting up. This helps automate recovery and reduce downtime.

By understanding these commands and what to look for, you can effectively troubleshoot Pods in Kubernetes and get them back to a healthy state. Troubleshooting Pods is a critical skill and a frequent topic in technical interviews. Interviewers may ask this to assess your practical knowledge of Kubernetes and your problem-solving approach. So, it's beneficial to have a clear strategy for diagnosing and resolving issues with Pods, which are at the core of Kubernetes operations.

Container probes — Ensuring Pod health

Probes are used by Kubernetes to perform regular health checks on containers within a Pod. There are three types of probes:

- **Liveness probes:** These determine whether the container is running. If a liveness probe fails, the kubelet kills the container, and the container is subjected to its restart policy.
- **Readiness probes:** These determine whether the container is ready to handle requests. If a readiness probe fails, Kubernetes stops sending traffic to the pod until it passes the readiness check.
- **Startup probes:** These are used to determine whether a container application has started. If a startup probe is configured, it disables liveness and readiness checks until it succeeds, ensuring those probes don't interfere with the application startup.

> **Interview tip**
>
> **Question:** *What's the difference between a liveness probe and a readiness probe?*
>
> **Answer:** A liveness probe checks whether the container is running, and restarts it if it's not. A readiness probe checks whether the container is ready to serve traffic and removes it from service if it's not.

The following diagram visually summarizes the outcome when a liveness probe or readiness probe fails.

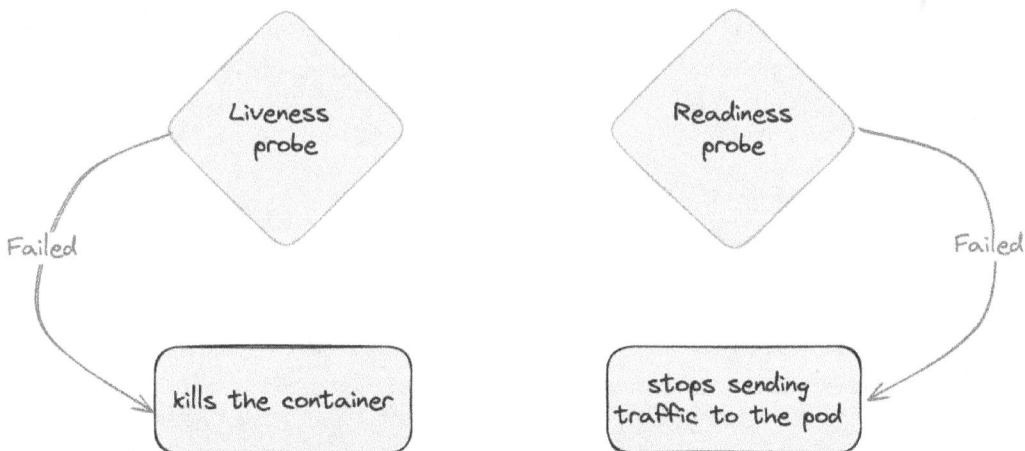

Figure 3.3 – Kubernetes health checks: liveness and readiness probes

Container probes in action — A code sample

Here's an example of defining a liveness probe with an HTTP GET request:

```yaml
apiVersion: v1
kind: Pod
metadata:
  name: liveness-http
spec:
  containers:
  - name: liveness
    image: registry.k8s.io/e2e-test-images/agnhost:2.39
    args:
    - /server
    livenessProbe:
      httpGet:
        path: /healthz
        port: 8080
        httpHeaders:
        - name: Custom-Header
          value: Awesome
      initialDelaySeconds: 3
      periodSeconds: 3
```

This snippet configures Kubernetes to perform an HTTP GET request to the /healthz endpoint of the application running in the container every three seconds, starting three seconds after the container starts. If the probe fails, the kubelet will kill the container and restart it, according to the Pod's restart policy.

> **Interview tip**
>
> **Question:** *When should you use a startup probe in a container?*
>
> **Answer:** Use startup probes for applications that take a long time to start. It prevents Kubernetes from killing the container during its slow boot by temporarily disabling other probes.

Integrating probes with your application

It's essential to integrate these probes into your application's operation logic to take full advantage of Kubernetes' self-healing capabilities. Your application should expose endpoints for liveness and readiness checks and handle these checks appropriately.

The Pod lifecycle is a fundamental concept that every Kubernetes practitioner must understand. It provides insights into application deployment, stability, and recovery. By integrating lifecycle concepts and probes into your application deployment, you can create robust systems that maximize Kubernetes' capabilities to build resilient and scalable applications.

Now that we have a good understanding of Pods and their lifecycles, we're ready to scale up. In a production environment, it's not practical to have just one pod for an application due to risks such as traffic surges or hardware failures. Here's where Kubernetes' auto-healing capability comes into play – it ensures high availability and scalability. The ReplicaSet is the key resource that enables this by maintaining a stable set of replica Pods running at any given time. We'll cover this next.

Managing stateless applications

A single Pod is a point of failure. If the node it's on crashes, the Pod and your application are gone. To build resilient, production-ready systems, you need a way to manage Pods automatically—ensuring a desired number of replicas are always running and healthy. This is the job of Kubernetes controllers. This section focuses on controllers designed for **stateless applications**, such as web servers or API gateways, where any Pod is interchangeable. We'll start with the foundational controller, the **ReplicaSet**, which guarantees a specific number of Pods are running. Then, we'll build on that concept to explore the **Deployment**, the most common and powerful controller you'll use daily for handling rolling updates, rollbacks, and declarative application management.

Foundation of scaling: ReplicaSets

ReplicaSets are a foundational Kubernetes concept that facilitates scaling and self-healing functionality for your applications. The purpose of a ReplicaSet is to maintain a stable set of replica Pods running at any given time. This is particularly useful in a production environment where the availability and scaling of your application are critical.

> **Interview tip**
>
> **Question:** *What is the primary function of a ReplicaSet in Kubernetes?*
>
> **Answer:** A ReplicaSet ensures a specified number of identical Pods are always running. It automatically replaces failed or deleted Pods to maintain the desired replica count.

The ReplicaSet specification block defines the desired state of how many replicas of a Pod should be running. It also includes a selector to identify the Pods it should manage, and a template to create new Pod replicas if necessary.

The following ReplicaSet manifest demonstrates how the replicas, selector, and template fields work together to maintain two backend Pods in the cluster:

```yaml
apiVersion: apps/v1
kind: ReplicaSet
metadata:
  name: backend-replicaset
spec:
  replicas: 2
  selector:
    matchLabels:
      type: backend
  template:
    metadata:
      labels:
        type: backend
    spec:
      containers:
      - name: backend-app
        image: nginx:1.25
        ports:
        - containerPort: 80
```

Here's a breakdown of the specifications:

- `replicas: 2` specifies that two instances of the Pod should be running.
- `selector` defines how the ReplicaSet identifies which Pods to manage. In this case, it's selecting Pods with a `type: backend` label.
- `template` specifies the data the ReplicaSet uses to create new Pods when needed. The template includes a label for the Pod and the container image to use.

Now that we've broken down the key fields, let's see how a ReplicaSet uses them in practice.

Auto-healing with ReplicaSets

If a Pod in a ReplicaSet is deleted, the ReplicaSet notices the change and creates a new Pod to replace it. This ensures the number of desired replicas is maintained, which is a crucial feature for fault tolerance and availability.

When there are more Pods running than specified in the ReplicaSet, Kubernetes will terminate the extra Pods to match the desired count. Conversely, if there are fewer Pods, it will create new ones.

When you create a ReplicaSet, a series of events unfolds:

1. The request to create a ReplicaSet is sent to the Kubernetes API server.
2. The ReplicaSet controller detects a new ReplicaSet creation event.
3. The controller creates new Pod definitions based on the specified number in the ReplicaSet definition.
4. The scheduler assigns these Pods to appropriate nodes.
5. The kubelet on the assigned nodes creates containers as per the Pod definitions.
6. Once the containers are created, Kubelet updates the API server with the status of the Pods.

Now that you understand the lifecycle and auto-healing process, let's put this into practice by defining and managing a ReplicaSet.

Creating and managing a ReplicaSet

Listing ReplicaSets and their details, scaling them, and managing their lifecycle can be done using various kubectl commands.

Here's an example of a ReplicaSet definition that ensures two backend-type Pods are always running:

```
apiVersion: apps/v1
kind: ReplicaSet
metadata:
  name: backend-replicaset
spec:
  replicas: 2
  selector:
    matchLabels:
      type: backend
  template:
```

```
metadata:
  labels:
    type: backend
spec:
  containers:
  - name: httpd-yup
    image: httpd
```

To create this ReplicaSet, you'd save it to a file and use kubectl apply -f replicaset.yaml. Once created, you can monitor and manage the ReplicaSet with kubectl commands, such as the following:

```
kubectl get rs                        # List all ReplicaSets
kubectl describe rs backend-replicaset # Get detailed info about the
                                      # backend-replicaset
kubectl delete rs backend-replicaset --cascade=false  # Delete ReplicaSet
                                                      # without deleting
                                                      # its Pods
```

Understanding the output of kubectl get rs is vital for troubleshooting. For instance, if the READY column is at 0, the Pods are not ready to handle traffic, which could be due to an application error or simply because the container is still starting up.

With ReplicaSets, we've ensured that our Kubernetes cluster maintains a specified number of Pod replicas to handle our application workload. But what happens when we need to update the application running within these Pods? How do we manage different versions or roll back to a previous version if something goes wrong? This is where Kubernetes Deployments come into play. Deployments provide us with the capability to update and iterate our applications seamlessly and manage changes to our Pods and ReplicaSets. Let's dive into the next section to explore Deployments, which will show us how to manage our application releases and updates gracefully in a Kubernetes environment.

Deployments in Kubernetes: Managing application lifecycles

You rarely create Pods directly for production applications. Why? Because a raw Pod has no self-healing or scaling capabilities. If its node goes down, the Pod is gone forever. Instead, you declare the desired state for your application using a higher-level controller. The most common controller for stateless apps is the **Deployment**, which automates updates, scaling, and rollbacks by managing Pods for you.

A Deployment provides a declarative way to manage your application's lifecycle. You tell the Deployment what you want your end state to look like—for example, "I want three replicas of my application running version 1.2.0"—and the Deployment controller works to make that happen. It automates deploying, updating, scaling, and rolling back your application, making it a cornerstone of modern Kubernetes operations.

Under the hood, a Deployment manages ReplicaSets. When you create or update a Deployment, it creates a new ReplicaSet. This ReplicaSet is then responsible for creating the actual Pods. This layered approach is what enables powerful features such as rollbacks and update history.

Interview tip

Question: *What's the difference between a Deployment and a ReplicaSet?*

Answer: A ReplicaSet's only job is to ensure a specific number of identical Pods are running at all times. A Deployment is a higher-level controller that manages ReplicaSets. You use a Deployment to handle updates, rollbacks, and scaling, and the Deployment, in turn, creates and manages the underlying ReplicaSets to achieve the desired state. You almost always interact with Deployments, not ReplicaSets directly.

Creating and inspecting a Deployment

You can create a Deployment imperatively using `kubectl`, which is great for quick tests. For example, to create a simple nginx Deployment, you would run the following:

```
kubectl create deployment nginx-deployment --image=nginx:alpine
```

This command instructs Kubernetes to create a Deployment named `nginx-deployment` using the `nginx:alpine` image. To verify its creation, you can run the following:

```
kubectl get deployments
```

This will list all Deployments in the current namespace, showing their desired, current, and ready states. You'll also see that a corresponding ReplicaSet and Pod have been created automatically.

Deployment strategies: RollingUpdate versus Recreate

The real power of a Deployment comes from how it handles updates. When you need to release a new version of your application—perhaps by changing the container image—the Deployment controller manages the transition gracefully. The way it performs this update is defined by its chosen strategy.

The Deployment resource has two built-in strategies you can specify in the manifest under `spec.strategy.type`:

- `Recreate`: This is the simplest strategy. The Deployment terminates all old Pods at once and then creates new ones. This approach is fast and straightforward, but results in **downtime** while old Pods are gone and new ones are starting up. It's generally only suitable for development or non-critical environments where service interruption is acceptable.

- `RollingUpdate`: This is the default and most common strategy. The Deployment updates Pods incrementally, ensuring that a certain number of Pods are always running. It gradually brings up new Pods while taking down old ones, achieving a **zero-downtime** update. This controlled process is ideal for production applications where availability is critical.

While `Recreate` and `RollingUpdate` are strategies built directly into the Deployment object, they form the foundation for more advanced deployment patterns, such as **Blue/Green**, **Canary**, and **A/B Testing**. These patterns offer greater control over release risk and are often implemented using a combination of deployments, services, and other tooling.

> **Note**
>
> For a deep dive into these advanced patterns, their trade-offs, and how to implement them, we cover them in detail in *Chapter 10*.

Controlling a rolling update

For a rolling update, you can fine-tune the update process using two key parameters in your Deployment manifest, `maxSurge` and `maxUnavailable`:

- `maxSurge`: Defines the maximum number of extra Pods that can be created beyond the desired replica count during an update. For example, if you have 10 replicas and `maxSurge` is 2, the Deployment can create 2 new Pods before it starts terminating old ones.

- `maxUnavailable`: Specifies the maximum number of Pods that can be unavailable during the update process. If you have 10 replicas and `maxUnavailable` is 1, the Deployment will ensure that at least 9 Pods are always running and ready to serve traffic.

By tuning these parameters, you can balance deployment speed against resource consumption and application availability. *Figure 3.4* visualizes this process step by step, showing how Kubernetes maintains availability while introducing the new version.

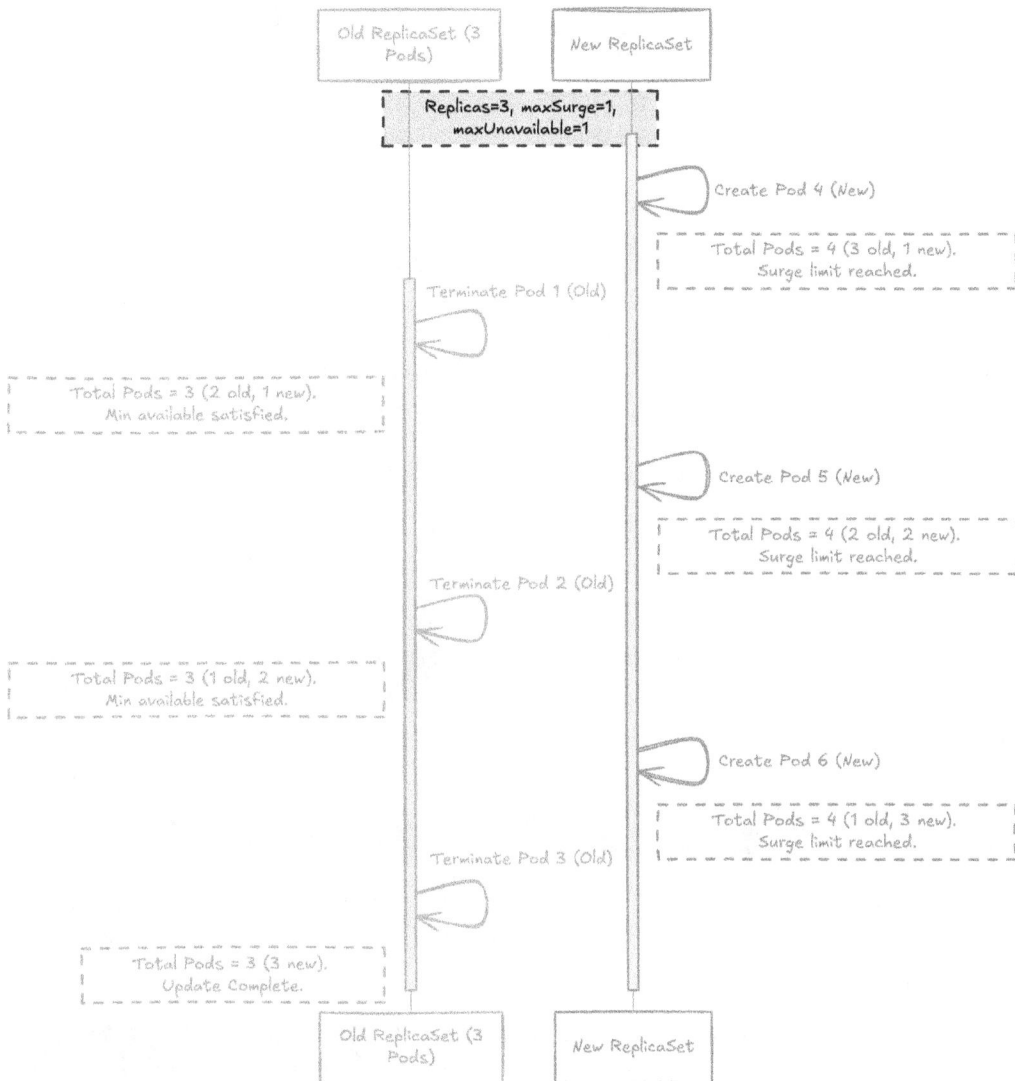

Figure 3.4 – Step-by-step flow of a rolling update with Replicas=3, maxSurge=1, and max-Unavailable=1

Interview tip

Question: *What are* maxSurge *and* maxUnavailable *in a rolling update strategy?*

Answer: The maxSurge parameter defines how many extra Pods can be added during an update, while maxUnavailable sets how many can be unavailable. These values help control update speed and stability.

Here's an example snippet from a Deployment manifest showing these settings:

```
spec:
  replicas: 4
  strategy:
    type: RollingUpdate
    rollingUpdate:
      maxSurge: 1        # Can create 1 extra pod (total of 5)
      maxUnavailable: 1  # At most 1 pod can be unavailable
```

With your update strategy configured, the next crucial step is to monitor the update's progress in real time and know how to react if something goes wrong.

Monitoring rollouts and handling rollbacks

A critical feature of Deployments is the ability to monitor updates and revert them if something goes wrong.

To update an existing Deployment's image, you can use the set image command:

```
kubectl set image deployment/nginx-deployment nginx=nginx:1.19.2
```

This command triggers the rolling update process defined by the Deployment's strategy. You can watch the status of this rollout in real time:

```
kubectl rollout status deployment/nginx-deployment
```

If you detect a problem with the new version, you can quickly roll back to the previously deployed, stable version. Deployments maintain a history of revisions, allowing for easy rollbacks.

To see the history of a deployment, run the following:

```
kubectl rollout history deployment/nginx-deployment
```

To roll back to the previous version, execute the following command:

```
kubectl rollout undo deployment/nginx-deployment
```

This command tells the Deployment to revert to the configuration of the previous ReplicaSet, effectively and safely rolling back the application. This rollback capability is a crucial safety net for production operations.

Deployments are the ideal choice for stateless applications where any Pod can be replaced by another without issue. However, many critical applications, such as databases, are not stateless and require stable, persistent identities. This brings us to a different kind of workload and a specialized controller designed to manage it.

Managing specialized workloads

Deployments are the workhorse for stateless applications, but they aren't a one-size-fits-all solution. Real-world systems involve many kinds of tasks that don't fit the simple stateless model. What about a database that needs a stable network identity and persistent storage? What about a monitoring agent that must run on *every single node* in the cluster? Or a data processing task that needs to run once and then terminate? For these scenarios, Kubernetes provides a toolkit of specialized controllers. In this section, we'll move beyond the basics to cover these essential workloads. You will learn when to use a **StatefulSet** for applications that remember data, a **DaemonSet** for node-level services, and **Jobs** or **CronJobs** for batch and scheduled tasks.

Stateful applications: StatefulSets (versus Deployments)

Managing stateful applications such as databases in Kubernetes is a common challenge. *Can I deploy my MySQL database on Kubernetes? Is it safe to do so?* These questions come up frequently at conferences and interviews. Let's address these by diving into StatefulSets and their role in managing stateful applications in Kubernetes.

What are StatefulSets?

StatefulSets are Kubernetes objects designed to manage stateful applications. They provide guarantees about the ordering and uniqueness of these Pods. Unlike Deployments, which are suited for stateless applications and where Pods are often interchangeable, StatefulSets maintain a sticky identity for each of their Pods. These Pods are created from the same spec, but they are not fungible—each has a persistent identifier that it maintains across any rescheduling.

> **Interview tip**
>
> **Question:** *Why would you use a StatefulSet instead of a Deployment in Kubernetes?*
>
> **Answer:** StatefulSets are designed for workloads that require stable identities, persistent storage, and ordered startup/shutdown, such as databases or stateful applications.

The primary feature that distinguishes StatefulSets from Deployments is the orderly, graceful deployment and scaling. StatefulSets assign a unique ordinal number to each Pod, which helps to maintain a stable identity, consistent network, and stable storage. These ordinal indexes are used to name Pods, such as `mysql-0`, `mysql-1`, and so forth.

When you use a StatefulSet, the persistent volume associated with a Pod in a StatefulSet is not deleted when the Pod is deleted. This means that when the Pod is rescheduled, it can reattach to its persistent storage and maintain the necessary state.

Here's a basic example of a StatefulSet manifest for a MySQL database:

```yaml
apiVersion: apps/v1
kind: StatefulSet
metadata:
  name: mysql
spec:
  selector:
    matchLabels:
      app: mysql
  serviceName: "mysql"
  replicas: 3
  template:
    metadata:
      labels:
        app: mysql
    spec:
      containers:
      - name: mysql
        image: mysql:5.7
        ports:
        - containerPort: 3306
        volumeMounts:
        - name: mysql-persistent-storage
          mountPath: /var/lib/mysql
  volumeClaimTemplates:
  - metadata:
      name: mysql-persistent-storage
    spec:
      accessModes: ["ReadWriteOnce"]
      resources:
        requests:
          storage: 10Gi
```

This manifest describes a StatefulSet that will create three replicas of a MySQL Pod, each bound to a persistent volume to maintain state.

> **Interview tip**
>
> **Question:** *What happens to the storage of a Pod managed by a StatefulSet after it is deleted?*
>
> **Answer:** The associated persistent volume is retained and not deleted, allowing the Pod to reattach to it if recreated.

StatefulSets vs Deployments

While Deployments are good for stateless applications and provide features such as rolling updates and rollbacks, StatefulSets are specifically designed for stateful applications and provide the following features:

- **Consistent and unique network identities**: Each Pod in a StatefulSet is given a unique and stable hostname, which ensures that each Pod can be uniquely identified across the network. This is crucial for applications that require stable network identifiers for communication and data replication purposes.

- **Persistent and stable storage**: StatefulSets ensure that each Pod has its own dedicated storage that persists across Pod rescheduling and restarts. This means that even if a Pod fails and is recreated, the data remains intact and is reattached to the Pod, ensuring data durability.

- **Sequential and graceful scaling**: Scaling operations for Pods within a StatefulSet are performed in a controlled sequential manner. Pods are created or terminated in a specific order, respecting the sequential numbering of the Pods. This is particularly important for applications that require a specific startup or shutdown sequence.

- **Automated and sequential updates**: When updates are applied to a StatefulSet, they are rolled out to the Pods in a predictable order. This allows for careful control over the update process, ensuring that updates do not disrupt the application's stability and that each Pod is updated in turn.

Having covered StatefulSets, we now understand the safety and efficacy of deploying stateful applications on Kubernetes. But what about ensuring certain services, such as monitoring or logging solutions, run on every worker node within the cluster? This is where DaemonSets come into play, offering a robust solution for node-wide service deployment. In the upcoming section, we'll dive into DaemonSets, exploring how they guarantee the presence of specific applications on all or some nodes in your Kubernetes cluster. Let's move forward to uncover the workings and benefits of DaemonSets in detail.

Node-bound workloads: DaemonSets

In the realm of Kubernetes, ensuring the smooth operation of a cluster involves more than just managing the applications it hosts. Critical services such as security enhancements, monitoring, logging, storage provisioning, and network management play a significant role in maintaining the health and efficiency of the cluster. This is where DaemonSets come into the picture as a powerful tool.

DaemonSets are a Kubernetes feature designed to ensure that some or all of your nodes run a copy of a Pod. When nodes are added to the cluster, Pods are automatically added to them. When nodes are removed from the cluster, those Pods are garbage collected. Deleting a DaemonSet will clean up the Pods it created.

This model is perfect for cases where you want every node in the cluster to run a copy of a Pod, which could include utility applications such as log collectors, monitoring agents, or even specific networking setups.

Interview tip

Question: *Why are DaemonSets useful in Kubernetes clusters?*

Answer: DaemonSets ensure that specific Pods, such as logging or monitoring agents, are automatically deployed to every node in the cluster.

Key differentiators of DaemonSets

DaemonSets offer the following differentiators:

- **Cluster-wide coverage**: DaemonSets ensure that every node in your cluster runs a copy of a specified Pod, providing a blanket coverage that's particularly useful for implementing cluster-wide logging, monitoring, or a network proxy

- **Automatic scaling**: As you add nodes to your cluster, DaemonSets automatically scale to accommodate new nodes, ensuring that your essential services are consistently deployed across the cluster without manual intervention

- **Resource optimization**: By running on each node, DaemonSets can optimize resource usage, ensuring that monitoring or logging tools have minimal impact on the cluster's performance

Figure 3.5 shows how a DaemonSet automatically deploys a Pod onto every worker node in the cluster, ensuring consistent coverage across the entire Kubernetes environment.

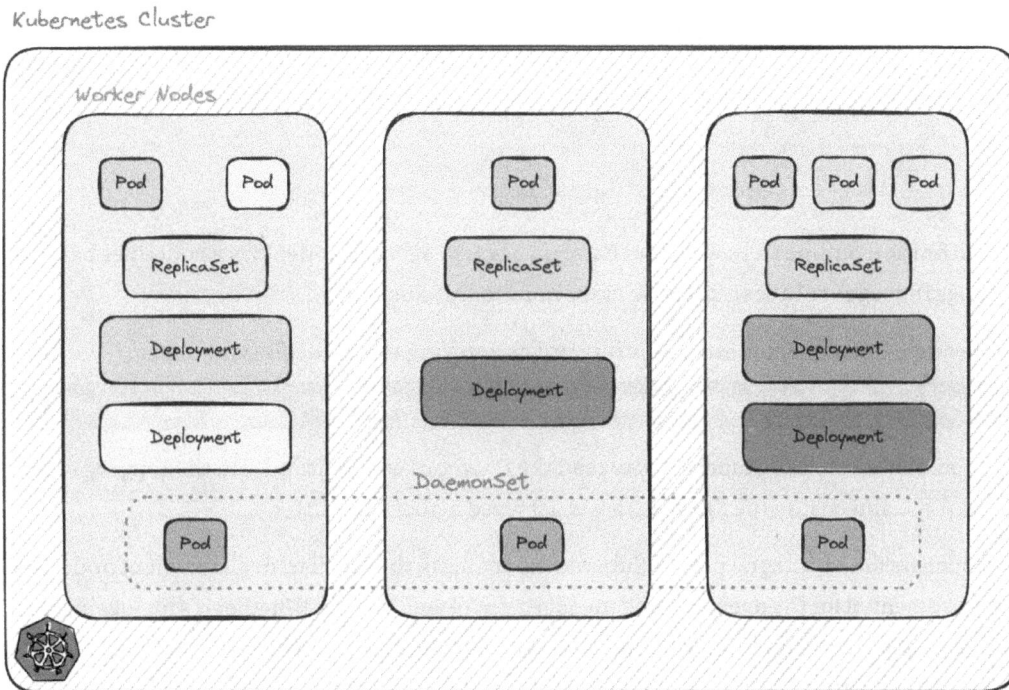

Figure 3.5 – Overview of Kubernetes cluster architecture with DaemonSet pods on each node

Creating a DaemonSet involves defining a YAML file that specifies the desired state, much like any other Kubernetes object. Here's a simplified example of a DaemonSet definition that ensures a logging agent is present on every node:

```
apiVersion: apps/v1
kind: DaemonSet
metadata:
  name: logging-agent
  labels:
    app: logging
spec:
 .selector:
    matchLabels:
      name: logging-agent
```

```
template:
  metadata:
    labels:
      name: logging-agent
  spec:
    containers:
    - name: agent
      image: logging-agent:latest
```

This definition outlines a DaemonSet named `logging-agent` that deploys a container based on the `logging-agent:latest` image to every node in the cluster.

Deploying a DaemonSet is as straightforward as applying the YAML file via `kubectl`:

```
kubectl apply -f logging-agent-ds.yaml
```

This command instructs Kubernetes to read the DaemonSet definition from the `logging-agent-ds.yaml` file and ensure the desired state is achieved across the cluster.

DaemonSets are an integral part of Kubernetes, enabling the efficient deployment of node-level services essential for the operation and management of your cluster. Whether it's for logging, monitoring, or any form of node-specific operation, DaemonSets provide a reliable and automated way to ensure these critical services are always running and up to date across all nodes in your cluster.

However, many applications are designed around **event-driven architecture** (**EDA**) and require tasks to run at specific times or in response to particular events. This need for scheduled and event-driven tasks leads us into the realm of Kubernetes Jobs and CronJobs. In the next part of our exploration, we will delve into how Jobs and CronJobs enable us to handle workloads that run to completion and how they schedule tasks at predetermined intervals. Let's explore capabilities and configurations that make event-driven workflows a breeze in Kubernetes.

Batch and scheduled tasks: Jobs and CronJobs

In the evolving world of Kubernetes, orchestrating and automating tasks is essential. Jobs and CronJobs in Kubernetes provide powerful tools for running tasks that need to execute once or repeatedly at specified times.

Kubernetes Jobs for one-off tasks

A Kubernetes Job creates one or more Pods and ensures that a specified number of them successfully terminate. When the specified number of Pods terminate successfully, the Job is complete. Jobs are ideal for batch processing, data analysis, batch image rendering, or any other workload that does not require a long-running service.

Creating a Job is straightforward. Here's an example Job manifest that executes a simple batch task:

```
apiVersion: batch/v1
kind: Job
metadata:
  name: example-job
spec:
  template:
    spec:
      containers:
      - name: batch-processor
        image: batch-processor:latest
        command: ["sh", "-c", "echo Hello, Kubernetes! && sleep 60"]
      restartPolicy: Never
  backoffLimit: 4
```

This Job runs a container that prints a message and then sleeps for 60 seconds. The restartPolicy parameter is set to Never, so if the container exits, the Job will not restart it unless the Pod fails.

Kubernetes CronJobs for scheduled tasks

CronJobs take the concept of Jobs a step further by allowing you to schedule Jobs to run periodically at fixed times, dates, or intervals. They are akin to cron tasks in Unix-like operating systems.

Interview tip

Question: *How do CronJobs differ from regular Kubernetes Jobs?*

Answer: Jobs run once and complete, while CronJobs run Jobs on a scheduled basis using a cron expression.

An example of a CronJob that runs every hour might look like this:

```yaml
apiVersion: batch/v1
kind: CronJob
metadata:
  name: hourly-job
spec:
  schedule: "0 * * * *"
  jobTemplate:
    spec:
      template:
        spec:
          containers:
          - name: hello
            image: busybox
            args:
            - /bin/sh
            - -c
            - date; echo Hello from the Kubernetes cluster
          restartPolicy: OnFailure
```

This CronJob uses the busybox image to print the current date and a hello message every hour. The schedule field in a CronJob's configuration specifies when and how often the job should run. It's written in the cron format, which is composed of five fields separated by spaces, representing different units of time.

Here's how to read the schedule: "0* * * *" line:

- The first field represents the minute of the hour (0-59). The 0 here means the job will run when the minute hand points to zero, which is at the top of the hour.

- The second field is the hour of the day (0-23). The asterisk (*) means every hour.

- The third field is the day of the month (1-31). The asterisk (*) signifies every day of the month.

- The fourth field is the month of the year (1-12). The asterisk (*) indicates every month.

- The fifth field is the day of the week (0-7, where both 0 and 7 stand for Sunday). The asterisk (*) means every day of the week.

Putting it all together, "0 * * * *" means the job will run once every hour at the beginning of the hour.

You can visualize this schedule in the following diagram, which helps clarify how each part of the cron schedule determines the job's timing.

How to read the schedule: "0 * * * *" line

day of week (0-7)

month (1-12)

day of month (1-31)

hour (0-23)

min (0-59)

Figure 3.6 – Guide to reading cron schedules

Now, let's move on to how Kubernetes efficiently manages resource cleanup after the job has completed, using the ttlSecondsAfterFinished feature.

Ensuring job completion with TTL

With the addition of the ttlSecondsAfterFinished feature, Kubernetes allows for the automatic cleanup of Jobs and their associated Pods after they finish executing. This helps in keeping the cluster tidy by preventing the accumulation of finished Jobs.

Here's how you might specify a **time-to-live (TTL)** in your Job manifest:

```yaml
apiVersion: batch/v1
kind: Job
metadata:
  name: example-job-with-ttl
spec:
  ttlSecondsAfterFinished: 100
  template:
    spec:
      containers:
      - name: temp-job
        image: busybox
      restartPolicy: Never
```

With this configuration, the Job and its Pods will be automatically deleted 100 seconds after the completion of the Job.

> **Interview tip**
>
> **Question:** *What is the purpose of the* `ttlSecondsAfterFinished` *field in Kubernetes Jobs?*
>
> **Answer:** It sets a TTL after the Job completes, automatically cleaning up completed Jobs and Pods to reduce resource clutter.

After exploring dynamic ways to run and schedule tasks in Kubernetes through Jobs and CronJobs, it's time to shift our focus to a more persistent presence within the cluster: Static Pods. Static Pods are managed directly by the kubelet daemon on a specific node, without the API server observing them. In the next section, we'll delve into what Static Pods are, why they're important, and their use cases.

Control-plane-independent Pods: Static Pods

In Kubernetes, there is a special type of Pod known as a Static Pod. These Pods are managed directly by the kubelet service on a specific node, rather than by the API server. The kubelet on the node automatically restarts the Static Pod if it fails. This direct node-level management of Static Pods makes them independent of the control plane, which is especially useful for cluster bootstrapping or maintenance.

The distinction between Static Pods and other resources

Unlike resources such as Deployments and ReplicaSets, which are dynamic and managed by Kubernetes' control plane, Static Pods do not have cluster-level objects. This means there are no Static Deployments or Static ReplicaSets. The kubelet daemon on each node is solely responsible for the lifecycle of Static Pods on that node.

Static Pods are particularly useful for running the Kubernetes control-plane components themselves, such as `kube-apiserver`, `kube-scheduler`, and `etcd`. Since these components must be running for the Kubernetes control plane to function, managing them as Static Pods ensures they remain operational even if the cluster's control plane has issues.

Static Pods are typically identified by their naming convention. They usually have a name that includes the node's name as a suffix. This is a clue that the Pod is managed directly by the kubelet on that particular node.

For example, if you see a Pod named `kube-apiserver-my-node-name`, it's a strong indication that this is a Static Pod running on the `my-node-name` node.

Static Pods manifests' location

The manifests for Static Pods are often located in the `/etc/kubernetes/manifests` directory, but this can vary based on the configuration of the kubelet. To confirm the directory, you can check the kubelet's configuration file or look at the kubelet process's command-line arguments.

Deleting a Static Pod involves manual intervention. Since they are not managed by the API server, you cannot delete them with `kubectl`. Instead, you remove the Pod's manifest file from the node's filesystem where the Static Pods' manifests are stored. The kubelet will then recognize the file's absence and stop the Pod.

For example, to delete a Static Pod, you would remove its manifest file like so:

```
rm /etc/kubernetes/manifests/<POD_DEFINITION_FILE>
```

After deleting the file, the kubelet stops the Pod almost immediately.

Summary

In this chapter, we journeyed through various methods available for launching pods in Kubernetes. It's crucial to grasp that a pod is the smallest deployable unit in Kubernetes, confined to a single node. Yet, the true power of Kubernetes is unlocked when we manage multiple pods, and we uncovered eight distinct ways to achieve this.

We started with the basics of pod creation, moved on to ReplicaSets and Deployments for managing stateless applications, and then to StatefulSets for those requiring persistent storage. We explored DaemonSets for node-wide services and Jobs and CronJobs for task scheduling. We also touched upon the self-cleaning mechanism provided by TTL and the direct node-level management of Static Pods.

While we covered fundamental aspects of pod deployment, we intentionally paused before discussing scaling strategies, such as how ReplicaSets and Deployments can adjust the number of pod instances. This sets the stage for our next chapter, where we will delve into the dynamic world of autoscaling in Kubernetes, learning how to ensure our applications can adapt to workload demands automatically.

By now, you should feel confident in understanding the differences between Deployments and StatefulSets, the scenarios that call for DaemonSets, and how to orchestrate scheduled tasks with Jobs and CronJobs. As we progress, keep in mind that each method serves a specific purpose, and choosing the right one is key to a robust and efficient Kubernetes environment.

Stay tuned, as we're about to explore how Kubernetes not only maintains but also intelligently scales our applications to meet the ever-changing demands of users and systems.

4

Principles of Scaling: Horizontal vs Vertical

This chapter provides a comprehensive guide to scaling in Kubernetes, focusing on horizontal and vertical autoscaling. It explains the working of the **Horizontal Pod Autoscaler (HPA)** and the **Vertical Pod Autoscaler (VPA)**, including their respective advantages, disadvantages, and practical use cases. This chapter is a must-read for DevOps engineers, cloud architects, and anyone interested in optimizing resource utilization in a Kubernetes environment.

Learning the ideas in this chapter will help you build Kubernetes applications that use resources better, stay stable under heavy load, and save costs. Knowing how autoscaling works is important for doing well in Kubernetes job interviews and for running real projects in the cloud.

Throughout this chapter, we will address the following questions and topics:

- Scaling your workloads in Kubernetes
- What are HPA and VPA?
- Best practices and common pitfalls

Scaling your workloads in Kubernetes

This section aims to comprehensively understand how scaling operates at a high level in Kubernetes. We'll delve deeper into scheduler basics and address fundamental questions often arising in Kubernetes technical interviews. We'll also touch on some fundamental aspects of scaling to set the stage for a deeper understanding of the topics we'll explore further in the upcoming questions of this chapter. Along the way, we'll demystify the theory and offer practical insights to empower you to navigate Kubernetes scaling scenarios confidently.

So, let's explore the intricacies of scaling in the Kubernetes ecosystem and unravel the theory.

What is scaling in general?

Scaling, in its essence, signifies a system's capability to manage a growing workload or demand. This inquiry aims to gauge the candidate's foundational understanding of scaling concepts. Now, let's delve into an exploration of diverse strategies for scaling workloads. This exploration applies to Kubernetes and the underlying infrastructure components it relies upon. Going beyond the surface into these strategies, we aim to provide a comprehensive understanding of optimizing performance and adapting to varying demands effectively.

Companies make significant efforts in the scaling strategies design to improve the following aspects of their applications:

- **Performance optimization**: Scaling ensures that systems remain responsive even under varying workloads. It prevents bottlenecks and guarantees optimal performance, contributing to a positive user experience.

- **Cost-efficiency and resource utilization**: Organizations can optimize resource utilization by scaling resources dynamically based on demand. This, in turn, leads to cost efficiency, avoiding unnecessary expenses associated with over-provisioning.

- **Adaptability to demand**: Scaling provides the flexibility to adapt to changing demands. Whether facing peak usage periods or experiencing reduced activity, scaling allows the infrastructure to align with the current workload.

- **Availability and reliability**: Scaling contributes to high availability by distributing workloads across multiple resources. This redundancy ensures that if one component fails, others can seamlessly take over, minimizing downtime.

- **Future-proofing**: As organizations grow, their computational demands evolve. A scalable infrastructure ensures that the IT environment can quickly expand, accommodating increased workloads and supporting future growth.

Scaling refers to a system's ability to handle increased workload or demand. This concept is crucial for understanding how to optimize performance and adapt to changing demands in Kubernetes and its underlying infrastructure. Effective scaling strategies enhance performance, ensure cost-efficiency, improve resource utilization, adapt to varying demand levels, maintain high availability and reliability, and future-proof the IT environment for growth.

Understanding scaling is essential for passing Kubernetes interviews as it demonstrates a candidate's ability to manage dynamic workloads, optimize resource usage, and ensure system reliability and efficiency. Proficiency in scaling strategies showcases the capability to design resilient and adaptable infrastructures, which are critical skills for any Kubernetes professional.

> **Interview tip**
>
> **Question**: *Why is understanding scaling important in Kubernetes?*
>
> **Answer:** Because Kubernetes runs dynamic workloads, knowing how to scale applications ensures you can keep them responsive, cost-efficient, and reliable under changing demand – skills every Kubernetes professional is expected to have.

Now that we understand why scaling is important, let's start by exploring **horizontal scaling** and how scaling out and scaling in help manage changing workloads in Kubernetes.

Horizontal scaling: Scaling out and scaling in

Scaling out focuses on *expanding* the system by adding more instances or nodes. This horizontal scaling approach is deployed to accommodate increasing workloads or to enhance system performance and reliability. Organizations can ensure optimal response times and uphold service availability by distributing the workload across additional resources, especially during peak usage periods. Kubernetes excels in orchestrating the scaling-out process, enabling the seamless integration of new nodes to meet the growing demands of applications and services.

Scaling in, on the other hand, involves *reducing* the number of instances or application instances within a system. This approach is particularly advantageous during times of decreased demand or to optimize resource utilization. By consolidating resources, organizations can enhance cost-efficiency and streamline operations. In the context of Kubernetes, scaling in can be orchestrated seamlessly, allocating resources based on actual requirements and contributing to a more sustainable and economical infrastructure. In the diagram in *Figure 4.1*, we see how it works in reality: some new load is increasing (**1**) and the application scales out (**2**). After the load decreases (**3**), we just scale the application back in (**4**).

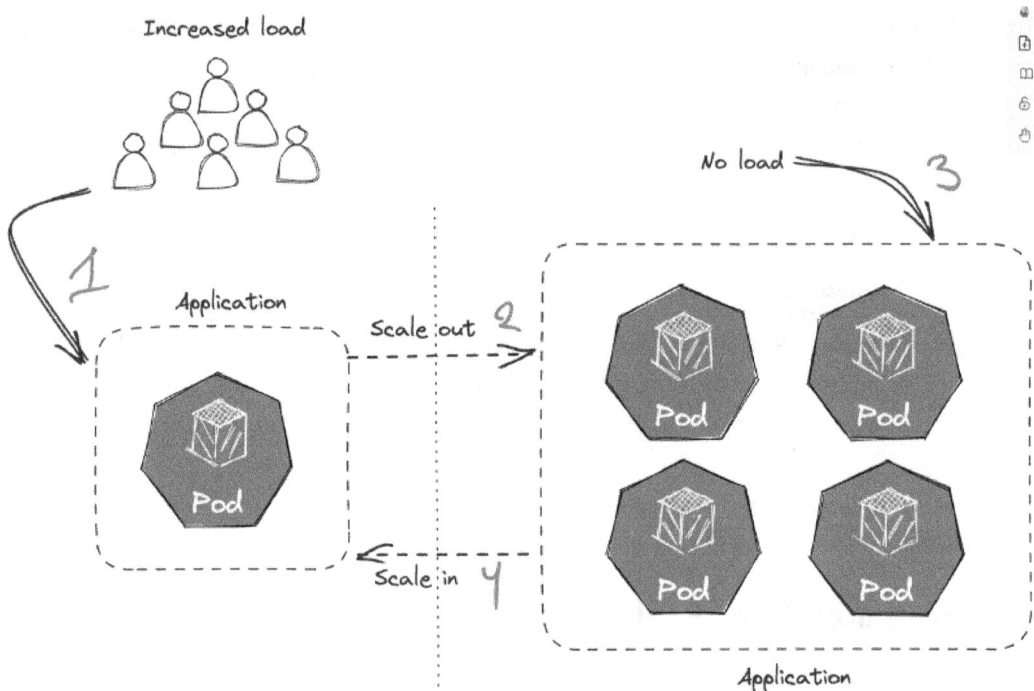

Figure 4.1 – Horizontal scaling in action

Interview tip

Question: *What is the difference between scaling out and scaling in Kubernetes?*

Answer: Scaling out means adding more Pods or nodes to handle higher loads, whereas scaling in removes them during low demand to save resources. Kubernetes automates both to match current workload needs efficiently.

After covering horizontal scaling, let's move on to **vertical scaling** and see how adjusting resource limits can help optimize the performance of individual Pods in Kubernetes.

Vertical scaling: Scaling up and scaling down

Scaling up or **vertical scaling** involves increasing the capacity or power of existing resources within a system. This approach often includes upgrading hardware components, such as adding CPU, memory, or storage to a single server. Scaling up is advantageous when specific system components require enhanced performance to handle increased workloads. Scaling up offers a straightforward solution in scenarios where a single server's capabilities can be augmented to meet demand. However, it's essential to note that there are limitations to how much a single resource can be scaled vertically. As applications and services grow in complexity, organizations may need to combine vertical scaling with horizontal scaling strategies for a comprehensive and sustainable approach. In Kubernetes, scaling up can be efficiently managed, ensuring that individual components receive the necessary enhancements to address the evolving requirements of the applications hosted on the cluster. You can find the visualization of that approach right after this sentence.

On the opposite end is **scaling down**, a vertical scaling strategy aimed at reducing the capacity of resources within a system. This approach is instrumental during reduced-demand periods or when optimizing resource utilization is prioritized. Scaling down typically involves decreasing the power or capacity of existing hardware components, such as reducing the number of CPU cores or lowering memory allocations. In practical terms, scaling down offers cost-efficiency benefits during non-peak hours or when the system experiences lighter workloads. Organizations can minimize operational costs by consolidating resources while maintaining the necessary infrastructure to handle baseline demands. In Kubernetes, scaling down is seamlessly orchestrated, allowing for the dynamic adjustment of resources based on real-time requirements. This adaptability ensures the cluster efficiently allocates resources, contributing to an optimized, responsive, and economically viable IT environment. In the diagram in *Figure 4.2*, we see that the difference here is in how we handle the load – instead of adding more replicas, we give our Pod more resources.

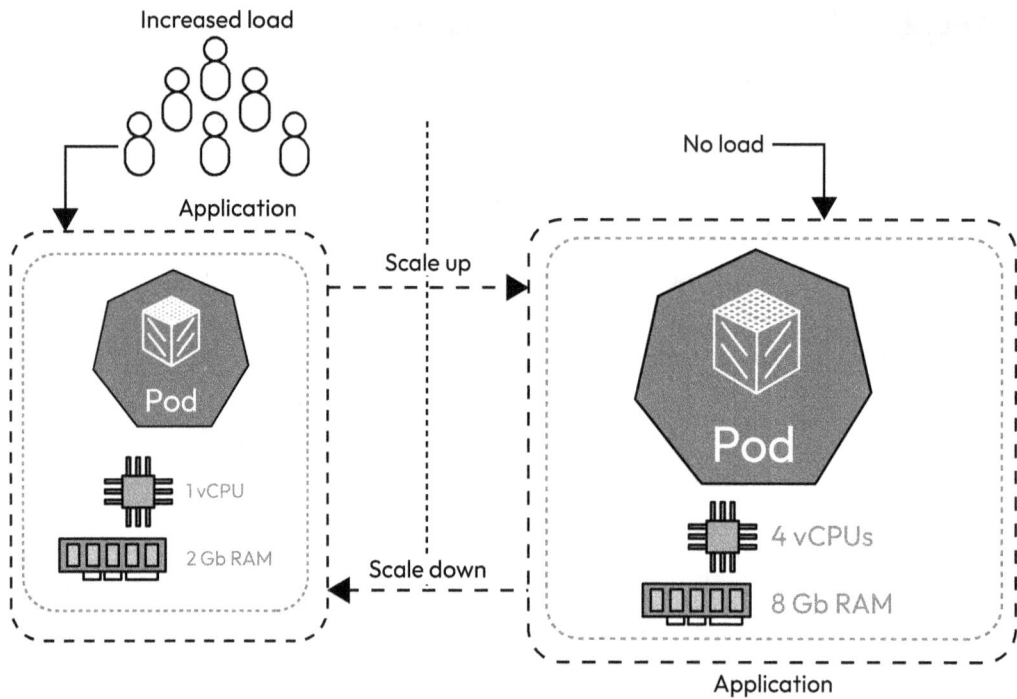

Figure 4.2 – Vertical scaling in action

Interview tip

Question: *What is vertical scaling in Kubernetes, and how is it different from horizontal scaling?*

Answer: Vertical scaling increases or decreases the resources (such as CPU or memory) assigned to existing Pods, while horizontal scaling adds or removes Pod replicas. Kubernetes can manage both, but vertical scaling is limited by the node's capacity.

Now that we've discussed how scaling works in practice, it's a good time to cover a common interview question: *What types of scaling do you know in Kubernetes?* It's really important to understand this part because you can meet this type of question in almost every Kubernetes-related interview.

What types of scaling do you know in Kubernetes?

Let me clarify the theory we discussed earlier to help answer this question more efficiently. When asked this question, you can provide two possible answers: scaling nodes and Pods in general or about the specific usage of HPA and VPA. We recommend asking for clarification from the interviewer by saying, "*Could you please specify which approach you're looking for? I can answer your question in two ways: by discussing scaling nodes and Pods or by explaining how to use HPA and VPA.*"

When adjusting the scale of your Pods and nodes in Kubernetes, you can lean on those high-level concepts we just walked through – scaling up, down, in, and out. In the world of Kubernetes, you've got a couple of ways to make it happen. If you're feeling hands-on, you can roll up your sleeves and manually handle Pod scaling with trusty kubectl commands. Need more Pods? Use kubectl scale with the increased number of replicas. Too many? Use kubectl scale with fewer replicas.

Let's look at several command examples that can be used to scale our replicas out and in:

```
$ kubectl scale deployment example --replicas=2 # scale out
$ kubectl scale deployment example --replicas=0 # scale in
```

There's also an automated way to do it – using HPA and VPA. It's like having your Pods on auto-pilot. Don't worry; we're diving into the nitty-gritty of HPA and VPA in the upcoming chapters of this saga. So, buckle up – automation is just around the corner!

Which Kubernetes components are responsible for scaling capabilities?

In the dynamic realm of Kubernetes, several vital components take center stage, each playing a crucial role in bestowing the platform with its robust scaling capabilities. Let's spotlight the main characters responsible for orchestrating the Kubernetes workload scaling:

1. Users send the request to the API server to scale Pods out – we're triggering scaling and the journey begins. This is the starting point for increasing the number of replicas for a specific workload.

2. The API server checks and processes the scaling request and then interacts with etcd to store the user's scaling intent.

3. etcd acts as a reliable storage system for Kubernetes cluster data, including configuration details.

4. The controller manager continuously watches the cluster's current state. Upon detecting the scaling intent in etcd, it activates the relevant controller to manage the desired number of replicas.

5. The controller manager ensures the cluster moves toward the desired state based on observed conditions.

6. Now the scheduler takes charge, organizing the allocation of additional Pods to nodes. It considers factors such as resource availability and load distribution, ensuring the increased replicas find their designated spots within the cluster.

7. At the end (on the target node the scheduler has chosen), the kubelet receives instructions from the control plane (specifically, the controller manager) about necessary scaling actions.

In this sequential process, the user's scaling request moves through the Kubernetes control plane components, each playing a critical role in executing the scaling intent. This ensures the cluster dynamically adapts to the changing needs of hosted applications.

Now that we understand the key components responsible for scaling in Kubernetes, let's move on to real implementation examples in Kubernetes. In the next chapter, we will explore HPA and VPA in detail. HPA helps by adjusting the number of Pod replicas based on workload metrics, ensuring that the application can handle varying loads. VPA, on the other hand, changes the resource requests and limits of existing Pods to better match the current demands.

By learning about HPA and VPA, you'll gain deeper insights into how Kubernetes manages resources effectively, making sure applications run smoothly and efficiently.

Interview tip

Question: *Which Kubernetes components are involved in the scaling process?*

Answer: The API server receives the scaling request and stores it in etcd, and the controller manager acts on it by adjusting replicas. The scheduler assigns new Pods to nodes, and the kubelet ensures those Pods are created on the selected nodes.

To better understand how scaling works in an automatic way in Kubernetes, let's dive into two important tools that make it possible: HPA and VPA.

What are the HPA and VPA?

In the lively world of Kubernetes, the HPA emerges as a star performer, orchestrating dynamic adjustments to the number of Pod replicas based on observed metrics. Picture it as your automated scaling wizard, ensuring your applications gracefully sway with the current workloads' demand. An HPA acts as a computerized conductor, dynamically scaling the number of Pod replicas to maintain optimal performance and responsiveness. Here's a spotlight on when (in what cases) you need to use the HPA in your clusters and for your workloads:

- **Varying workloads:** Your applications experience fluctuations in demand throughout the day or week. The HPA ensures your application can gracefully scale out during peak times and down during periods of lower activity, optimizing resource utilization.

- **Seasonal peaks:** Your workload experiences periodic spikes during product launches, promotions, or seasonal events. The HPA provides an automated response to handle sudden increases in demand, preventing performance bottlenecks during critical business periods.

- **Cost efficiency:** You want to optimize resource usage and control costs in a cloud-native environment. By dynamically adjusting the number of Pod replicas based on demand, the HPA prevents over-provisioning, ensuring you only consume resources when needed.

- **Unpredictable traffic:** Your application attracts varying levels of user traffic that are challenging to predict. The HPA adapts to unpredictable traffic patterns, providing a responsive and efficient scaling mechanism without manual intervention.

- **Custom metrics-based scaling:** You require scaling decisions based on custom metrics tailored to your application's performance indicators. The HPA supports custom metrics, allowing you to define scaling criteria aligned with your application's unique characteristics.

- **Resource optimization:** You aim to maintain optimal resource utilization without compromising performance. The HPA adjusts the number of Pod replicas dynamically, preventing resource wastage during periods of low demand and ensuring responsiveness during peaks.

- **Cluster efficiency:** You want to optimize the overall efficiency of your Kubernetes cluster by preventing resource bottlenecks. The HPA contributes to cluster efficiency by allocating resources based on demand, preventing underutilization or overload.

- **Simplified operations:** You prefer automated solutions to reduce the manual effort required for scaling decisions. The HPA automates scaling decisions, reducing the operational burden and allowing your team to focus on higher-level tasks.

So, let's start with exploring the HPA implementation details to understand why most companies today use the HPA and horizontal scaling for their workloads.

How does the HPA work?

In the dynamic universe of Kubernetes, where workloads flow, the HPA emerges as a potent enchantress, wielding the power to orchestrate the scaling of pod replicas dynamically. As the maestro of automated scaling decisions, the HPA dances to the rhythm of observed metrics, seamlessly adapting your applications to the ever-changing demand cadence.

The HPA's journey begins with the Metrics Server, where it diligently collects and exposes vital metrics, such as CPU and memory utilization, from the Kubernetes nodes using **cAdvisor** (short for **Container Advisor**). cAdvisor is an open source container monitoring and performance analysis tool designed by Google. It provides real-time information about resource usage and performance metrics for running containers, making it a valuable tool for managing and optimizing containerized applications. cAdvisor supports various container runtimes, including Docker and Kubernetes, and offers a user-friendly web interface for easy visualization of container metrics. These metrics become the canvas upon which the HPA paints its scaling masterpiece. As the architect of responsiveness, you, the Kubernetes sorcerer, define scaling policies within the HPA configuration. Here, you set the criteria: the desired metrics, the sacred thresholds, and the number of desired Pod replicas. This incantation shapes the spell that the HPA will cast upon your applications.

Next, the HPA becomes the vigilant observer, continuously monitoring and comparing the metrics against the defined thresholds. Like a seasoned oracle, it interprets these signals, triggering scaling decisions when the metrics cross the mystical boundaries of demand. When the demand crescendos, the HPA gracefully orchestrates the "scaling out," conjuring additional Pod replicas to join the performance. This ensures the workload is met with resilience and optimal performance. In moments of tranquility, the HPA harmonizes the "scaling in" gracefully reducing the number of Pod replicas to prevent resource extravagance. The HPA's magic unfolds as it optimizes resource utilization. Preventing underutilization during periods of low demand and ensuring responsiveness during peaks, the HPA crafts an efficient and resourceful performance worthy of a standing ovation.

The HPA operates in an autopilot mode, a guardian spirit that autonomously adjusts the number of Pod replicas based on real-time demand. This hands-off approach minimizes manual intervention, allowing your applications to dance seamlessly in response to the ever-shifting melodies of your workloads.

Beyond the conventional, the HPA supports custom metrics, allowing you to weave bespoke scaling criteria tailored to your application's unique characteristics. This bespoke flexibility ensures that your enchantment aligns perfectly with the distinct heartbeat of your workloads.

In Kubernetes, where demand is ever-shifting, the HPA stands as a guardian, ensuring your applications perform a graceful dance, scaling effortlessly to meet the crescendo of demand and elegantly waltzing back when tranquility reigns. As we peel back the layers, we'll delve deeper into the enchanting workings of the HPA, unlocking the secrets behind its automated scaling symphony.

In *Figure 4.3*, you see all participants in one place. Please review it one more time to summarize the gathered knowledge.

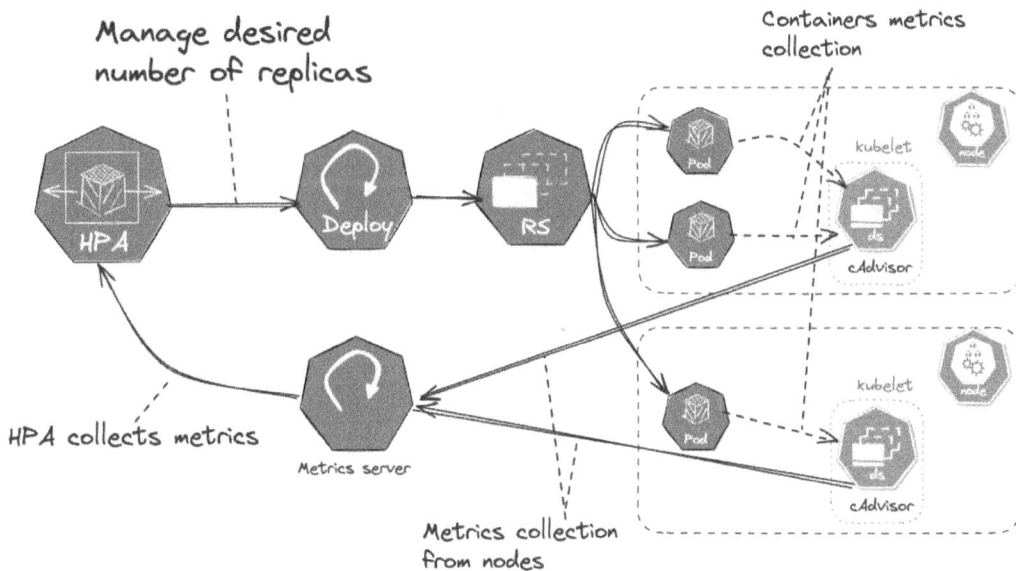

Figure 4.3 – HPA in action

Interview tip

Question: *How does the HPA work in Kubernetes?*

Answer: The HPA watches metrics such as CPU or memory usage and automatically increases or decreases the number of Pod replicas to match the current demand.

How do I start to use the HPA?

In general, you need to remember that there are two hard requirements to start using the HPA in a new cluster:

- Confirm the Metrics Server availability. Ensure the Metrics Server is up and running in your Kubernetes cluster. The HPA relies on this magical source of metrics to make informed scaling decisions. Don't have the metrics server installed? Just install it according to official documentation using Helm or manifests.

- All the Pods you want to scale based on the container resources consumption (such as CPU or memory) should have appropriate resource requests configured. The HPA uses this boundary with the current resource consumption to determine the need for scaling in or out of an event.

If you have it already defined and clear, you can start using the HPA for Pods. Here is the example "to-do" list you can use as a reference in your projects:

1. **Define metrics and targets**: Within your HPA configuration, specify the metrics you want to observe, such as CPU or memory utilization. Set target thresholds that trigger scaling actions based on your application's requirements. For instance, you can configure to scale out workloads horizontally if your current memory utilizes more than 80% of the configured requests. Please see the manifest example here:

```
apiVersion: autoscaling/v2
kind: HorizontalPodAutoscaler
metadata:
  name: example
spec:
  scaleTargetRef:
    apiVersion: apps/v1
    kind: Deployment
    name: example
  minReplicas: 1
  maxReplicas: 2
  metrics:
    - type: Resource
      resource:
        name: memory
        target:
          type: Utilization
          averageUtilization: 80
```

2. **Install the HPA resource definition**: Deploy the HPA resource definition in your Kubernetes cluster.

3. **Observe and tweak**: Deploy your application and observe how the HPA reacts to varying workloads. Tweak your configuration and thresholds as needed to fine-tune the HPA's responsiveness.

4. **Explore custom metrics**: if your application demands bespoke metrics, explore the realm of custom metrics with the HPA. Define and integrate metrics that align with your application's unique characteristics.

5. **Monitor and celebrate**: Keep a watchful eye on your HPA-enabled deployment. Monitor how it gracefully scales in response to demand surges and elegantly scales back during periods of calm. Celebrate the newfound efficiency and resilience.

6. **Iterate and refine**: As your application evolves, iterate on your HPA configuration. Refine the metrics, thresholds, and scaling targets to ensure your automated scaling symphony remains finely tuned.

To provide a good and short answer to this question, it is enough to go through this ordered list. It follows the typical process of the HPA adoption and answers the question according to the expectations. Sometimes, companies that actively use the HPA want to scale faster and in a more proactive way. To do so, they can use some queues, load balancer metrics, or database metrics to react to anomalies or unexpected traffic spikes. The HPA out of the box gives you the ability to use custom metrics for that, but it also will be a benefit for you to know more flexible and accurate tools such as **Kubernetes Event-Driven Autoscaler (KEDA)**.

So, if the interviewer asks you something like *Can I scale Pods horizontally based on the size of some queues (such as RabbitMQ)?*, your short response is yes – there are two ways to do that:

- **Using custom metrics**: You need to install a custom or external metrics adapter for the application you want to integrate. More information about that can be found in the documentation.

- **Using a CNCF application called KEDA project**: With this application, you install an operator that manages the HPA using more high-level abstraction objects. KEDA can work with dozens of different applications and scale workloads based on metrics from these sources.

The HPA is a crucial component in Kubernetes that automatically adjusts the number of Pod replicas based on current workloads. The HPA monitors metrics such as CPU utilization or custom metrics and scales the application horizontally by adding or removing Pods. This ensures that applications can handle varying loads efficiently, maintaining performance and responsiveness.

Understanding the HPA is vital for managing dynamic workloads in Kubernetes. It demonstrates a candidate's ability to configure and optimize scaling based on real-time metrics, ensuring resource efficiency and high availability.

In the next section, we will cover the VPA, which complements the HPA by adjusting the resource requests and limits of existing Pods. Mastering the VPA is equally important for passing Kubernetes technical interviews, as it shows a comprehensive understanding of both horizontal and vertical scaling strategies, enabling optimal resource management and application performance.

How does the VPA help to optimize resources?

The VPA is a valuable tool in the Kubernetes ecosystem designed to optimize resource utilization at the individual Pod level. Unlike the HPA, which focuses on adjusting the number of Pod replicas, the VPA delves into fine-tuning resource requests and limits for each Pod. Here are some points to explain how the VPA works:

- **Dynamic adjustment of resource requests and limits**: The VPA dynamically adjusts the resource requests and limits for individual containers within a Pod based on observed metrics. It analyzes the historical resource usage patterns of the container to determine the optimal resource allocations. By continuously adapting resource requests and limits, the VPA ensures that each Pod receives the right resources to meet its needs. This prevents over-provisioning and underutilization, optimizing resource utilization at the granular level.

- **Monitoring and learning from Pod behavior**: The VPA continuously monitors the resource utilization patterns of Pods, taking into account factors such as CPU and memory usage. It learns from the historical behavior of each container to make informed decisions. Through intelligent observation, the VPA gains insights into the actual resource requirements of Pods. This learning process allows the VPA to tailor resource allocations for optimal performance, adapting to the changing demands of the workload.

- **Prevention of resource bottlenecks**: The VPA aims to prevent resource bottlenecks by ensuring that each container within the Pod has adequate resources to operate efficiently. The VPA proactively addresses potential bottlenecks by adjusting resource allocations based on historical patterns. It allocates resources dynamically, preventing scenarios where containers struggle due to insufficient resources.

- **Fine-tuning for efficiency**: The VPA fine-tunes the resource requests and limits to balance efficiency and performance. It adjusts allocations based on observed behavior to avoid overcommitting and underutilizing resources. The fine-tuning capability ensures that resources are used efficiently. The VPA helps achieve optimal performance without wasting resources, resulting in a more cost-effective and responsive Kubernetes environment.

In summary, the VPA enhances resource optimization by dynamically adjusting resource requests and limits for individual containers within Pods. Through continuous monitoring, learning, and fine-tuning, the VPA contributes to a Kubernetes environment that is responsive to changing workloads but also resource-efficient and cost-effective.

The next figure visualizes the VPA functionality step by step.

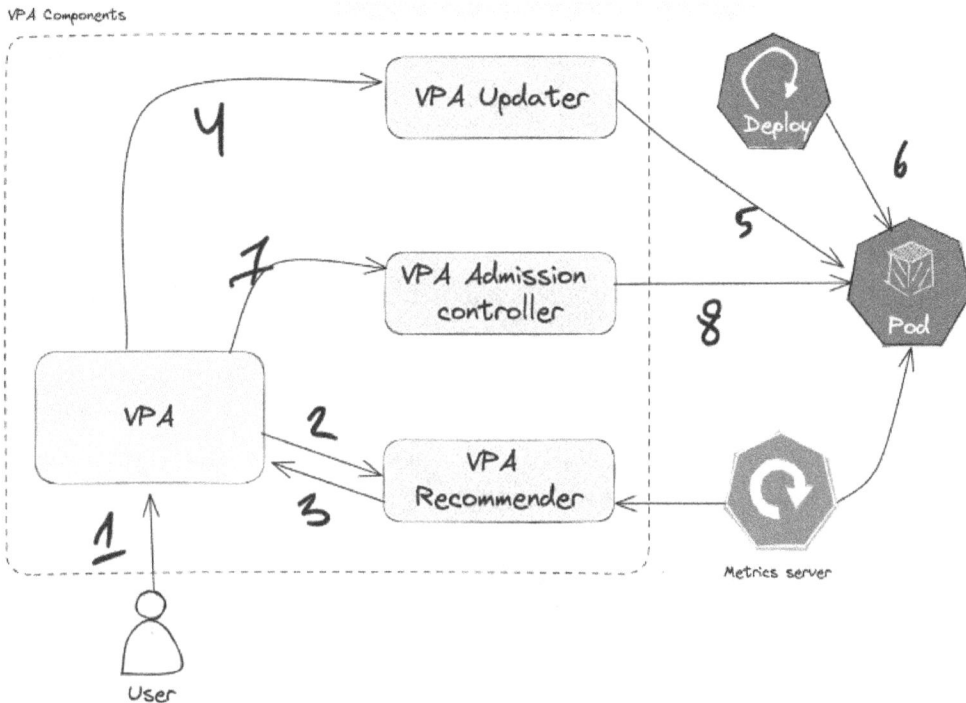

Figure 4.4 – VPA in action

Let's dive into some technical details about the VPA implementation details represented in *Figure 4.4*:

1. The user (aka operator) configures the VPA.

2. Meanwhile, the **VPA Recommender** component constantly listens for configuration changes and updates the compute information it is responsible for.

3. After that, it returns the Pod resource recommendation to the VPA.

4. Based on this information, the VPA triggers the **VPA Updater** to apply this recommendation.

5. The VPA Updater evicts the Pod and causes the Deployment to perform rollout action.

6.   Before new Pod provisioning (from the Kubernetes events), the VPA informs the **VPA Admission Controller** about the desired configuration for a new Pod.

7.   The VPA Admission Controller patches the Pod specification during the Pod creation, creating the Pod with increased resources.

8.   Deployment terminates the old replica (which has been evicted).

Overall, we have covered all the necessary theoretical topics related to horizontal and vertical autoscaling in Kubernetes. Now, let's review and summarize what we've learned, enhance it with key best practices, and take a look at common pitfalls to avoid.

Interview tip

Question: *How does the VPA help to optimize resources in Kubernetes?*

Answer: The VPA automatically adjusts CPU and memory requests and limits for Pods based on their actual usage, helping avoid both over-provisioning and un-derutilization.

Now that we understand how autoscaling works in Kubernetes, let's go over some best practices and common pitfalls to help you use scaling effectively and avoid typical mistakes.

Best practices and common pitfalls

In this section, we want to share some best practices and common pitfalls from our production experience.

Here are some of the best practices:

- Configure probes (liveness, readiness) and control resource requests and limits (HPA and VPA):

  - Ensure that your Pods have properly configured liveness and readiness probes. The HPA relies on these probes to make accurate scaling decisions.

  - Have explicit resource requests and limits set for your containers. This helps the HPA make informed scaling decisions based on accurate resources. For the VPA, it gives you more understanding of everything the VPA can do with your workloads.

- Define meaningful metrics and realistic scaling thresholds (HPA): Choose metrics that align with the performance characteristics of your application, such as CPU utilization or custom metrics. Define scaling thresholds based on your application's behavior and expected load. Avoid overly aggressive or conservative thresholds. It can cause pretty unpredictable and flaky behavior of your workloads and, as a result, your end users can suffer even more.

- Gradual implementation and testing in non-production environments (HPA and VPA): Introduce scaling for your applications gradually, starting with less critical workloads. This allows you to observe its impact and fine-tune configurations. Test all scaling adjustments in lower environments before applying them to production. This helps in identifying any unexpected behaviors or conflicts.

- Monitor and tweak (HPA and VPA): Regularly monitor HPA and VPA behavior and adjust configurations as needed. This includes observing scaling events and assessing the impact on application performance.

- Adopt VPA and HPA in the same cluster for different workloads: It is recommended to use the VPA along with the HPA to improve the scaling capabilities of your cluster for different workloads. However, it's crucial to note that configuring the HPA and VPA for the same workload, such as the same Deployment, can cause unpredictable behavior. Therefore, it's not recommended to use the HPA and VPA together for the same workload. On the other hand, it's highly recommended to use both approaches in the cluster because some applications perform better when scaled out horizontally, while others can only be scaled up vertically. Employing both approaches creates a comprehensive resource management strategy.

Following these best practices will enable organizations to be flexible and scalable to provide high-level quality platforms on top of the Kubernetes ecosystem.

Next, let's look at some common pitfalls:

- Wrong application configuration (HPA and VPA): Inadequate liveness and readiness probes can prevent the HPA and VPA from making incorrect scaling decisions. Ensure probes are configured correctly for accurate pod health assessment.

- Incorrect metrics selection and overlooking resources (requests and limits) and thresholds (HPA): Choosing metrics that don't accurately represent your application's performance can lead to ineffective scaling decisions. Not defining resource requests and limits can result in inaccurate metrics and scaling decisions. It may lead to overcommitting or underutilizing resources.

- No monitoring (HPA and VPA): This is critical because wrongly configured scaling can worsen your application availability and your end users' satisfaction. Keep an eye on the events happening with your applications with HPA and VPA participation.

- Not enough available resources on nodes in the cluster (HPA and VPA): The HPA and VPA do not consider your current cluster setup and the amount of available (schedulable) resources (e.g., node size, available size, and available quota) and their actions can cause Pods to go pending. This can be partly addressed by using VPA together with Cluster Autoscaler or other projects to scale nodes to handle this kind of demand. We will dive deeper into the way it works in the next chapter.

Summary

In this chapter, we learned the principles of scaling in Kubernetes, focusing on both horizontal and vertical autoscaling. The chapter covered the general concept of scaling and its importance in managing workloads and optimizing resources. Detailed workings of the HPA were explained, including how it adjusts the number of Pod replicas based on workload metrics. The principles of vertical scaling, including the VPA, which adjusts resource requests and limits for Pods, were also covered. Additionally, the chapter provided practical implementation details, best practices, and common pitfalls related to the HPA and VPA in Kubernetes.

This information is crucial for anyone involved in managing Kubernetes clusters, such as DevOps engineers and cloud architects. Understanding the HPA and VPA is essential for optimizing resource utilization, ensuring cost-efficiency, and maintaining the high performance and reliability of applications. This knowledge is also vital for passing Kubernetes technical interviews, as it demonstrates a comprehensive understanding of scaling strategies and resource management in a Kubernetes environment.

In the next chapter, you will gain a comprehensive understanding of autoscaling in Kubernetes and its importance. The chapter will cover the fundamentals of autoscaling and the reasons it is essential for managing dynamic workloads. It will provide guidance on implementing best practices for autoscaling, particularly in managed Kubernetes environments. You will also learn about advanced autoscaling solutions and their advantages over traditional methods. Additionally, the chapter will cover how to set up and configure autoscaling tools for optimal performance, and how to monitor auto-scaling activities and manage costs effectively through billing alarms.

By mastering these skills, you will be well prepared for Kubernetes technical interviews, demonstrating a solid understanding of implementing and managing autoscaling strategies to ensure efficient resource utilization and optimal application performance.

Unlock this book's exclusive benefits now

UNLOCK NOW

Scan this QR code or go to `https://packtpub.com/unlock`, then search
for this book by name.

Note: Keep your purchase invoice ready before you start.

5

Autoscaling in Action

Let's journey further into Kubernetes autoscaling. Imagine your app hits the spotlight and user numbers soar. You'd want it to handle this new popularity seamlessly. That's where Kubernetes autoscaling proves invaluable. It scales your app's resources up or down based on traffic, ensuring solid performance without wasting money.

We've touched on how to scale within a Kubernetes cluster using the **Horizontal Pod Autoscaler (HPA)** and **Vertical Pod Autoscaler (VPA)** in earlier chapters. Now, we'll zoom out to see how to expand the cluster's capacity itself, ensuring it can handle the increased load.

Remember, Kubernetes is a dual-structured system. There's the control plane and the worker nodes. In a cloud service scenario, the provider usually scales the control plane for you. Many cloud services, such as AWS, offer managed solutions that handle the scaling for you. This is highly recommended, as it offloads a complex task that can be critical to the stability and reliability of your applications.

However, it's crucial to understand that while AWS handles the scaling, managing the load on the control plane still falls within our purview. This means we need to be mindful of how our actions—such as how often we create new Pods or query the API server—affect the load. Efficiently managing these operations can help maintain the control plane's performance, ensuring that our applications remain responsive and stable.

On to the worker nodes: these are where your workloads run. As your applications grow, you might also run cluster services such as Helm charts for compliance and integrations. These services, vital for your workloads, will need to scale accordingly, which might require external resources—such as virtual machines on a cloud platform.

Two main tools assist in scaling the cluster:

- **Cluster Autoscaler**: Adds or removes machines to match Pod needs, akin to adjusting the number of desks based on staff in an office
- **Karpenter**: Tailored for AWS, this tool dynamically manages the machine count for optimal application performance

This chapter will delve into these autoscaling tools. We'll dissect how they function and guide you on when to apply each. By the end of this chapter, you'll know how to use autoscaling to simplify management and boost efficiency.

But there's more. Sometimes, merely adding new instances isn't enough. We need to consider other components such as networking, storage, cluster limits, load balancing, and so on. We will address these complex topics later in this chapter, equipping you with comprehensive knowledge for both interviews and real-world application management.

We'll kick off with the Cluster Autoscaler, breaking it down to its core functions and implications. Ready to get started? Let's scale up our Kubernetes expertise.

Cluster Autoscaler

Let's break down the **Cluster Autoscaler (CA)**, a tool that automatically resizes your cluster to match workload demand. The CA's job is to make sure every Pod has a place to run, which cuts waste and optimizes costs.

The CA is adept at managing the delicate act of scaling a cluster up or down. It takes action to scale up the cluster when it detects Pods that are unable to find a home on existing nodes due to a lack of resources. Conversely, it scales down the cluster when it notices nodes are being underutilized, thus conserving resources.

This Kubernetes feature doesn't directly measure resource usage such as CPU or memory. Instead, it focuses on the Pods' state, specifically looking for those that are pending and unable to schedule due to resource constraints. When such Pods are found, the CA triggers the addition of new nodes, allowing these pending Pods to be scheduled and run.

The mechanics of the CA

The process of the CA includes a cyclical check for pending Pods at regular intervals—typically every **10 seconds by default**, though this is adjustable. Here's a succinct rundown of how the CA functions:

1. The CA perpetually monitors for pending Pods—those awaiting resources to run

2. Upon identifying the need for more resources, and within the set constraints, the CA instructs the addition of new nodes

3. As new nodes are provisioned, they're incorporated into the cluster by the Kubernetes control plane

4. These fresh nodes are then considered by the Kubernetes scheduler, which allocates the previously pending Pods to them

> **Interview tip**
>
> **Question**: *My cluster's CPU usage is at 95%, but the Cluster Autoscaler hasn't added any new nodes. Is this expected behavior?*
>
> **Answer:** Yes, this is entirely expected behavior. The Cluster Autoscaler's trigger is not high resource utilization such as CPU or memory. It only acts when the Kubernetes scheduler cannot place a Pod due to insufficient resources, resulting in a Pending Pod. As long as all existing Pods are running—no matter how high their resource usage—the Cluster Autoscaler will remain idle. A scale-up will only occur when a new Pod arrives that cannot be scheduled.

This process is visually illustrated in the referenced diagram, highlighting the CA's decision-making flow during a scale-up event. A parallel process exists for scaling down, where the CA seeks to efficiently reallocate Pods and remove surplus nodes:

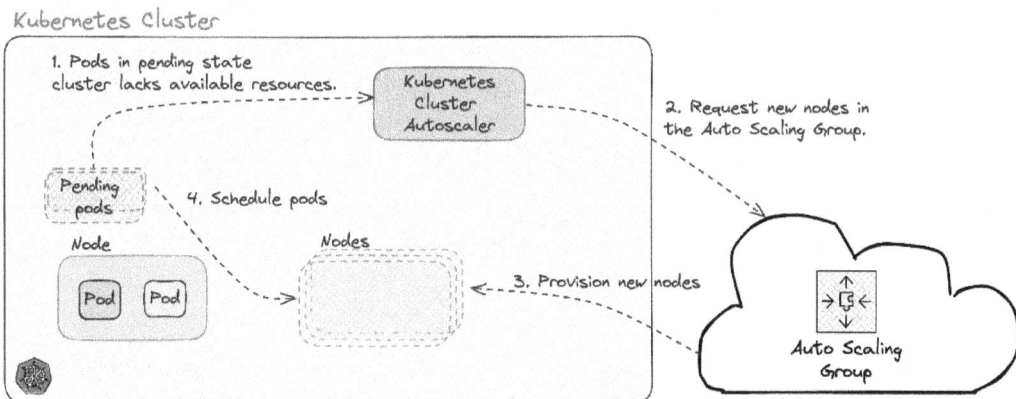

Figure 5.1 – The process of the Cluster Autoscaler

🔍 **Quick tip**: Need to see a high-resolution version of this image? Open this book in the next-gen Packt Reader or view it in the PDF/ePub copy.

🔒 **The next-gen Packt Reader** and a **free PDF/ePub copy** of this book are included with your purchase. Scan the QR code OR visit `https://packtpub.com/unlock`, then use the search bar to find this book by name. Double-check the edition shown to make sure you get the right one.

In our upcoming sections, we'll delve into how the CA integrates with various cloud providers, such as AWS, to use their native scaling capabilities such as AWS Auto Scaling groups. These integrations allow the CA to seamlessly add or remove EC2 instances, further extending the cluster's capabilities.

With a firm grasp on the theory of the CA within Kubernetes, let's transition to practical application. On AWS, employing the CA with the **Elastic Kubernetes Service (EKS)** involves a series of methodical steps, each significant to ensuring seamless scalability for your applications.

Now that you understand the theory behind the CA, let's put it into practice. In an interview, describing the high-level steps is good, but walking through a concrete deployment proves your hands-on skill. We'll build a secure, production-ready CA on Amazon EKS. This mini-lab will arm you with the talking points and confidence to answer any "how-to" question.

Deploying the CA on AWS EKS

You'll often be asked to "walk me through how you'd enable node autoscaling on EKS." The strongest answers show you can wire **IAM Roles for Service Accounts (IRSA)**, tag node groups for auto-discovery, deploy the CA safely, and prove it works.

Plan: What we'll build and why

We will configure CA on an **Amazon EKS** cluster, using IRSA for secure, password-free authentication. This setup ensures that when Pods cannot be scheduled due to resource shortages, the CA will securely request new nodes from AWS. Conversely, when nodes are underutilized for a defined period, it will safely remove them to optimize costs.

Here are the high-level milestones we will cover, which you can use as a narrative guide in an interview:

- **Foundation and guardrails**: Define our EKS cluster configuration, including the essential tags the CA needs for auto-discovery and the minimum/maximum size to prevent unexpected costs or outages.
- **Establishing trust (IRSA)**: Enable the OIDC provider for our cluster in AWS IAM, creating the foundation for secure communication between our cluster and the AWS APIs.
- **Principle of least privilege**: Craft a fine-grained IAM policy that grants the CA only the permissions it needs, strictly scoped to the resources it's supposed to manage.
- **Creating the identity**: Generate the specific IAM role and Kubernetes ServiceAccount, linking them together through the power of IRSA.
- **Deployment**: Install the CA using its official Helm chart, configuring it to use our IRSA setup and setting safe, production-sensible arguments.
- **Proof of work**: Trigger a scale-up event by deploying a workload that exceeds our cluster's capacity and watch the logs to confirm the CA is making intelligent decisions.
- **Troubleshooting**: Discuss common failure modes and how to quickly diagnose them—a key skill for any operational role.

> **Note—Why we use eksctl here**
>
> There are many ways to create and manage an EKS cluster—Terraform (including EKS Blueprints), AWS CDK/CDKTF, Pulumi, and CloudFormation. To keep the hands-on examples short and repeatable, we'll use *eksctl*, which gives us a single declarative config and an idempotent CLI. The autoscaling concepts you'll learn here map directly to IaC tools if your team prefers Terraform or AWS CDK.

We'll reference *Figure 5.2* – IRSA flow for Cluster Autoscaler on EKS as the mental model throughout.

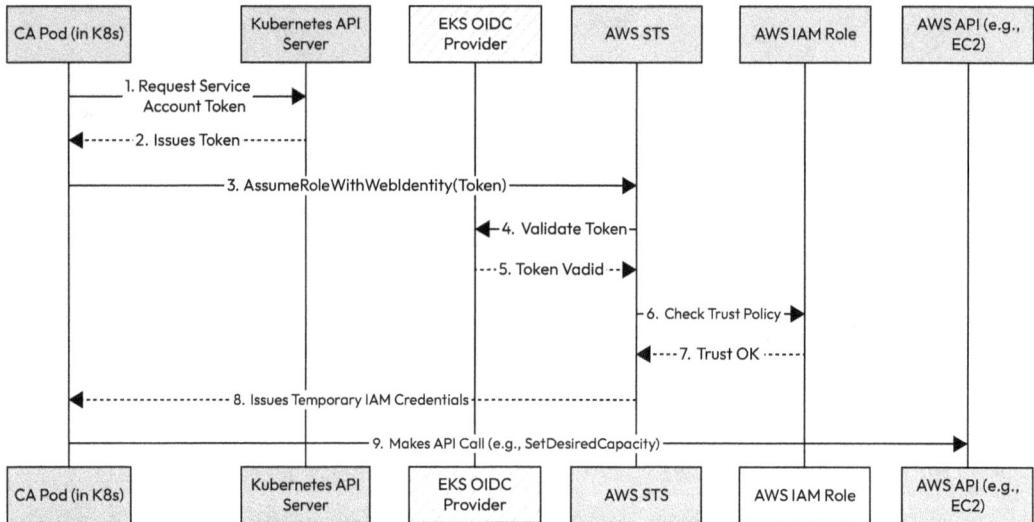

Figure 5.2 – IRSA flow for Cluster Autoscaler on EKS

Step 1: Prepping the environment and cluster

Before we create the cluster, we'll set up some environment variables to make our commands clean and reusable. This is also a good practice to demonstrate in an interview, as it shows you value consistency and avoid manual errors.

First, we define our cluster's name, region, and AWS account ID. We then programmatically detect the latest supported Kubernetes version for EKS in our target region. This is a robust approach that avoids hardcoding versions, though we include a safe fallback.

```
set -Eeuo pipefail
# Basic context for our cluster
export CLUSTER_NAME="interview-ca-cluster"
export AWS_REGION="us-east-1"
export AWS_ACCOUNT_ID="$(aws sts get-caller-identity --query Account
--output text)"
# Discover the latest supported Kubernetes version for EKS
export EKS_LATEST_VERSION="$( aws eks describe-addon-versions
--region "$AWS_REGION"
--query 'addons[].compatibilities[].clusterVersion'
--output text | tr '\t' '\n' | sort -uV | tail -1 || true )"
# Fallback to a recent version if discovery fails
```

```
: "${EKS_LATEST_VERSION:=1.33}"
echo "Using: Account=$AWS_ACCOUNT_ID Region=$AWS_REGION Cluster=$CLUSTER_
NAME K8s=$EKS_LATEST_VERSION"
```

Step 2: Creating the EKS cluster with auto-discovery tags

The CA doesn't automatically manage every node group in your cloud account. You must explicitly tell it which ones to control. It discovers these managed node groups using a specific set of AWS tags. The presence of these tags is non-negotiable; without them, the autoscaler will not detect or manage the Auto Scaling group.

There are two mandatory tags:

- `k8s.io/cluster-autoscaler/enabled`: A true value on this tag signals, "This Auto Scaling Group is available for management."

- `k8s.io/cluster-autoscaler/<cluster-name>`: This tag, with a value of owned, associates the node group with a specific EKS cluster, preventing a single Cluster Autoscaler from trying to manage nodes belonging to another cluster.

> **Interview tip**
>
> **Question:** *How does the Cluster Autoscaler discover which AWS Auto Scaling Groups it is allowed to manage?*
>
> **Answer:** The Cluster Autoscaler discovers manageable **Auto Scaling Groups (ASGs)** using a specific set of **AWS tags**. These tags must be applied directly to the ASG, not just the instances, and their presence is non-negotiable for discovery. There are two mandatory tags:
>
> - `k8s.io/cluster-autoscaler/enabled` must be set to `"true"`.
>
> - `k8s.io/cluster-autoscaler/<cluster-name>` must be set to `"owned"` to associate the group with a specific cluster.
>
> If these tags are missing or incorrect, the autoscaler will completely ignore the node group.

We'll embed these tags directly into our cluster configuration file (`demo-cluster.yaml`):

```
apiVersion: eksctl.io/v1alpha5
kind: ClusterConfig
metadata:
name: ${CLUSTER_NAME}
```

```yaml
region: ${AWS_REGION}
version: "${EKS_LATEST_VERSION}"
managedNodeGroups:
- name: managed-ng-1
minSize: 1
desiredCapacity: 1
maxSize: 5
instanceType: t3.medium
volumeSize: 20
labels: { role: worker }
# Required tags for Cluster Autoscaler autodiscovery
tags:
k8s.io/cluster-autoscaler/enabled: "true"
k8s.io/cluster-autoscaler/${CLUSTER_NAME}: "owned"
```

> 💡 **Quick tip:** Enhance your coding experience with the **AI Code Explainer** and **Quick Copy** features. Open this book in the next-gen Packt Reader. Click the **Copy** button
>
> **(1)** to quickly copy code into your coding environment, or click the **Explain** button
>
> **(2)** to get the AI assistant to explain a block of code to you.

Copy   Explain

❶   ❷

```javascript
function calculate(a, b) {
  return {sum: a + b};
};
```

🔒 **The next-gen Packt Reader** is included for free with the purchase of this book. Scan the QR code OR go to https://packtpub.com/unlock, then use the search bar to find this book by name. Double-check the edition shown to make sure you get the right one.

Let's break down the key fields in this `managedNodeGroups` definition:

- `minSize: 1` and `maxSize: 5`: These are our safety rails. The CA will never scale the node count below 1 or above 5 for this group. This is crucial for controlling costs and ensuring a baseline capacity.

- `tags`: Here, we apply the two essential discovery tags. When `eksctl` creates the underlying AWS ASG, it will attach these tags, making the node group visible to the CA.

Now, let's create the cluster. This process can take 15-20 minutes as AWS provisions the control plane and worker nodes.

```
eksctl create cluster -f ./demo-cluster.yaml
```

Once the cluster is ready, we'll configure `kubectl` to communicate with it:

```
aws eks update-kubeconfig --region "$AWS_REGION" --name "$CLUSTER_NAME"
```

Interview tip

Question: *You've deployed the Cluster Autoscaler, but your nodes aren't scaling up when Pods are pending. You suspect it's a discovery issue. How would you troubleshoot this?*

Answer: My first step would be to verify the AWS tags on the ASG for my managed node group. I'd go to the EC2 console, find the ASG, and check its tags tab. I would confirm that the two required tags, `k8s.io/cluster-autoscaler/enabled` and `k8s.io/cluster-autoscaler/my-cluster-name`, are present and correctly spelled. If they're missing, the CA won't see the ASG and will never attempt to scale it. I would also check the CA Pod logs for messages indicating it can't find any node groups to manage.

Step 3: Setting up IRSA and a least-privilege IAM policy

To modify ASGs, the CA Pod needs AWS credentials. The most secure and recommended method for granting these permissions is IRSA. IRSA links a Kubernetes `ServiceAccount` to an AWS IAM role. This allows any Pod using that `ServiceAccount` to inherit the role's permissions without needing static secret keys.

Enable the IAM OIDC provider

The first step is to create an OIDC identity provider for your cluster in IAM. This establishes a trust relationship, allowing IAM to accept identity tokens from your Kubernetes cluster's OIDC provider. `eksctl` makes this a one-step process:

```
eksctl utils associate-iam-oidc-provider \
  --region "$AWS_REGION" \
  --cluster "$CLUSTER_NAME" \
  --approve
```

Craft a least-privilege IAM policy

Next, we'll create an IAM policy that grants the CA only the permissions it needs. A common mistake is to grant overly broad permissions ("Resource": "*" everywhere). A stronger, more secure policy limits powerful actions to only the resources that are tagged for autoscaling.

```json
// cluster-autoscaler-policy.json
{
  "Version": "2012-10-17",
  "Statement": [
    {
      "Effect": "Allow",
      "Action": [
        "autoscaling:DescribeAutoScalingGroups",
        "autoscaling:DescribeAutoScalingInstances",
        "autoscaling:DescribeLaunchConfigurations",
        "autoscaling:DescribeScalingActivities",
        "autoscaling:DescribeTags",
        "ec2:DescribeImages",
        "ec2:DescribeInstanceTypes",
        "ec2:DescribeLaunchTemplateVersions",
        "ec2:GetInstanceTypesFromInstanceRequirements",
        "eks:DescribeNodegroup"
      ],
      "Resource": "*"
    },
    {
      "Effect": "Allow",
      "Action": [
        "autoscaling:SetDesiredCapacity",
        "autoscaling:TerminateInstanceInAutoScalingGroup",
        "autoscaling:UpdateAutoScalingGroup"
      ],
```

```
      "Resource": "*",
      "Condition": {
        "StringEquals": {
          "aws:ResourceTag/k8s.io/cluster-autoscaler/enabled": "true"
        },
        "StringLike": {
          "aws:ResourceTag/k8s.io/cluster-autoscaler/*": "owned"
        }
      }
    }
  ]
}
```

This IAM policy follows the principle of least privilege. It has two parts:

- **Read-only actions**: It allows the autoscaler to read (`Describe*`) information about any node group or instance type. This is safe and necessary for it to see what's available.

- **Tag-restricted write permissions**: It only grants powerful actions—such as changing capacity or terminating instances—to resources that have our specific autoscaling tags. This is a critical security measure that prevents the autoscaler from accidentally modifying the wrong set of machines.

Now, let's create this policy in IAM:

```
# Create the policy and capture its ARN
export CA_POLICY_ARN="$(
aws iam create-policy
--policy-name AmazonEKSClusterAutoscalerPolicy
--policy-document file://./cluster-autoscaler-policy.json
--query "Policy.Arn" --output text 2>/dev/null ||
aws iam list-policies --scope Local
--query "Policies[?PolicyName=='AmazonEKSClusterAutoscalerPolicy'].Arn |
[0]"
--output text
)"
echo "CA policy ARN: $CA_POLICY_ARN"
```

Step 4: Create the IRSA and service account

With the policy created, we can now create the final piece of the IAM puzzle. We need an IAM role that our service account can assume, and that role needs our new policy attached to it.

Once again, eksctl simplifies this into a single, powerful command:

```
eksctl create iamserviceaccount
--cluster "$CLUSTER_NAME"
--region "$AWS_REGION"
--namespace kube-system
--name cluster-autoscaler
--attach-policy-arn "$CA_POLICY_ARN"
--approve
--override-existing-serviceaccounts
```

This command performs three actions:

- Creates a new IAM role with a trust policy that allows the EKS OIDC provider to assume it
- Attaches AmazonEKSClusterAutoscalerPolicy to this new role
- Creates a Kubernetes ServiceAccount named cluster-autoscaler in the kube-system namespace and, most importantly, annotates it with the ARN of the IAM role it just created

You can verify this by inspecting the ServiceAccount in Kubernetes:

```
kubectl -n kube-system get sa cluster-autoscaler -o yaml
```

You should see an annotation like this, which is the magic that links Kubernetes to IAM:

```
annotations:
  eks.amazonaws.com/role-arn: arn:aws:iam::123456789012:role/eksctl-
interview-ca-cluster-addon-iamserviceac-Role1-ABCDEFGHIJKL
```

Step 5: Install the CA via Helm

With the permissions correctly configured, we can now deploy the CA application itself. The recommended method is to use the official Kubernetes Helm chart.

First, add the Helm repository:

```
helm repo add autoscaler https://kubernetes.github.io/autoscaler
helm repo update
```

Now, we'll install the chart. The parameters we pass via --set are crucial for a correct and secure installation.

```
helm upgrade --install cluster-autoscaler autoscaler/cluster-autoscaler \
    --namespace kube-system \
    --set nameOverride=aws-cluster-autoscaler \
    --set cloudProvider=aws \
    --set awsRegion="$AWS_REGION" \
    --set autoDiscovery.clusterName="$CLUSTER_NAME" \
    --set expander=least-waste \
    --set rbac.serviceAccount.create=false \
    --set rbac.serviceAccount.name=cluster-autoscaler \
    --set extraArgs.balance-similar-node-groups=true \
    --set extraArgs.scale-down-unneeded-time=5m \
    --set extraArgs.skip-nodes-with-local-storage=false \
    --set extraArgs.skip-nodes-with-system-pods=false
```

Let's highlight the most important settings for an IRSA-based setup:

- `autoDiscovery.clusterName="$CLUSTER_NAME"`: This tells the autoscaler which ownership tag to look for when discovering node groups.
- `rbac.serviceAccount.create=false`: This is critical. We are telling the Helm chart, "Do not create a new `ServiceAccount`."
- `rbac.serviceAccount.name=cluster-autoscaler`: This tells the chart, "Instead, use the existing `cluster-autoscaler` `ServiceAccount` we already created and configured with IRSA."

Forgetting these two settings is a very common error. If the Helm chart creates its own `ServiceAccount`, it won't have the IRSA annotation, and the CA Pod will fail with permission errors when trying to call AWS APIs.

Interview tip

Question: *You're installing the Cluster Autoscaler Helm chart on a cluster with IRSA already configured. Which two* `rbac.serviceAccount` *values are the most important to set, and why?*

Answer: The two most critical values are `--set rbac.serviceAccount.create=false` and `--set rbac.serviceAccount.name=cluster-autoscaler`. This is because I have already created a `ServiceAccount` and linked it to a specific IAM role via IRSA. I need to instruct Helm to use my existing, pre-configured `ServiceAccount`. If I let Helm create a new one, it won't have the necessary `eks.amazonaws.com/role-arn` annotation, and the Pod will fail with `AccessDenied` errors because it won't have any permissions to interact with AWS ASGs.

Step 6: Smoke test—Prove that it works!

A deployment isn't done until you've proven it works. We need to create a scenario that forces a scale-up, observe the Cluster Autoscaler's response, and confirm the result.

Remember, the trigger for the CA isn't high CPU or memory; it's **unschedulable Pods**. We will create a Deployment that requests more resources than our single node can provide.

```yaml
# scale-test.yaml
apiVersion: apps/v1
kind: Deployment
metadata:
  name: scale-test
  namespace: default
spec:
  replicas: 20
  selector:
    matchLabels: { app: scale-test }
  template:
    metadata:
      labels: { app: scale-test }
    spec:
      containers:
        - name: pause
          image: registry.k8s.io/pause:3.9
```

```
    resources:
      requests: { cpu: "200m", memory: "256Mi" }
      limits:   { cpu: "200m", memory: "256Mi" }
```

This manifest attempts to create 20 Pods, each requesting 200m CPU. Our t3.medium instance only has 2 vCPUs (2000m), so it can only fit a handful of these Pods. The rest will get stuck.

Apply the test deployment:

```
kubectl apply -f ./scale-test.yaml
```

Confirm that some Pods are pending:

```
kubectl get pods -l app=scale-test
```

You should see several Pods with the status pending. This is our trigger. Now, let's watch the CA's logs in real time to see its decision-making process.

```
# Tail the logs of the Cluster Autoscaler deployment
kubectl -n kube-system logs -f deploy/cluster-autoscaler-aws-cluster-
autoscaler
```

You are looking for key messages like the following:

- `Pod scale-test-xxxxxxxx-xxxxx is unschedulable`
- `Scale-up: setting group managed-ng-1 size to 4`
- `Expanding Node Group managed-ng-1 from 1 to 4`

While the logs are running, open a new terminal and watch the nodes join the cluster:

```
kubectl get nodes -w
```

You will see new nodes appear and transition to the Ready state. Shortly after, the pending scale-test Pods will be scheduled on these new nodes. This completes the verification loop: we created demand, the autoscaler saw the need, it provisioned new supply (nodes), and Kubernetes scheduled the Pods.

Finally, to test scale-down, simply remove the load:

```
kubectl delete -f ./scale-test.yaml
```

After the scale-down-unneeded-time we set in the Helm chart (5 minutes), the CA will identify the now-empty nodes and issue commands to terminate them, scaling the group back down towards its minSize.

Troubleshooting in the trenches: Quick hits for when things go wrong

After deploying the CA, you might be asked, *"Okay, you've deployed it, but it's not scaling. What are the first three things you check?"* This tests your diagnostic process. A great answer moves logically from the most likely cause to the more nuanced ones.

Here are some common failure modes and how to address them.

1. **Problem: Scale-up isn't happening despite pending Pods**

   This is often an issue with discovery. The CA simply can't find the ASG it's supposed to manage.

   - **Verification**: The link between the CA and an ASG is a set of specific tags. You need to confirm they are correctly applied to the ASG itself, not just the instances.

     1. Navigate to the **EC2 Console** in AWS.
     2. Under **Auto Scaling**, select **Auto Scaling Groups**.
     3. Find the ASG corresponding to your EKS node group.
     4. Select it and go to the **Tags** tab.
     5. Confirm these two tags exist and are spelled correctly:

        - `k8s.io/cluster-autoscaler/enabled` with a value of `true`.
        - `k8s.io/cluster-autoscaler/interview-ca-cluster` (or your cluster's name) with a value of `owned`.

   If these tags are missing or incorrect, the CA will ignore the node group completely.

2. **Problem: The CA Pod is crash-looping or its logs show AccessDenied errors**

   This is almost always an IRSA permissions problem. The Pod is trying to call AWS APIs (such as `DescribeAutoScalingGroups`) but is being told it doesn't have the authority.

   - **Verification**: The magic link in the IRSA chain is the annotation on the Kubernetes `ServiceAccount`. This annotation tells the EKS control plane to swap the Pod's default token for temporary IAM credentials.

- Run this command to inspect the ServiceAccount:

```
kubectl -n kube-system get sa cluster-autoscaler -o
yaml
```

- You **must** see an annotation that looks like this: eks.amazonaws.com/
  role-arn: arn:aws:iam:::.... If that annotation is missing, it means
  you either forgot to create the IRSA mapping or, more likely, you let the
  Helm chart create a new, un-annotated ServiceAccount instead of using
  the one you prepared.

3. **Problem: Scale-up works, but scale-down never happens**

   This is a more subtle issue, as the autoscaler might be intentionally blocked from removing a node.

   - **Verification:** The CA won't remove a node if it can't safely evict all the Pods. Check
     for these common blockers:

     - minSize **constraint:** First, check the obvious: is minSize of your ASG set
       to a value that prevents further scale-down?

     - **PodDisruptionBudgets (PDBs):** A PDB can prevent the autoscaler from
       evicting a Pod if it would violate the budget (e.g., "always keep at least 3
       replicas of this app running"). This is a legitimate safety feature, but it
       can pin a node.

     - **"Unsafe to evict" Pods:** The autoscaler respects certain Pods that it consid-
       ers unsafe to evict. This includes Pods with local storage (emptyDir doesn't
       count) or any Pod with the annotation cluster-autoscaler.kubernetes.
       io/safe-to-evict: "false". You can check for this by describing the
       Pods on the underutilized node.

Tip: Avoid autoscaler turf wars

Here's a critical operational rule: *never run two different node autoscalers* (e.g., Cluster
Autoscaler and Karpenter) managing the same set of nodes. They will fight for control
over the same resources, leading to unpredictable and chaotic scaling behavior where
one system adds a node and the other immediately tries to remove it.

Step 7: Cleaning up your environment

A crucial part of any demonstration or project is responsible resource management. Leaving cloud resources running incurs costs, so always clean up when you're done.

- **Uninstall the CA application:** This command uses Helm to remove the Deployment, Services, and other Kubernetes resources associated with the CA.

```
helm -n kube-system uninstall cluster-autoscaler || true
```

- **Delete the EKS cluster and nodes:** This is the main cleanup command. It instructs `eksctl` to deprovision all AWS resources it created for the cluster, including the EKS control plane, the worker nodes in the ASG, IAM roles, and security groups.

```
eksctl delete cluster --name "$CLUSTER_NAME" --region "$AWS_REGION"
```

- **Remove the IAM policy (optional):** After the cluster that used the policy is gone, it's good practice to remove the now-orphaned IAM policy to keep your AWS account tidy.

```
aws iam delete-policy --policy-arn "$CA_POLICY_ARN"
```

From practice to theory: understanding the "why" behind the "how"

Navigating the detailed setup, deployment, and troubleshooting process reveals both the power and the inherent design philosophy of the CA. It is a robust, mature, and highly effective tool for managing capacity in a predictable way. You have proven you can configure it securely and make it work.

However, this hands-on success also highlights its specific mode of operation. It's *reactive*, waiting for the Kubernetes scheduler to fail before it acts. Its actions are constrained by *pre-defined groups* (Auto Scaling Groups), which means you must decide on your instance types ahead of time. Finally, its speed is ultimately limited by how fast the cloud provider can provision and boot a new virtual machine.

Understanding these operational characteristics is just as important as knowing how to deploy the tool. This leads us directly to a critical discussion for any senior engineering interview: the *limitations of the Cluster Autoscaler*, and when you might choose a more advanced alternative.

CA limitations

When discussing the CA during interviews, it's common for interviewers to probe into its limitations. Like any technological solution, the CA has its constraints, which are essential to understand for comprehensive Kubernetes management. Let's delve into some of the key limitations:

- **Limited on-premise support**: Primarily designed for cloud environments, the CA's functionality for on-premise Kubernetes clusters is not as robust, which might restrict its applicability in certain infrastructures.

- **Scaling delays**: Adjusting the size of a cluster is not instantaneous; it can take a few minutes, particularly for larger or more complex setups. This delay might impact the system's ability to swiftly respond to sudden workload increases.

- **Performance at scale**: While CA excels in dynamically managing cluster sizes, its efficiency can diminish as the cluster's scale increases. At a certain point, the CA may struggle with effectively adding or removing nodes, though strategies such as vertically scaling the CA deployment or streamlining node groups can mitigate this issue.

- **Disruption tolerance assumption**: The CA assumes it's safe to restart your Pods on new nodes when it scales down. This can break applications that are sensitive to disruption.

- **Resource-based, not utilization-based, scaling**: CA scales clusters based on the requested resources of Pods rather than their actual usage. This approach could lead to resource overprovisioning if Pod requests are not meticulously calibrated.

- **Challenges with node constraints**: Nodes that have specific dependencies or configurations preventing their removal pose a challenge for the CA, which may find it difficult to scale down such nodes despite them being underutilized.

The CA's main goal is to match resource availability to the demands of various applications within a Kubernetes cluster. This balancing act becomes more challenging with a mix of applications that have differing resource requirements, from lightweight web services to resource-intensive database applications.

Moving on, Karpenter is gaining attention as an efficient alternative for Kubernetes scaling, offering faster and more flexible adjustments than the CA. In the next part of our discussion, we'll delve into how Karpenter compares with the CA, highlighting how it overcomes some of the CA's challenges by more effectively responding to the changing needs of workloads.

Karpenter

Karpenter is a flexible, high-performance Kubernetes cluster autoscaler that quickly provisions nodes to meet the demands of pending Pods. By analyzing the combined resource needs of these Pods, Karpenter smartly selects the most suitable instance types for execution. It enhances resource utilization by scaling down or terminating instances that are no longer hosting essential Pods, thereby minimizing unnecessary resource consumption. Additionally, its consolidation feature actively rearranges Pods to optimize and possibly downsize nodes to more cost-effective options, further driving down expenses.

Before Karpenter's advent, managing Kubernetes cluster compute resources was largely handled through **Amazon EC2 Auto Scaling groups** alongside the Kubernetes Cluster Autoscaler. Karpenter is a major upgrade in flexibility and efficiency. Instead of you managing many different node groups for different needs, Karpenter handles it automatically. It's also less tied to specific Kubernetes versions than the Cluster Autoscaler, simplifying upgrades and reducing the headache of managing controls in both AWS and Kubernetes.

Karpenter brings under one umbrella the task of instance management with an eye for simplicity, stability, and a keen understanding of cluster demands. It's engineered to address the Cluster Autoscaler's limitations by doing the following:

- Tailoring node provisioning directly to workload needs, sidestepping the one-size-fits-all node group approach
- Offering versatile node configuration possibilities without the overhead of managing a plethora of specialized node groups
- Enhancing Pod scheduling efficiency and scalability through rapid node provisioning and deployment

It's a good time to look at how Karpenter works and see how it's different from the Cluster Autoscaler. We'll take a closer look to understand their main features, how they help manage Kubernetes clusters, and what makes them different from each other. This comparison will help us see which tool might be better for certain situations when working with Kubernetes.

How it differs from the Cluster Autoscaler

Exploring the nuanced distinctions between the Cluster Autoscaler and Karpenter reveals key operational differences, particularly in how they interact with AWS EC2 to manage Kubernetes clusters.

In our exploration, we find that the Cluster Autoscaler engages with EC2 indirectly, via Auto Scaling groups. This process involves the Auto Scaling group acting as an intermediary, receiving directives from the Cluster Autoscaler before communicating with EC2 to adjust resources as needed.

Karpenter, on the other hand, streamlines this communication. It directly interfaces with the EC2 API, allowing it to promptly assess available resources within a specific region. This direct line not only facilitates a quicker response to resource demands but also enables Karpenter to efficiently tap into cost-saving options such as **spot instances**. Spot instances, known for their affordability, can be dynamically allocated by Karpenter based on real-time availability in the designated region.

> **Interview tip**
>
> **Question:** *How does Karpenter's method of provisioning nodes fundamentally differ from the Cluster Autoscaler's, and what key advantage does this provide?*
>
> **Answer:** The Cluster Autoscaler works **indirectly** by managing pre-defined ASGs. It tells the ASG to scale up or down, and the ASG handles the interaction with EC2. In contrast, Karpenter works **directly** with the EC2 Fleet API without needing ASGs. This direct approach is a major advantage because it allows Karpenter to provision the most optimal and cost-effective instance type based on the exact needs of pending Pods, rather than being limited to the instance types defined in a node group.

Moreover, Karpenter offers the flexibility to set various constraints for application deployment, such as insisting on spot instances. These constraints can be meticulously defined within Karpenter's custom resource definitions or directly in your deployment configurations.

The visual representations provided further illustrate this pivotal difference. Karpenter's ability to directly communicate with the EC2 API underscores its core advantage: provisioning resources precisely when needed, at the most favorable costs, and suited to the regional availability.

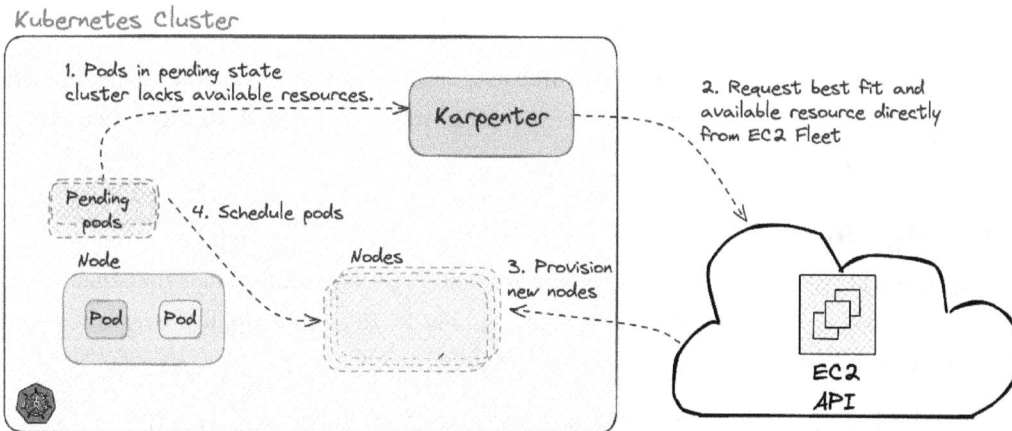

Figure 5.3 – Karpenter's interaction with EC2

This approach lets Karpenter overcome key Cluster Autoscaler limitations, such as being stuck with pre-defined node sizes, and allows it to provision the perfect-sized node just in time. Karpenter's design principle centers around offering just-in-time resources, optimizing both cost and performance by leveraging the best available options within the AWS region.

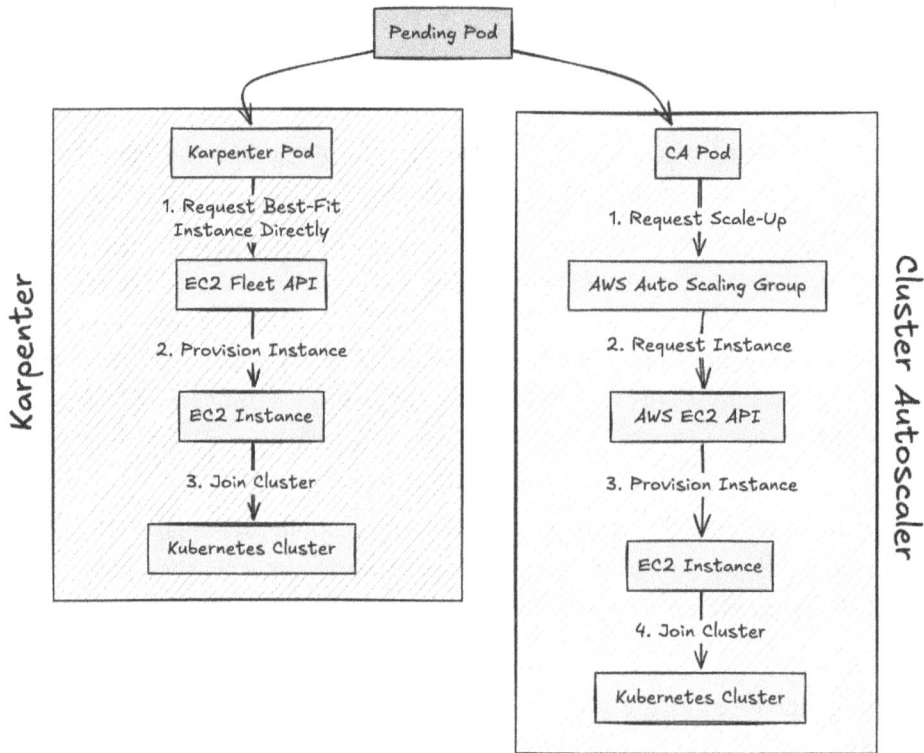

Figure 5.4 – A comparison between CA and Karpenter

Such capabilities underscore the strategic value Karpenter brings to Kubernetes cluster management, especially for organizations looking to optimize their cloud resource usage and cost-efficiency dynamically.

Working with Karpenter

Setting up Karpenter on your Kubernetes cluster involves a few essential steps that enable it to efficiently provision new nodes based on workload needs. Here's a simplified overview to get you started with Karpenter:

1. **Initial setup**: Karpenter operates directly within your Kubernetes cluster. For it to function, it requires permissions to interact with the underlying cloud provider—AWS in this case—to manage resources.

2. **Granting permissions**: The process involves setting up AWS IRSA. This setup allows your cluster to securely make requests to AWS services, empowering Karpenter to access necessary information about EC2 instance types and to create or terminate EC2 instances as required.

3. **Deploying Karpenter**: With the necessary permissions configured, Karpenter is installed using a Helm chart. This step integrates Karpenter into your Kubernetes environment, ready to manage node provisioning.

NodePool configuration

Karpenter introduces the concept of **NodePools** to define how it should manage unschedulable Pods and the provisioning of nodes. You'll need to specify various behaviors and constraints for these NodePools, such as node disruption policies and resource limits.

Upon initializing Karpenter, a default NodePool configuration is established, which plays a crucial role in dictating the characteristics of nodes that Karpenter can provision, as well as determining the types of Pods that are eligible to run on these nodes. *Figure 5.5* provides a visual walk-through of this decision-making process, showing how Karpenter uses the constraints from a matching NodePool to filter all available instance types and select the perfect one for the pending Pod.

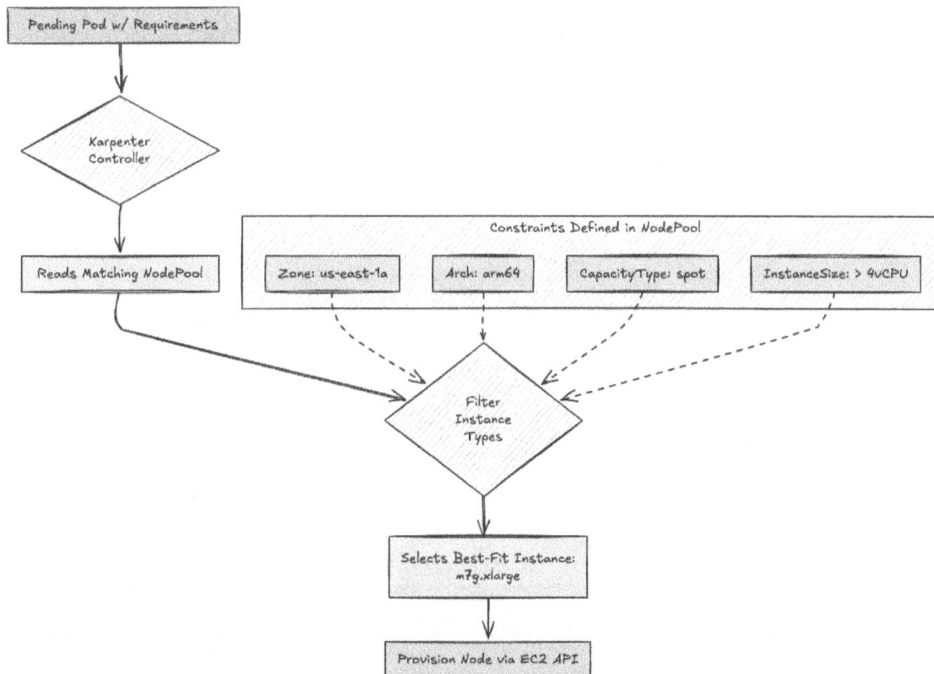

Figure 5.5 – The decision-making flow for Karpenter node provisioning

Through NodePools, Karpenter gains the flexibility to do the following:

- Impose taints to selectively permit certain Pods on its nodes
- Apply initial taints that Karpenter should place on a node at startup, indicating these taints are intended to be temporary
- Restrict node provisioning to specific zones, instance types, or computing architectures
- Establish default guidelines for when nodes should expire

> **Interview tip**
>
> **Question:** *What is a NodePool in Karpenter, and what are two key constraints you can define within it to control which nodes get provisioned?*
>
> **Answer:** A NodePool is a Karpenter resource that defines how it should manage unschedulable Pods and provision nodes. It sets the rules and characteristics for the nodes Karpenter creates. Two key constraints you can define are as follows:
>
> - **Instance types:** You can specify a list of allowed instance types or families (e.g., only t3 or m5 instances) to control costs and performance profiles.
> - **Zones:** You can restrict node provisioning to specific availability zones, which is critical for applications that rely on persistent volumes or have other zone-specific dependencies.

Modifying your existing NodePool or incorporating additional NodePools into Karpenter allows for tailored cluster management.

Diving into the configuration possibilities within a NodePool for Karpenter, there are several essential components to understand, ensuring that the nodes provisioned match the specific needs of your Kubernetes cluster.

- **NodePool essentials:** Remember, Karpenter needs at least one NodePool to begin provisioning nodes. Without it, the system won't activate the node creation process.
- `nodeClassRef`: The NodeClass is a blueprint for nodes, varying per cloud provider. It contains details about the type of instance that will be integrated into your Kubernetes cluster, including options for operating systems, networking, and storage configurations.
- **Taint management:** Taint management in Kubernetes is a crucial mechanism that allows you to control the scheduling of Pods onto nodes. By using taints and tolerations, you can ensure that Pods are only scheduled on appropriate nodes, which helps in maintaining

the stability and performance of your cluster. Taints are applied to nodes, making them less desirable for scheduling unless a Pod explicitly tolerates the taint.

- `taints`: Nodes provisioned by Karpenter will come with predefined taints. These taints are key in determining which Pods can be scheduled on these nodes, depending on their toleration settings.

- `startupTaints`: Distinct from regular taints, startup taints are applied to nodes upon initialization. These are not required to be tolerated by Pods for scheduling and are typically removed by other processes, such as a DaemonSet, once the node setup is complete. A common use case is for configuring network interfaces before Pod deployment commences.

- **Constraint configuration** (`requirements`): A critical section within NodePool setup is defining the requirements that shape your nodes. These constraints work alongside Kubernetes features such as topology spread constraints, node affinity, and node selectors. Within these constraints, you have the ability to use different operators such as `In`, `NotIn`, `Exists`, `DoesNotExist`, `Gt`, and `Lt`. This range offers extensive flexibility in dictating the precise conditions under which your nodes should operate.

Interview tip

Question: *How would you use a Karpenter NodePool to ensure that only specific, high-priority Pods can run on newly provisioned nodes?*

Answer: I would use taints within the `NodePool` configuration. By applying a specific taint to the `NodePool`—for example, `priority-workload-only=true:NoSchedule`—any node that Karpenter creates from that pool will be marked with this taint. This prevents normal Pods from being scheduled on it. To complete the setup, I would ensure my high-priority application's Pods have the corresponding **toleration**, which would allow them to be scheduled on these reserved, newly created nodes. This is an effective strategy to dedicate capacity for specific workloads.

For optimal operation, it's advisable to design NodePools with exclusivity in mind, ensuring that a Pod matches only a single NodePool. In scenarios where a Pod qualifies for multiple NodePools, Karpenter selects the NodePool with the highest assigned weight for provisioning. This approach enhances Karpenter's ability to manage node resources effectively and ensures Pods are scheduled in the most suitable environment based on the predefined constraints.

Within the NodePool, there's an opportunity to fine-tune the behavior of the kubelet, the agent that runs on each node in a Kubernetes cluster. This customization is optional, but it caters to specific requirements or constraints that may be unique to your Kubernetes setup. A common scenario for kubelet customization is managing the maximum number of Pods per node.

Here's how you can manage this:

- **Dynamic kubelet configuration**: You can adjust kubelet settings dynamically based on your cluster's characteristics. For instance, if you're operating within a cloud environment where there are IP address limitations per node, you can configure kubelet to limit the number of Pods relative to the amount of available CPU resources to prevent node saturation.
- **Static pod limit**: Alternatively, you can set a static upper limit on the number of Pods per node. This method is straightforward and ensures you don't exceed the count, avoiding issues such as IP address shortages, which can prevent Pod deployment.

By leveraging these kubelet argument configurations in Karpenter, you're able to optimize the allocation of Pods to nodes, ensuring efficient resource use and stable cluster operation.

The **disruption** settings within Karpenter play a crucial role in managing your Kubernetes cluster's efficiency and cost-effectiveness. These settings govern how boldly Karpenter can act when performing tasks such as recycling nodes past their lifespan or downsizing to cut costs.

Understanding disruption in Karpenter

Disruption settings in Karpenter are designed to manage and minimize the impact on workloads during node consolidation and scaling. These settings ensure that critical applications stay available and stable while Karpenter optimizes resource usage. Next, we will review all the settings and strategies involved in managing disruptions effectively.

Node consideration

Karpenter decides which nodes to evaluate for cost-saving consolidation based on their utilization levels. Nodes running at low capacity might be flagged for potential removal or replacement to optimize expenditure.

Node consolidation is the process of optimizing resource usage by reducing the number of underutilized nodes in a cluster. By consolidating nodes, Karpenter can lower operating costs and improve efficiency.

> **Interview tip**
>
> **Question**: *Explain Karpenter's consolidation feature. What is its main purpose and what are the two modes it can operate in?*
>
> **Answer**: Consolidation is a feature in Karpenter that actively works to reduce cluster costs by optimizing resource utilization. Its main purpose is to identify underutilized nodes and replace them with cheaper alternatives or terminate them if the workloads can fit elsewhere. The two primary operating modes are as follows:
>
> - **WhenUnderutilized:** This mode flags nodes for potential consolidation when they are running at low capacity.
>
> - **WhenEmpty:** This mode targets nodes that are not hosting any workload Pods, making consolidation decisions much simpler.

There are different configurations that Karpenter uses to determine which nodes to consolidate:

- `WhenUnderutilized`: Nodes running under capacity are assessed by Karpenter for potential consolidation to lower the cluster's operating costs.

- `WhenEmpty`: Karpenter may also target nodes that are not hosting any workload Pods, simplifying consolidation decisions.

Here are a few strategies for node consolidation:

- *Deletion and replacement*: Nodes may be marked for deletion if Karpenter determines their workloads can be accommodated by the spare capacity on other nodes. Alternatively, nodes might be replaced with more cost-efficient ones if the combined capacity of other nodes and a new, less expensive node can support the existing workloads.

- *Heuristics for multi-node consolidation*: Given the complexity of multi-node consolidation, Karpenter employs heuristic methods to identify likely candidates for consolidation rather than attempting to evaluate all possible combinations.

- *Consolidation preferences*: When considering multiple nodes for consolidation, Karpenter aims to minimize workload disruption by prioritizing the removal of nodes that have fewer Pods, are nearing the end of their lifespan, or are running lower-priority workloads.

- By implementing these strategies, Karpenter ensures that node consolidation is performed efficiently and with minimal disruption to your workloads.

- As we have seen, managing node consolidation is key to optimizing your Kubernetes cluster's performance and cost-efficiency. However, it is equally important to control the speed and the way nodes are scaled down. This is where scaling control comes into play.

Scaling control

The speed at which Karpenter can scale down nodes is controlled by **budgets**. These settings help regulate the pace of scaling down, ensuring that the cluster's stability and workload needs are not compromised.

Karpenter takes a calculated approach to managing disruptions in your Kubernetes cluster, ensuring that it respects the constraints defined within your NodePool budgets. The logic Karpenter uses is all about maintaining the right balance—it looks at the total number of nodes in a NodePool and adjusts for any nodes that are currently being deleted or are in a NotReady state.

Here's a breakdown of how Karpenter handles budgets:

- **Budget calculations**: If a NodePool's disruption budget is based on a percentage, Karpenter rounds up the product of the total node count and the percentage to get the number of nodes that can be disrupted. It then subtracts the number of nodes already being deleted and those marked as NotReady.

- **Non-percentage budgets**: When a budget is a fixed number instead of a percentage, the calculation is straightforward: Karpenter subtracts the number from the total node count, accounting for nodes that are being deleted and those in a NotReady state..

- **Minimum values for multiple budgets**: For NodePools with several budgets, Karpenter applies the most restrictive (or the minimum) value among them.

As an example, consider a NodePool with a trio of budgets—the first allows 15% of nodes to be disrupted, the second caps disruptions at 6 once there are over 40 nodes, and the third prevents any disruptions during the first 15 minutes of each day. Karpenter would calculate the allowable disruptions based on these budgets, ensuring it doesn't exceed any of the specified limits.

```
apiVersion: karpenter.sh/v1
kind: NodePool
metadata:
  name: default
spec:
  disruption:
    consolidationPolicy: WhenUnderutilized
    expireAfter: 720h # 30 * 24h = 720h
    budgets:
    - nodes: "15%"
      schedule: "@daily"
      duration: 15m
```

> **Interview tip**
>
> **Question:** *How can you use Karpenter to ensure nodes are regularly recycled, and why is this a good practice?*
>
> **Answer:** You can use the `expireAfter` setting within a NodePool's disruption configuration. By setting a duration, such as `720h` for **30 days**, you instruct Karpenter to automatically drain and terminate nodes after they reach that age. This is a valuable best practice for maintaining cluster health and security. Regularly recycling nodes helps to apply the latest security patches from a new AMI, reduces configuration drift, and prevents potential issues that can arise on long-running nodes.

By adhering to these budgeting rules, Karpenter can smartly scale down your cluster without disrupting more nodes than your applications can handle, thus optimizing the cluster's performance and cost without compromising on reliability.

By fine-tuning these disruption and consolidation settings, you can instruct Karpenter on how to manage node turnover efficiently—whether that's through swift replacement of resources or more gradual adjustments, all tailored to your specific operational requirements and cost considerations.

For more hands-on examples and guidance on implementing Karpenter in your Kubernetes setup, our associated GitHub repository is a valuable resource. There, you'll find demonstrations on adding new resources with Karpenter, how it efficiently manages resource consolidation, and more. Visit our GitHub repository for detailed steps on deploying Karpenter in your own clusters.

It's important to note that while Karpenter automates node provision and management, you also have the option to maintain application availability through `PodDisruptionBudgets`. These are Kubernetes features that limit the number of concurrently disrupted Pods in a replicated application, ensuring high availability. We will delve deeper into `PodDisruptionBudgets` and how to implement them effectively later in this book. They are crucial tools in maintaining stable services, especially during voluntary disruptions such as upgrades or scaling down.

Beyond addition: The dynamics of Kubernetes scaling

Karpenter demonstrates an impressive suite of features that enable granular control over node management within Kubernetes. We've explored the depth of customization available—from node consolidation strategies to detailed node configuration, showing how Karpenter equips us to fine-tune our clusters' scaling behaviors and resource utilization.

While Karpenter offers a high degree of flexibility compared to the Cluster Autoscaler, it's also a relatively new solution, evidenced by its version number indicating ongoing development towards stabilization. As with any rapidly evolving tool, users should be prepared for regular updates, which are part and parcel of Kubernetes ecosystem tools.

Although we have not yet delved into event-driven scaling mechanisms such as **KEDA**, which scales applications based on event metrics, rest assured, this topic will be covered as we progress in our book. The world of Kubernetes scaling is rich and multifaceted, with event-driven approaches offering yet another dimension of adaptability.

Summary

Scaling, as we've seen, isn't just about adding resources; it's also about the smart removal of resources when they're no longer needed. This balance of cost and efficiency is key. Karpenter excels in this area by managing both stateless and stateful applications effectively. It's smart enough to understand factors such as persistent volumes and their availability zone constraints, which are critical for stateful applications.

In this chapter, we explored how tools such as the Cluster Autoscaler and Karpenter help optimize Kubernetes cluster performance by dynamically adjusting node counts. The Cluster Autoscaler works well with predefined Auto Scaling groups, while Karpenter offers greater flexibility and efficiency by directly interacting with the EC2 API. Karpenter's ability to handle cost-effective spot instances and its configuration through NodePools provide a tailored scaling solution.

We have also covered the critical role of disruption settings and scaling controls. These ensure that scaling activities do not impact the stability and availability of your applications. By using disruption budgets and consolidation strategies, Karpenter maintains optimal performance without compromising on reliability.

As we close this chapter, we acknowledge the relative simplicity of scaling stateless applications. However, the challenges of scaling stateful applications, particularly those with persistent storage requirements, are more complex. This leads us to the next chapter, where we will dive into managing storage and persistence in Kubernetes. We will explore best practices and strategies to ensure data resilience and availability, equipping you with the knowledge to handle these advanced scaling scenarios effectively.

Unlock this book's exclusive benefits now

Scan this QR code or go to https://packtpub.com/unlock, then search for this book by name.

Note: Keep your purchase invoice ready before you start.

Part 3

Networking, Services, and Security

This part equips you with the practical knowledge needed to understand how services communicate, how traffic is routed and exposed, and how to keep your workloads secure. Whether you're prepping for interviews or building production-ready clusters, you'll come away ready to answer tough questions and make smart architectural choices.

This part of the book includes the following chapters:

- *Chapter 6, Essentials of Kubernetes Networking*
- *Chapter 7, Kubernetes Network Architecture: Services and Ingresses*
- *Chapter 8, Storage: Persistence and CSI Drivers*
- *Chapter 9, Security Best Practices in Kubernetes and RBAC*

6

Essentials of Kubernetes Networking

Think of Kubernetes as a busy city full of containers, each one needing to talk to the others. In this fast-moving world of microservices, how does all communication stay organized and efficient? That's where Kubernetes networking comes in—an essential topic for anyone preparing for a technical interview.

In this chapter, we'll go beyond the basics and dive into how Kubernetes handles container communication. You'll learn how networking in Kubernetes differs from traditional virtual machines and why that matters when solving real-world problems or answering interview questions. We'll also cover **Container Network Interface (CNI)** plugins, which are key to connecting your applications to the network. You'll see how they work and why they're so important, giving you the confidence to discuss them clearly and effectively when it counts.

By the time you finish this chapter, you'll have the knowledge and practical understanding to answer networking questions in interviews and explain Kubernetes internals with confidence.

Let's get started and unlock the full power of Kubernetes networking!

We will discuss the following in this chapter:

- How does Kubernetes networking work?
- What is **Container Network Interface (CNI)**?
- What is the kube-proxy component?

How does Kubernetes networking work?

Imagine a Kubernetes cluster as a group of containers talking to each other. Knowing how this talking happens is important because you will likely come across this kind of question in almost every technical session where Kubernetes knowledge is a must. So, it's essential to understand everything from top to bottom.

In the following sections, we'll dive deeper into things such as Pods and Services, which are messengers that help containers communicate. It's like understanding the different roads data takes within a Kubernetes neighborhood. We'll break down the basics, from how containers communicate to the layers of the networking system.

How does Kubernetes networking look at a high level?

When faced with the question "How does Kubernetes networking work?" you can begin by explaining the fundamentals. As the conversation unfolds, you can then use additional questions to cover all the specific aspects the interviewer is interested in (we will expand on every aspect in this chapter).

Kubernetes networking forms the bedrock of communication within a cluster, orchestrating seamless interactions for containerized applications. At its essence, Kubernetes networking includes the following key components:

- **Pod communication**: Containers are grouped into Pods, allowing unrestricted communication within the same Pod and requiring networking solutions for inter-node communication. We will expand on this in the next question, "How do Pods communicate in Kubernetes?"

- **Services and Ingresses**: Services act as abstractions, defining sets of Pods and facilitating load balancing and service discovery through different types of exposure. Ingresses govern external traffic routing to internal Services, serving as an entry point for HTTP and HTTPS traffic. Ingress controllers manage web server settings for you and create appropriate settings and rules for external access based on the Ingress specification. It's also important to mention that Kubernetes is continuously improving, and a new way of exposing services called Gateway API has been introduced. It's a better way to handle traffic routing, designed to eventually replace Ingress with a clearer and more flexible approach. We will deeply review these components in *Chapter 7*.

- **Network policies**: Define rules governing communication between Pods, enhancing security and segmentation within the cluster, with control over Ingress and Egress traffic. We will also expand on that in detail and give examples in the next chapter.

- **kube-proxy**: This is critical in managing network connectivity for services and implementing load balancing and proxy features to ensure efficient communication.

- **Domain Name System (DNS) components**: These are used for service discovery, enabling communication between Pods using service names, and maintaining adaptability in dynamic environments.

- **CNI plugins**: Handle networking functionalities, providing necessary interfaces to connect containers to the network and establish connectivity within the cluster.

This high-level perspective encapsulates the foundational elements of Kubernetes networking, which is essential for orchestrating efficient and secure containerized environments.

How do Pods communicate in Kubernetes?

This question is common, and if you were asked it, you would first need to request clarification (as usual) from the interviewer. You can ask what specific type of communication they want to hear about, or you can say something such as, "The Pod's communication can be split into multiple types of scenarios..." These scenarios are detailed as follows.

How do containers within one Pod communicate?

Containers within the same Pod in Kubernetes can communicate with each other using the localhost network interface. When multiple containers are part of a single Pod, they share the same network namespace. This means they can reach each other using the loopback address (127.0.0.1) and communicate over the localhost network.

Essentially, it's as if all the containers within a Pod are running on the same host, enabling them to interact seamlessly without external networking. This local communication within the Pod is fast and efficient and doesn't involve the complexities of external network routing.

This design promotes cohesiveness within the Pod, allowing containers to collaborate and share information as if running on a single machine. It's a key feature in Kubernetes for enabling communication and coordination between tightly coupled components within the same application or service.

You can see this process visualized in the following figure:

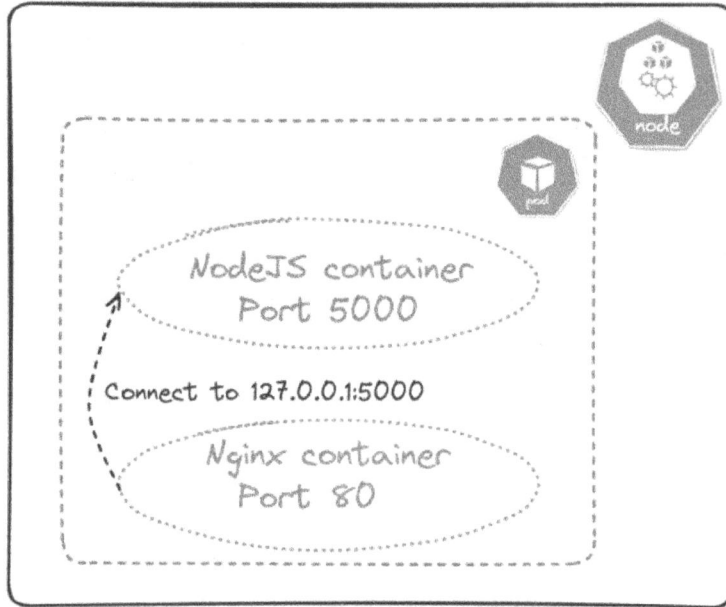

Figure 6.1 – Container-to-container communication within one Pod

You can return to *Chapter 3* to refresh your memories about the Pod itself.

How do Pods on the same node communicate?

Pods on the same node in Kubernetes can communicate with each other directly over the host machine's network. Each Pod on a node is assigned a unique IP address within the node's network space. Containers within these Pods can use this IP address to communicate.

When containers in one Pod want to communicate with containers in another Pod on the same node, they can use the destination Pod's IP address directly. This communication occurs without external routing since the Pods are co-located on the same machine.

Let's compare this setup with the one shown in *Figure 6.1* by examining how the same containers—Node.js and Nginx—operate when they are deployed in separate Pods that are co-located on the same Kubernetes node.

In the following figure, each container runs in its own Pod: the Node.js Pod exposes port 5000, and the Nginx Pod exposes port 80.

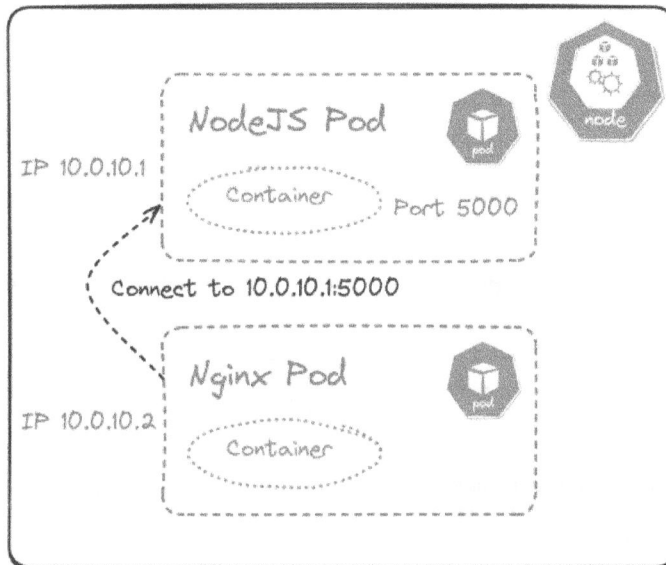

Figure 6.2 – Pod-to-Pod communication within one node

Because the Pods are on the same node, they can communicate directly via the node's virtual network using each other's Pod IP addresses. This contrasts with *Figure 6.1*, where both containers shared the same network namespace and used 127.0.0.1 for communication. This new setup introduces stronger isolation between containers, while still allowing efficient local communication at the node level.

How do Pods on different nodes communicate?

Pods on different nodes in Kubernetes communicate with each other over the cluster network. When Pods are spread across multiple nodes, inter-node communication becomes essential. Kubernetes facilitates this communication through various networking components. Here's a simplified overview:

- Pods have unique IP addresses within the cluster network, and containers within Pods communicate using these IP addresses.
- kube-proxy is a Kubernetes component responsible for managing network connectivity. It ensures that communication requests from one Pod to another are correctly routed. We will talk in detail about that closer to the end of this chapter.

- Kubernetes establishes a cluster network that connects all nodes. This network enables communication between Pods on different nodes.

- When a Pod on one node wants to communicate with a Pod on another node, the network routing ensures the message reaches the destination.

- A Kubernetes Service (again, this will be discussed in more detail in *Chapter 7*) might be involved in load balancing for replicated copies of Pods.

- Pods on different nodes can communicate using the external IP addresses of their respective nodes.

Now that we have reviewed in detail inner cluster network communication, we will dive deeper into the next important topic in Kubernetes networking—DNS.

How does Kubernetes handle DNS?

In Kubernetes, DNS facilitates service discovery and communication between Pods. Here's an overview of how Kubernetes handles DNS:

- **Pod names**: Each Pod in Kubernetes is assigned a unique hostname, such as the Pod's name. For example, a Pod named "nginx" would have the hostname "nginx" too.

- **DNS resolution**: Containers within a Pod can communicate with each other using the Pod's hostname. Kubernetes automatically configures the DNS to map Pod names to their respective IP addresses.

- **Service discovery**: When a Pod wants to communicate with another Pod or a Service, it can use the DNS name. Services are assigned DNS names that follow the pattern `<service-name>.<namespace>.svc.cluster.local`.

- **The cluster domain**: Usually, `cluster.local` is appended to DNS names to form the full DNS address. For example, if a Pod wants to communicate with a Service named "nginx" in the "web" namespace, it will use the DNS name "`nginx.web.svc.cluster.local`".

- **External DNS resolution**: Kubernetes DNS can also be configured to allow Pods to communicate with external services or resources. Kubernetes can be configured to use an external DNS server for resolution beyond the cluster domain.

Kubernetes allows configuring **DNS policies**, defining how DNS requests are handled within the cluster in the Pods' specification. You will encounter policies such as the following:

- **Default**: Uses the node's DNS settings and is suitable for basic setups where Pods inherit node configuration. No custom DNS configuration is required.

- **ClusterFirst**: The default for Pods, this prioritizes cluster DNS and falls back on external DNS. It is ideal for most applications needing access to cluster services and external domains. No custom DNS configuration is required.

- **ClusterFirstWithHostNet**: Same as `ClusterFirst`, but only for Pods with `hostNetwork` set to `true`. This is useful for host-networked Pods needing both cluster and external access. No custom DNS configuration is required.

- **None**: No automatic DNS configuration is required. It is fully customizable via `dnsConfig` and suitable for advanced setups needing custom DNS servers and search domains. It requires manual DNS settings.

> **Interview tip**
>
> **Question:** *How does DNS work inside a Kubernetes cluster?*
>
> **Answer:** Kubernetes uses a built-in DNS service (usually CoreDNS) to resolve internal service names and Pod hostnames. Every service gets a DNS entry such as `service-name.namespace.svc.cluster.local`, allowing Pods to discover and communicate with each other by name.

What is the role of the kube-dns or CoreDNS service in Kubernetes networking?

Both kube-dns and CoreDNS are DNS servers used in Kubernetes to facilitate service discovery and DNS resolution within the cluster.

kube-dns was the original DNS server used in Kubernetes for service discovery. It consists of containers running on the Kubernetes cluster, including a DNS server (SkyDNS) and a service discovery component. kube-dns automatically creates DNS records for each Service and Pod in the cluster, allowing for accessible DNS-based communication.

CoreDNS is a more flexible and extensible DNS server that gradually replaced kube-dns as the default DNS server starting from Kubernetes version 1.11. But even today, companies sometimes prefer kube-dns in modern Kubernetes installations primarily because of some legacy reasons. CoreDNS is a general-purpose DNS server that supports various plugins, providing features beyond essential DNS resolution. It is highly configurable, allowing administrators to customize DNS behavior based on their cluster requirements.

Both types of DNS play a vital role in ensuring that Pods and Services can communicate with each other using human-readable names rather than IP addresses. Mainly, they are responsible for the following:

- **Service discovery**: Both DNS servers automatically create DNS records for Services in the cluster, enabling Pods to discover and communicate with each other using DNS names
- **DNS resolution**: They handle DNS resolution requests, translating human-readable DNS names into IP addresses for Pods and Services within the cluster
- **Cluster domain:** They append the cluster domain (e.g., `svc.cluster.local`) to DNS names to form **fully qualified domain names (FQDNs)** for internal cluster communication

In Kubernetes, DNS is a core component that enables reliable service discovery, allowing Pods and Services to communicate with one another using easy-to-remember hostnames instead of IP addresses. By managing DNS records dynamically, Kubernetes makes it possible for applications to resolve service names into cluster IP addresses, promoting a seamless, stable communication layer even as services scale up or down. DNS serves as the foundation for service discovery, ensuring that applications can locate and interact with each other efficiently across the cluster. As Kubernetes clusters grow, however, basic DNS capabilities alone are often insufficient to meet all networking requirements. This is where CNI plugins come into play, enabling Kubernetes to handle more complex networking demands by extending capabilities beyond simple DNS resolution. In the next section, we'll dive into CNI and how it supports advanced networking functionality for robust, scalable Kubernetes environments.

What is Container Network Interface (CNI)?

CNI is a specification and set of libraries that define how network connectivity is provided to containers. Kubernetes uses CNI plugins to manage Pod networking, regardless of the container runtime in use—such as containerd, cri-o, or Docker (which relied on the dockershim component, *deprecated* in Kubernetes v1.20).

Kubernetes uses CNI as its networking interface for managing container networking. CNI plugins are employed to set up networking for Pods, facilitating communication within the cluster. CNI provides a standardized way for different container runtimes to use various networking plugins seamlessly, allowing containers to communicate with each other and the broader network.

CNI plugins themselves are executable files that implement the CNI specification. These plugins handle tasks such as setting up network interfaces, configuring routes, and managing container networking namespaces. Container runtimes interact with CNI plugins during the container creation process. When a container starts, the runtime calls the appropriate CNI plugin to configure the network.

CNI enables network providers to create plugins that can be easily integrated with container runtimes. This enables a **plug-and-play model** where different networking solutions can be used interchangeably.

Let's try to demonstrate how it works on a high level, using the following figure:

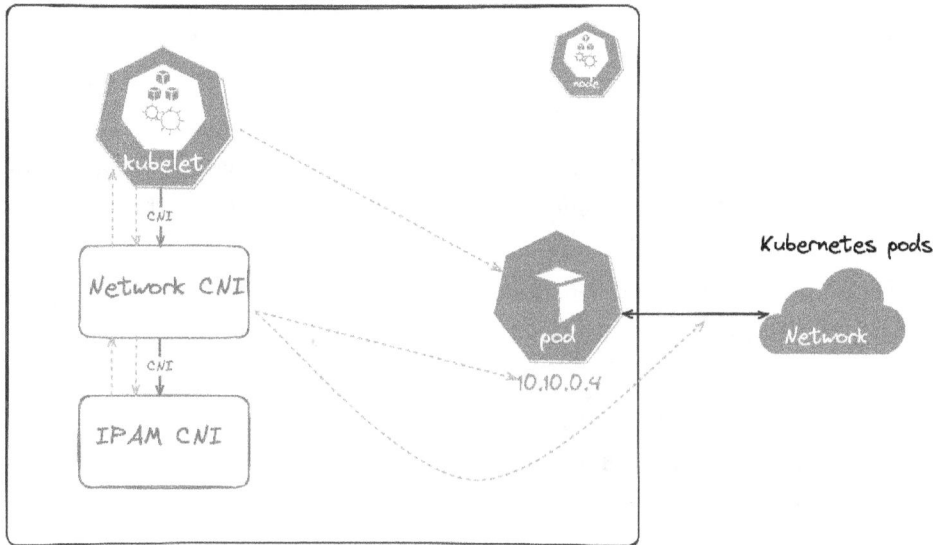

Figure 6.3 – CNI at a high-level glance

In the figure, you can see how the kubelet to spin up a new Pod first goes to the network CNI plugin to request the network creation and asks the **IP Address Management (IPAM)** system to provide the IP address (it can be dynamic or static, depending on the CNI plugin implementation and configurations). As a result, the kubelet can spin up the Pod with network connectivity to other cluster components.

Now, let's start exploring the most important aspects of CNI that you will come across in Kubernetes technical interviews.

What are the functions provided by CNI?

CNI primarily focuses on the primary network setup for containers, including IP address allocation, routes, and DNS configuration. Let's expand each key functionality one by one:

- CNI sets up the container network configuration, including IP addresses, routes, and DNS settings. This ensures that containers can communicate with each other and the external network.

- CNI creates separate network namespaces for each Kubernetes Pod. This isolation allows containers to have their network stack, preventing interference with other containers on the same host.

- CNI supports bridge-based networking, where containers are connected to a virtual bridge that facilitates communication within the same host and, if needed, with the external network.

- CNI enables overlay networks, allowing containers across different hosts to communicate securely over an overlay network.

- Containers can be attached directly to the host network, bypassing **Network Address Translation (NAT)** and allowing them to use the host's IP address, which translates private IP addresses to public ones (and vice versa).

- CNI supports the dynamic loading of plugins, allowing administrators to switch between different networking solutions easily without requiring changes to container runtime configurations.

- CNI manages container assignment and the release of IP addresses (known as IP management). This ensures containers have unique and accessible IP addresses within the designated network.

- CNI is designed to be dynamically extendable, allowing new plugins to be added without modifying the CNI core. This extensibility fosters a diverse ecosystem of networking solutions.

- CNI interfaces with various container runtime tools, including Docker and containerd, provide a common networking abstraction that works across different runtime environments.

- Network plugins that integrate with CNI provide the necessary functionality for policy enforcement and extension, offering a comprehensive solution for securing and controlling container communication (we will talk about network policies in the next chapter).

Interview tip

Question: *What is the* **Container Network Interface (CNI)***, and why is it important in Kubernetes?*

Answer: CNI is a specification and plugin interface used by Kubernetes to provide networking for containers. It handles tasks such as assigning IP addresses, setting up network interfaces, and configuring routing so that Pods can communicate within the cluster and externally. Kubernetes uses CNI plugins regardless of the container runtime.

What is the container overlay network?

Even though overlay networks mainly relate to computer networking and container fundamentals in general, you may still be asked this question in the technical interview session. That's why a basic understanding of this topic can benefit you during the interview.

So, the **container overlay network** is a type of network architecture used in containerized environments, providing communication and connectivity between containers running on different hosts within a cluster. Overlay networks enable container-to-container communication across multiple nodes in a distributed system. Overlay networks allow containers to communicate seamlessly regardless of the physical host they are running on. This is essential for distributed applications where containers may be deployed across multiple nodes.

Overlay networks also create a virtual network abstraction that spans the entire container cluster. Containers within this overlay network can communicate with each other using virtual IP addresses independent of the underlying physical network. Communication across the overlay network often involves encapsulation and tunneling techniques. This means that data packets are encapsulated within another packet (tunneled) to traverse the physical network infrastructure.

Overlay networks are designed to dynamically scale as containers are added or removed from the cluster. This makes them well suited for dynamic and elastic containerized environments.

Various solutions provide overlay network capabilities for container orchestration platforms. Examples are Flannel, Calico, and Weave. These solutions implement different overlay network strategies, such as VXLAN or GRE encapsulation.

What CNI implementations do you know?

When asked this question, you should first name any CNI solution you work with and have personal experience with, concentrating your response on those.

But it also makes sense to name at least the most frequently encountered solutions and their pros and cons. Let's list the most used CNI solutions today and then review in more detail the most famous of them:

- Calico is a versatile CNI plugin known for its scalability and support for various networking topologies. It leverages BGP routing for efficient communication and provides network policies for security.

- Flannel is a straightforward and lightweight CNI solution commonly used in Kubernetes clusters. It utilizes overlay networking, often employing VXLAN, for connecting containers across different nodes.

- Weave offers a simple and easy-to-use solution for container networking. It provides network segmentation and encryption and can be seamlessly integrated into various container orchestration platforms.

- Cilium stands out for its focus on providing secure networking and API-aware network visibility. It incorporates load balancing, network security, and even HTTP-aware network policies.

- Canal is a networking solution that combines the best features of Flannel and Calico. It provides users with a unified networking solution that includes Calico's network policy enforcement capabilities and the rich connectivity options offered by both Calico (unencapsulated) and Flannel (encapsulated) networks.

- The AWS VPC CNI is a specific CNI plugin designed for Kubernetes clusters running on **Amazon Web Services** (**AWS**), also known as **Elastic Kubernetes Service** (**EKS**). It is tailored to leverage the networking capabilities of AWS **Virtual Private Clouds** (**VPCs**) to provide efficient and secure communication between containers.

- Other cloud providers (such as Azure) also provide solutions for CNI functionality for their managed Kubernetes services, but they are less frequently encountered.

What CNI should you choose for production projects?

The choice of a CNI solution for production projects depends on various factors, including the specific requirements of your environment, the characteristics of your workloads, and your familiarity with the plugin.

When choosing a CNI plugin for production, consider the following:

- **Scalability**: Ensure the plugin can handle the scale of your production environment

- **Security**: Evaluate the security features, such as network policies and encryption, provided by the CNI plugin

- **Ease of use**: Consider the ease of deployment, configuration, and maintenance, especially if you prefer simplicity

- **Community support**: A vibrant and active community often indicates ongoing development, support, and shared knowledge

Let's look at the features and pitfalls of the top three CNI solutions today:

CNI	Pros	Cons	Best fit for...
Calico	Known for scalability, security, and support for various network topologies. Utilizes Border Gateway Protocol (BGP) for efficient routing. Offers rich network policies for enhanced security.	It may have a steeper learning curve for beginners.	In environments that require high availability and scalability, Calico's rich feature set makes it an excellent choice for large clusters where maintaining performance at scale is critical.
Flannel	Lightweight and easy to set up. Suitable for simpler deployments. Utilizes overlay networking, often using VXLAN.	Best suited for smaller-scale or less complex scenarios.	An excellent choice for simplified Kubernetes networking requirements where ease of use is paramount. Its compatibility with various backends makes it adaptable to different environments. It also has the highest network bandwidth performance.
Cilium	Focuses on secure networking and API-aware visibility. Offers features such as load balancing, network security, and HTTP-aware network policies.	Advanced features may only be necessary for some use cases.	In high-security and scalable environments, application protocols are crucial for securing modern microservice architectures where traditional network-layer controls are insufficient.

Table 6.1 – Top three CNI plugins (Calico, Flannel, and Cilium) comparison table

What exactly makes Cilium so different in comparison to other solutions?

Answering this question can be tricky for those who are not profoundly familiar with networking and Linux kernel fundamentals because the most significant difference is that Cilium leverages the power of **extended Berkeley Packet Filter (eBPF)**. When you have to answer a question like this, you should be honest and tell the interviewer about your knowledge of the Linux kernel field. Using terms such as iptables and eBPF can trigger the interviewer to ask more questions in this area. So, just tell the truth and provide your high-level knowledge of Cilium's specific features.

While other CNI solutions use the Linux iptables networking solution and a firewall, ePBF is a highly efficient and programmable framework in the Linux kernel that allows for dynamic and customizable packet processing without kernel modifications, which slightly improves the network performance for high-loaded systems.

Cilium, using eBPF, has the following features and advantages:

- Cilium is known for its API-aware network security capabilities. It can enforce security policies at the HTTP and API layers, enabling fine-grained control over communication between microservices based on API semantics.

- Cilium includes built-in load-balancing capabilities. It can distribute traffic across multiple instances of a service, enhancing availability and performance.

- Cilium can provide transparent encryption for inter-Pod communication, ensuring that traffic between microservices is secure and confidential.

- Cilium offers distributed Layer 7 visibility (according to the OSI model), providing insights into microservices' communication patterns and behavior across the entire cluster.

- Cilium is designed to integrate seamlessly with service mesh architectures, such as Istio. This integration enhances observability, security, and control over microservices communication.

- Cilium allows the definition of security policies based on network and transport layer attributes. This enables a flexible and context-aware approach to securing communication between services.

- Cilium generates a dynamic API-aware network graph, visually representing the relationships between microservices and their communication patterns.

Figure 6.4 illustrates the difference between iptables-based networking and its modern alternative using eBPF for more efficient packet routing and filtering. While iptables has traditionally been used in Kubernetes for handling network traffic, **IP Virtual Server (IPVS)** has also emerged as an alternative, particularly for kube-proxy's service load balancing. However, eBPF represents a more fundamental shift by enabling faster, programmable packet processing in the kernel without relying on traditional iptables/IPVS chains.

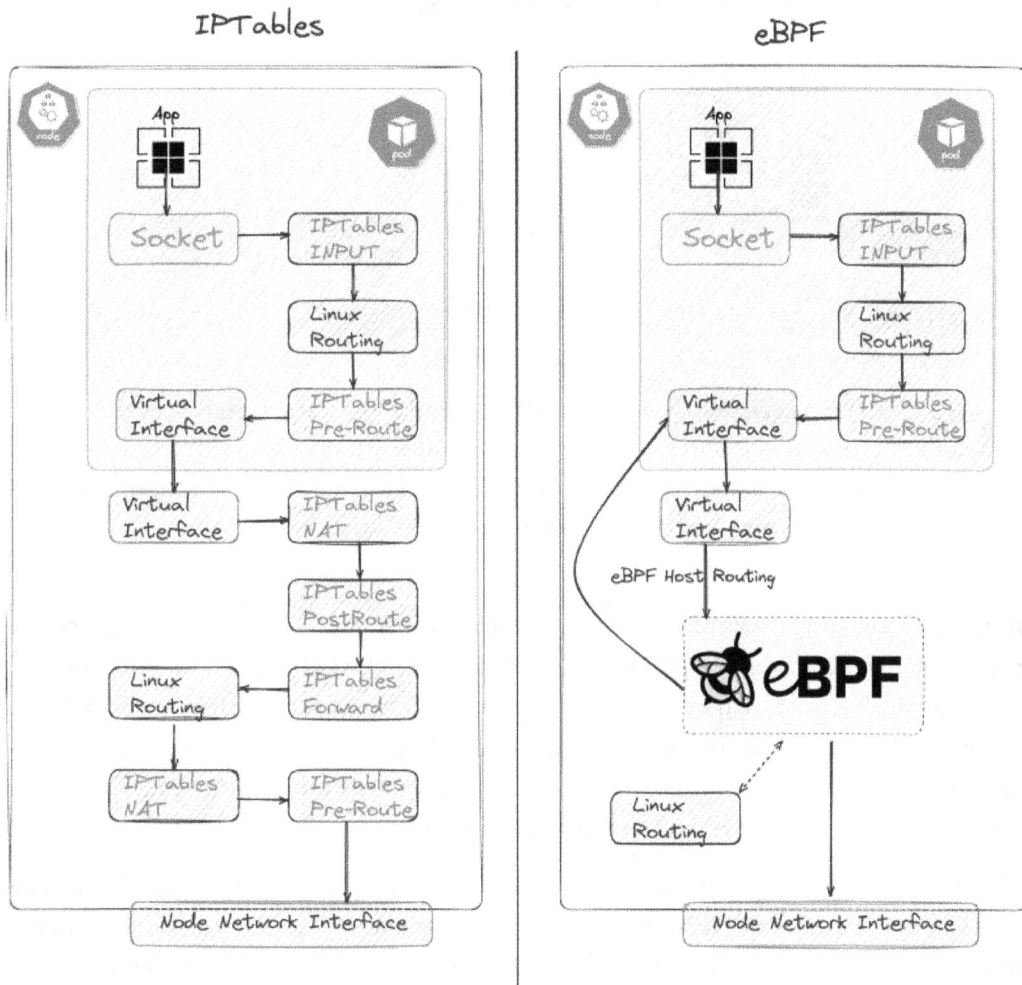

Figure 6.4 – iptables and eBPF differences at a glance

🔍 **Quick tip**: Need to see a high-resolution version of this image? Open this book in the next-gen Packt Reader or view it in the PDF/ePub copy.

🔒 **The next-gen Packt Reader** and a **free PDF/ePub copy** of this book are included with your purchase. Scan the QR code OR visit `https://packtpub.com/unlock`, then use the search bar to find this book by name. Double-check the edition shown to make sure you get the right one.

Note

We cannot expand on some network concepts here because that is beyond the scope of this book. There are plenty of books and other materials available, but our recommendation is Andrew S. Tanenbaum's books on networking and operating systems. These are large works but provide really vital knowledge in this area.

In summary, selecting the right CNI plugin is crucial for shaping how your Kubernetes cluster manages networking. Each CNI option brings unique strengths: Calico provides scalability and robust security features for large clusters, Flannel offers a lightweight and straightforward solution for simpler setups, and Cilium enables advanced security controls suitable for complex, microservices-based architectures. Choosing the appropriate CNI solution depends on your specific networking needs, cluster size, and security requirements.

With the foundational networking setup covered, we can now move on to another key component of Kubernetes networking: kube-proxy. This component plays a vital role in managing the network connections for services within a Kubernetes cluster, ensuring stable communication between services and handling traffic distribution. Let's explore how kube-proxy functions and how it contributes to Kubernetes' service networking model.

What is the kube-proxy component?

kube-proxy is a critical component in a Kubernetes cluster, responsible for managing network connectivity to and from Pods. It operates at the network layer (Layer 4) and performs essential functions to enable communication between Pods within the cluster and between external clients and Services.

What is kube-proxy strictly responsible for?

kube-proxy primarily provides a Service abstraction within the Kubernetes cluster. Services in Kubernetes define sets of Pods and a policy by which to access them (Services abstraction). Also, it's responsible for the following:

- It supports different types of Services, including the following:

    - **ClusterIP**: Internal-only Service accessible within the cluster
    - **NodePort**: Exposes a Service on each node's IP at a static port
    - **LoadBalancer**: Exposes a Service externally using a cloud provider's load balancer
    - **ExternalName**: Maps a Service to a DNS name

- kube-proxy relies on the underlying networking infrastructure to implement its functionality. It typically uses IP tables directly or IPVS to set up rules for packet forwarding, load balancing, and service abstraction.

- kube-proxy maintains associations between Services and the corresponding sets of Pods (endpoints). It dynamically updates this association based on cluster changes, ensuring traffic is directed to the correct Pods.

- kube-proxy implements simple load balancing. It distributes incoming requests among the available Pods (for multi-replica deployment models), ensuring even distribution of traffic.

- In the case of NodePort Services, kube-proxy ensures that the selected port on each node is accessible from external clients. It forwards the traffic to the appropriate Pod within the cluster.

- It can be configured to support session affinity (sticky sessions). This ensures traffic from the same client is consistently directed to the same Pod, facilitating stateful communication.

- kube-proxy supports different proxy modes, including userspace, iptables, and IPVS. The chosen mode depends on the underlying infrastructure and specific requirements.

- It may perform health checking on the available Pods to ensure that traffic is directed only to healthy Pods, improving the overall reliability of the application.

Under the hood, kube-proxy is a critical component in Kubernetes networking, providing efficient routing and load balancing for service traffic. By maintaining iptables or IPVS rules, kube-proxy ensures that traffic within the cluster is consistently directed to the correct Pods, adapting dynamically to changes in the cluster. This enables Kubernetes to handle service networking seamlessly and reliably, regardless of the scale or complexity of the workload.

Summary

In this chapter, we explored the foundational elements that make Kubernetes networking both powerful and flexible. We began with an overview of DNS in Kubernetes, understanding how it enables reliable service discovery within the cluster, allowing Services and Pods to communicate seamlessly. We then examined the different DNS policies available, highlighting how each policy can be tailored to fit various network needs, from simple setups to highly customized configurations. Moving beyond DNS, we introduced CNI plugins, such as Calico, Flannel, and Cilium, and discussed their unique strengths in providing scalable, secure, and adaptable networking options for Kubernetes clusters.

Finally, we delved into the workings of kube-proxy, the component responsible for managing network rules and load balancing traffic across service endpoints, ensuring stable communication within the cluster. kube-proxy's ability to route and balance traffic dynamically plays a vital role in maintaining service availability and performance.

Altogether, understanding these networking essentials—from DNS configurations to CNI plugins and kube-proxy—equips you with the knowledge to make informed decisions about how to structure and manage network traffic within your Kubernetes clusters. This knowledge forms a strong foundation for tackling more advanced Kubernetes networking topics and ensures you're ready to design resilient, scalable, and efficient networking setups in your environments.

Let's jump into the next chapter and dive deeper into the traffic flow in Kubernetes, learn more about the Kubernetes services we mentioned in this chapter, and complete our knowledge of Kubernetes networking.

7

Kubernetes Network Architecture: Services and Ingresses

Welcome to *Chapter 7* of our journey through Kubernetes. In this chapter, we will delve deep into the intricate network of Kubernetes Services and Ingresses, exploring how traffic flows inside and around the cluster. As Kubernetes continues to revolutionize how we build, deploy, and scale applications, understanding how services and Ingresses facilitate communication and routing within the cluster is essential for mastering the platform's networking capabilities.

This chapter will explore Kubernetes Services, which act as an abstraction layer for accessing pods and enable seamless communication between application components. We'll delve into the various types of services, including `ClusterIP`, `NodePort`, and `LoadBalancer`, and examine their use cases, advantages, and implementation details.

Specifically, we will cover the following main topics:

- What are the main Kubernetes service types and their key differences?
- How exactly do Kubernetes Services interact with pods?
- What is an Ingress controller in Kubernetes, its types, functionality, and service routing?
- What does the new Gateway API approach bring to the Kubernetes world?

By the end of this chapter, you'll have a deep understanding of how Kubernetes Services and Ingresses facilitate communication and traffic routing within the cluster. This will empower you to design, deploy, and manage cloud-native applications with confidence and efficiency. So, let's dive in and unlock the secrets of Kubernetes networking together.

What are the Kubernetes Services?

We have already touched on this topic in the previous chapter when talking about kube-proxy; answering this question will slightly overlap with the last chapter, but it's essential. Moreover, we will dive deeper into every Kubernetes service type to elaborate on their use cases and working methods.

So, Kubernetes Services are essential for facilitating communication between various parts of an application running within a Kubernetes cluster. They provide a stable endpoint by abstracting away the details of individual pods and enabling dynamic load balancing and service discovery. Kubernetes Services ensures the application remains accessible and functional even as pods are added, removed, or replaced.

There are several types of Kubernetes Services:

- **ClusterIP**: This is the default type of Service. It exposes the Service on an internal IP within the cluster and is accessible only within the Kubernetes cluster. Another kind of sub-service is called a **headless Service**. It is a special kind of service where no ClusterIP is assigned. Instead of providing a single stable IP and load balancing across pods, a headless service directly returns the IP addresses of the associated pods. This allows clients to connect directly to individual pods, which is particularly useful for scenarios such as StatefulSets or when applications need to handle their own load balancing.

- **NodePort**: This service exposes the service to each node's IP address at a static port. It allows external traffic to reach the Service outside the cluster using the node's IP address and the allocated port.

- **LoadBalancer**: This Service type exposes the Service externally using a cloud provider's load balancer. The cloud provider assigns a unique external IP address to the Service, allowing it to be accessed from outside the cluster.

- **ExternalName**: This type of Service maps the Service to the contents of the externalName field. It allows access to external services by returning a CNAME record with the configured value.

Kubernetes Services operate based on labels and selectors. Services select pods based on their labels, enabling dynamic scaling and reconfiguration without disrupting service availability. By abstracting the complexity of individual pod addresses and providing a consistent endpoint, Services simplify networking and allow seamless communication within Kubernetes clusters.

What is the ClusterIP service type?

The `ClusterIP` service type in Kubernetes exposes a service on an internal IP address within the cluster. It makes the service reachable only from within the cluster, meaning that applications inside the cluster can access the service using `ClusterIP`.

A high-level visualization of the traffic flow using `ClusterIP` is shown in *Figure 7.1* (the complete source code can be found here in our GitHub repo:`chapter-7/cluster-ip-svc.yaml`). The source code representing this figure is the following:

```yaml
---
apiVersion: apps/v1
kind: Deployment
metadata:
  name: nginx-sample
  namespace: default
spec:
  ...
  template:
    metadata:
      labels:
        app: nginx
    spec:
      containers:
      - name: nginx
        image: nginx:1.25.4
        ports:
          - containerPort: 80
---
apiVersion: v1
kind: Service
metadata:
  name: nginx-sample
  namespace: default
spec:
  selector:
    app: nginx
  ports:
```

```
      - protocol: TCP
        port: 80
        targetPort: 80
---
apiVersion: apps/v1
kind: Deployment
metadata:
  name: hello-sample
  namespace: default
spec:
  ...
  template:
    metadata:
      labels:
        app: hello
    spec:
      containers:
      - name: hello
        image: gcr.io/google-samples/node-hello:1.0
        ports:
          - containerPort: 8080
            name: http
---
apiVersion: v1
kind: Service
metadata:
  name: hello-sample
  namespace: default
spec:
  selector:
    app: hello
  ports:
    - protocol: TCP
      port: 80
      targetPort: 8080
```

The following diagram illustrates the `ClusterIP` service type in Kubernetes and demonstrates how pods communicate with the service. It shows the internal network flow within a cluster.

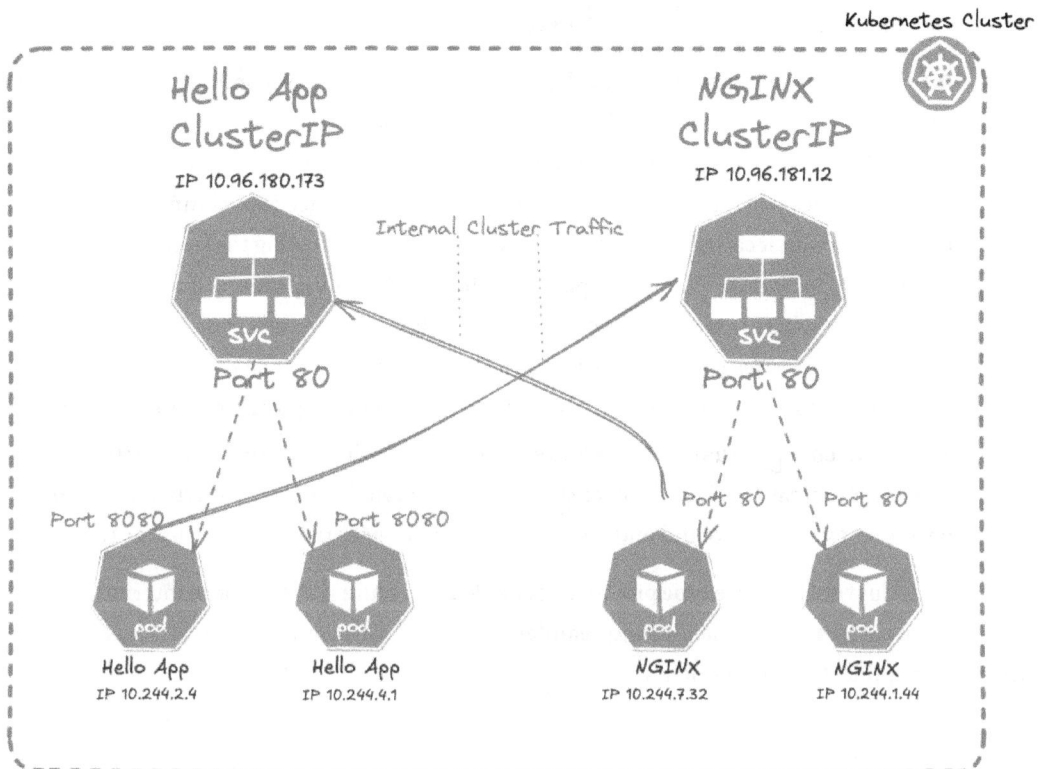

Figure 7.1 – Kubernetes ClusterIP Service

In this example, we deploy two sample web servers and test the connectivity:

```
> kubectl apply -f chapter-7/cluster-ip-svc.yaml
> kubectl exec svc/nginx-sample -- curl hello-sample
# This part specifies that we want to execute the command in a pod that's part of the nginx-
sample service. Kubernetes will choose one of the pods behind this service. And call hello-sample service.
Hello Kubernetes!


> kubectl exec svc/hello-sample -- curl nginx-sample
# On one of the pod from hello-sample service call nginx-sample service
...
<title>Welcome to nginx!</title>
...
```

Here are some use case scenarios for the ClusterIP service type:

- **Internal communication within the cluster**: When different components of an application need to communicate with each other but their pods are not directly reachable due to dynamic IP assignments or scaling, ClusterIP services provide a stable endpoint for communication. For instance, if a frontend application needs to communicate with a backend service, it can be exposed as a ClusterIP service, allowing the frontend to reliably access it regardless of changes in pod IP addresses or scaling events. In a microservices architecture where multiple services interact, each service can be exposed as a ClusterIP service. This ensures that services remain isolated within the cluster and are not directly accessible from outside, enhancing security and reducing exposure to potential threats.

- **Service discovery**: ClusterIP services enable other services within the cluster to discover and communicate with each other dynamically. Services can use Kubernetes DNS or environment variables to find and connect to other services using their ClusterIP.

Overall, the ClusterIP service type provides a reliable and secure way to expose internal services within a Kubernetes cluster, facilitating seamless communication and service discovery among distributed application components.

Interview tip

Question: *What is a ClusterIP service in Kubernetes and when should you use it?*

Answer: The ClusterIP service exposes an application on an internal IP, making it reachable only within the Kubernetes cluster. It is typically used for internal service-to-service communication, improving reliability and security by isolating access from the outside world.

What is the NodePort service type?

The NodePort service type in Kubernetes exposes a service on a specific port on all nodes (VMs or physical machines) in the cluster. This means the service is accessible from outside the cluster using each node's IP address and the NodePort allocated.

The NodePort type is not recommended for production workloads (especially for publicly exposing services) because it creates additional security attack vectors; the exposed port range is well-known (30000 to 32767), so potential attackers can use it for scanning.

Use case scenarios for the `NodePort` service type include the following:

- **External access to services:** When applications or services running within the cluster must be accessed from outside the cluster, `NodePort` services provide a straightforward way to expose them. External clients can access the service using any node's IP address and the allocated `NodePort` by allocating a specific port on each node.

- **Testing and development:** `NodePort` services can be helpful during the testing and development phases when developers need to access services running within the cluster from their local machines or testing environments. By exposing services via `NodePort`, developers can easily access and test their applications without complex networking configurations.

- **Load balancing:** While not typically used as a primary load balancing mechanism, `NodePort` services can be combined with external load balancers to distribute traffic across multiple nodes in the cluster. External load balancers can be configured to distribute traffic to the nodes' IP addresses and the allocated `NodePort`, providing a basic form of load balancing.

- **Legacy application integration:** In some cases, legacy applications or systems may require access to services running within a Kubernetes cluster. `NodePort` services can bridge legacy systems and modern containerized applications, allowing legacy systems to communicate with services exposed via `NodePort`.

Let's deploy our `hello` service using the `NodePort` service to see the exact differences we have here:

```
---
apiVersion: apps/v1
kind: Deployment
metadata:
  name: hello-sample
  namespace: default
spec:
  ...
  template:
    ...
    spec:
      containers:
      - name: hello
        image: gcr.io/google-samples/node-hello:1.0
        ...
```

```
---
apiVersion: v1
kind: Service
metadata:
  name: hello-sample
  namespace: default
spec:
  type: NodePort
  ...
  ports:
    - protocol: TCP
      port: 80
      targetPort: 8080
      nodePort: 30000
```

To better understand how the NodePort service works, let's examine the following diagram, which illustrates the network flow for both internal and external traffic in a Kubernetes cluster.

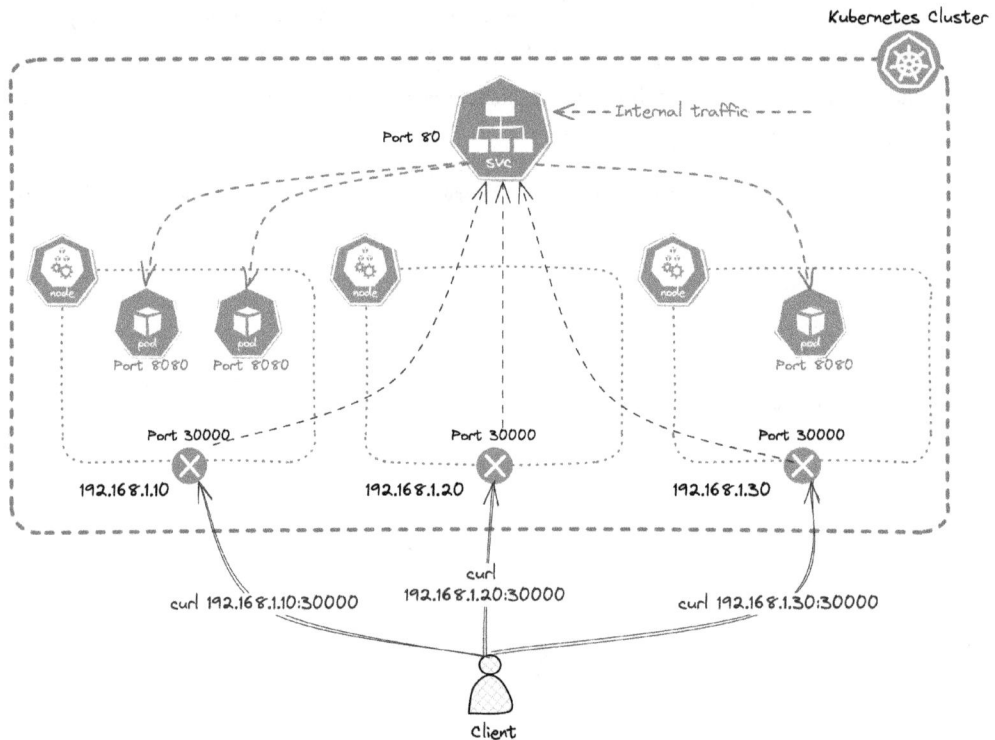

Figure 7.2 – The NodePort Service type

As a result, we can access the service not only internally (using internal DNS) but also using the port exposed on any of the nodes (even empty nodes) we have in the cluster:

```
> curl 192.168.1.10:30000
Hello Kubernetes!
> curl 192.168.1.20:30000
Hello Kubernetes!
```

In summary, the NodePort service type provides a simple and flexible way to expose services running within a Kubernetes cluster to external clients, facilitating communication and integration with external systems and applications.

> **Interview tip**
>
> **Question:** *Why is using* NodePort *services in production environments generally discouraged?*
>
> **Answer:** NodePort services expose a known range of ports (30000–32767) on all nodes, which can increase security risks by making services easier to discover and attack during port scanning.

What is the LoadBalancer service type?

The LoadBalancer service type in Kubernetes provisions an external load balancer from a cloud provider and assigns it a unique external IP address. This allows external clients to access the service via the load balancer, distributing traffic across multiple pods serving the service within the cluster. The LoadBalancer service type is widely used in production Kubernetes environments, particularly in cloud-based deployments where cloud providers offer managed load balancer services. While it may incur additional costs due to the provisioning of external load balancers, the benefits of high availability, scalability, and ease of integration make LoadBalancer services a popular choice for exposing services externally in Kubernetes clusters.

Use case scenarios for the LoadBalancer service type include the following:

- **High availability and fault tolerance**: LoadBalancer services ensure high availability and fault tolerance by distributing incoming traffic across multiple pods. The external load balancer automatically detects healthy pods and directs traffic to them, helping to prevent service disruptions and downtime.

- **External access to services**: LoadBalancer services are commonly used to expose services running within a Kubernetes cluster to external clients, such as web applications or APIs. Provisioning an external load balancer allows external clients to access the service via a stable external IP address, providing a seamless and reliable user experience.

- **Public-facing applications**: LoadBalancer services are well-suited for public-facing applications or services that require high levels of availability and scalability. By distributing traffic across multiple pods and leveraging the scalability of cloud-based load balancers, LoadBalancer services can handle large volumes of incoming requests without degradation in performance.

- **Elastic scaling**: LoadBalancer services facilitate elastic scaling by automatically adjusting the number of pods serving the service based on demand. As traffic increases, Kubernetes can automatically scale up the number of pods, and the external load balancer distributes incoming traffic across the newly created pods, ensuring that the application can handle increased load effectively.

- **Integration with external systems**: LoadBalancer services can be integrated with external systems or applications that require access to services running within the Kubernetes cluster. By exposing services via an external load balancer, external systems can communicate with the services seamlessly, enabling integration with third-party services or legacy systems.

Let's look at the sample deployed in the **Amazon Web Services (AWS)** cloud using the **Elastic Kubernetes Service (EKS)**:

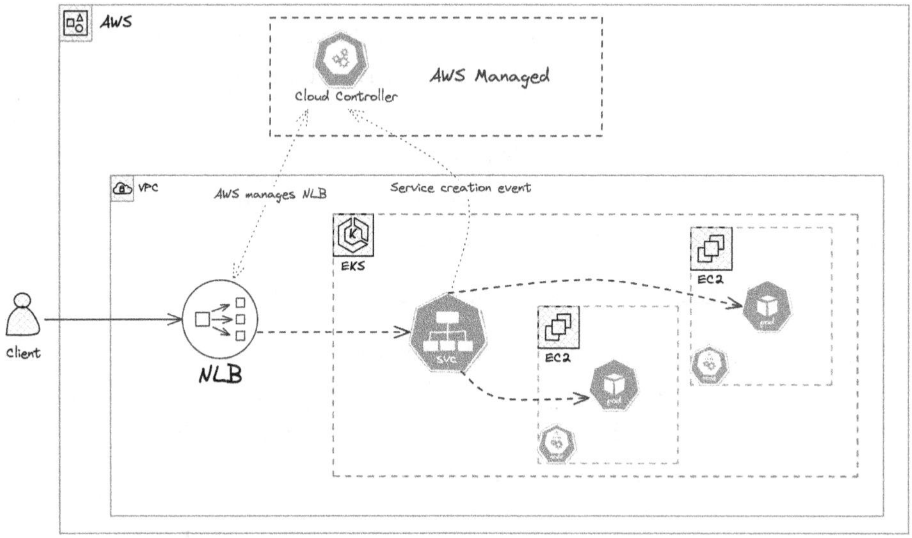

Figure 7.3 – Amazon EKS LoadBalancer Service architecture

When we create some service type with type: LoadBalancer, the AWS services automatically (using the Cloud Controller component on the AWS side), make the cloud **Network Load Balancer (NLB)** for us, and manage its configuration based on the Kubernetes object settings. After the successful reconciliation, we will have the EXTERNAL-IP attribute for our service, which we can use to access our pods. Here is a small piece of code that can deploy this type of service:

```
---
apiVersion: v1
kind: Service
metadata:
  name: hello-sample
  namespace: default
spec:
  type: LoadBalancer
  ...
  ports:
    - protocol: TCP
      port: 80
      targetPort: 8080
```

At the end, we can check the status of the service and use its external IP to access our pods:

```
> kubectl get svc hello-sample

NAME            TYPE          CLUSTER-IP       EXTERNAL-IP       PORT(S)
AGE
hello-sample    LoadBalancer  10.251.125.130   129.159.206.213   80:30287/
TCP    105s
```

In the status of the LoadBalancer service, you can see external IP addresses that you can use to test your application:

```
> curl 129.159.206.213
Hello Kubernetes!
```

Your application is now accessible to external users.

What is the ExternalName service type?

The `ExternalName` service type in Kubernetes maps a service to an external DNS name. Unlike other service types, `ExternalName` does not expose any internal cluster IP or provide load balancing or routing capabilities within the cluster. Instead, it acts as a DNS alias for an external service.

Use case scenarios for the `ExternalName` service type include the following:

- **Integration with external services**: `ExternalName` services are commonly used to integrate Kubernetes Services with external services or resources hosted outside the cluster. By mapping a Kubernetes service to an external DNS name, applications running within the cluster can access external services seamlessly as if they were part of the cluster.

- **Legacy system integration**: `ExternalName` services can integrate Kubernetes clusters with legacy systems or applications that are not containerized or managed within the cluster. By mapping a Kubernetes service to an external DNS name, Kubernetes workloads can communicate with legacy systems without complex networking configurations.

- **Service abstraction**: `ExternalName` services provide a level of abstraction for accessing external services, allowing Kubernetes applications to interact with external resources without being aware of their specific network addresses or configurations. This simplifies application development and deployment, as developers can refer to services using familiar DNS names rather than IP addresses or URLs.

- **Load balancing and failover**: `ExternalName` services do not provide cluster load balancing or failover capabilities. However, they can indirectly leverage external DNS providers' load balancing, failover mechanisms, or load balancers. By mapping a Kubernetes service to an external DNS name, traffic can be distributed across multiple endpoints or failover to backup endpoints as configured by the external service provider.

Overall, the `ExternalName` service type provides a flexible and convenient way to integrate Kubernetes clusters with external services, enabling seamless communication and interoperability between Kubernetes workloads and external resources.

Let's imagine that the company is in the process of migration between clouds. Some of their integrations currently rely on some managed service (such as API gateway), which we cannot replace but should migrate everything else. This integration uses the same DNS but a different path. Everything else on this domain migrated to the new cloud's Kubernetes. To do so, we must re-route only one request to another location.

Let's assume we have some external site (such as `google.com`) we want to make accessible using the internal **Service (SVC)** endpoint.

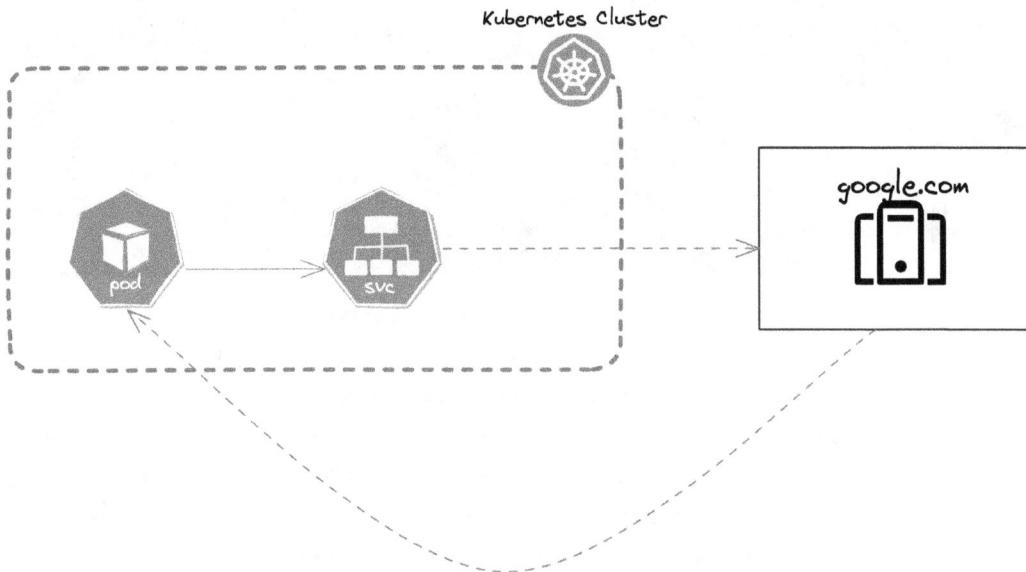

Figure 7.4 – The ExternalName Service type

The manifest is tiny and looks like this:

```
---
apiVersion: v1
kind: Service
metadata:
  name: hello-sample-ext
  namespace: default
spec:
  type: ExternalName
  externalName: google.com
```

Using that, we can access this external website using extended DNS features of this kind of service:

```
> kubectl run -it --rm test --image alpine

# apk add curl
# curl hello-sample-ext

...
<title>Error 404 (Not Found)!!1</title>
```

```
...

# curl hello-sample-ext -H 'Host: google.com' -L -I

HTTP/1.1 301 Moved Permanently
...
HTTP/1.1 200 OK
```

In the preceding example, we've created an ExternalName service that points to google.com. When we try to curl the service without specifying the Host header, we get a 404 error. This is because the request is being sent to the Kubernetes cluster's internal DNS, which doesn't know how to handle the request for google.com. However, when we add the 'Host: google.com' header, we get a successful response. The first request results in a 301 Moved Permanently status, which is a redirect. Following this redirect with the -L flag, we ultimately receive a 200 OK status. This demonstrates that our ExternalName service is successfully routing requests to the external google.com site, but we need to ensure the correct Host header is set for it to work properly. This behavior is crucial to understand when working with ExternalName services, especially in scenarios involving complex routing or migrations between environments.

Interview tip

Question: *What is an* ExternalName *service in Kubernetes and when would you use it?*

Answer: The ExternalName service maps a Kubernetes service to an external DNS name, allowing pods to access external services as if they were part of the cluster, without managing IPs or complex network settings.

How exactly do Kubernetes Services interact with pods?

Kubernetes Services facilitate traffic forwarding to pods using label selectors and IP table rules managed by kube-proxy. When a service is created, a cluster IP (for ClusterIP services), a Node port (for NodePort services), or an external IP (for LoadBalancer services) is assigned.

Pods within the cluster discover and communicate with services using DNS-based service discovery. Each service is assigned a DNS record that pods can access. kube-proxy intercepts traffic sent to the service's ClusterIP and applies IP table rules to route it to the appropriate pods based on the service's selector criteria.

For services with multiple pods, kube-proxy implements load-balancing strategies to distribute traffic among them. NodePort and LoadBalancer services involve additional IP table rules to forward traffic from the specified port to the ClusterIP Service and then to the relevant pods.

The main load-balancing strategies kube-proxy uses are as follows:

- **Round-robin**: This is the default and most common strategy. kube-proxy cycles through the list of available pod endpoints one by one, sending each new connection to the next pod in the list. It's simple and works well for most typical workloads.

- **Random selection**: When depending on the version and configuration, kube-proxy may also randomly select an endpoint from the available ones, which can help avoid predictable traffic patterns.

- **Session affinity (optional)**: This can be also configured with sessionAffinity: ClientIP. kube-proxy can ensure that requests from the same client IP are consistently sent to the same pod. This is useful when the application needs session persistence (sticky sessions).

In summary, Kubernetes Services abstract pod infrastructure and provide a stable endpoint for communication. At the same time, kube-proxy handles traffic forwarding and load balancing, ensuring seamless communication between services and pods within the cluster.

If you still need more information about Kubernetes' services, please return to *Chapter 6* and read about the Kubernetes kube-proxy component to bridge this gap.

How do Ingress controllers work in Kubernetes?

In Kubernetes, an **Ingress** is an API object that serves as a collection of rules for routing external HTTP and HTTPS traffic to services within the cluster. It acts as a layer of abstraction between external clients and services, defining how incoming requests should be directed to different services based on criteria such as hostnames, paths, or other HTTP header values.

An Ingress resource typically consists of the following components:

Rules: Ingress rules define how incoming requests should be routed to different services based on criteria such as hostnames and paths. Each rule specifies a set of conditions (such as a specific hostname or URL path) and the corresponding backend service to which the request should be forwarded.

Backend Services: Backend services are the Kubernetes Services to which incoming requests should be forwarded based on the matching criteria defined in the rules. These services represent the target applications or microservices that handle the incoming traffic.

TLS configuration (optional): Ingress resources can optionally include TLS configuration to enable secure communication over HTTPS. TLS configuration specifies details such as SSL certificates and private keys for encrypting and decrypting traffic.

Annotations (optional): Ingress resources may include annotations and key-value pairs that provide additional configuration options or directives for the Ingress controller. Annotations can be used to customize behavior, configure advanced routing rules, or integrate with external services or components.

In summary, Kubernetes Ingress provides a flexible and powerful way to manage external access to services within a cluster. It allows administrators to define routing rules and configure SSL termination for incoming HTTP and HTTPS traffic. By abstracting away the complexities of networking and routing, Ingress enables more efficient management of external connectivity and enhances the scalability, security, and flexibility of applications running in Kubernetes clusters.

Let's look at the high-level explanation of this new object for you.

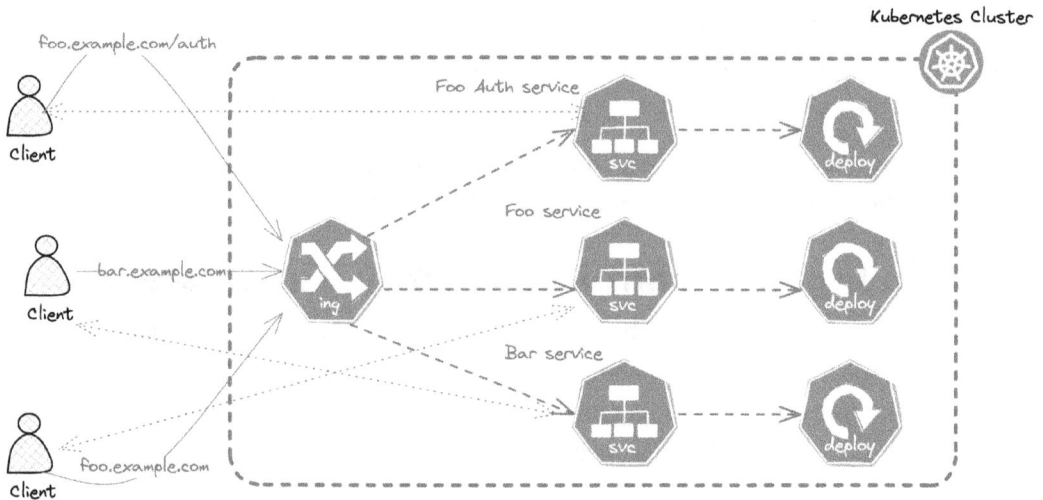

Figure 7.5 – The Ingress flow at a glance

In this figure, we have the same "entry point" for all clients—our Ingress endpoint. Based on the HTTP request (the hostname and the path), the Ingress components route the requests to appropriate Kubernetes Services and connect the client with the required pod containing the required application.

What is an Ingress controller?

Ingress controllers play a crucial role in Kubernetes networking by providing an additional abstraction layer and functionality for managing external access to services within the cluster. Here's why we need Ingress controllers:

- **Single entry point:** In Kubernetes, services typically expose applications within the cluster. However, managing access to these services from outside the cluster can become complex, especially as the number of services and routes increases. Ingress controllers act as a single entry point for external traffic, simplifying the management of inbound connections.

- **HTTP and HTTPS routing:** Ingress controllers can route HTTP and HTTPS traffic to different services based on the request's path, host, or other attributes. This enables more sophisticated routing configurations, such as directing requests to specific services based on URL patterns or domain names.

- **SSL/TLS termination:** Ingress controllers can handle SSL/TLS termination, decrypting incoming HTTPS traffic and forwarding it to services over plain HTTP within the cluster. This offloads the burden of SSL/TLS encryption and decryption from individual services, improving performance and security.

- **Load balancing:** Ingress controllers often include built-in load balancing capabilities, distributing incoming traffic across multiple pods or services based on configurable rules. This helps optimize resource utilization and improve application availability and scalability.

- **Path-based routing:** Ingress controllers allow for path-based routing, enabling different paths in a URL to be directed to other services or versions of an application. This facilitates the deployment of multiple microservices behind a single external endpoint, simplifying application management and deployment.

- **Integration with external services:** Ingress controllers can integrate with external services or components, such as external authentication providers, **web application firewalls (WAFs)**, or **content delivery network (CDN)** providers, to enhance security and performance for applications running within the cluster.

Ingress controllers provide a powerful and flexible mechanism for managing external access to Kubernetes Services, enabling advanced routing, load balancing, and SSL termination capabilities. They streamline exposing applications to the outside world while enhancing security, scalability, and manageability within Kubernetes clusters.

> **Interview tip**
>
> **Question:** *What is the role of an Ingress controller in Kubernetes?*
>
> **Answer:** The Ingress controller manages external access to services by routing HTTP and HTTPS traffic based on rules, handling SSL/TLS termination, and providing load balancing to ensure efficient and secure connectivity to applications inside the cluster.

What Ingress controllers do you know?

You might be asked this question. You should share your experience here, but knowing the modern landscape is always good. So, here is the list of most frequently used Ingress controllers today:

- **NGINX Ingress Controller** is one of the most popular and widely adopted Ingress controllers. It is based on the NGINX open source software and provides advanced features such as SSL termination, path-based routing, and traffic load balancing. NGINX Ingress Controller is highly configurable and suitable for various use cases.

- **Traefik** is a modern, cloud-native Ingress controller designed to be lightweight, easy to use, and highly scalable. It supports dynamic configuration updates and automatic SSL certificate management and integrates seamlessly with Kubernetes and other container orchestration platforms. Traefik is particularly well suited for microservices architectures and cloud-native environments.

- **HAProxy Ingress** is a high-performance and feature-rich Ingress controller that leverages the HAProxy load balancer to route traffic to backend services. It offers advanced traffic routing capabilities, SSL termination, and powerful customization options. HAProxy Ingress is known for its performance and reliability, making it suitable for high-traffic and mission-critical applications.

- **Contour** is an Envoy-based Ingress controller with advanced routing and load balancing capabilities. It is designed to work seamlessly with Kubernetes and leverages the Envoy proxy to provide features such as HTTP/2 support, gRPC routing, and WebSockets. Contour offers a declarative configuration model and is well-suited for modern application architectures.

- **Kong** is an open source API gateway and Ingress controller providing comprehensive features for managing API traffic in Kubernetes clusters. It offers rate limiting, authentication, and authorization capabilities, making it suitable for building secure and scalable API-driven applications. Kong can be deployed as a standalone service or as an Ingress controller within Kubernetes.

Also, all modern cloud providers (AWS, Azure, Google Cloud Platform, Oracle Cloud, etc.) provide their Ingress controllers for their managed Kubernetes Services to provision cloud load balancers that act as the entry point for your application requests from the Internet.

How does the Ingress controller work?

This is a complicated topic, and the answer always depends on the specific Ingress controller specified and used. It will be essential to highlight this before answering the question. There is a list of high-level steps that the Ingress controller executes to provide the required result:

- **Ingress resource creation**: A Kubernetes user creates an Ingress resource by defining routing rules, backend services, and optional TLS configuration using YAML or JSON manifests.

- **API interaction**: The Ingress controller continuously watches the Kubernetes API server for changes to Ingress resources. When a new Ingress resource is created, updated, or deleted, the controller retrieves the corresponding configuration and updates its routing rules accordingly.

- **Routing configuration**: Based on the Ingress resource specifications, the controller configures its underlying software component (e.g., NGINX or Traefik) to implement the defined routing rules. This involves configuring listeners, virtual hosts, path-based routing, and other routing policies as specified in the Ingress resource.

- **Traffic handling**: The Ingress controller intercepts incoming HTTP and HTTPS traffic destined for the cluster's external IP address or hostname. It inspects the HTTP request headers (e.g., host or path) to determine the appropriate backend service based on the configured routing rules.

- **Load balancing and SSL termination**: If the Ingress resource specifies multiple backend services or SSL termination, the Ingress controller may perform load balancing across the backend pods and handle SSL/TLS encryption and decryption as required.

- **Proxying requests**: Once the backend service is determined, the Ingress controller forwards the incoming request to the appropriate pod(s) serving the backend service within the Kubernetes cluster. This involves proxying the request through the cluster's internal networking infrastructure.

- **Response handling**: After the backend pod(s) process the request and generate a response, the Ingress controller proxies the response to the client, ensuring that the appropriate headers and status codes are set according to the Ingress resource configuration.

- **Monitoring and logging**: The Ingress controller may also provide monitoring and logging capabilities to track incoming traffic, identify errors or anomalies, and generate logs or metrics for analysis and troubleshooting.

How does the Ingress find the appropriate Service?

Typically (as always in Kubernetes), it's based on labels, but you can answer in more detail. So, when a request arrives at the cluster's external IP address or hostname, the Ingress controller determines the appropriate backend service to route the request to. The Ingress controller relies on a Kubernetes resource called `Endpoints` to specify the backend service's network address.

In Kubernetes, **endpoints** represent a set of network addresses (IP addresses and port numbers) corresponding to the pods' service targets. They essentially act as a mapping between a service and the actual pods that serve the traffic for that service.

Here's how it works:

- **Service creation**: When you create a Kubernetes service, Kubernetes automatically creates an `Endpoints` object associated with that service. The `Endpoints` object initially contains the IP addresses and port numbers of all pods that the service's label selector selects.

- **Pod IP address and port**: Each pod in the cluster has its IP address and listens on specific ports to serve traffic. When a pod is created, Kubernetes adds its IP address and port to the `Endpoints` object associated with any services that target that pod.

- **Service discovery**: When the Ingress controller receives an incoming request, it looks up the desired backend service in the Kubernetes API server. The service definition contains a reference to the corresponding `Endpoints` object.

- **Endpoint resolution**: The Ingress controller queries the `Endpoints` object associated with the targeted service to retrieve the list of IP addresses and ports of the pods serving that service.

- **Routing traffic**: Using the list of pod IP addresses and ports obtained from the `Endpoints` object, the Ingress controller can forward the incoming request to one of the pods serving the backend service. It typically uses a load-balancing algorithm to distribute traffic across multiple pods if needed.

Endpoints are dynamic and automatically updated by Kubernetes as pods are added, removed, or scaled within the cluster. This ensures that the Ingress controller always has the most up-to-date information about the network addresses of the pods serving a particular service, enabling reliable and efficient traffic routing within the Kubernetes cluster.

What is the Gateway API in Kubernetes?

As Kubernetes has evolved, so has the need for a more flexible and extensible way to manage traffic entering a cluster. The Gateway API is a newer standard developed to address some of the limitations of the classic Ingress resource. It provides a more powerful, expressive, and role-oriented model for handling routing and load balancing. The Gateway API defines a set of resources that model how external traffic should be routed to Kubernetes Services. It aims to improve flexibility, scalability, and portability across different environments (on-premises, cloud, etc.). It allows for better separation of concerns, enabling different teams (networking, platform, application) to manage parts of the network configuration independently.

Advantages compared to the classic Ingress are as follows:

- **More expressive routing rules:** The Gateway API supports advanced routing capabilities out of the box, such as traffic splitting, header-based routing, and more detailed match conditions
- **Separation of responsibilities:** The Gateway API introduces distinct resources such as GatewayClass, Gateway, HTTPRoute, and so on, allowing infrastructure teams to manage infrastructure-level settings (gateways) and application teams to manage traffic rules (routes) separately
- **Better standardization:** The Gateway API is designed to work consistently across different vendors and platforms, reducing reliance on vendor-specific annotations that are common with traditional Ingress
- **Built-in status and health reporting:** Resources in the Gateway API provide better visibility into the status of traffic configurations, making it easier to troubleshoot and monitor

Key differences from classic Ingress are illustrated in the following table:

Feature	Classic Ingress	Gateway API
Routing capabilities	Limited (basic path and host-based routing)	Advanced (headers, query parameters, and traffic splitting)
Role separation	Single resource (Ingress)	Multiple resources (`GatewayClass`, `Gateway`, `HTTPRoute`, etc.)
Extensibility	Vendor-specific via annotations	Native, consistent extensibility
Resource health/status	Limited	Rich, detailed status fields

Table 7.1 – Differences between classic Ingress and Gateway API

Common Implementations of the Gateway API are as follows:

- **Istio Gateway Controller:** Integrates tightly with the Istio service mesh to handle routing, mTLS, and advanced traffic management using Gateway API resources

- **NGINX Gateway Fabric:** A modern implementation from the NGINX team that supports the Gateway API while leveraging NGINX's advanced load balancing features

- **Kong Gateway Operator:** A Kubernetes-native operator from Kong that supports Gateway API for managing Ingress, load balancing, and API gateway capabilities at scale

How does the traffic flow inside Kubernetes when using the Ingress?

Let's assume that some client from the internet initiated the HTTPS request to the web application hosted in our Kubernetes cluster. We expanded every step in more detail in this and the previous chapters. Let's look at the detailed explanation of every event after.

Incoming request from an external client

When a user interacts with an application hosted on Kubernetes, the journey begins with an incoming request from an external client, typically over the internet. This request can take various forms, such as an HTTP GET request for a web page, a POST request to submit form data, or a WebSocket connection for real-time communication.

The journey often starts with DNS resolution, where the client's browser resolves the application's domain name to an IP address. This IP address corresponds to the external-facing endpoint of the Kubernetes cluster, typically managed by an external load balancer or DNS service.

Ingress Controller processing

Upon reaching the Kubernetes cluster, the Ingress Controller intercepts the incoming request. The Ingress Controller acts as the entry point for external traffic and is responsible for routing requests to the appropriate backend services within the cluster.

The Ingress Controller examines the request headers, including the hostname, URL path, and other metadata, to determine which Ingress resource should handle the request. Ingress resources define routing rules and policies for incoming traffic, specifying how requests should be directed to different backend services based on criteria such as hostnames and paths.

If SSL/TLS termination is configured, the Ingress Controller may decrypt HTTPS traffic, ensuring secure communication between the client and the backend services.

Service discovery and endpoint resolution

Once the appropriate Ingress resource is identified, the Ingress Controller queries the Kubernetes API server to locate the backend Service associated with the Ingress rule. Kubernetes Services abstract the underlying pods and provide a stable endpoint for communication.

The Ingress Controller retrieves the list of network addresses (IP addresses and port numbers) of the Pods serving the backend Service from the corresponding Endpoints object in the Kubernetes API. Endpoints represent a set of IP addresses and ports corresponding to the Pods selected by the Service.

Load balancing and Pod selection

With the list of Pod IP addresses obtained from the Endpoints object, the Ingress Controller performs load balancing to distribute incoming traffic across multiple Pods serving the backend Service. Load balancing ensures optimal utilization of resources and enhances application availability and scalability.

The Ingress Controller may use various load balancing algorithms, such as round-robin or least connections, to evenly distribute traffic among the Pods. Additionally, the Ingress Controller may consider Pod health and resource utilization factors when selecting Pods to handle incoming requests.

Containerized web application processing

Once a Pod is selected to handle the incoming request, the containerized web application running inside the Pod processes the request. The application logic executes business logic, retrieves data from backend services or databases, and generates a response to the client's request.

The containerized web application interacts with other components within the Kubernetes cluster, such as databases, caching layers, or external APIs, to fulfill the request and provide the client with the requested content or functionality.

Response back to the client

Finally, the containerized web application formulates an HTTP response with the requested content or functionality. The response is then proxied back through the Ingress Controller, which forwards it to the external client over the internet.

The Ingress Controller ensures the response is delivered reliably and efficiently, handling any necessary transformations or modifications to the response headers or content. Once the reaction reaches the client's browser, the user can interact with the application and receive the desired experience.

Interview tip

Question: *What are the main steps in the traffic flow when a client accesses a Kubernetes application through an Ingress?*

Answer: The client request is resolved by DNS to the cluster's endpoint, intercepted by the Ingress controller, matched to the right Ingress rule, routed through the Service to the appropriate Pod, and the Pod's response is sent back through the Ingress controller to the client.

Summary

In this chapter, you've explored the intricate world of Kubernetes network architecture, focusing on Services and Ingresses. You've learned how these components facilitate communication and routing within and around the cluster, enabling seamless application deployment and management.

You've explored the various types of Kubernetes Services—`ClusterIP`, `NodePort`, `LoadBalancer`, and `ExternalName`—along with their specific use cases. You've come to understand how Services abstract pod details and provide stable endpoints for communication. Practical examples (complete with code snippets and traffic flow diagrams) have shown you how to implement each Service type. You've also learned about Ingress resources and Ingress controllers, gaining an understanding of their critical role in managing external access to services within the cluster, along with an overview of popular Ingress controllers and their unique features. Additionally, you've gained insight into the traffic flow from external clients through the Ingress controller to Services and, finally, to Pods, which is essential for effective troubleshooting and network optimization. Real-world scenarios and use cases throughout the chapter have further illustrated when and how to apply these networking concepts in Kubernetes deployments.

By mastering these concepts, you're now better equipped to work with internal and external services and communication within a Kubernetes cluster. This means we can deploy and manage cloud-native applications with confidence and efficiency. However, we can't do this without persistent storage.

It's a good time to move on to the next chapter, where we'll review storage topics in Kubernetes. You'll learn how to create your first stateful application on Kubernetes without worrying about data loss. Remember, data management is one of the most challenging topics during interviews.

8

Storage: Persistence and CSI Drivers

Welcome to this chapter, where we delve into the critical aspects of managing data persistence and **Container Storage Interface (CSI)** drivers within Kubernetes environments. This chapter will equip you with the knowledge and skills to tackle storage-related questions during Kubernetes interviews. We'll start by exploring the fundamentals of Kubernetes objects such as **Persistent-Volumes (PVs)** and **PersistentVolumeClaims (PVCs)**. These are essential components for ensuring data persistence in Kubernetes clusters. Additionally, we'll delve into the complexity of Storage-Classes and dynamic provisioning, empowering you to optimize storage resources effectively.

Furthermore, we'll unravel the complexities of CSI drivers, providing insights into integrating external storage systems seamlessly with Kubernetes. We will deepen your understanding of storage persistence and CSI drivers, unlocking new opportunities for success in Kubernetes interviews. With a focus on best practices for managing stateful applications and ensuring data integrity, this chapter prepares you to confidently address storage-related challenges in Kubernetes interviews.

As such, we will cover the following main topics in the chapter:

- How do you manage stateful applications in Kubernetes?
- What is CSI?
- What are the best practices for stateful applications?

Technical requirement

This chapter's source code is available here:

```
https://github.com/PacktPublishing/Cracking-the-Kubernetes-Interview/tree/main/
chapter-8
```

How do you manage stateful applications in Kubernetes?

Managing stateful applications in Kubernetes requires a clear understanding of all the risks of putting the stateful components in the container environment. For a relational database with business-critical information, we'd recommend using managed services or dedicated hosts to deploy it. For everything else (caches, NoSQL databases, and so on), you should know what kind of options Kubernetes provides you to maintain a stateful application.

We'll begin this section with a quick overview of the key concepts for managing stateful applications in Kubernetes, then dive deeper into these topics in the following subsections.

Stateful applications typically require **persistent storage** to store data beyond the life cycle of individual Pods. Kubernetes provides PVs and PVCs to manage persistent storage. PVs represent storage resources provisioned by the cluster, while PVCs are requests for storage by Pods. By creating PVCs and binding them to appropriate PVs, you can ensure that your stateful application's data persists even if Pods are restarted or rescheduled. We will talk about that later in this chapter.

StatefulSets are a Kubernetes resource designed specifically for managing stateful applications. They ensure that each Pod in the StatefulSet has a stable, unique identity and can maintain its state through restarts and rescheduling. StatefulSets also support ordered Pod creation, scaling, and termination, which is crucial for maintaining data consistency and integrity in stateful applications.

When deploying stateful applications, you often must expose individual Pods directly to clients or other Services. **Kubernetes Headless Services** enable this by assigning stable DNS names to each Pod in a StatefulSet, allowing clients to discover and connect to Pods directly. This is particularly useful for applications such as databases, where each instance has its unique identity and state.

This component will also be covered in this chapter.

Stateful applications may require additional **data management tasks** such as backups, restores, and migrations. Kubernetes operators or external tools can automate these tasks by leveraging Kubernetes APIs to interact with stateful applications and their underlying storage resources. Operators such as RabbitMQ Operator and MySQL Operator are examples of tools designed to automate the management of specific stateful applications.

Monitoring and alerting are critical for ensuring the health and availability of stateful applications. Kubernetes allows users to implement a variety of monitoring capabilities through tools such as **Prometheus** and **Grafana**, or via some SaaS solutions such as **Datadog**, which can monitor application metrics, storage usage, and Pod health. Additionally, you can set up alerts to notify you of any issues or anomalies, allowing you to address them before they proactively impact your application's availability.

What is a Headless Service?

A Headless Service is a Kubernetes Service that doesn't allocate a cluster IP to itself. Instead, it exposes the Pods' endpoints (IP addresses) directly to the client or other Services. This type of Service is beneficial for stateful applications where each Pod has its unique identity and requires direct communication.

Unlike typical Kubernetes Services, which allocate a cluster IP to route traffic to a set of Pods, a Headless Service does not have a cluster IP. This means only one entry point for accessing the Service from within the cluster. Instead of a cluster IP, a Headless Service assigns stable DNS names to each Pod in the Service. These DNS names are automatically created based on the Pod's name and namespace, allowing other Pods or Services to discover and connect to individual Pods directly.

Headless Services enable direct communication between Pods without going through a load balancer or proxy. This is particularly useful for stateful applications such as databases, where each Pod has its unique identity, and clients must communicate directly with specific Pods. Kubernetes automatically manages DNS resolution for Headless Services, ensuring that clients can reliably find and connect to Pods.

Headless Services are commonly used with StatefulSets, but are not limited to them. Sometimes, they can also be helpful in stateless applications (if needed).

Figure 8.1 shows the visualization of the Headless Service type integration for some stateful applications.

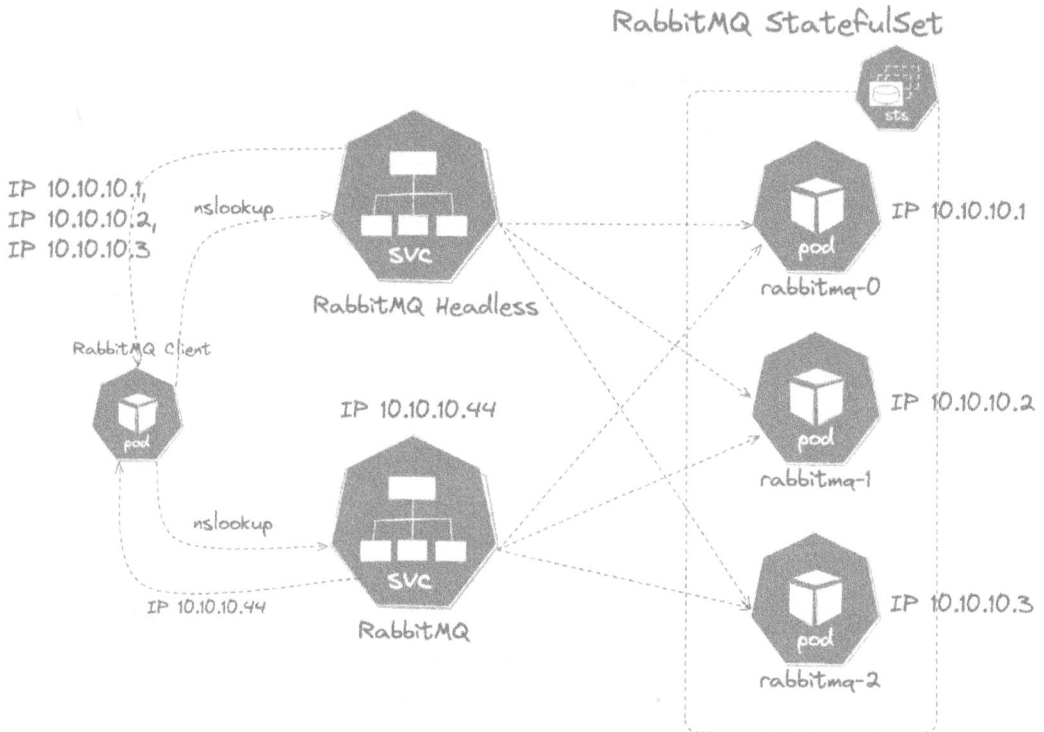

Figure 8.1 – A Headless Service using RabbitMQ StatefulSets as the example

In *Figure 8.1*, we see what the RabbitMQ cluster can look like in real, production-ready Kubernetes clusters, and the following shows what it looks like inside the cluster (you can find this YAML sample in our GitHub repository):

```
> kubectl apply -f chapter-8/headless-service.yaml
> kubectl run --rm -it --image busybox busybox
/ # nslookup sample-rabbitmq.default.svc.cluster.local
Server:         10.10.0.10
Address:        10.10.0.10:53


Name:   sample-rabbitmq.default.svc.cluster.local
Address: 10.10.10.44


/ # nslookup sample-rabbitmq-headless.default.svc.cluster.local
Server:         10.10.0.10
Address:        10.10.0.10:53
```

```
Name:    sample-rabbitmq-headless.default.svc.cluster.local
Address: 10.10.10.1
Name:    sample-rabbitmq-headless.default.svc.cluster.local
Address: 10.10.10.2
Name:    sample-rabbitmq-headless.default.svc.cluster.local
Address: 10.10.10.3
```

Interview tip

Question: *What is a Headless Service in Kubernetes, and when would you use it?*

Answer: A Headless Service is a Kubernetes Service without a cluster IP. It exposes individual Pod endpoints directly, allowing clients to connect to specific Pods using DNS. It's typically used in stateful applications such as databases, where Pods need stable identities and direct communication.

What types of volumes in Kubernetes do you know?

When asked this question, you're probably expected to describe the types of PVs you can attach to your Pods. Here is a short list of the most frequently used objects and approaches you can use as the volume within the Pod configuration:

- An **emptyDir volume** is created when a Pod is created and exists for the lifetime of that Pod. It is initially empty but can be written to by any container in the Pod. emptyDir volumes are useful for storing temporary data only needed for a Pod's execution.

- A **hostPath volume** mounts a directory from the host node's filesystem into the Pod. This allows Pods to access files and directories on the host machine. hostPath volumes help share files between containers running on the same node or accessing host-specific resources.

- **PVs and PVCs** are used to provide persistent storage to Pods. A PV is a piece of networked storage provisioned by an administrator, while a PVC is a request for storage by a Pod. PVs can be dynamically or statically provisioned, depending on the storage class and configuration. We will expand on this later in this chapter. StatefulSets have a **volume-ClaimTemplates** setting, which allows you to automatically create PVs and PVCs when you scale out your StatefulSets.

- A **local volume** represents locally attached storage on the node where the Pod is scheduled. Unlike network-based storage solutions such as NFS and iSCSI, which provide storage resources over the network, local volumes utilize storage devices directly attached to the node.

- **Network File System (NFS)** volumes allow Pods to access files stored on remote NFS servers. They help share files between Pods or access shared storage resources in a distributed environment.

- **Internet Small Computer System Interface (iSCSI)** is a protocol for accessing block-level network storage. In Kubernetes, iSCSI volumes allow Pods to access storage resources provided by iSCSI storage arrays or targets.

- While they are not traditional volumes, Kubernetes also provides **Secrets** and **ConfigMaps** to store sensitive information and configuration data. Secrets and ConfigMaps can be mounted as Pod volumes, allowing applications to access their data as files.

There are more ways, but most have already been deprecated or will be deprecated soon. In Kubernetes (and in Linux in general), literally everything is a file or a folder.

What are the differences between emptyDir and hostPath volumes?

emptyDir and **hostPath** are both types of volumes in Kubernetes, but they have different characteristics and use cases. Here are the critical differences between emptyDir and hostPath volumes:

- **Scope:** An emptyDir volume is scoped to a single Pod and exists for the lifetime of that Pod. It is created when the Pod is created and deleted when it is deleted.

  A hostPath volume is scoped to the node where the Pod is scheduled. It mounts a directory from the host node's filesystem into the Pod and persists beyond its life cycle.

- **Persistence:** An emptyDir volume is temporary and does not persist data across Pod restarts or rescheduling. When a Pod is deleted or restarted, the data stored in the emptyDir volume is lost.

  A hostPath volume persists data on the node's filesystem, even if the Pod using the volume is deleted. The data remains on the node until manually deleted or the node itself is decommissioned.

- **Accessibility:** An emptyDir volume is accessible only to containers running within the same Pod. It cannot be shared across multiple Pods or accessed by containers running on other nodes.

A hostPath volume is accessible to all containers running on the same node. It can be shared across multiple Pods or accessed by containers running on other nodes, making it suitable for scenarios where data needs to be shared between Pods or nodes.

- **Use cases:** emptyDir volumes are commonly used for caching, temporary storage, or sharing data between containers in a Pod.

  hostPath volumes are commonly used to access host-specific resources, share configuration files, or mount host directories into containers.

> **Interview tip**
>
> **Question:** *What types of storage volumes does Kubernetes support?*
>
> **Answer:** Kubernetes supports several volume types, such as emptyDir for temporary data, hostPath for mounting host files, and PVs such as PV/PVC for durable storage. It also supports remote options such as NFS and ways to mount configs or secrets using ConfigMaps and Secrets.

What is a PV and how do Pods claim it?

In Kubernetes, a PV is a storage resource within the cluster, either set up by an administrator or dynamically provisioned using StorageClasses (which we'll cover later in the chapter). Like a node, it's a resource in the cluster. PVs ensure data is stored in a way that remains intact beyond the life cycle of individual Pods.

PVs are decoupled from the Pod life cycle, meaning they can persist even if the Pod is deleted. This decoupling allows Pods to claim and use PVs without concern for the underlying storage mechanisms.

Here's a basic workflow for how Pods claim PVs:

1. First, an administrator defines one or more PVs within the cluster by creating PV objects. Some Storage Class should be defined (with or without dynamic provisioning). If we do not have a Storage Class defined, we must start by creating one (more details about Storage Classes will be provided later in this chapter).

2. Users or developers define PVC objects to request storage resources. A PVC is a request for storage by a user, such as how a Pod requests CPU and memory – it specifies the amount of storage required and some other settings (see the next step).

3. The cluster then binds the PVC object to an appropriate PV object. The binding process is either implemented statically by an administrator or dynamically by Kubernetes, depending on how the PV was provisioned. The following factors should match to bind the PVC to the PV successfully:

   - The PVC specifies the minimum amount of storage required (using the *capacity* setting) and may identify additional constraints such as storage class, access mode, and labels. The control plane matches PVCs to PVs that meet or exceed the requested capacity.

   - The *access mode* specified in the PVC must be compatible with the access modes supported by the PV.

   - If a specific *storage class* is requested in the PVC, the control plane will try to match it with a PV provisioned with the same storage class. The control plane will consider PVs with any storage class if no storage class is specified.

   - PVCs and PVs can be *annotated* or *labeled* to provide additional metadata. The control plane can use labels and annotations to match PVCs to PVs based on custom criteria defined by the cluster administrator.

   - PVCs can specify *selector criteria* to match PVs with specific labels. PVs can also have labels, and the control plane can match PVCs to PVs based on these labels.

4. Once a PVC is bound to the PV, the volume can be mounted into the desired Pod(s).

The Pod can now use the PV to store data. It can be read from and written to the volume as needed. If the Pod is deleted, the data can be persisted in the PV, allowing another Pod to claim and use the same volume later.

Overall, PVs provide a way for Pods to access durable storage in a Kubernetes cluster, enabling stateful applications that require data persistence.

How are PVs/PVCs configured?

PVs and PVCs have different settings, but initially, you can operate at least the most critical ones to manage stateful applications in the Kubernetes clusters:

- **Access modes** (*accessModes*):

  - **ReadWriteOnce (RWO)**: This mode allows the volume to be mounted as read-write by a single node. It means that the volume can be mounted by only one node in the cluster and read from and written to by that node's Pods. Other nodes in the cluster cannot mount the volume concurrently.

- **ReadOnlyMany (ROX)**: This mode allows the volume to be mounted as read-only by multiple nodes simultaneously. Numerous Pods on different nodes can read from the volume, but none can write. This mode is helpful for scenarios where various Pods need read-only access to the same data, such as for sharing configuration files or static assets.

- **ReadWriteMany (RWX)**: This mode allows the volume to be simultaneously mounted as read-write by multiple nodes. Multiple Pods on different nodes can simultaneously read from and write to the volume. This mode is helpful for scenarios where various Pods, such as shared file storage, must access and modify the same data concurrently.

- **ReadWriteOncePod (RWOP)**: In this mode, Kubernetes will attach the volume to only one Pod within the cluster.

- **Capacity** (`capacity`): This is just the storage size according to your needs.

- **Reclaiming** (`PVReclaimPolicy`): This is the most crucial setting that defines how Kubernetes should behave if the Pod is being deleted. The policy can be as follows:

  - **Retain policy**: The PV is not automatically deleted when the associated claim is released or deleted. Instead, the PV is retained and its data is preserved. This allows an administrator to reclaim the volume manually. The administrator can manually delete the PV when it's no longer needed.

  - **Delete policy**: The PV is deleted automatically when the associated claim is released or deleted. When the claim is released or deleted, Kubernetes deletes the PV and any associated storage resources (such as Amazon **Elastic Block Store (EBS)** volumes or GCP Persistent Disk). This is the default behavior if no reclaim policy is specified.

  - **Recycle policy**: This policy has been deprecated in recent versions of Kubernetes and should be avoided. With this policy, the PV is formatted and made available again for a new claim. However, it does not guarantee data privacy as the data isn't securely wiped. Alternatively, it's recommended to use dynamic provisioning (see the following questions, where we will touch on this topic).

- **Storage class name** (`storageClassName`): This specifies the Storage class that should handle dynamic provisioning of this PV/PVC – we will also talk about this later.

- **Volume mode** (`volumeMode`): This specifies whether the volume should be mounted in a filesystem (default mode) path (Filesystem mode) or as a raw block device (Block mode). The volume is exposed directly to the Pod as a raw block device in Block mode. This mode is helpful for applications that need direct access to block devices, such as databases or high-performance storage systems.

- Let's talk about a specific Kubernetes API called Downward that allows users to mount some meta information from the cluster inside the Pod being run.

> **Interview tip**
>
> **Question:** *What is a PV in Kubernetes, and how does a Pod use it?*
>
> **Answer:** A PV is a cluster resource that provides durable storage, independent of the Pod's life cycle. Pods use it by creating a PVC, which is then bound to a matching PV based on storage size, access mode, and storage class.

What is the Downward API?

The **Downward API** in Kubernetes is a mechanism that allows Pods to expose information about themselves to containers running inside them and to the container runtime environment. The Downward API is commonly used by applications running inside Pods to access metadata about the Pod or the Kubernetes environment. For example, applications may use Pod labels or annotations to customize their behavior based on the Pod's configuration or IP address to establish network connections with other Pods or Services. Here are some typical use cases for the Downward API:

- The Downward API enables Pods to expose metadata about themselves as environment variables or as files in a specific directory accessible to containers running inside the Pod. The metadata exposed by the Downward API includes information such as the Pod's name, namespace, IP address, labels, annotations, resource limits, and more. This metadata can provide valuable insights into the Pod's identity, configuration, and runtime environment.

- Pods can expose metadata as environment variables by specifying them in the Pod's `spec.containers[].env` field. These environment variables are injected into the container's environment when the Pod is created.

- Alternatively, Pods can expose metadata as files in a specific directory by mounting the Downward API volume into containers. The metadata is written to files inside the volume, which containers can then read to access the information.

- By exposing metadata through the Downward API, Pods can dynamically configure themselves based on their environment without requiring manual intervention. This enables greater flexibility and automation in managing applications deployed in Kubernetes clusters.

- Overall, the Downward API in Kubernetes provides a powerful mechanism for Pods to expose metadata about themselves to containers running inside them. By leveraging this metadata, applications can gain insights into their runtime environment and adapt their behavior accordingly, enhancing the flexibility and automation of Kubernetes Deployments.

Here is a YAML example that deploys the application and exposes some of the information about the Kubernetes environment it's running inside in logs:

```
> cat chapter-8/downward-api.yaml

---
apiVersion: v1
kind: Pod
metadata:
  name: downward-sample
  namespace: default
  labels:
    foo: bar
spec:
  containers:
    - name: ubuntu
      image: ubuntu
      args:
        - "bash"
        - "-c"
        - "echo Namespace: $MY_NAMESPACE && echo Labels: $(cat /etc/pod/
labels)"
      env:
        - name: MY_NAMESPACE
          valueFrom:
            # Exposing via fieldRef directly
            fieldRef:
              fieldPath: metadata.namespace
```

```
    volumeMounts:
      - name: labels
        mountPath: /etc/pod
volumes:
  - name: labels
    # Exposing via api mount
    downwardAPI:
      items:
        - path: labels
          fieldRef:
            fieldPath: metadata.labels
```

> 💡 **Quick tip:** Enhance your coding experience with the **AI Code Explainer** and **Quick Copy** features. Open this book in the next-gen Packt Reader. Click the **Copy** button
>
> (1) to quickly copy code into your coding environment, or click the **Explain** button
>
> (2) to get the AI assistant to explain a block of code to you.

Copy   Explain
①   ②

```
function calculate(a, b) {
  return {sum: a + b};
};
```

> 🔒 **The next-gen Packt Reader** is included for free with the purchase of this book. Scan the QR code OR go to https://packtpub.com/unlock, then use the search bar to find this book by name. Double-check the edition shown to make sure you get the right one.

```
> kubectl apply -f chapter-8/downward-api.yaml
> kubectl logs downward-sample
Namespace: default
Labels: foo="bar"
```

What is ConfigMap?

In Kubernetes, a ConfigMap is a resource object that stores configuration data in key-value pairs that Pods, containers, and other Kubernetes objects can consume. ConfigMaps provide a convenient way to decouple configuration from containerized applications, allowing for greater flexibility, portability, and manageability. They're not directly connected to the topic, but we haven't covered them yet, so let's bridge this gap.

ConfigMaps are primarily used to store configuration data such as environment variables, command-line arguments, configuration files, and any other settings that must be provided to Pods or containers at runtime. They consist of key-value pairs where each key represents a configuration parameter and its associated value. ConfigMaps can contain multiple key-value pairs, making them suitable for storing complex configurations with different parameters.

Once created, ConfigMaps can be mutable (by default) or immutable (using a particular setting: `immutable: true`), meaning their data cannot be modified directly. Instead, if you need to update configuration data, you must create a new ConfigMap with the updated values. This ensures consistency and predictability in the configuration of Pods and applications.

ConfigMaps can be consumed by Pods and containers in several ways:

- As environment variables in Pod specifications, containers can access configuration values as environment variables at runtime. A sample YAML document demonstrates how it works:

```
---
apiVersion: v1
kind: ConfigMap
metadata:
  name: env-sample
  namespace: default
data:
  K8S_FOO: bar
  K8S_BAR: foo
```

```yaml
---
apiVersion: v1
kind: Pod
metadata:
  name: env-sample
  namespace: default
spec:
  containers:
    - name: sample
      image: busybox
      command: [ "/bin/sh", "-c", "env" ]
      # One way we expose all keys from the configMap as
      # environment variables
      envFrom:
      - configMapRef:
          name: env-sample
      env:
        - name: K8S_FOO
          valueFrom:
            # Another way to instruct what values from the
            # configMap should be used for this key
            # In that case it takes precedence and K8S_FOO will be
            # equal to K8S_BAR's value
            configMapKeyRef:
              name: env-sample
              key: K8S_BAR
  restartPolicy: Never
```

Let's apply this manifest, and then you can check the logs and see the following results:

```
> kubectl apply -f chapter-8/config-map-env-vars.yaml
> kubectl get logs env-sample | grep K8S
K8S_BAR=foo
K8S_FOO=foo
```

- ConfigMaps' data can be mounted as volumes in Pod specifications, making configuration files or data available to containers as files in a specific directory. Let's briefly look at how this can be done:

```yaml
---
apiVersion: v1
kind: ConfigMap
metadata:
  name: volume-sample
  namespace: default
data:
  1-file.txt: |
    One two three
    I'm not the Superman :(
  2-file.txt: hello
---
apiVersion: v1
kind: Pod
metadata:
  name: volume-sample
  namespace: default
spec:
  containers:
    - name: sample
      image: busybox
      command: [ "/bin/sh", "-c", "cat /data/test/*" ]
      volumeMounts:
      - name: volume-sample
        mountPath: /data/test
        readOnly: true
  volumes:
    - name: volume-sample
      configMap:
        name: volume-sample
  restartPolicy: Never
```

After applying, you can check the logs and see the following:

```
> kubectl apply -f chapter-8/config-map-env-volume.yaml
> kubectl get logs env-volume | grep K8S
One two three
I'm not the Superman :(
hello%K8S_FOO=foo
```

- ConfigMaps' data can also be passed as command-line arguments to containers when starting up, allowing containers to access configuration values directly using the particular syntax format presented as follows:

```
---
apiVersion: v1
kind: ConfigMap
metadata:
  name: args-sample
  namespace: default
data:
  TEST_VAR: hello from the book
---
apiVersion: v1
kind: Pod
metadata:
  name: args-sample
  namespace: default
spec:
  containers:
    - name: sample
      image: busybox
      command: [ "/bin/sh", "-c", "echo $(TEST_VAR)" ]
      envFrom:
      - configMapRef:
          name: args-sample
  restartPolicy: Never
```

This example will have the following logs:

```
> kubectl get logs args-sample
hello from the book
```

ConfigMaps are commonly used for managing application configuration, including database connection strings, API endpoints, feature flags, log levels, and more. They provide a centralized and flexible way to manage configuration across multiple Pods and environments, simplifying the deployment and management of containerized applications.

You can find all the examples from this chapter in the GitHub repository of the book.

Note

It's also useful to mention that Pods do not automatically detect changes to a Config-Map after they start running. This is because ConfigMaps are mounted as files, and Kubernetes does not dynamically notify containers about updates. As a result, any changes to the ConfigMap will not be reflected in a running Pod unless additional mechanisms are used:

- Delete or restart the Pod manually to force it to reload the ConfigMap on startup.

- Trigger a rollout of the Deployment to recreate Pods and pick up the new ConfigMap.

- Include a hash of the ConfigMap content in a Pod spec annotation. When the ConfigMap changes, the hash changes, triggering a redeployment.

How and what should be monitored in the Kubernetes stateful application?

Monitoring stateful applications in Kubernetes involves tracking various metrics related to the application's health, performance, and resource utilization. Monitoring helps detect issues, optimize performance, and ensure the availability and reliability of stateful workloads. We will talk about this topic in *Chapter 14*, but there are some key aspects and metrics to monitor in Kubernetes stateful applications:

- *Resource utilization metrics such as CPU and memory usage* for stateful application Pods. Identify any resource constraints or bottlenecks that may impact application performance or scalability.

- The *health and status of stateful application Pods* to ensure they are running as expected. Track metrics such as Pod status, restart count, and container life cycle events to detect any issues or failures.

- *PV usage metrics, including capacity, utilization, and throughput,* for storage volumes used by stateful applications. Ensure that storage resources are adequately provisioned and optimized for performance and reliability. Monitor network traffic metrics such as Ingress and Egress bandwidth, packet loss, and latency for stateful application Pods. Identify any network-related issues or bottlenecks that may affect application performance or connectivity.

- *Application logs and events generated by stateful application Pods* to identify errors, warnings, and anomalies. Logging solutions such as EFK (Elasticsearch, Fluentd, and Kibana) and LGP (Loki, Grafana, and Promtail) can centralize and analyze logs for troubleshooting and debugging.

- For database components, *database performance metrics* such as query throughput, latency, and transaction rates. Track database-specific metrics such as connections, locks, and buffer pool usage to optimize database performance and reliability.

- *Security-related metrics* such as authentication failures, unauthorized access attempts, and compliance violations. Use audit logs, security events, and intrusion detection systems to detect and respond to security threats and vulnerabilities.

- *Long-term trends and historical data* to perform capacity planning and scaling for stateful application workloads. Identify patterns and trends in resource utilization, workload growth, and performance metrics to anticipate future resource requirements and scale resources accordingly.

By monitoring these key aspects and metrics, you can gain insights into the health, performance, and behavior of Kubernetes stateful applications and proactively address issues to ensure their availability, reliability, and scalability. Don't forget to configure the alert rules and notification channels for critical and essential events.

Now that we've covered PVCs and how they enable Pods to request persistent storage in Kubernetes, it's time to look at the next layer of storage management: CSI. CSI provides a standardized way for Kubernetes to interact with various storage systems, making it easier to integrate and manage different types of storage. By moving on to the CSI topic, we'll explore how Kubernetes can leverage a wide range of storage solutions, extending flexibility and control over storage beyond what PVCs alone provide.

> **Interview tip**
>
> **Question:** *What should be monitored in a Kubernetes stateful application?*
>
> **Answer:** Key areas include CPU/memory usage, Pod health (status, restarts), PV metrics (capacity, **Input/Output Operations Per Second (IOPS)**), network traffic, logs (using EFK or LGP stacks), and database-specific performance. Monitoring helps detect bottlenecks, ensure reliability, and guide your capacity planning. Always configure alerts for critical events.

What is CSI?

CSI is a standardized API that allows storage vendors to develop plugins for container orchestration platforms such as Kubernetes. Before CSI, storage systems had to be tightly integrated directly into the Kubernetes code base (or the code base of other orchestrators), which made supporting new storage backends difficult. Any change or addition required modifications to the core orchestration system itself, resulting in slower development and limited flexibility.

With CSI, storage providers can build standalone plugins that conform to the CSI specification. These plugins can be deployed independently alongside Kubernetes, enabling dynamic provisioning, attachment, and management of storage volumes – *without modifying Kubernetes itself*. This decoupling allows a much broader range of storage options, including block, file, and even object storage, to be supported more easily.

CSI empowers Kubernetes to provision storage volumes on demand. When a Pod requests persistent storage, Kubernetes uses the CSI plugin to create and attach the appropriate volume. CSI also supports operations such as attaching/detaching, mounting/unmounting, resizing volumes, and taking snapshots.

Additionally, CSI enables multi-tenancy by supporting secure and isolated volume management per workload or user group, allowing multiple applications to share the same underlying storage infrastructure without interfering with each other.

Let's explore one of the key components that enables dynamic provisioning in CSI: **StorageClass**.

What is StorageClass in Kubernetes?

In Kubernetes, a StorageClass object is an object that defines the different storage classes available in the cluster, and the provisioner is responsible for dynamically provisioning storage resources of that class. It allows administrators to define the different classes of storage they provide and the methods by which they are provisioned.

Here are the main aspects of a StorageClass object:

- A StorageClass object *specifies the provisioner* responsible for dynamically provisioning storage volumes when PVCs are created. The provisioner determines the type of storage (e.g., cloud-based storage, local storage, etc.) and manages the creation, attachment, and deletion of storage volumes.
- StorageClasses can include *parameters that specify configuration options* for the provisioner, such as storage type, performance characteristics, and other vendor-specific settings.

- StorageClasses also specify a *volume binding mode*, determining how PVCs are bound to PVs. The two available modes are Immediate and WaitForFirstConsumer. In the Immediate mode (the default), a PV is dynamically provisioned as soon as a matching claim is created. In the WaitForFirstConsumer mode, the volume is provisioned only when a Pod using the claim is created.

How does dynamic provisioning work?

Let's look at the following diagram to summarize the overall workflow in modern Kubernetes clusters using CSI controllers to manage the PV/PVC life cycle. In this example, we use the **Amazon Web Services (AWS)** CSI driver based on the EBS service.

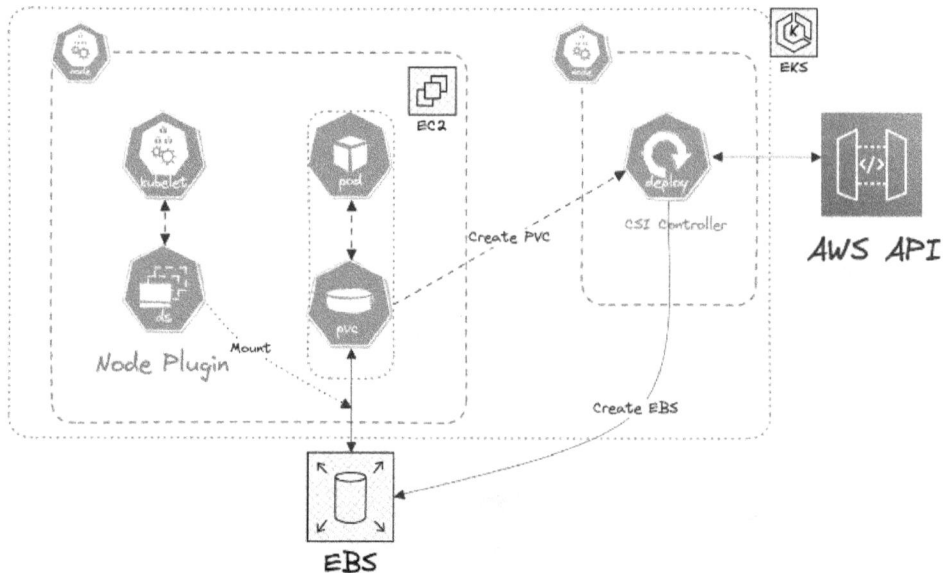

Figure 8.2 – Dynamic PV provisioning in the AWS EKS service with EBS CSI

Let's wrap up this part with some best practices that will summarize the knowledge gained in this chapter and give you a significant advantage in real-world technical interviews.

Interview tip

Question: *What is CSI in Kubernetes?*

Answer: CSI is a standard API that lets storage vendors develop plugins to manage storage in Kubernetes without touching the core code. It enables dynamic provisioning, mounting, snapshots, and more, making it easier to support diverse storage systems such as block and file storage.

What are the best practices for stateful applications?

These types of questions are tricky. We recommend you keep in mind a few outcomes from this chapter:

- Different databases (relational and non-relational, key-value, in-memory, caches, etc.) can work in Kubernetes if you understand what you do 100%. However, it's still recommended that more stable and durable methods, such as managed database services (e.g., Amazon **Relational Database Service (RDS)**), be used for critical databases. In general, Kubernetes today can work with stateful components and all other container workloads.

- Deploying stateful applications requires you to have a clear understanding and adoption of the following recommendations and processes:

    - Use tested and trusted StorageClass configurations to control how PVs are provisioned. Choose the right reclaim policy (Retain, Delete, or Recycle), volume binding mode (Immediate or WaitForFirstConsumer), and storage backend (e.g., **Solid State Drive (SSD)** or **Hard Disk Drive (HDD)**) to match your workload's performance and durability needs. Also, consider setting a default StorageClass to streamline dynamic provisioning.

    - Use StatefulSets and PV/PVCs provisioned dynamically by your StorageClass.

    - Configure all required health checks to ensure the health of your applications by implementing detailed monitoring systems, allowing you to track the state of your applications.

    - Implement auto-scaling (if applicable) and control resource requests and limits to prevent unexpected performance issues.

    - Follow all existing security practices (we will talk about these in the next chapter) to ensure the security of your stateful applications and the data at rest.

As you can see, the list of best practices is really small and clear because nowadays, companies don't trust Kubernetes enough to run business-critical stateful applications inside it. Anyway, the trend is that at some point any company will face a situation when it should run some stateful applications inside Kubernetes, and these best practices allow the company to do it in the correct way from the beginning. However, how do we make sure that it works with no issues? It's something we will dive deeper into in *Chapter 14*. For now we're done with this chapter and let's move forward.

Summary

In this chapter, we explored the essentials of storage in Kubernetes, focusing on persistence through PVs and PVCs, as well as the role of CSI drivers. We discussed how PVs and PVCs work together to provide stable, long-term storage solutions for Kubernetes applications, ensuring data remains intact across Pod life cycles. The introduction of CSI drivers expanded our view of storage management by providing a standardized, flexible way to integrate various storage systems within Kubernetes, from cloud-based storage to on-premises solutions.

With a solid foundation in storage and persistence, we are now ready to move on to other core aspects of managing Kubernetes clusters. The next chapters will cover security best practices in Kubernetes and **role-based access control (RBAC)**, where we'll explore the use of critical security principles and RBAC to protect cluster resources. Following that, we'll dive into understanding deployment processes in Kubernetes, examining best practices and strategies for deploying applications reliably and efficiently. Together, these next steps will build upon our knowledge of storage, further strengthening the management and security of our applications in Kubernetes.

9

Security Best Practices in Kubernetes and RBAC

Security is a critical aspect of managing Kubernetes deployments. In today's landscape, where threats and vulnerabilities are constantly evolving, ensuring that your Kubernetes cluster is secure is more important than ever. This chapter will provide you with comprehensive insights into securing your Kubernetes environment, equipping you with the knowledge to protect your deployments effectively.

We will begin by exploring the core components of Kubernetes security, including securing the Kubernetes API server, which acts as the central management entity of your cluster. You'll learn how to implement authentication and authorization mechanisms to control access to the API server and ensure that only authorized personnel can make changes.

Next, we will cover strategies for securing the nodes in your cluster. Nodes are the machines, physical or virtual, that run your containerized applications. Properly securing these nodes involves configuring them to minimize vulnerabilities, regularly updating them, and monitoring them for suspicious activity. A part of this chapter will focus on **role-based access control** (**RBAC**), a fundamental mechanism for managing permissions and access within Kubernetes. RBAC allows you to define roles and assign them to users or groups, ensuring that each entity has the minimum necessary permissions.

Lastly, we will delve into network security policies; these are crucial for controlling traffic between different parts of your cluster. These policies help ensure that only authorized communication occurs between services, preventing unauthorized access and potential breaches. You will learn how to define and apply network policies to create a secure network environment within your cluster.

By the end of this chapter, you will have a solid understanding of the key security practices to be followed to protect your Kubernetes deployments. You will be equipped with the knowledge to pass technical interviews about Kubernetes and answer questions surrounding security.

In this chapter, we will be covering the following topics:

- How to secure a Kubernetes cluster
- How to manage network security within the Kubernetes cluster
- Best practices for securing Kubernetes workloads

Technical requirements

The code for this chapter is available at:

https://github.com/PacktPublishing/Cracking-the-Kubernetes-Interview/tree/main/
chapter-9

How to secure a Kubernetes cluster

Securing a Kubernetes cluster involves adopting a range of best practices that safeguard its various components from potential threats. A cluster's security spans several layers, including the control plane, worker nodes, and the Kubernetes API. To help you understand how to implement these best practices effectively, we'll break down the key areas that need your attention.

In the upcoming subsections, we'll guide you through securing the control plane, which is the heart of the cluster's operations; the worker nodes, where your applications and workloads run; and the Kubernetes API, which is part of the control plane and is the central interface for managing the cluster. By covering these critical areas, you'll gain a comprehensive understanding of how to mitigate risks and enhance the overall security of your Kubernetes environment.

Here are some key security aspects to consider:

- **Access control:** Talk about the importance of RBAC in defining and managing user permissions within the cluster.
- **Network security:** Highlight the need for implementing network policies to control traffic between Pods and protect against unauthorized access.
- **Authentication and authorization:** Emphasize the use of authentication mechanisms, such as TLS certificates and service accounts, alongside RBAC for robust access control.

- **Container security**: Discuss strategies for securing container images, including vulnerability scanning, image signing, and runtime security measures.

- **API server security**: Mention securing the Kubernetes API server with authentication, authorization, and encryption mechanisms to protect against unauthorized access and data breaches.

- **Logging and monitoring**: Discuss the importance of logging and monitoring to promptly detect and respond to security incidents.

- **Updates and patch management**: Stress the significance of regularly updating Kubernetes components and applying security patches to mitigate known vulnerabilities.

Each of these aspects will be explored in detail in the upcoming sections, where we'll provide actionable steps to implement these practices and secure your Kubernetes clusters effectively.

Interview tip

Question: *Why is securing the Kubernetes API server critical for cluster security?*

Answer: The Kubernetes API server, part of the control plane, is the central point for managing cluster operations. Securing it ensures that only authenticated and authorized users can make changes, preventing unauthorized access to sensitive cluster components and data.

How to secure the Kubernetes control plane

Securing the Kubernetes control plane is paramount to safeguarding the entire cluster against threats and unauthorized access. Ensuring the security of the control plane components is essential to maintaining the integrity and confidentiality of cluster data and resources.

Interview tip

Question: *Why is securing the Kubernetes control plane critical for overall cluster security?*

Answer: The control plane manages the entire cluster's operations, including scheduling, networking, and resource management. If compromised, an attacker could gain full control over the cluster. Securing components such as the API server, etcd datastore, and scheduler ensures the integrity, availability, and confidentiality of the cluster's data and workloads.

So, what exactly should we do to keep our control plane secure? Let's take a look at the most essential items we should do:

- **Restrict access to the Kubernetes API server**, which serves as the primary interface for cluster management. Implement authentication mechanisms such as client certificates, bearer tokens, or integration with external identity providers such as **Lightweight Directory Access Protocol (LDAP)** or **OpenID Connect (OIDC)**. Additionally, authorization policies should be enforced using RBAC to limit the actions of user and service accounts.

- **Encrypt communications between all Kubernetes components**, including the API server, etcd, and kubelet, using TLS certificates. Ensure that certificates are regularly rotated and adhere to best practices for certificate management, such as using robust encryption algorithms and secure key storage. We will discuss this topic in more detail later in the *How to implement in-transit encryption in Kubernetes* section later in this chapter.

- **Protect the etcd datastore**, which stores the cluster's configuration and state, by implementing access controls, encryption, and network segmentation. Consider deploying etcd in a secure network environment and regularly backing up the etcd data to prevent data loss in case of failures or breaches.

- **Apply security best practices to the nodes hosting control plane components** (control plane hardening), such as the API server, scheduler, and controller manager. Utilize tools such as Kubernetes security contexts and Pod Security Policies to enforce least privilege and restrict control plane components' capabilities and access levels.

- **Enable auditing features in the Kubernetes API server** to log all requests and actions against the control plane. Store audit logs securely and regularly review them for suspicious activities or potential security incidents. Auditing helps maintain accountability and provides valuable insights into the cluster's security posture.

- **Stay vigilant about security updates and patches** released for Kubernetes and its dependencies. Regularly update the control plane components to mitigate known vulnerabilities and ensure that the cluster remains resilient against emerging threats.

- **Implement network segmentation** to isolate the control plane components from untrusted networks and apply firewall rules to restrict inbound and outbound traffic to essential services. Utilize network policies within Kubernetes to control Pod-to-Pod communication and limit exposure to potential attacks.

By implementing these measures, administrators can strengthen the security of the Kubernetes control plane and minimize the risk of unauthorized access, data breaches, and other security incidents.

How to granularly configure access to the Kubernetes API

This is an important topic because interviewers regularly ask questions about it. Granularly configuring access to the Kubernetes API involves implementing fine-grained controls to restrict and manage user permissions based on roles, responsibilities, and specific resource requirements. This is typically achieved through RBAC, a Kubernetes feature that allows administrators to define custom roles and bind them to users or service accounts. Here's how to granularly configure access to the Kubernetes API:

1. **Define custom roles**: Start by defining custom roles that encapsulate specific permissions required for various tasks or operations within the cluster. Roles can be scoped at the cluster or namespace levels, depending on the desired level of granularity. Every Kubernetes distribution comes with predefined roles that you can use, but they cover only general cases. Define role permissions with precision, ensuring that users only have access to the resources necessary for their tasks while preventing unauthorized access to sensitive resources.

    Here is an example:

    ```
    apiVersion: rbac.authorization.k8s.io/v1
    kind: Role
    metadata:
     namespace: dev
      name: pod-reader
    rules:
    - apiGroups: [""]
      resources: ["pods"]
      verbs: ["get", "list", "watch"]
    ```

    This role allows reading Pod information (get, list, watch) in the dev namespace.

2. **Create role bindings**: Once roles are defined, bind them to specific entities using RoleBinding (for namespace-scoped access) or ClusterRoleBinding (for cluster-wide access). Entities can be either of the following:

    *   Users (individual human users)
    *   Groups (collections of users)
    *   Service accounts (identities for applications/Pods running in the cluster)

Here is an example:

```
apiVersion: rbac.authorization.k8s.io/v1
kind: RoleBinding
metadata:
  name: read-pods-binding
  namespace: dev
subjects:
- kind: User
  name: jane.doe@example.com  # Binding to a specific user
  apiGroup: rbac.authorization.k8s.io
roleRef:
  kind: Role
  name: pod-reader
  apiGroup: rbac.authorization.k8s.io
```

This `RoleBinding` grants user `jane.doe@example.com` read-only access to Pods in the dev namespace.

3. **Use service accounts for applications**: Grant permissions to applications and services running inside the cluster using **service accounts**. By default, each namespace has a default service account, but it's a best practice to create dedicated ones for specific applications.

Here is an example:

```
apiVersion: v1
kind: ServiceAccount
metadata:
  name: app-service-account
  namespace: dev
```

Now, bind it to a role, as follows:

```
apiVersion: rbac.authorization.k8s.io/v1
kind: RoleBinding
metadata:
  name: app-read-pods
  namespace: dev
subjects:
```

```
- kind: ServiceAccount
  name: app-service-account  # Binding to a service account
  namespace: dev
roleRef:
  kind: Role
  name: pod-reader
  apiGroup: rbac.authorization.k8s.io
```

This gives `app-service-account` read access to Pods in the `dev` namespace.

4. **Attribute-based access control (ABAC)**: In addition to RBAC, ABAC can be used for more dynamic access control based on user attributes, labels, or custom metadata. For example, you can define policies allowing access based on user roles or project affiliations.

   Here is an example of an ABAC policy (JSON):

```
{
  "apiVersion": "abac.authorization.kubernetes.io/v1beta1",
  "kind": "Policy",
  "spec": {
    "user": "jane.doe@example.com",
    "namespace": "dev",
    "resource": "pods",
    "verb": "get"
  }
}
```

   This allows `jane.doe@example.com` to get Pod information in the `dev` namespace.

5. **Audit and review access policies**: Regularly audit user permissions and role bindings to identify misconfigurations or unauthorized access. Enable RBAC audit logging to track and monitor user interactions with the Kubernetes API.

Let's look at an example of enabling RBAC audit logging.

In the `kube-apiserver` configuration, add the following:

```
--audit-log-path=/var/log/kubernetes/audit.log
--audit-policy-file=/etc/kubernetes/audit-policy.yaml
```

Here is an example of an audit policy (YAML):

```yaml
apiVersion: audit.k8s.io/v1
kind: Policy
rules:
# Log all RBAC-related API requests
- level: Metadata
  verbs: ["create", "update", "patch", "delete", "get",
"list", "watch"]
  resources:
    - group: "rbac.authorization.k8s.io"
      resources: ["roles", "rolebindings", "clusterroles",
"clusterrolebindings"]
# Log all authorization decisions
- level: Metadata
  resources:
    - group: "authorization.k8s.io"
      resources: ["*"]
# Optionally log all configmap changes
(e.g., where RBAC might be configured indirectly)
- level: Request
  resources:
    - group: ""
      resources: ["configmaps"]
# Default rule: drop everything else
- level: None
```

6. **Follow the principle of least privilege**: This principle involves configuring access controls and granting users only the permissions necessary to perform their tasks. For instance, if an application only needs to read the Pod status, don't grant it permissions to delete or modify Pods.

For more information on API access control, feel free to read the official documentation at `https://kubernetes.io/docs/reference/access-authn-authz`.

How to secure the Kubernetes worker nodes

Securing Kubernetes worker nodes is essential to protect the integrity and availability of containerized workloads running within the cluster. Let's look at some practices and ways to enhance the security of Kubernetes worker nodes, ensuring that they remain resilient against potential threats and unauthorized access:

1. **Harden the operating system (OS):**

    Start by securing the OS running on your worker nodes. This includes regularly applying security patches, disabling unnecessary services, and configuring firewalls. Follow these steps:

    1. Update the packages:

        ```
        sudo apt update && sudo apt upgrade -y
        ```

    2. Disable unnecessary services:

        ```
        sudo systemctl disable --now bluetooth.service
        sudo systemctl disable --now cups.service
        ```

    3. Configure the firewall with the **Uncomplicated Firewall (UFW)**, which is a simple command-line tool for managing firewall rules on Linux systems:

        ```
        sudo ufw allow 6443/tcp  # Allow Kubernetes API server
        sudo ufw enable
        ```

    For comprehensive OS hardening guidelines, refer to the CIS Kubernetes Benchmark at `https://www.cisecurity.org/benchmark/kubernetes`.

2. **Secure the container runtime:**

    Configure security settings and options to secure the container runtime, such as `containerd`. Features such as AppArmor and SELinux can enforce mandatory access controls and restrict container processes' capabilities.

    Follow these steps to enable AppArmor profiles:

    1. Create a `/etc/apparmor.d/containerd-profile` profile:

        ```
        # Profile for containerd
        profile containerd-default flags=(attach_disconnected) {
            # Add security rules here
        }
        ```

2. Load the profile:

```
sudo apparmor_parser -r /etc/apparmor.d/containerd-profile
```

Note

For a deeper dive into configuring container security, see the *Best practices for securing Kubernetes workloads* section later in this chapter.

3. **Ensure secure container images**:

Regularly scan container images for vulnerabilities. Regularly update base images and enforce image signing and verification mechanisms. Implement container image registries with access controls and image scanning capabilities to prevent the deployment of compromised or malicious images.

Use the following to scan images using Trivy:

```
trivy image nginx:latest
```

In a modern cloud-native environment, ensuring the integrity and authenticity of container images is a critical part of securing the software supply chain. Tools such as **Cosign** allow you to sign container images and verify those signatures before deployment, helping to protect against tampering, impersonation, and supply chain attacks. Here's a usage example:

```
cosign sign --key cosign.key myregistry/myimage:latest
cosign verify --key cosign.pub myregistry/myimage:latest
```

4. **Enable strong node authentication**:

Implement strong authentication mechanisms to verify the identity of worker nodes before allowing them to join the cluster. Use tools such as TLS certificates or token-based authentication to authenticate nodes and establish trust between them and the Kubernetes control plane. Additionally, authorization policies should be enforced to restrict which nodes can join the cluster based on their credentials.

Follow these steps to implement node authentication:

1. Generate TLS certificates:

```
openssl genrsa -out kubelet.key 2048
openssl req -new -key kubelet.key -out kubelet.csr
openssl x509 -req -in kubelet.csr -CA ca.crt -CAkey ca.key
-CAcreateserial -out kubelet.crt -days 365
```

2. Join the node to a cluster:

```
kubeadm join <master-ip>:6443 --token <token> --discovery-
token-ca-cert-hash sha256:<hash>
```

3. Deploy nodes in a **virtual private cloud (VPC)**:

    Deploy worker nodes in a dedicated network segment or in a VPC in cloud environments to isolate them from unauthorized access. Utilize network segmentation and firewall rules to control inbound and outbound traffic to and from worker nodes, minimizing their exposure to external threats.

5. **Encrypt communications:**

    Encrypt communications between worker nodes and the Kubernetes control plane to protect sensitive data and credentials transmitted over the network. Utilize TLS encryption and mutual authentication to secure API server communications, kubelet connections, and other control plane interactions with worker nodes.

> **Reference**
>
> For a deeper dive into configuring encrypted communications, see the *How to implement in-transit encryption in Kubernetes* section later in this chapter.

6. **Audit and monitor node activity:**

    Conduct regular security audits and monitor worker nodes to detect and respond to potential security incidents in real time. Utilize tools such as Kubernetes audit logs, system logs, and intrusion detection systems to monitor node activity, identify anomalies, and investigate security breaches promptly.

Here's how to implement it:

- Enable audit logging. Add extra arguments to API server flags list (we reviewed commands and policy examples previously in this chapter).

- Use Falco (an open source runtime security tool designed to monitor and detect unexpected behavior in containers, Kubernetes clusters, and Linux systems) for real-time threat detection. Here is a sample of the installation via Helm (Helm is the package manager for Kubernetes, which we will talk more about in *Chapter 10*):

```
helm repo add falcosecurity https://falcosecurity.github.io/
charts
helm install falco falcosecurity/falco
```

7. **Apply the principle of least privilege**:

As for the Kubernetes control plane and the API, you should also follow the principle of least privilege when configuring access controls and permissions on worker nodes. Limit user access and permissions to only what is necessary for their tasks, reducing the risk of privilege escalation and unauthorized access to sensitive resources.

To implement it, you need to enforce the **restricted** Pod Security Admission (PSA) level on your namespaces. For example:

```
apiVersion: v1
kind: Namespace
metadata:
  name: restricted-ns
  labels:
    pod-security.kubernetes.io/enforce: restricted
```

At this stage, we're finalizing essential recommendations and have already covered simple answers to widespread questions related to the Kubernetes RBAC and security best practices. Now, we will dive deeper into the implementation details and discuss more production-related aspects of this topic, touching on more technical context rather than some industry-wide theory.

How to manage network security within the Kubernetes cluster

In general, computer networks in the IT world, particularly Kubernetes networks, are the foundation for Kubernetes workloads (we have already discussed Kubernetes networking basics in *Chapter 6*). Cluster administrators should control everything that happens within their clusters, and network security is also one of their highest priorities. When the interviewer asks you a question about this topic, your answer can go in multiple directions, so it's (again) essential to clarify the exact aspect of the Kubernetes network security you're expected to expand upon. First, you can start by listing the main reasons for taking care of network security in the Kubernetes clusters and workloads:

- **Effective isolation**: Proper isolation will prevent unauthorized access between applications, teams, or departments. This isolation is essential for maintaining data privacy, confidentiality, and regulatory compliance.

- **Protecting sensitive data**: This can also be a solid reason to control network security. Many applications hosted within Kubernetes handle sensitive data, such as **personally identifiable information** (**PII**) or proprietary intellectual property. Secure networking prevents data interception, tampering, or unauthorized access while safeguarding the organization's assets and reputation.

- **Minimizing attack spread**: Network security controls limit attackers' ability to move laterally within the cluster, containing potential threats and minimizing their impact on critical resources or services. Kubernetes clusters face various external threats, including DDoS attacks, brute-force attempts, or unauthorized access. Securing network ingress and egress points mitigates these risks, ensuring cluster availability, performance, and operational continuity.

- **Ensuring availability and reliability**: Network security is essential for maintaining the availability and reliability of applications and services running within the Kubernetes cluster. Organizations can ensure uninterrupted operation and customer satisfaction by preventing unauthorized access and network disruptions.

- **Maintaining reputation and credibility**: Security breaches can have devastating consequences for an organization's reputation and credibility. By investing in robust network security, organizations demonstrate their commitment to protecting data privacy, integrity, and trustworthiness, thereby maintaining customer loyalty and stakeholder confidence.

Let's now try to expand on how you can improve your network security using encryption and network policies.

How to implement in-transit encryption in Kubernetes

In-transit security in Kubernetes is crucial for safeguarding sensitive data and maintaining the integrity of communications within the cluster. By encrypting data in transit using protocols such as TLS, organizations can prevent unauthorized access, interception, or tampering of data exchanged between components, Pods, and services. This helps mitigate the risk of data breaches, unauthorized access, and data manipulation, ensuring the confidentiality, integrity, and availability of critical information and resources within the Kubernetes environment. In-transit security measures are essential for meeting regulatory compliance requirements, protecting organizational assets, and maintaining trust and confidence in the integrity of Kubernetes-based applications and services.

Let's break this topic down into sub-sections based on the encryption segments within the Kubernetes cluster.

TLS encryption for the API server and etcd

We have mentioned this several times—TLS encryption for communications between Kubernetes components and the API server is essential and implemented out of the box (the same for etcd). This process ensures that data exchanged between elements, such as kubelet, kube-proxy, API, etcd, and controllers, is encrypted and protected from interception or tampering.

Pod-to-Pod encryption and mutual TLS authentication

Encrypt network traffic between Pods within the cluster to protect sensitive data transmitted between applications. You can achieve Pod-to-Pod encryption using network overlays such as Calico and Flannel, or service meshes such as Istio and Linkerd, which provide out-of-the-box encryption capabilities. Some service meshes and **container network interface (CNI)** plugins also support mutual TLS authentication to authenticate clients and servers during communication within the cluster. Mutual TLS ensures that both parties verify each other's identity using X.509 certificates, preventing unauthorized access and man-in-the-middle attacks.

In the following figure, you can see how mutual TLS works on the mTLS Pod-to-Pod encryption example using Envoy and Istio:

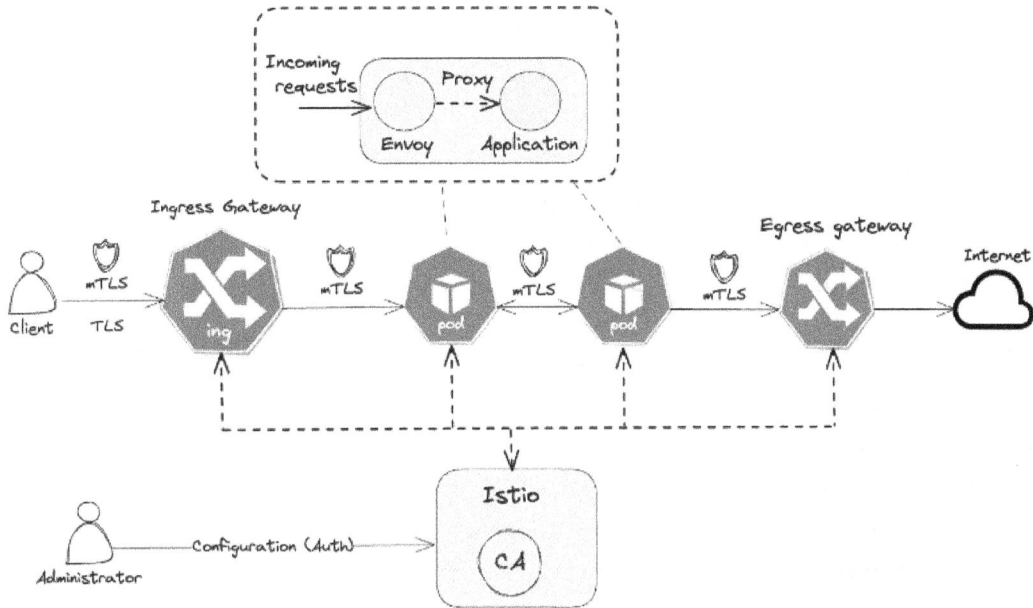

Figure 9.1 – mTLS implementation using Envoy and Istio

So, everything starts with the clients establishing the HTTPS connection (or mTLS if needed) with the ingress gateway endpoint. All components within the cluster are integrated with the Istio **certificate authority (CA)**, which cluster administrators typically manage. Using this CA, Istio issues the necessary certificates and keys to enable mTLS within the cluster. Every Pod involved in this communication has a sidecar container receiving all incoming requests and proxying them to the application container. The egress gateway is optional to securely control the egress connection from the cluster to the external (internet-located) systems.

> **Interview tip**
>
> **Question:** *How does TLS encryption protect Kubernetes API communications?*
>
> **Answer:** TLS encryption secures communications between Kubernetes components and the API server by encrypting data in transit. This prevents unauthorized interception, ensuring that sensitive information such as authentication tokens and cluster configurations remains confidential.

Service encryption for external traffic

Enforcing encryption for traffic routed through Kubernetes services secures communications between services within the cluster. Implement ingress controllers with TLS termination capabilities to encrypt incoming traffic to services, ensuring data confidentiality and integrity. This type of encryption depends on the ingress controller used (some support only classical HTTP-secured protocols, and some can also work with mTLS). Today, it has become the industry standard to use HTTPS instead of HTTP-only endpoints for your applications.

How to implement network policies to control the traffic flow between Pods and nodes

Controlling traffic flow between Pods and nodes in Kubernetes is essential for securing applications, enforcing isolation, and ensuring only authorized communications occur within the cluster. This is achieved by implementing network policies. Network policies are Kubernetes resources that define rules for how Pods can communicate with each other and other network endpoints. These policies define rules for how traffic should be allowed or denied between Pods based on various criteria, such as Pod labels, namespaces, IP addresses, and port numbers. Kubernetes network policies rely on the CNI plugin installed in the Kubernetes cluster. The CNI plugin is responsible for implementing network policies and enforcing network segmentation and isolation between Pods within the cluster. This plugin enforces the network policy rules, monitors network traffic, and ensures that traffic flowing between Pods adheres to the specified policies.

The Kubernetes API has the default `NetworkPolicy` kind (part of the `networking.k8s.io/v1` API version), which can be enforced by any installed CNI plugin. Additionally, some CNI plugins, such as Cilium, offer custom resources and enhanced capabilities for more advanced traffic control within the cluster.

Let's look at the implementation details of applying network policies in the Kubernetes cluster:

1. Create network policies and define which Pods can communicate with each other and external services. Network policies use labels and selectors to identify Pods and apply rules based on their characteristics.

2. Label Pods with specific identifiers that match the selectors defined in network policies. These labels determine which Pods are subject to the rules specified in the network policies. Network policies can target Pods based on their labels and namespaces. You can specify Pod and namespace selectors in network policies to apply rules to specific groups of Pods or namespaces within the cluster.

3. Within network policies, define ingress and egress rules to control incoming and outgoing traffic to and from Pods. Ingress rules specify the sources from which traffic can enter Pods, while egress rules specify the destinations to which traffic can exit Pods.

4. It's highly recommended that the default "deny-all" policy be defined to apply this policy to Pods not selected by other policies. This zero-trust approach helps prevent unauthorized access and reduces the attack surface within the cluster.

Let's review a few samples of network policies and start with outgoing connections (egress) from our Pods to internet resources. Let's assume we only must allow outgoing connections from some Pods to `https://github.com`.

Our sample deployment will use `curl` to check the connectivity to the GitHub HTTPS endpoint. Here, we've shown just part of this Deployment (the full copy is available in the official book GitHub repository in the `chapter-9/basic-policy.yaml` file at `https://github.com/PacktPublishing/ Cracking-the-Kubernetes-Interview/blob/main/chapter-9/basic-policy.yaml`):

```yaml
---
apiVersion: apps/v1
kind: Deployment
metadata:
  name: test-github
  namespace: test-github
  labels:
    app: test
    component: github
spec:
  ...
  selector:
    matchLabels:
      app: test
      component: github
  template:
    ...
    spec:
      containers:
        - name: curl
          image: curlimages/curl
          command:
```

```
              - /bin/sh
              - -c
              - "set -e; while true; do curl --fail https://github.
  com -I -L --connect-timeout 5; sleep 5; done"
```

Here is a quick explanation of this code:

- A deployment named `test-github` runs in the `test-github` namespace
- Labels help apply network policies to the correct Pods
- The `curl` container repeatedly checks connectivity to GitHub every 5 seconds, allowing us to confirm whether the egress policy is correctly enforced

This setup ensures that only authorized Pods can reach external endpoints such as GitHub. It will produce logs indicating whether the Pod can connect to GitHub:

```
kubectl logs -l component=github –namespace test-github
HTTP/2 200
server: GitHub.com
```

When we don't have any policies applied for the Pod (or don't have a default policy defined for the entire cluster), everything is allowed (the Pod can communicate with any networks, and all incoming requests are allowed). Everything else will be forbidden as soon as we apply the network policy to this Pod. Now, let's deploy `NetworkPolicy`, allowing only connections to the GitHub public IP (right now, it's `140.82.121.4`):

```
---
apiVersion: networking.k8s.io/v1
kind: NetworkPolicy
metadata:
  name: test-github-deny
  namespace: test-github
spec:
  podSelector:
    matchLabels:
      component: github
  policyTypes:
    - Egress
  egress:
    - to:
```

```
      - ipBlock:
          cidr: 140.82.121.4/32 <- correct GitHub IP
    ports:
      - protocol: TCP
        port: 443
        endPort: 443
```

Here is a quick explanation of the code:

- podSelector targets Pods labeled component: github in the test-github namespace
- policyTypes: Egress means this policy controls outgoing connections
- ipBlock restricts egress to GitHub's public IP
- Port 443 (HTTPS) is the only allowed port; all other traffic will be denied

This policy ensures that the Pod can only connect to GitHub and nowhere else.

It looks okay. But after applying it, we see the curl: (28) Resolving timed out after 5002 milliseconds error in the logs. Why? The policy should also allow internal cluster DNS traffic to resolve the github.com domain in the appropriate public IP address (because, as we said, after applying the policy, everything else is forbidden).

Let's update the policy and add one more egress rule to allow DNS queries from the Pod to the Kubernetes DNS system (if you don't remember how it works, please return to *Chapter 6*, where we covered the topic of DNS):

```
  egress:
    ...
    # We have to allow the DNS requests as well
    - to:
      - namespaceSelector:
          matchLabels:
            kubernetes.io/metadata.name: kube-system
        podSelector:
          matchLabels:
            k8s-app: kube-dns
      ports:
      - protocol: UDP
        port: 53
```

After this update, everything will recover, and we will see the desired 200 status codes in the logs. Feel free to play with the policy and change the IP in the rules to see how it will fail.

> **Interview tip**
>
> **Question:** *How do network policies improve Kubernetes cluster security?*
>
> **Answer:** Network policies control traffic flow between Pods and external endpoints. By defining rules for ingress and egress traffic, administrators can isolate workloads, prevent unauthorized communication, and limit the attack surface within the cluster.

The default NetworkPolicy object allows you to handle basic scenarios and works the same way in any CNI you use. Some CNI plugins, such as Cilium, expand network policy configuration capabilities and will enable you to create more complicated and flexible policies using custom resource definitions that the CNI provider brings inside your cluster during the installation. Cilium is the best example because it allows the creation of policies based not only on IP addresses but also on **fully qualified domain names** (**FQDNs**), HTTP paths and headers, and so on. All of the following examples were prepared using Cilium.

> You can follow the official Cilium installation guide at:
>
> https://docs.cilium.io/en/stable/installation/k8s-toc/.

In the following example, we will replace the IP with the FQDN to simplify the management because IP addresses can be changed occasionally, and it's not a good practice to operate IP addresses. So, we will operate full domain names to limit connections to the GitHub endpoint only. We will use the same test deployment. We will change the policy and will replace the default Kubernetes NetworkPolicy object with the Cilium CiliumNetworkPolicy custom Kubernetes object manifest (the full copy is available in the official repository in the chapter-9/fqdn-policy.yaml file at https://github.com/PacktPublishing/Cracking-the-Kubernetes-Interview/blob/main/chapter-9/fqdn-policy.yaml):

```
---
apiVersion: "cilium.io/v2"
kind: CiliumNetworkPolicy
metadata:
  name: test-github-deny
  namespace: test-github
```

```
spec:
  endpointSelector:
    matchLabels:
      component: github
  egress:
    - toFQDNs:
      - matchPattern: "github.com"
    # We have to allow the DNS requests as well
    - toEndpoints:
      - matchLabels:
          "k8s:io.kubernetes.pod.namespace": kube-system
          "k8s:k8s-app": kube-dns
      toPorts:
        - ports:
          - port: "53"
            protocol: ANY
          rules:
            dns:
              - matchPattern: "*"
```

This will produce the same results as we had before, but will simplify management over a long distance. When using the TLS HTTPS protocol for our websites, we cannot use other settings such as HTTP headers, methods, and paths because of the HTTPS protocol encryption (only the host is known). Let's deploy one more test deployment and limit access from one Pod to another only for POST requests under the /test path (a full copy of the manifest is available in the repository in the chapter-9/basic-policy.yaml file at https://github.com/PacktPublishing/Cracking-the-Kubernetes-Interview/blob/main/chapter-9/basic-policy.yaml):

```
---
apiVersion: apps/v1
kind: Deployment
metadata:
  name: test-http-server
  namespace: cilium-test
  labels:
    app.kubernetes.io/name: http-server
spec:
  replicas: 1
```

```yaml
  ...
  template:
    ...
    spec:
      containers:
      - name: http
        image: mendhak/http-https-echo

        ...
        ports:
          - containerPort: 8080
            name: http
---
apiVersion: v1
kind: Service
metadata:
  name: test-http-server

  ...
spec:
  selector:
    app.kubernetes.io/name: http-server
  ports:
    - name: http
      protocol: TCP
      port: 80
      targetPort: http
---
apiVersion: apps/v1
kind: Deployment
metadata:
  name: test-http-post

  ...
spec:

  ...
  template:

    ...
    spec:
      containers:
```

```
        - name: curl
          image: curlimages/curl
          command:
          - /bin/sh
          - -c
          - "set -e; while true; do curl --fail http://test-http-server/
test -I --connect-timeout 5 -X POST; sleep 1; done"
---
apiVersion: "cilium.io/v2"
kind: CiliumNetworkPolicy
metadata:
  name: test-http-post
  namespace: cilium-test
spec:
  endpointSelector:
    matchLabels:
      app.kubernetes.io/name: http-server
  ingress:
    - fromEndpoints:
      - matchLabels:
          "k8s:io.kubernetes.pod.namespace": cilium-test
      toPorts:
        - ports:
          - port: "8080"
            protocol: TCP
          rules:
            http:
              - method: "POST"
                path: "/test"
  egress:
    - toEndpoints:
      - matchLabels:
          "k8s:io.kubernetes.pod.namespace": cilium-test
```

As a result, we will have 100% control of all incoming requests to the test-HTTP-server Pods and allow only HTTP POST connections to the web server on the /test HTTP path.

By adopting a comprehensive approach to network security, organizations can create a resilient and trusted infrastructure for deploying and managing applications in Kubernetes. As Kubernetes continues to evolve and become more prevalent in modern cloud-native environments, ensuring network communication integrity, confidentiality, and availability remains paramount. Let's become more familiar with securing workloads (Pods and containers) next.

Best practices for securing Kubernetes workloads

When securing workloads in Kubernetes, the principle of least privilege is key, granting each workload only the permissions it needs to perform its tasks. While we've already discussed this in the context of RBAC, the same principle applies to how we configure workload manifests and container specifications.

In this final section of the chapter, we'll explore three essential areas for securing Kubernetes workloads:

- **Security contexts**: How to define privilege and access control settings at the Pod or container level, including configurations such as `runAsUser`, `capabilities`, and `readOnlyRootFilesystem`

- **Pod Security Admission**: How Kubernetes enforces security policies using Pod Security Standards (`privileged`, `baseline`, and `restricted`) to control Pod behavior during creation and updates

- **Service accounts**: Best practices for managing service accounts to securely authenticate Pods and control access to the Kubernetes API using fine-grained RBAC policies

These practices help ensure that your workloads run securely, limiting potential attack vectors and enforcing compliance with organizational security policies.

What is the security context?

The security context is part of the workload Kubernetes object that defines a Pod or container's privilege and access control settings. It allows administrators to specify security-related configurations at the Pod or container level, such as the following:

- `hostNetwork`, `hostPID`, and `hostIPC`: These control how Pods interact with the host system's network, process namespace, and **Inter-Process Communication (IPC)** namespace, respectively.

- `runAsUser`: This defines the **user ID (UID)** the container's process should run as. This setting helps enforce the least privilege by running the container as a non-root user to minimize the impact of potential security vulnerabilities or exploits. runAsNonRoot can deny or allow running Pods or containers using the root user (UID 0).

- runAsGroup: This specifies the **group ID (GID)** the container's process should run as. Like runAsUser, this setting allows administrators to restrict the privileges of the container by specifying a non-root group.

- capabilities: This defines the Linux kernel capabilities that are available to the container. Kubernetes can enable administrators to add or drop specific capabilities to limit the container's actions, reducing the attack surface and potential impact of security breaches.

- sysctls: This can be used to configure kernel parameters (sysctl settings) for the containers within the Pod. Sysctl settings control various aspects of the Linux kernel's behavior and configuration, such as network settings, filesystem parameters, process scheduling, and so on.

- **SELinux and AppArmor profiles**: These specify the SELinux or AppArmor security profiles to apply to the container. These profiles enforce **mandatory access control (MAC)** and restrict the container's interactions with the host system, enhancing security by isolating the container's processes and resources.

- privileged: This determines whether the container can run in privileged mode, with access to all Linux kernel capabilities. Running a container in privileged mode can pose security risks, so administrators should carefully consider whether it is necessary for its functionality.

- readOnlyRootFilesystem: This specifies whether the container's root filesystem should be mounted in read-only mode. This setting helps prevent unauthorized modifications to the container's filesystem, reducing the risk of tampering or compromise.

- fsGroup: This defines the permissions for volumes mounted into the container. Administrators can specify whether the container should have read, write, or execute permissions on mounted volumes, helping to control access to sensitive data and resources.

Some security context items can be applied to the Pod only, and some can be used to specific containers (take precedence) within this Pod.

What is Pod Security Admission?

The **Pod Security Admission** feature in Kubernetes is a mechanism that helps enforce security policies on Pod creation and updates within a cluster. It works by intercepting requests to create or update Pods and evaluating them against a set of predefined security policies called **Pod Security Standards** (this was known as Pod Security Policies before the 1.21 version).

Here's how the Pod Security Admission process works:

1. Cluster administrators define Pod Security Standards, which specify the security requirements that Pods must meet. These standards are defined using **custom resource definitions (CRDs)** and can be customized to fit the organization's security policies and requirements.

2. The Kubernetes cluster enforces the Pod Security Standards by validating Pods against the defined standards during Pod creation or update using the Pod Security Admission controller. If a Pod's configuration does not meet the requirements specified in the Pod Security Standards, Kubernetes rejects the Pod creation or update request.

Interview tip

Question: *How does the principle of least privilege apply to securing Kubernetes workloads?*

Answer: The principle of least privilege limits permissions for users, services, and workloads to only what's necessary to perform their tasks. This reduces the risk of privilege escalation, unauthorized access, and accidental misconfigurations in Kubernetes clusters.

When discussing Pod Security Standards in Kubernetes, terms such as *privileged*, *baseline*, and *restricted* are often used to categorize the level of security enforced for pods. Here's an overview of what each of these terms typically represents:

- Pods labeled `privileged` have the highest level of access and privileges within the Kubernetes cluster. These Pods can perform actions that are typically restricted, such as accessing the host system's network namespace, PID namespace, or IPC namespace. They may also have access to sensitive system resources and capabilities. Due to the elevated privileges, `privileged` Pods pose a higher security risk and should be used sparingly and only when necessary.

- Pods labeled `baseline` adhere to a set of security policies and best practices defined by the Kubernetes cluster administrator. These policies typically include requirements such as running containers as non-root users, mounting the root filesystem as read-only, and restricting kernel capabilities. `baseline` Pods provide a reasonable level of security for most workloads and are suitable for general-purpose applications.

- Pods labeled `restricted` have the most stringent security requirements enforced by the Kubernetes cluster administrator. These Pods are subject to strict security policies that may include additional restrictions on network access, volume mounts, container capabilities, and more. `restricted` Pods are typically used for highly sensitive workloads or in environments with strict compliance requirements.

In summary, `privileged` Pods have the highest level of access and privileges, `baseline` Pods adhere to standard security policies, and `restricted` Pods are subject to strict security requirements. By categorizing Pods into these different security levels, organizations can effectively manage the security posture of their Kubernetes clusters and ensure that workloads are deployed with the appropriate level of security based on their sensitivity and risk profile.

What is a Kubernetes service account?

A Kubernetes service account is an object that allows Pods to authenticate and communicate securely with the Kubernetes API server. It provides an identity for Pods running within the cluster, allowing them to interact with other Kubernetes resources and perform various actions within the cluster. This is the recommended best practice when you need to grant your Pod the ability to interact with the Kubernetes API inside the cluster.

Each Pod in Kubernetes is associated with a service account, which provides a unique identity. When a Pod requests the Kubernetes API server, the Pod authenticates using the credentials associated with its service account. By default, Kubernetes creates a service account for each namespace in the cluster. If a Pod does not explicitly specify a service account, the Pod uses the default service account for its namespace.

As Kubernetes uses RBAC to control access to cluster resources, service accounts are subject to RBAC policies, allowing administrators to define granular permissions and restrict Pods' actions within the cluster. Administrators can create custom service accounts with specific roles and permissions tailored to the needs of their applications. Pods can specify which service account they want to use by including the `serviceAccountName` field in their Pod specifications.

Service accounts authenticate with the Kubernetes API server using bearer tokens. Kubernetes generates and manages these tokens automatically, ensuring secure communication between Pods and the API server.

Kubernetes service accounts are crucial in securing communication between Pods and the Kubernetes API server. They provide identity and authentication mechanisms that enable secure interaction with cluster resources. They are an essential component of Kubernetes security and access control mechanisms, helping to enforce the least privilege and ensure the integrity and confidentiality of cluster operations.

Interview tip

Question: *What is the role of service accounts in Kubernetes, and how do they improve security?*

Answer: Service accounts provide an identity for Pods to interact securely with the Kubernetes API. By associating Pods with specific service accounts and applying RBAC policies, administrators can control and limit what actions Pods can perform, enhancing workload security.

Summary

This chapter explored various aspects of securing Kubernetes clusters and workloads, focusing on best practices, security features, and mechanisms to enhance the overall security posture. We learned about the importance of securing Kubernetes clusters and workloads to protect against threats, vulnerabilities, and unauthorized access. We also covered a range of security best practices, including ensuring the security of the Kubernetes control plane, implementing RBAC, managing updates and patches, securing networking, enforcing security policies, and so on.

The concepts and techniques discussed in this chapter directly apply to real-world Kubernetes projects and deployments. Organizations can create a secure and resilient Kubernetes environment for running their applications by implementing these security best practices and features. Understanding Kubernetes security is essential for technical interviews, especially for roles involving Kubernetes administration, DevOps, or cloud-native development. Demonstrating knowledge of security best practices, features, and implementation details can help candidates stand out and showcase their expertise in Kubernetes security.

In the following chapters, we will dive into other practical aspects of the Kubernetes world and will be prepared for any questions on actual technical interviews.

In the next chapter, we will explore the real-world deployment scenarios and will understand how to answer questions about **continuous deployment (CD)** processes in the Kubernetes clusters.

Unlock this book's exclusive benefits now

UNLOCK NOW

Scan this QR code or go to `https://packtpub.com/unlock`, then search for this book by name.

Note: Keep your purchase invoice ready before you start.

Part 4

Deployment, Application Management, and GitOps

By the end of this part, you'll be equipped to manage deployments and infrastructure using GitOps—the modern way to deliver applications.

You'll learn how to automate, version, and track your changes using Git as the single source of truth, enabling faster, more reliable, and fully auditable software delivery in real-world projects.

This part of the book includes the following chapters:

10

Real-World Deployment Scenarios and Continuous Deployment

In the previous chapter, we delved into the essential security best practices in Kubernetes, focusing on **Role-Based Access Control (RBAC)** to ensure that our clusters are secure and robust against unauthorized access. Now that you've secured your Kubernetes environment, you need to know how to deploy your applications in real-world scenarios effectively. This chapter guides you through various deployment strategies, emphasizing best practices and addressing common pitfalls that can arise during Kubernetes deployment interviews.

We'll begin with a comprehensive overview of all possible deployment strategies within Kubernetes. We'll cover a wide spectrum of techniques, from basic approaches such as manual deployments to more sophisticated methods such as blue-green deployments, canary releases, and rolling updates. Understanding each strategy's strengths and use cases will help you choose the best approach for different situations.

As we progress through this chapter, we'll review these deployment strategies and dive into real-world implementations. This will provide us with practical insights into how these strategies are applied in various scenarios, enhancing our ability to answer tricky interview questions with confidence and clarity.

This chapter will also emphasize best practices to ensure our deployments are efficient, reliable, and maintainable. Additionally, we'll address common interview questions related to Kubernetes deployments, providing insights into what interviewers typically look for and how to articulate our knowledge effectively.

We will cover the following main topics:

- The core problem: How to update a live application
- Advanced strategies for zero downtime and low-risk releases
- How to manage configurations across environments
- Understanding Helm as the de facto standard for Kubernetes deployments

By the end of this chapter, you will have a solid understanding of the various deployment strategies in Kubernetes, practical experience with real-world scenarios, and the confidence to tackle deployment-related questions in any Kubernetes interview. Let's start mastering Kubernetes deployments and **continuous deployment (CD)** practices.

The core problem: How to update a live application

When you've deployed your application to a Kubernetes cluster, the journey doesn't end there. Development is an ongoing process that involves fixing bugs, adding new features, and responding to user needs. So, how do you deploy these changes to your cluster? While we've already reviewed the basic deployment processes available in Kubernetes out of the box, such as recreating and rolling updates, it's essential to explore the other deployment strategies available on the market that can be implemented in Kubernetes.

The simplest (but riskiest): The Recreate deployments strategy

This is the simplest strategy. Here, when a new version is ready, the old version is stopped and removed, and the new one is deployed. This straightforward approach, however, involves **downtime**. During deployment, the application is unavailable. If a rollback is needed, we must repeat the procedure, resulting in further downtime. This can significantly impact our end users, as the application might be down or read-only. Despite these drawbacks, the Recreate strategy is straightforward and suitable for non-critical environments where downtime is acceptable. Let's see how it looks when used in real-world clusters.

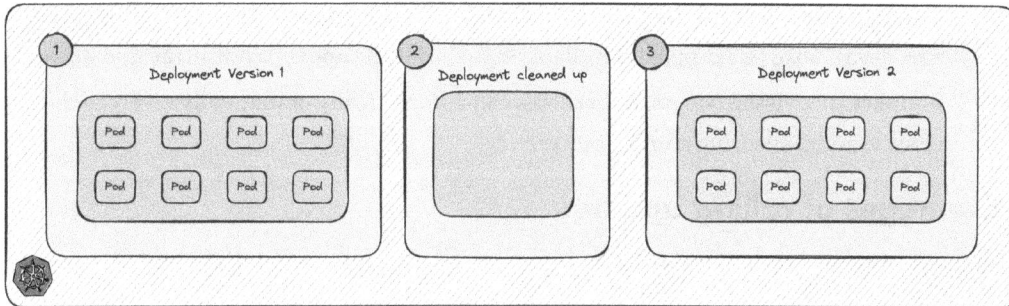

Figure 10.1 – The Recreate deployments strategy

Interview tip

Question: *When is the "Recreate" deployments strategy an acceptable choice, despite the downtime it causes?*

Answer: The Recreate strategy is an acceptable choice for **non-critical environments** where downtime is not a major concern. This could include development, testing, or staging environments where developers are the primary users and scheduled downtime is permissible. Because it is the simplest strategy—it stops the old version completely before starting the new one—it's very straightforward to implement and troubleshoot. You would never use it for a critical, user-facing production application due to the service interruption.

The default: Rolling updates (and why they're not always enough)

A **rolling update** is a strategy in Kubernetes that updates Pods with zero downtime by incrementally replacing old Pods with new ones. This approach ensures high availability for applications. Here's a concise overview of the rolling update process in real clusters:

- **Incremental replacement:** New Pods replace old ones gradually. Kubernetes decreases the number of old Pods while increasing the number of new Pods in a controlled manner.
- **Readiness probes:** Before switching completely to new Pods, Kubernetes verifies their readiness. Only Pods that pass these checks replace old ones. It's important to configure the readiness probe correctly, as it does not allow us to test the application directly. Instead, it checks whether the new Pod is ready to handle traffic. Recall that we discussed the difference between readiness and liveness probes in previous chapters.

- **Configuration**: Parameters such as `maxSurge` (maximum extra Pods allowed) and `maxUnavailable` (maximum unavailable Pods during the update) control the update's pace.

- **Rollback**: If an issue occurs, Kubernetes can automatically or manually revert to the previous version, ensuring continuous service.

Advantages of rolling updates

Rolling updates have various advantages:

- **Zero downtime**: Users experience no interruption during updates, making this ideal for critical applications.

- **Version control and testing**: New versions are easier to manage and test. Poorly performing Pods can be replaced quickly.

- **Resource efficiency**: Only part of the cluster is updated at any time, optimizing resource use.

Interview tip

Question: *In a Kubernetes rolling update, what are the* `maxSurge` *and* `maxUnavailable` *parameters, and how do they let you control the deployment?*

Answer: The `maxSurge` and `maxUnavailable` parameters are key settings that control the speed and safety of a rolling update:

- `maxSurge` defines the maximum number of extra Pods that can be created beyond the desired replica count during an update. This allows you to add new Pods before removing old ones, ensuring capacity remains high.

- `maxUnavailable` specifies the maximum number of Pods that can be unavailable during the update process. This setting ensures that a minimum level of service availability is maintained at all times.

By tuning these two parameters, you can balance the trade-off between deployment speed and resource consumption. For example, a higher `maxSurge` value can speed up the deployment but will temporarily consume more cluster resources.

Use cases

The following are some use cases related to rolling updates:

- **CI/CD environments**: Perfect for continuous updates in dynamic development settings
- **User-facing services**: Ensures seamless transitions without disrupting user experience

Since we reviewed how to implement rolling updates in Kubernetes in *Chapter 3*, we will skip the detailed steps here and continue by looking at more advanced deployment strategies.

Advanced strategies for zero downtime and low-risk releases

While rolling updates are your default for zero-downtime deployments, they aren't a silver bullet. They mix old and new code, which can cause unpredictable behavior, and a rollback can be slow. For critical, user-facing applications, you need more control and greater safety.

This is where advanced deployment strategies come in. These patterns are designed to solve specific, high-stakes problems: how do you roll back an entire system instantly? How do you test a new feature on just 1% of your users? How do you validate performance under real production load without a single user noticing?

Let's break down these strategies, starting with the one that offers the ultimate safety net: the instant rollback.

Blue-green deployments

First up is **blue-green deployments**, which minimize release risk by maintaining two identical production environments: **blue** (the current version) and **green** (the new version). Only one environment is live at any time. To release, you simply switch your router or service so that it sends all traffic from blue to green. This provides near-zero downtime and an instant, one-step rollback if issues arise—just switch the traffic back to blue.

There are various reasons to use blue-green deployments:

- **Reduced downtime**: Switching from the blue to the green environment involves updating DNS or load balancer settings, typically resulting in no downtime. However, switching environments using an external network service or device can lead to session loss, affecting current users.
- **Instant rollback**: If the green environment (new version) fails, you can instantly revert to the blue environment (old version). This quick switch minimizes disruption and maintains service availability.
- **Testing in production**: The green environment mirrors the production environment, allowing for last-minute checks. Live traffic can be gradually routed to the green environment, ensuring everything works under production conditions.

The following diagram provides a visual high-level representation of how blue-green deployments are implemented in real Kubernetes clusters. It shows all the components involved in the rolling process, so you can easily return to this diagram if you need help memorizing any aspect of this strategy.

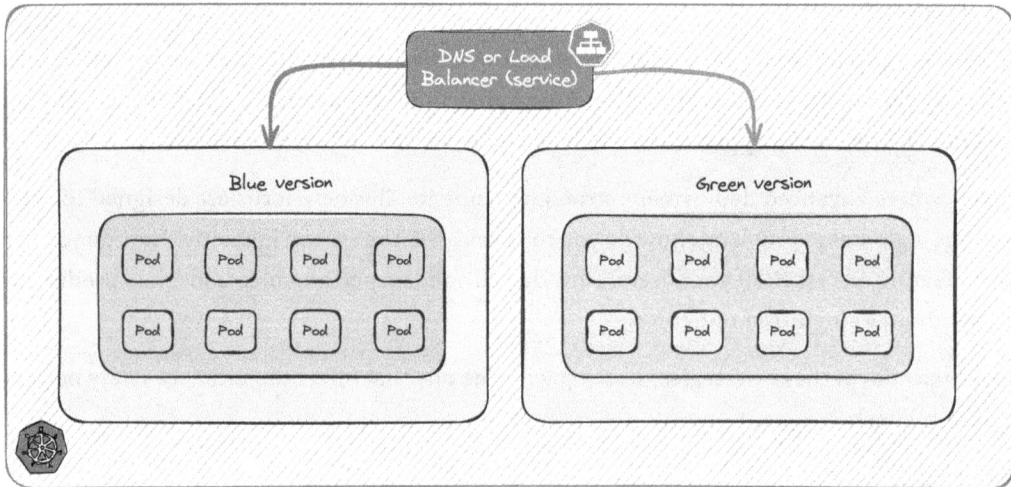

Figure 10.2 – Blue-green deployments

Best practices for blue-green deployments in Kubernetes

Here are some best practices you should know about:

- **Environment parity**: Ensure both the blue and green environments are identical in terms of hardware, configurations, and databases to avoid inconsistencies. Note that this strategy can be expensive, as it requires maintaining two environments simultaneously.

- **Automated testing**: Run automated tests before switching traffic to the green environment to verify that the deployment meets all quality standards.

- **Monitoring and logging**: Implement comprehensive monitoring and logging to detect issues early. This includes monitoring application performance, error rates, and user feedback.

- **Decouple components**: Decouple services to minimize the impact of updates on any single service, enhancing overall deployment stability.

- **Use Kubernetes features**: Utilize Kubernetes resources such as Deployments, Services, and Ingress controllers to manage blue-green deployments efficiently.

> **Interview tip**
>
> **Question:** *You've just switched traffic to the green environment in a blue-green deployment, and your monitoring tools immediately detect a spike in critical errors. What is the rollback procedure, and what is its primary advantage?*
>
> **Answer:** The rollback procedure in a blue-green deployment is to simply redirect traffic back to the stable blue environment. This is typically done by updating a load balancer or, in Kubernetes, patching the service's selector so that it points back to the Pods of the old version. The primary advantage of this is **speed**. The rollback is nearly instantaneous because the old version is still running and ready to handle traffic. This allows you to minimize user disruption and maintain service availability while you investigate the failure in the green environment offline.

Managing data can be challenging in blue-green deployments. Switching environments quickly is feasible for the application layer, but the data layer often requires more careful handling to ensure consistency and integrity.

Implementing a blue-green deployment in Kubernetes

Implementing a blue-green deployment in Kubernetes involves several components, including Deployments, Services, and possibly Ingress controllers. Here's a basic example:

1. **Define the deployments:** Define two deployments: one for the blue version and one for the green version. These deployments manage the life cycle of your Pods:

```
# Blue Deployment
apiVersion: apps/v1
kind: Deployment
metadata:
  name: app-blue
spec:
...
    spec:
      containers:
      - name: my-app
        image: my-app:blue
...
```

```
# Green Deployment
apiVersion: apps/v1
kind: Deployment
metadata:
  name: app-green
spec:
...

    spec:
      containers:
      - name: my-app
        image: my-app:green

...
```

You can find the complete code here: https://github.com/PacktPublishing/Cracking-the-Kubernetes-Interview/blob/main/chapter-10/blue-green-deployment.yml.

2. **Create a service**: Initially, this service must point to the blue version. This service acts as a stable address for your Pods:

```
apiVersion: v1
kind: Service
metadata:
  name: my-app-service
spec:
  type: LoadBalancer
  ports:
  - port: 80
    targetPort: 80
  selector:
    app: my-app
    version: blue   # Initially set to blue
```

You can find the complete code here: https://github.com/PacktPublishing/Cracking-the-Kubernetes-Interview/blob/main/chapter-10/blue-green-service.yml.

3. **Update the service so that it points to the green deployment**: When you're ready to switch to the green version, update the service's selector so that it redirects traffic to the green deployment:

```
kubectl patch service my-app-service -p
'{"spec":{"selector":{"version":"green"}}}'
```

This command updates the service configuration so that it directs all incoming traffic to the green version of your application.

4. **Roll back**: If something goes wrong, quickly revert the service selector so that it points back to the blue version:

```
kubectl patch service my-app-service -p
'{"spec":{"selector":{"version":"blue"}}}'
```

This quick switchback ensures minimal disruption in terms of service availability.

A **blue-green deployment** is incredibly safe, but it's an all-or-nothing switch. You're moving 100% of your traffic at once, and it requires you to run double the infrastructure, which is expensive. What if you're not quite that confident in a new release? You need to expose it to a small fraction of real traffic to see how it behaves first. This is precisely the problem the **canary deployment** strategy solves.

Canary deployments

Canary deployments are used in software development to minimize risk when new features are released. The name "canary deployment" comes from an old practice used by coal miners in the early 1900s. Miners would carry canaries down into mine tunnels. Since canaries are particularly sensitive to toxic gases such as methane and carbon monoxide, their reactions served as an early warning system for miners. If the canary became ill or died, that was a signal that the air quality was dangerous, and miners would evacuate.

In the context of software development, canary deployments serve a similar early warning purpose. Instead of risking all users' experiences with a new software release, developers release the new version to a small percentage of users. This allows them to monitor the performance and stability of the update in a controlled way, mitigating potential widespread issues.

As for all previous examples, the following diagram shows the canary deployment rollout process, including all the components involved:

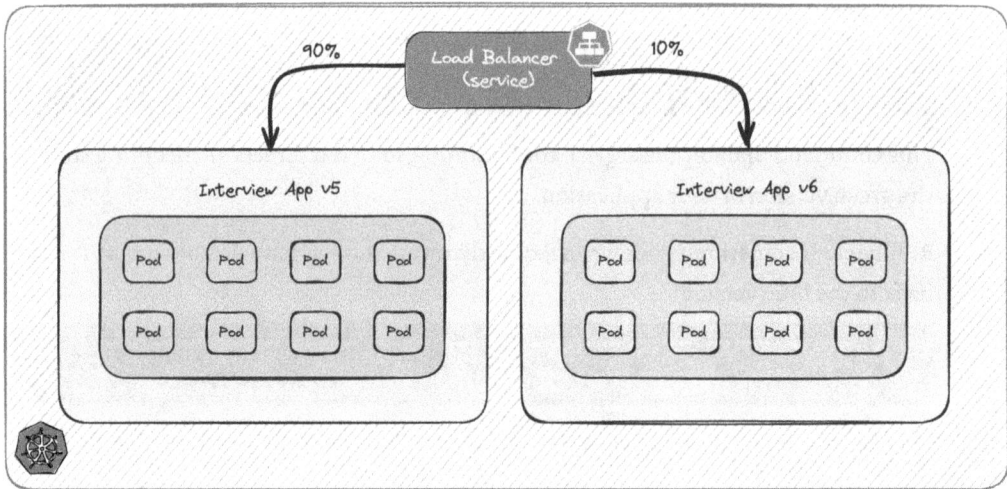

Figure 10.3 – Canary deployment

Principles of canary deployments

The principles behind a canary deployment are relatively straightforward:

- **Less exposure:** The new version of the software is rolled out to a small subset of users, typically 5% to 10%. This helps in isolating any negative impact.

- **Real traffic:** This subset of users is exposed to the new version under real operational conditions. This provides genuine feedback and metrics on the performance and stability of the new release.

- **Gradual rollout:** Depending on the initial results, the deployment can be gradually expanded to more users or rolled back if issues arise. This flexibility in management helps with maintaining system stability and user satisfaction.

Interview tip

Question: *How does a canary release offer a more resource-efficient way to test in production compared to a blue-green deployment?*

Answer: A **canary** release is more resource-efficient because you don't need to run two full, identical production environments simultaneously. In a **blue-green** deployment, you must have enough capacity to run both the old and new versions, which can be expensive. In a **canary** deployment, you only deploy a small number of new version instances alongside the existing stable version. For example, you might have nine instances of your stable version and just one instance of the new canary version, directing **only 10%** of traffic to it. This allows you to validate the new release with real traffic while minimizing both resource costs and the potential impact (or **blast radius**) of any bugs.

Standard Kubernetes objects implementation

To implement a canary deployment using standard Kubernetes objects, you typically use Deployments, Services, and possibly Ingress controllers. This section provides a step-by-step guide on how to do this, as well as sample YAML configurations to help demonstrate a basic canary setup.

Step 1: Define the deployments

You'll need two deployments: one for the stable version of your application and another for the canary version. Here's an example of how you might define these in YAML:

```
# Deployment for the stable version
apiVersion: apps/v1
kind: Deployment
metadata:
  name: frontend-app
spec:
  replicas: 9
  ...
      labels:
        app: interview-app
        layer: frontend
        version: stable
    spec:
      containers:
```

```
      - name: interview-app
        image: interview:v5
# Deployment for the canary version
apiVersion: apps/v1
kind: Deployment
metadata:
  name: frontend-app-canary
spec:
  replicas: 1
...
      labels:
        app: interview-app
        layer: frontend
        version: canary
    spec:
      containers:
      - name: interview-app
        image: interview:v6
```

You can find the complete code here: https://github.com/PacktPublishing/Cracking-the-Kubernetes-Interview/blob/main/chapter-10/canary-deployments.yml.

Step 2: Configure the service

A Kubernetes Service will route traffic to both the stable and the canary Pods. Here's how you might configure this Service:

```
apiVersion: v1
kind: Service
metadata:
  name: interview-app-service
spec:
  ports:
  - port: 80
    targetPort: 80
  selector:
    app: interview-app
    layer: frontend
```

You can find the complete code here: `https://github.com/PacktPublishing/Cracking-the-Kubernetes-Interview/blob/main/chapter-10/canary-service.yml`.

With that, we have seen how to easily implement a canary deployment using just Kubernetes objects. In our example, version 5 (stable version) will process 90% of the traffic, since we defined 9 Pods for that version, while the new version will handle only 10% with its single pod. Using `kubectl patch`, we can manage the number of Pods for the stable and new versions to adjust traffic distribution. However, if we need a more complex implementation, a service mesh or Gateway API can help.

In our earlier discussion on blue-green deployments, we mentioned Istio. Now is a good time to look at how to implement canary deployments using Istio for more advanced traffic management and control.

Using Istio for canary deployments

Istio offers more advanced traffic routing capabilities using VirtualServices and DestinationRules. Here's how you can set up a canary deployment using Istio:

1. **Install Istio in your cluster**: Make sure Istio is properly installed and configured to manage your Kubernetes cluster.

2. **Deploy your applications**: You can use the same deployment definitions provided in the previous Kubernetes example.

3. **Define DestinationRules**: DestinationRules determine policies that apply to traffic intended for a service after routing has occurred:

```
apiVersion: networking.istio.io/v1alpha3
kind: DestinationRule
metadata:
  name: interview-app-destination
spec:
  host: interview-app-service
  subsets:
  - name: stable
    labels:
      version: stable
  - name: canary
    labels:
      version: canary
```

You can find the complete code here: `https://github.com/PacktPublishing/`
`Cracking-the-Kubernetes-Interview/blob/main/chapter-10/canary-deploy-istio-`
`destination-rule.yml`.

4. **Configure VirtualServices**: VirtualServices control how requests are routed to various subsets of the same service within the mesh:

```
apiVersion: networking.istio.io/v1alpha3
kind: VirtualService
metadata:
  name: interview-app-virtualservice
spec:
  hosts:
  - interview-app-service
  http:
  - route:
    - destination:
        host: interview-app-service
        subset: stable
      weight: 90
    - destination:
        host: interview-app-service
        subset: canary
      weight: 10
```

You can find the complete code here: `https://github.com/PacktPublishing/Cracking-the-`
`Kubernetes-Interview/blob/main/chapter-10/canary-deploy-istio-destination-rule.yml`.

This configuration routes 90% of the traffic to the stable version and 10% to the canary version. You can adjust these weights based on real-time monitoring and performance metrics.

Monitoring and adjusting

As we process real traffic from users—in our case, 10%—it's crucial to set up a robust monitoring solution to ensure the new version of our application works correctly. Whether you're using Kubernetes directly or Istio, tools such as Prometheus, Grafana, and Kubernetes metrics are essential for observing the behavior of your canary deployments. You can then adjust the traffic weights, scale up the canary, or roll back based on your observations. We will review how to implement monitoring in detail in *Chapter 14*.

Canary deployments are perfect for testing the *technical stability* of a new release—does it crash? Are the error rates low? But what if your goal isn't just to prove the code works, but to test whether a new feature actually improves business metrics, such as user engagement or sales conversions? This requires more than just a random percentage of traffic; you need to target specific user segments for a controlled experiment. This moves us from canary deployments to an **A/B testing** strategy.

A/B deployments

An **A/B deployment**, also known as **split testing** or **bucket testing**, is a deployment strategy that's used to compare two versions of an application or feature against each other to determine which one performs better. Here are some of the key principles of A/B deployments:

- **Controlled experiments**: Two versions (A and B) are released simultaneously to different segments of users
- **User segmentation**: Traffic is split between the two versions based on specific criteria or randomly
- **Performance metrics**: The performance of each version is monitored and measured against predefined metrics such as user engagement, conversion rates, or system performance

Use cases

A/B deployment strategies are particularly useful in the following scenarios:

- **Feature testing**: When you want to test new features with a subset of users to gather feedback and measure impact
- **User experience improvements**: Comparing different UI designs or user flows to determine which one improves user satisfaction and engagement
- **Performance enhancements**: Testing backend changes or optimizations to see whether they improve application performance under real-world conditions
- **Marketing experiments**: Evaluating different marketing messages or offers to see which ones resonate more with users

Who needs to implement A/B deployments and when?

Let's take a look:

- **Product managers**: When they need to validate new features or changes before a full rollout
- **Marketing teams**: To test different promotional strategies or user acquisition techniques

- **Development teams**: When implementing performance optimizations or architectural changes
- **UX/UI designers**: To compare different design choices and their impact on user behavior

> **Interview tip**
>
> **Question:** *How is an A/B test different from a canary deployment, and which teams are most interested in its results?*
>
> **Answer:** An **A/B** test is a controlled experiment used to compare two or more versions of an application to determine which one performs better against specific business metrics, such as conversion rates or user engagement. A **canary** deployment, on the other hand, is a risk mitigation strategy used to detect bugs or performance issues in a new release before a full rollout. The key difference is intent: A/B testing is for making data-driven product decisions, while canary deployments are for ensuring technical stability. Because of this, product managers and marketing teams are typically the most interested in the results of A/B tests as they can use them to validate new features or promotional strategies.

Can Kubernetes help with implementing A/B deployments?

Kubernetes can facilitate A/B deployments to a certain extent, but it may require additional tools and configurations to fully implement this strategy. Here's how Kubernetes can help:

- **Traffic splitting**: Using Kubernetes Services and Ingress controllers, traffic can be routed to different versions of an application
- **Pod labels and selectors**: You can label Pods and use selectors to manage traffic distribution between different versions
- **Custom Resource Definitions (CRDs)**: Tools such as Istio and other service meshes can leverage CRDs to provide advanced traffic management and routing capabilities for A/B testing

Tools for A/B deployments

Several tools can aid in implementing A/B deployments:

- **Istio**: A service mesh that provides advanced traffic management, observability, and security for microservices. Istio can handle sophisticated traffic splitting and routing, both of which are necessary for A/B testing.

- **Flagger:** An open source progressive delivery tool for Kubernetes that automates the promotion of A/B deployments using Istio, Linkerd, or App Mesh.

- **Optimizely:** A popular A/B testing and experimentation platform that integrates well with modern web applications.

- **LaunchDarkly:** A feature management platform that allows for feature flagging and controlled rollouts, making it easier to implement A/B tests.

Drawbacks of A/B deployments

While A/B deployments offer significant benefits, there are some drawbacks to consider:

- **Complexity:** A/B deployment is one of the most complicated deployment strategies. It requires carefully selecting specific groups of users to test the new version, which can be challenging to manage and implement.

- **Resource intensive:** Running two versions in parallel requires additional resources, which can lead to increased costs.

- **Data management:** Collecting and analyzing data from A/B tests requires robust monitoring and analytics tools that can be challenging to set up and maintain.

- **User experience:** Some users may experience different versions of the application, which could lead to confusion or inconsistency in user experience.

The **blue-green**, **canary**, and **A/B** strategies all expose new code to users, even if it's a small group. But what if you need to test non-functional requirements, such as performance and latency, under heavy production load before any user is affected? You need a way to see how your new version holds up to real traffic without ever returning its response to a user. This is the unique and powerful purpose of a **shadow deployment**, also known as traffic mirroring.

Shadow deployments

Interviewers ask about shadow deployments to gauge your understanding of advanced, risk-averse testing strategies. Describing this pattern shows that you think deeply about validating new code under real-world conditions *before* it affects a single user. It separates you from candidates who only know the more common deployment patterns.

This is a powerful technique for testing non-functional requirements such as performance, latency, and resource consumption under true production load. Failing to mention the significant risks, particularly regarding data-modifying services, is a common pitfall. A strong answer will cover both the "how" and the critical "when *not* to."

Core explanation

A **shadow deployment** (also known as traffic mirroring) is a strategy where you deploy a new version (v2) alongside your stable production version (v1). The key difference from other strategies is that you fork or "mirror" a copy of the live production traffic from v1 to v2. The responses from v2 are completely ignored and never sent back to the user. This allows you to see how v2 behaves under a real production load without any risk to the end user experience.

> **Interview tip**
>
> **Question:** *When would you choose a shadow deployment over a canary release?*
>
> **Answer:** You should choose a **shadow deployment** when your main goal is to test the non-functional requirements of a new version, such as its performance, latency, or stability, under real production load, while ensuring there isn't any risk to users. In a shadow deployment, traffic is mirrored to the new version, but the responses are discarded, so users are never affected.
>
> You should choose a **canary** release when you need to test the functionality and user reception of a new feature with a small, controlled group of actual users. Canaries have a live impact on a subset of users, allowing you to gather real feedback and metrics on new features, which is something a shadow deployment cannot do.

The primary goal is to test for bugs, performance bottlenecks, or errors in the new version. Because v2 is receiving the same request stream as v1, you get a high-fidelity test of its stability and performance. The following diagram illustrates this traffic flow, showing how live traffic is mirrored without affecting the user's response.

Kubernetes Cluster

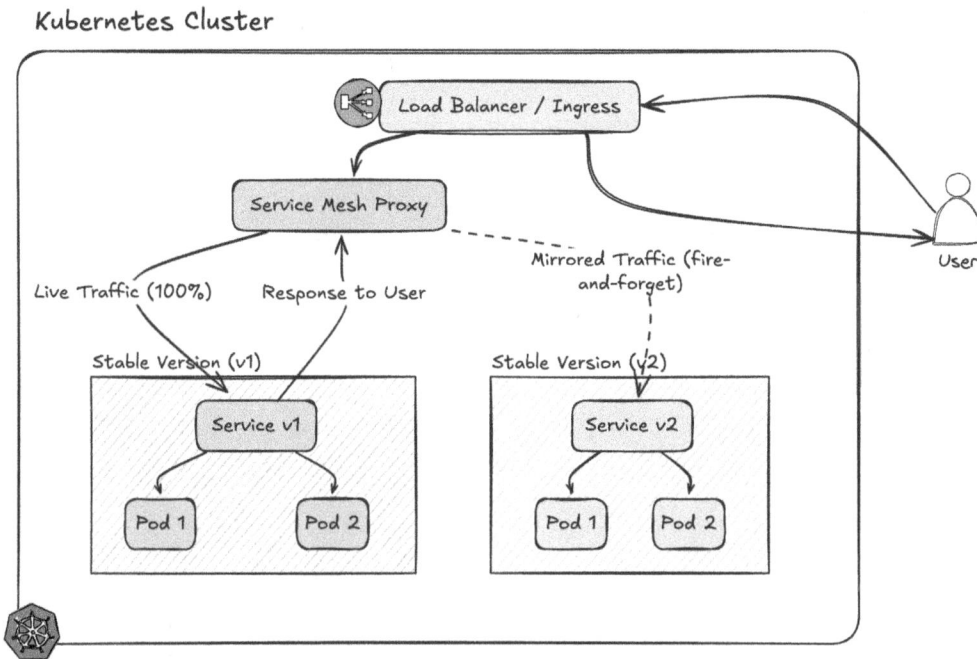

Figure 10.4 – Shadow deployment

However, this pattern comes with a major warning: **beware of side effects**. If your service writes to a database, calls a payment API, or sends an email, the shadow version will do it too. This could result in customers being charged twice or duplicate data being created. To mitigate this, you must ensure the shadow deployment targets read-only endpoints or uses mocked downstream services (stubs) for any stateful or external calls.

Example: Shadowing with Istio

To set up a shadow deployment, you need two distinct deployments running in your cluster: one for the stable version and one for the new (shadow) version. The magic happens in the Istio VirtualService resource, which controls the routing logic.

This VirtualService resource routes 100% of the actual traffic to the stable subset. Crucially, the mirror field tells Istio to also send a copy of that same traffic to the shadow subset. Istio handles this as a "fire-and-forget" operation, meaning it doesn't wait for a response from the shadow service before returning the stable service's response to the user:

```
apiVersion: networking.istio.io/v1beta1
kind: VirtualService
metadata:
  name: my-app-virtualservice
spec:
  hosts:
  - my-app-service # The Kubernetes service that receives traffic
  http:
  - route:
    - destination:
        host: my-app-service
        subset: stable # why it matters: This defines the primary destination
for live traffic.
        weight: 100
    mirror:
      host: my-app-service
      subset: shadow # why it matters: This defines the shadow destination.
Traffic is copied here.
    mirrorPercentage:
      value: 100.0 # why it matters: You can choose to mirror only a fraction
of traffic.
---
apiVersion: networking.istio.io/v1beta1
kind: DestinationRule
metadata:
  name: my-app-destinationrule
spec:
  host: my-app-service
  subsets:
  - name: stable
    labels:
      version: v1
  - name: shadow
    labels:
      version: v2
```

Once you've collected enough data from your monitoring tools (such as Prometheus and Grafana) to be confident in the stability of v2, you can proceed to a full rollout using a different strategy, such as a rolling update or blue-green deployment.

Interview tip

Question: *When would you choose a shadow deployment over a canary release?*

Answer: You should choose a **shadow deployment** when your primary goal is to validate the *performance and stability* of a new version under production load, without exposing any users to potential bugs. A canary release is better when you want to test the *functionality and user reception* of a new feature with a small, controlled group of actual users. Shadowing is for non-functional testing; canaries are for functional testing with live impact.

Key takeaways

Here are some key takeaways to consider regarding shadow deployments:

- **Shadow deployments are for risk-free performance testing**. They use real, live traffic to vet a new release without any user impact.
- **Responses from the shadow version are always discarded**. The user only ever sees the response from the stable version.
- **The biggest danger is unintended side effects**. You must carefully manage database writes, external API calls, and other stateful actions, often by using service mocks.
- **Implementation requires a service mesh**. Tools such as Istio and Linkerd are essential for managing the sophisticated traffic mirroring that this pattern requires.

Interview tip

Question: *What is the single biggest risk of shadow deployments, and how do you prevent it?*

Answer: The biggest risk is unintended side effects from **stateful operations**. For example, a shadow service could make duplicate database writes or call a third-party payment API, causing real-world problems. The best way to prevent this is by using mocked or stubbed-out downstream services for the shadow environment or by ensuring the mirrored traffic only hits read-only API endpoints.

Decision framework: Choosing the right strategy for the job

With that, we have reviewed all the deployment strategies that can be implemented using Kubernetes. Now, it's time to summarize what we have learned and provide a comprehensive overview of each strategy.

The following figure details the variations between these deployment strategies. Using this, depending on your specific situation, you can select the best one. If an interviewer asks you which deployment strategy is best, you need to understand the circumstances and requirements of the deployment. The right answer depends on these factors.

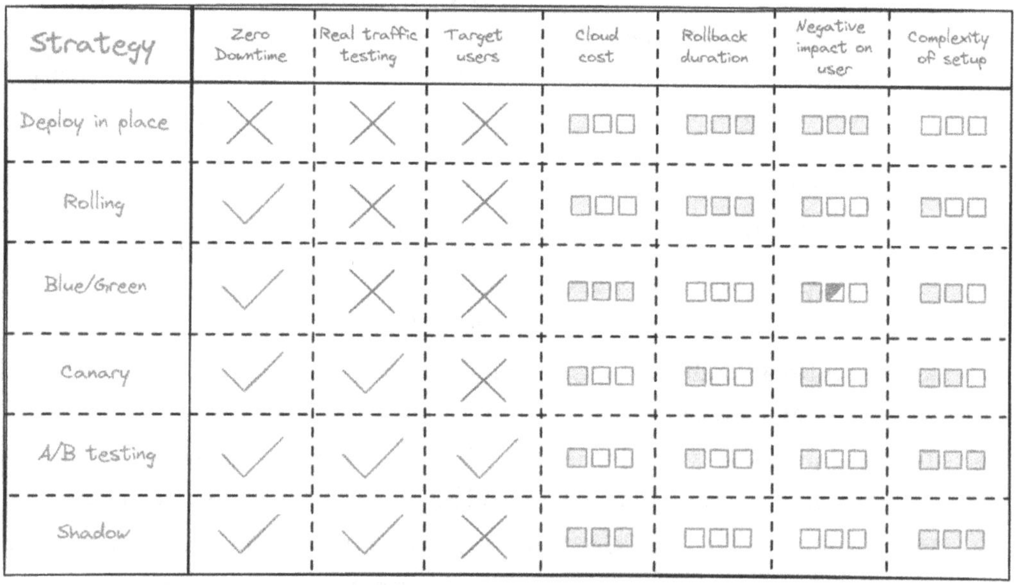

Strategy	Zero Downtime	Real traffic testing	Target users	Cloud cost	Rollback duration	Negative impact on user	Complexity of setup
Deploy in place	✗	✗	✗	☐☐☐	☐☐☐	☐☐☐	☐☐☐
Rolling	✓	✗	✗	☐☐☐	☐☐☐	☐☐☐	☐☐☐
Blue/Green	✓	✗	✗	☐☐☐	☐☐☐	☐■☐	☐☐☐
Canary	✓	✓	✗	☐☐☐	☐☐☐	☐☐☐	☐☐☐
A/B testing	✓	✓	✓	☐☐☐	☐☐☐	☐☐☐	☐☐☐
Shadow	✓	✓	✗	☐☐☐	☐☐☐	☐☐☐	☐☐☐

Figure 10.5 – Deployment strategies

While reviewing deployment strategies has been insightful, there's still the question of how to deploy applications to Kubernetes, especially when managing multiple environments such as development, staging, and production. Now is a good time to move on to the next step and review how to manage deployments in Kubernetes using tools such as Kustomize and Helm.

How to manage configurations across environments

Knowing these deployment strategies is half the battle. The other half is managing the YAML that defines them, especially across multiple environments, such as development, staging, and production. Manually editing manifests for each environment is slow, error-prone, and doesn't scale. A simple change, such as updating a container image tag or increasing a replica count, might require you to edit multiple files, risking inconsistencies that could bring down your application.

This is the configuration management problem that specialized Kubernetes tools are built to solve. They provide systematic, repeatable, and version-controlled ways to manage your application manifests.

There are two dominant tools in this space: Kustomize and Helm. We'll start with the simpler, template-free approach that's now built directly into kubectl: **Kustomize**. It allows you to define a standard "base" set of YAML and then apply declarative "overlays" so that you can customize it for each of your environments.

Kustomize

Kustomize is a powerful tool for managing Kubernetes configurations without the complexity of a templating engine. It lets you define a standard "base" set of YAML manifests and then apply environment-specific "overlays" or patches. For example, you can use an overlay to change the replica count for your production environment while leaving the base configuration untouched. This template-free, declarative approach makes managing configurations across environments simple and predictable.

Key concepts and components of Kustomize

Here's what you need to know:

- **Bases**: The base directory contains the original, template-free YAML files that represent your application's default configuration.
- **Overlays**: Overlays are directories that contain environment-specific modifications to the base configuration. Each overlay has a kustomization.yaml file specifying the changes.
- **Patches**: Patches are used within overlays to apply modifications to the base configurations. They can be strategic merge patches or JSON patches.
- **Resources**: These are the actual Kubernetes objects defined in YAML files.
- **Generators**: Generators create ConfigMaps and Secrets from files or literals, allowing dynamic generation of these resources based on the environment.

- These concepts and components have been compiled in the following diagram to provide you with a high-level representation so that they're easier to remember:

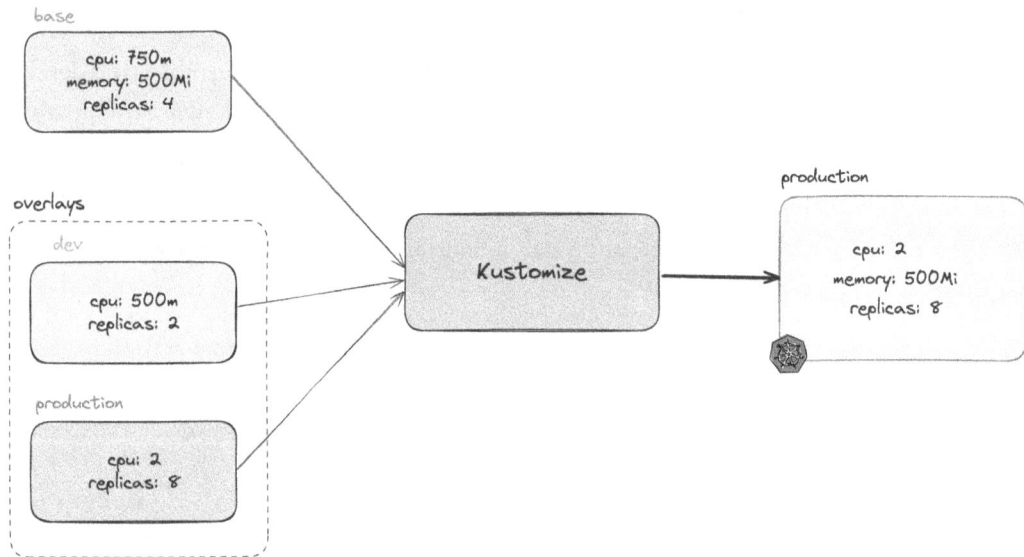

Figure 10.6 – Kustomize concept

Main benefits of using Kustomize

There are various benefits of using Kustomize. Here are some of them:

- **Template-free**: Simplifies configuration management by avoiding templating languages
- **Declarative customization**: Ensures configurations are easy to read and understand
- **Consistency across environments**: By reusing base configurations and applying environment-specific overlays, Kustomize maintains consistency
- **Reusability**: Base configurations can be reused across multiple environments with minimal changes

How overlays and bases work in Kustomize

In Kustomize, bases represent the core configuration of your application, while overlays represent environment-specific customizations. A base might include general configurations for a Kubernetes Deployment, Service, and ConfigMap. Overlays, on the other hand, might tweak these configurations for different environments, such as development, staging, and production. The kustomization.yaml file in each overlay directory specifies which base it builds on and what patches to apply, ensuring configurations remain consistent yet flexible across environments.

The purpose of the kustomization.yaml file

The `kustomization.yaml` file is central to Kustomize's functionality. It defines how Kubernetes resources should be customized and combined. Here are some of the key fields in this file:

- `resources`: A list of resource files to include
- `patches`: A list of patch files to apply
- `configMapGenerator` and `secretGenerator`: Instructions for generating ConfigMaps and Secrets
- `namePrefix` and `nameSuffix`: Prefixes and suffixes to add to resource names
- `commonLabels` and `commonAnnotations`: Labels and annotations to add to all resources

> **Interview tip**
>
> **Question:** *What is the core purpose of the* `kustomization.yaml` *file in Kustomize?*
>
> **Answer:** The `kustomization.yaml` file is the heart of Kustomize; it defines how to generate the final Kubernetes manifests. Its core purpose is to act as a declarative **instruction manual**. It specifies a list of base resource files to use, what patches to apply to them, and any generators for creating resources such as **ConfigMaps** and **Secrets**. By modifying this one file, you can manage complex customizations across different environments without ever touching the original base YAML files.

Kustomize best practices

Here are some best practices to consider:

- **Directory structure**: Use a consistent folder structure (e.g., `base/`, `overlays/`, `patches/`, `configs/`)
- **Resource storage**: Store each resource in its own YAML file, unless they are closely related
- **Naming scheme**: Use a consistent naming scheme for resource files (e.g., `<name>.<kind>.yaml`)
- **Generators**: Always use generators for ConfigMaps and Secrets to trigger rolling updates on changes
- **Version control**: Treat kustomizations as code—format with `kustomize cfg fmt`, and store them in version control
- **Patch usage**: Minimize the use of strategic merge and JSON patches; prefer other mechanisms when possible

How can Kustomize be integrated into CD pipelines?

In modern DevOps practices, CD pipelines are essential for delivering software efficiently and reliably. Integrating Kustomize into your CD pipeline can streamline the process of managing Kubernetes configurations across multiple environments. Here's a step-by-step guide on how to do this effectively.

Setting up your CD pipeline with Kustomize

You should follow these steps when setting up your CD pipeline with Kustomize:

1. **Define your base and overlay manifests**: Organize your Kubernetes manifests into base and overlay directories. The base directory should contain the common configuration files, while the overlays directory should contain subdirectories for each environment (e.g., development, staging, production).

2. **Version control**: Store your Kustomize configurations in a version-controlled repository (e.g., Git). This ensures that any changes to the configurations are tracked and can be reviewed.

3. **CI pipeline configuration**: Configure your CI/CD pipeline so that it uses Kustomize. For example, in a Jenkins pipeline, you can set up stages to check out the repository, build the manifests using Kustomize, and apply them to the appropriate Kubernetes cluster.

Example Jenkins pipeline configuration

Here's an example of how you might set up a Jenkins pipeline so that it uses Kustomize for CD:

```
pipeline {
    agent any
    stages {
        stage('Checkout') {
            steps {
                git 'https://your-repo-url.git'
            }
        }
        stage('Build Manifests') {
            steps {
                sh 'kustomize build overlays/staging > staging-manifest.
yaml'
            }
        }
```

```
        stage('Deploy to Staging') {
            steps {
                sh 'kubectl apply -f staging-manifest.yaml'
            }
        }
        stage('Run Tests') {
            steps {
                // Add steps to run your tests here
            }
        }
        stage('Promote to Production') {
            steps {
                input message: 'Promote to production?'
                sh 'kustomize build overlays/production > production-
manifest.yaml'
                sh 'kubectl apply -f production-manifest.yaml'
            }
        }
    }
    post {
        failure {
            mail to: 'dev-team@example.com',
                subject: "Failed Pipeline: ${currentBuild.
fullDisplayName}",
                body: "Something is wrong with ${env.BUILD_URL}"
        }
    }
}
```

All the code samples provided in this chapter, including the Jenkinsfile shown here, can be found in this book's GitHub repository (https://github.com/PacktPublishing/Cracking-the-Kubernetes-Interview/blob/main/chapter-10/Jenkinsfile). The Jenkins pipeline is **declarative** and uses core steps that are compatible with the most recent Jenkins versions.

Automating rollbacks

Incorporating automated rollback mechanisms is crucial for ensuring that deployments can be reverted quickly in case of failures. With Kustomize, you can store previous configurations and apply them if needed.

According to best practices, each version of your deployment manifests should be stored in a version-controlled repository (such as Git). Each version (or release) should have its own directory containing the relevant Kustomize configuration.

As an example, your repository should have a structure similar to the following:

```
kustomize/
├── base/
│   ├── deployment.yaml
│   ├── kustomization.yaml
├── overlays/
│   ├── dev/
│   ├── staging/
│   ├── prod/
├── releases/
│   ├── v1.0.0/
│   ├── v1.1.0/
│   ├── v2.0.0/
```

Real-world scenario using Kustomize

Consider a project where you need to deploy a multi-tier application across different environments. Each environment has specific configurations for resources such as ConfigMaps, Secrets, and container images.

Challenge

You need to maintain consistent configurations across environments while allowing for environment-specific customizations.

Solution

Here's a solution you could implement:

- **Define the base configuration**: Define the base configuration in the base directory. This includes common configurations for all environments.

- **Create environment-specific overlays**: Create overlays for each environment. For example, the development overlay might have fewer resources and lower resource limits, while the production overlay might have more replicas and higher resource limits.

- **Automate deployments**: Use a CI/CD pipeline to automate the deployment process. The pipeline checks out the configuration repository, builds the manifests using Kustomize, and applies them to the target environment.

Overcoming challenges

During the project, you might encounter challenges such as complex patching requirements or managing large configurations. Here are some strategies you can implement to overcome these challenges:

- **Modularize configurations**: Break down large configurations into smaller, manageable pieces. Use the Kustomize resource field to include these pieces in your `kustomization.yaml` file.

- **Use generators**: Leverage Kustomize generators to create ConfigMaps and Secrets dynamically. This reduces the need for manual updates and ensures consistency.

- **Review and test**: Implement thorough code reviews and testing for your configurations. Use tools such as `kubeval` to validate your Kubernetes manifests before applying them.

Kustomize is a powerful tool for managing Kubernetes configurations, offering a template-free, declarative approach that simplifies deployments. It allows for extensive customization, but still requires you to write everything in YAML. When deploying applications across multiple Kubernetes clusters in different locations, Helm becomes a valuable tool. Helm streamlines this process, providing a more scalable solution. Let's take a look.

Understanding Helm as the de facto standard for Kubernetes deployments

Helm is an essential tool in the Kubernetes ecosystem, simplifying the management of complex applications. It packages all the necessary resources into a single, reusable unit called a **chart**, making deployments and configurations more manageable. With its powerful templating capabilities using the Go template language, Helm offers extensive flexibility and customization, allowing applications to adapt to various environments.

Why Helm?

Here are some reasons you should use Helm:

- **Simplify deployments**: Helm packages, configures, and deploys applications on Kubernetes clusters with ease

- **Version control**: Helm encapsulates all Kubernetes resources into a single package, making it simple to manage versions

- **Reuse and share**: Applications can be shared and reused through repositories, fostering collaboration

- **Enable rollbacks:** Helm can easily roll back to previous application versions if needed, enhancing stability and control

What is the architecture of Helm?

Helm operates on a client-server model, providing a streamlined approach to managing Kubernetes applications:

- **Helm client:** This command-line tool runs locally, enabling you to manage Helm charts and releases effectively.
- **Helm library (Helm 3):** This contains the logic for executing Helm operations, such as combining charts and configurations to create releases. With Helm 3, the need for Tiller—a server-side component in Helm 2—was eliminated, allowing direct interaction with the Kubernetes API, simplifying security and deployment processes.

This architecture enhances user control and simplifies the overall management of Kubernetes environments.

The following diagram summarizes Helm in one place:

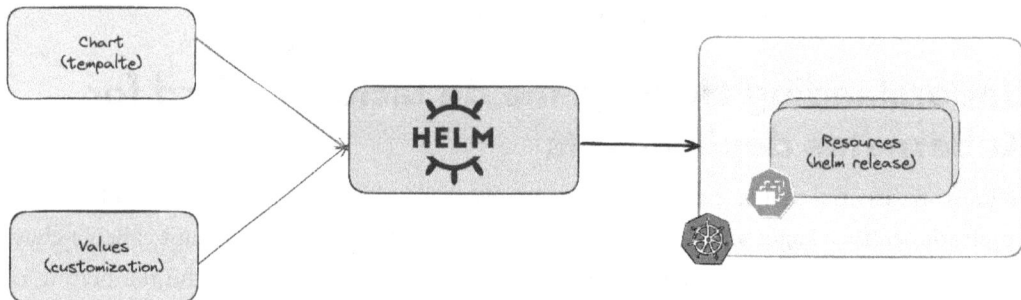

Figure 10.7 – Helm architecture

As you can see, the Helm client takes some templates and adds some variables provided by the user, resulting in resources being created in your Kubernetes cluster. This makes Helm the best templating tool in the Kubernetes world. Today, it is the worldwide standard for distributing and delivering complex Kubernetes deployments to thousands of Kubernetes clusters.

How to build a Helm chart

A Helm chart serves as a blueprint for your application that contains all the necessary components for deploying it on Kubernetes. The basic structure includes mychart/, which acts as the root directory for your chart. This root directory includes the following files and directories:

- `Chart.yaml`: Metadata about the chart, such as its name and version
- `values.yaml`: Default configuration values for the chart
- `charts/`: Subcharts or dependencies.
- `templates/`: Templates for Kubernetes resources

To start, use the `helm create mychart` command to scaffold a new chart, setting up the necessary structure efficiently. This approach helps streamline application deployment on Kubernetes.

Interview tip

Question: *An experienced colleague mentions that Helm 3 is much more secure and simpler than Helm 2. What major architectural change are they referring to, and why was it so important?*

Answer: They are referring to the **removal of Tiller**, which was the server-side component in Helm 2. In Helm 2, the Helm client on your machine would send commands to Tiller, a service running inside the Kubernetes cluster. Tiller would then execute those commands to create, update, or delete resources. The problem was that Tiller often needed broad, cluster-level permissions to manage applications, making it a significant security risk and a central point of failure. Helm 3 eliminated Tiller entirely. Now, the **Helm client interacts directly** with the Kubernetes API server, just like `kubectl` does. This was a crucial improvement because it means Helm now uses the user's own security credentials and permissions defined by **Kubernetes RBAC**. This simplifies the architecture, enhances security by removing the overly permissive shared service, and makes managing deployments a more standard and secure process.

How to develop templates in Helm

Templates in the `templates/` directory leverage the Go template language, offering powerful features:

- **Built-in objects**: Access chart and release metadata with objects such as `.Chart`, `.Values`, and `.Release`
- **Value references**: Insert configuration parameters using syntax such as `{{ .Values.key }}`
- **Functions and pipelines**: Transform data with functions such as `{{ quote .Values. key }}`
- **Flow control**: Use `if/else` conditionals and `range` loops for template logic

- **Named templates:** Reusable snippets for common tasks, promoting **Don't Repeat Yourself (DRY)** principles

Here's an extended example that showcases various template features:

```yaml
apiVersion: v1
kind: ConfigMap
metadata:
  name: {{ .Release.Name }}-config
  labels:
    app: {{ .Chart.Name }}
data:
  favoriteDrink: {{ .Values.favorite.drink | default "coffee" | quote }}
  greeting: {{ if .Values.greeting }}{{ .Values.greeting }}
{{ else }} "Hello, World!" {{ end }}
  items: |
    {{- range .Values.items }}
    - {{ . | quote }}
    {{- end }}


---


apiVersion: apps/v1
kind: Deployment
metadata:
  name: {{ .Release.Name }}-deployment
spec:
  replicas: {{ .Values.replicas | default 2 }}
  selector:
    matchLabels:
      app: {{ .Chart.Name }}
  template:
    metadata:
      labels:
        app: {{ .Chart.Name }}
    spec:
      containers:
        - name: {{ .Chart.Name }}-container
          image: {{ .Values.image.repository }}:{{ .Values.image.
```

```
tag | default "latest" }}
        ports:
          - containerPort: {{ .Values.service.port }}
        env:
          - name: CONFIG_GREETING
            valueFrom:
              configMapKeyRef:
                name: {{ .Release.Name }}-config
                key: greeting
```

You can find the complete code here: https://github.com/PacktPublishing/Cracking-the-Kubernetes-Interview/blob/main/chapter-10/helm-example.yml.

Let's take a closer look at some of the key components in this example:

- ConfigMap: Uses default values and conditional logic for configuration purposes
- Deployment: Illustrates the use of templates for the metadata and spec sections, employing .Values for configuration flexibility
- **Flow control**: Demonstrated with conditionals and loops to handle lists

This template structure allows for comprehensive customization, making it suitable for a wide range of applications.

What are the advanced features of Helm charts?

Helm charts offer several advanced capabilities that enhance Kubernetes application management:

- **Chart dependencies**: These allow you to build complex applications by composing **multiple charts**, each handling specific components. This modular approach allows for easy management and updates.
- **Hooks**: You can use these to execute tasks at specific points during a release's life cycle, such as when running database migrations before deploying a new version. This feature helps automate **pre- and post-deployment tasks**, ensuring smooth transitions.
- **Tests**: Helm charts define tests to verify that your chart deploys and functions correctly. These tests provide confidence in your deployments, ensuring stability and reliability.
- **Repositories**: Helm can host charts in remote repositories for easy sharing and reuse across teams and organizations. This facilitates collaboration and standardization, making it simpler to manage and distribute Helm charts within your organization.

These advanced features make Helm a powerful tool for Kubernetes application life cycle management, streamlining complex deployments and enhancing team collaboration.

How do Helm and Kustomize compare?

Although Helm is the de facto standard, some companies and people prefer to use Kustomize. Sometimes, they use these tools separately, though in some rare scenarios, they use them together. In technical interviews, you may be asked about the differences between them. The following easy-to-follow table compares Kustomize and Helm:

Property	Kustomize	Helm
Approach	Kustomize applies overlays to a base set of manifests, making customization straightforward.	Helm uses templating, leveraging Go templates to generate Kubernetes manifests.
Ease of use	Kustomize is simpler to start with as it uses intuitive YAML overlays.	Helm has a steeper learning curve due to its templating language.
Packaging and sharing	Kustomize focuses on per-application customization without a packaging concept.	Helm excels in packaging applications into reusable charts, which makes it ideal for version control and sharing.
Native integration	Kustomize integrates directly with kubectl, enabling easy application of Kustomizations.	Helm requires separate installations and commands to deploy charts.
Imperative versus declarative	Kustomize encourages a declarative approach, which is ideal for configuration variations.	Helm's templates allow for imperative logic and dynamic manifest generation.
Flexibility	Kustomize's overlays provide precise, constrained customizations.	Helm offers extensive flexibility with its templating.

Table 10.1 – Key differences between Kustomize and Helm

Interview tip

Question: *How does Helm's templating capability make it more flexible than Kustomize's overlay system? What is the trade-off?*

Answer: Helm's use of the Go template language allows for powerful, **imperative logic** to be implemented directly within your manifests, which makes it very flexible. You can use conditionals (if/else), loops (range), and functions to dynamically generate manifests based on the values provided. For example, you could deploy a secondary container, but only if a certain value is set to true. The trade-off for this flexibility is **complexity**. Helm has a steeper learning curve, and complex templates can become difficult to read and debug. Kustomize, by contrast, is template-free and purely declarative, making its customizations simpler and more predictable, though less powerful.

Summary

In this chapter, we explored various deployment scenarios in Kubernetes, emphasizing best practices and real-world applications. We discussed several deployment strategies, including rolling updates, blue-green deployments, canary deployments, and A/B deployments, each offering distinct benefits such as zero downtime, rapid rollbacks, and controlled testing of new features. These strategies empower us to choose the best approach for different use cases, ensuring efficient and reliable application management.

We also examined two powerful tools: Helm and Kustomize. Helm simplifies complex deployments through its templating capabilities, making it ideal for packaging and sharing reusable application components. Its ability to manage versioning and rollbacks enhances deployment flexibility. On the other hand, Kustomize provides a declarative, overlay-based approach, allowing for straightforward customization without the need for templating. This makes it an excellent choice for managing environment-specific configurations.

By comparing Helm and Kustomize, we highlighted their unique strengths and how they complement each other in Kubernetes workflows. Helm excels in packaging and dynamic configuration, while Kustomize focuses on simplicity and clarity with its YAML-based overlays.

In the next chapter, we'll learn about GitOps, a paradigm that applies Git-based workflows to Kubernetes operations. This approach promotes collaboration, enhances configuration management, and streamlines deployments. Understanding GitOps principles and practices will further strengthen our capabilities in managing Kubernetes environments effectively. So, let's get started and explore the world of GitOps!

Unlock this book's exclusive benefits now

UNLOCK NOW

Scan this QR code or go to `https://packtpub.com/unlock`, then search for this book by name.

Note: Keep your purchase invoice ready before you start.

11

Understanding GitOps: Principles and Practices

Configuration management systems such as Ansible and Puppet have long allowed DevOps specialists to configure their infrastructure using code inside **virtual machines (VMs)**. This was a significant step forward, enabling consistent and repeatable setups. The next step in this evolution was **Infrastructure as Code (IaC)**, which became very popular as cloud providers allowed the configuration of their resources using code. Tools such as Terraform and CloudFormation emerged, empowering DevOps specialists to set up entire infrastructures—from cloud resources to configurations inside VMs—using code.

With IaC, storing configurations in Git became a common practice. Many began applying GitOps principles to this code, using Git as the single source of truth and offering a declarative way to manage infrastructure and applications. However, the first iterations of GitOps faced limitations, particularly when applied to virtual machines and traditional infrastructures.

The advent of Kubernetes addressed many of these limitations. Kubernetes' design was a natural fit for GitOps, making it much easier to implement effectively. This alignment has made GitOps the main approach for delivering applications to Kubernetes clusters.

In this chapter, we'll explore GitOps in detail. We'll cover its principles, advantages, and practical implementations, particularly focusing on how Kubernetes has enabled GitOps to become a powerful framework for managing infrastructure and applications. You'll see how GitOps streamlines workflows to make your deployments more predictable, secure, and auditable. Whether you are an experienced Kubernetes user or new to the concept, this chapter will equip you with the knowledge and skills to effectively implement GitOps in your environment.

Specifically, we will cover the following main topics:

- Introduction to GitOps principles and benefits
- How are GitOps practices implemented and what challenges might arise?
- What is Argo CD and what is its role in the GitOps ecosystem?
- Practical use cases and scenarios with Argo CD in GitOps
- Delving deeper – Advanced topics and patterns in Argo CD

Introduction to GitOps principles and benefits

GitOps is a framework that applies familiar DevOps practices—such as version control and CI/CD—to infrastructure automation. These practices include version control, collaboration, compliance, and **continuous integration/continuous deployment (CI/CD)**. The core principles of GitOps revolve around making infrastructure and application management more predictable, secure, and efficient.

What are the key principles of GitOps?

On the technical interview, your interviewer could ask this question as the first question discussing the GitOps approach. Here is an easy-to-follow list describing the core features and principles of the GitOps approach.

- **Declarative descriptions**: In GitOps, the entire system—both infrastructure and applications—is described declaratively. This means that you specify the desired state of your system rather than the steps to achieve that state. This approach creates a clear, unambiguous definition of what your infrastructure and applications should look like.

- **Version control in Git**: The desired state of the system is versioned in Git. This serves as the single source of truth. All changes to the system are made through pull requests, reviewed, and then merged into the main branch. This practice ensures that every change is documented and traceable.

- **Automated application of changes**: Once changes are merged into the main branch, they are automatically applied to the system. This is achieved through continuous delivery pipelines that deploy the new configurations to the infrastructure.

- **Continuous reconciliation**: Software agents continuously monitor the actual state of the system and ensure it matches the desired state defined in Git. If there is any divergence, the system is automatically reconciled to align with the desired state.

Interview tip

Question: *Explain the four core principles of GitOps and why a pull-based model is preferred.*

Answer: Principles: (1) Declarative desired state, (2) Versioned and immutable storage (Git), (3) Automatic reconciliation, (4) Continuous drift detection and convergence. Pull-based is preferred for security (no CI creds to clusters), auditability (agents log changes), and scalability (agents reconcile locally with backoff and retries). Webhooks accelerate detection but do not push changes.

These core principles give GitOps significant advantages for managing infrastructure and applications. The use of declarative descriptions and version control in Git streamlines collaboration and boosts productivity, allowing team members to review and discuss changes before they are merged. Automated application of changes and continuous reconciliation ensure that deployments are stable and consistent, minimizing configuration drift. Moreover, the comprehensive documentation and version control inherent in GitOps simplify compliance and auditing, while automated, immutable infrastructure deployments enable quicker, more reliable rollbacks. *Figure 11.1* illustrates the pull-based model central to GitOps: CI updates Git; Argo CD detects changes, renders manifests, and reconciles the cluster—no CI credentials in the cluster.

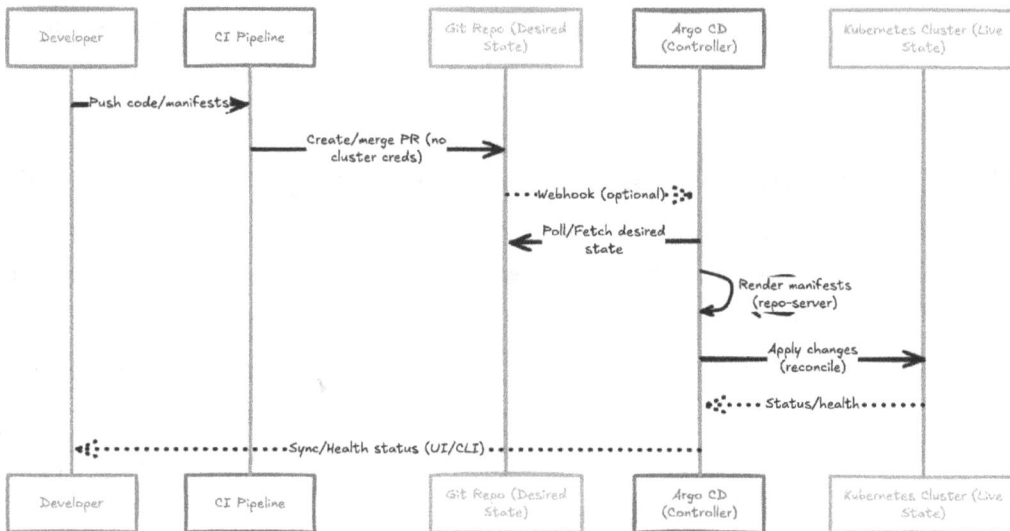

Figure 11.1 – GitOps pull-based reconciliation workflow

What are the benefits of adopting GitOps?

Adopting GitOps is a technically complex process that requires buy-in from the entire team. However, it also serves as an excellent opportunity to upskill members on modern, cutting-edge practices. Let's review the most important benefits of GitOps adoption:

- **Increased productivity and collaboration**: Using Git workflows enhances collaboration among team members. Changes are reviewed and discussed before being merged, improving code quality and team productivity.

- **Enhanced developer experience**: Developers can manage infrastructure using familiar Git tools, enabling self-service and reducing dependency on operations teams.

- **Improved stability and consistency**: With immutable infrastructure and continuous reconciliation, GitOps ensures that deployments are consistent and stable, reducing the chances of configuration drift. As shown in *Figure 11.1*, continuous reconciliation closes the loop and eliminates configuration drift.

- **Easier compliance and auditing**: Every change is version-controlled and documented in Git, simplifying compliance and auditing processes.

- **Simpler and faster deployments and rollbacks**: Automated deployments and the use of immutable infrastructure make rolling back to a previous state straightforward and quick.

Let's move forward and dive deeper into more important statements around GitOps. Understanding concepts such as IaC and declarative infrastructure provides a significant advantage in technical interviews.

What is declarative infrastructure and configuration as code?

Declarative infrastructure is a core concept in GitOps. Unlike an *imperative* approach (listing commands), a *declarative* approach lets you specify the desired end state. The system then automatically figures out the necessary steps to reach that state. This approach is known as IaC.

Tools such as Terraform, AWS CloudFormation, and Kubernetes facilitate the expression of infrastructure as declarative configuration files. These files can be stored in Git, reviewed via pull requests, and automatically applied. This process enables effective infrastructure management via GitOps.

Configuration management tools such as Ansible, Chef, and Puppet also allow defining the configuration of systems as code. You specify the desired state, and the tools ensure that the systems are configured accordingly. This declarative approach simplifies the management of complex environments and ensures consistency across deployments.

What is immutable infrastructure and how are deployments handled?

Immutable infrastructure is a cornerstone of GitOps. With immutable infrastructure, components are *replaced* for every deployment rather than being *updated in-place*. Once deployed, the infrastructure is *not changed*; any modifications are made by building new images with the required changes and deploying them.

This approach significantly reduces configuration drift, making deployments more consistent and reliable. If something goes wrong, rolling back is as simple as deploying the previous working version. Containerization plays a crucial role in enabling immutable infrastructure. Containers package applications along with their dependencies into immutable images. Deploying a new version involves building a new image and replacing the container, ensuring no configuration drift occurs.

GitOps leverages immutable infrastructure by storing the desired state in Git and using declarative tools to apply changes. This ensures that the running infrastructure always matches the state defined in Git, providing a robust and reliable deployment model.

Implementing GitOps involves setting up workflows that integrate closely with Kubernetes. This includes structuring repositories, defining Kubernetes manifests, and automating deployment processes. While GitOps offers significant advantages, it also presents challenges, such as managing secrets, handling complex workflows, and ensuring consistency across environments.

To overcome these challenges, it's essential to follow best practices and use appropriate tools. For instance, secrets management can be handled using tools such as Sealed Secrets or HashiCorp Vault. Complex workflows can be managed by breaking them down into smaller, manageable components and using GitOps operators such as Flux or Argo CD.

Putting these best practices into action requires a structured approach. The following sections will guide you through the key implementation steps and explore the common challenges you might encounter along the way.

How are GitOps practices implemented and what challenges might arise?

Implementing GitOps involves several critical steps. In this section, we'll cover setting up GitOps workflows with Kubernetes, structuring repositories, managing Kubernetes manifests, implementing promotion and deployment strategies, and handling secrets management. Let's explore these topics through a series of questions that you might encounter in an interview.

How do you set up GitOps workflows with Kubernetes?

Setting up a GitOps workflow with Kubernetes starts with defining your desired state in Git repositories. Here's how you can do it:

1. **Repository initialization:** How would you create and initialize a Git repository to store Kubernetes manifests and configurations?

   Start by creating a Git repository to act as the single source of truth for your infrastructure and applications.

2. **CI/CD Integration:** How do you integrate your repository with CI/CD pipelines?

   Use tools such as Jenkins, GitLab CI, or GitHub Actions to automate the validation and deployment of changes to your Kubernetes clusters.

3. **Deploying Argo CD or Flux:** What steps are involved in deploying a GitOps operator such as Argo CD or Flux into your Kubernetes cluster?

   Deploy Argo CD or Flux to monitor your Git repository and automatically apply changes to your cluster.

4. **Configuring webhooks:** How can webhooks be configured to trigger automatic deployments?

   Set up webhooks in your Git repository to trigger deployments whenever changes are pushed to the main branch. Webhooks only accelerate detection; reconciliation remains pull-based, as in *Figure 11.1*.

5. **Monitoring and alerting:** What tools can be used for monitoring and alerting in a GitOps workflow?

   Implement tools such as Prometheus and Grafana to monitor and visualize the status and performance of your GitOps workflows.

Beyond the general approach, interviewers often ask about best practices. Let's look at some key questions you might be asked.

How do you structure repositories for GitOps?

Properly structuring your Git repositories is crucial for efficient GitOps workflows. Consider these questions:

1. **Monorepo versus multi-repo**: Should you use a monorepo or multi-repo structure for GitOps, and why? Decide based on your needs: monorepos simplify dependency management, while multi-repos offer better isolation.

2. **Directory Structure**: How should you organize your repository's directory structure?

   Example structure:

   ```
   ├── environments
   │   ├── dev
   │   ├── staging
   │   └── production
   ├── applications
   │   ├── app1
   │   └── app2
   └── manifests
       ├── namespaces
       ├── services
       └── deployments
   ```

3. **Branching strategy**: What branching strategy should you adopt for managing deployments? Use branches such as `main`, `develop`, and `feature/*` to manage different stages of development and deployment.

4. **Git workflows**: How can Git workflows such as Git Flow or GitHub Flow improve your GitOps practices? Standardize how changes are proposed, reviewed, and merged to ensure consistency and collaboration.

> **Interview tip**
>
> **Question:** *Monorepo versus multi-repo for GitOps—trade-offs?*
>
> **Answer:** Monorepo: simpler discoverability, shared tooling, atomic changes across services; risk: larger CI scope, noisier history, permissioning complexity. Multi-repo: isolation, per-team autonomy, finer-grained access; risk: cross-repo coordination. Many orgs use multi-repo for apps plus a separate "infrastructure/live" repo.

Next, let's discuss the best practices for Kubernetes manifests management, the GitOps way.

How do you define and manage Kubernetes manifests in Git?

Kubernetes manifests define the desired state of your applications and infrastructure. Managing these in Git is essential. Ask yourself the following:

- **Declarative configuration:** What are the best practices for using declarative YAML files to define Kubernetes resources? Use declarative YAML files to describe the desired state of resources such as deployments, services, and config maps.

- **Modular manifests:** How can breaking down manifests into modular components help manage complexity? Modular manifests make it easier to manage and reuse configurations.

- **Templates and overlays:** How do tools such as Helm or Kustomize assist in creating templates and overlays? Templates and overlays allow for reusable components and environment-specific customizations.

- **Version control:** Why is it important to store Kubernetes manifests in Git and version them? Versioning provides an audit trail and simplifies rollbacks.

- **Validation and testing:** What tools can you use to validate and test Kubernetes manifests in a CI/CD pipeline? Tools such as kubeval or kube-score can validate manifests, while automated tests ensure correct deployments.

> **Interview tip**
>
> **Question:** *Kustomize versus Helm in GitOps?*
>
> **Answer:** Helm packages apps as charts with powerful templating and a rich ecosystem—great for third-party apps and platform add-ons—but templates can get complex and values can sprawl, so pin chart versions for deterministic GitOps. Kustomize composes plain YAML via bases and overlays, staying simple and deterministic for environment layering in first-party services, though it lacks dynamic templating. A common approach is to use Helm for vendor charts and Kustomize overlays for your own apps or to wrap those charts per environment.

After we decide how to store our code and manifests, we can discuss some best practices about the deployment strategies we can apply using the GitOps approach.

What are GitOps promotion and deployment strategies?

In the previous chapter, *Chapter 10*, we detailed deployment methods such as rolling updates, blue-green deployments, canary releases, and more. Here, we will briefly review which of these strategies are well-suited for GitOps workflows. Leveraging GitOps enhances these deployment methods with automated, declarative, and version-controlled practices, ensuring consistent, secure, and easily auditable deployments.

Promotion and deployment strategies are key to moving changes through different environments.

How do branch-based promotions work in a GitOps setup?

Branch-based promotions involve using branches to manage and promote changes through different environments. For example, you might promote changes from a `develop` branch to staging, and finally to main for production. This approach allows for systematic testing and validation at each stage, ensuring that only thoroughly vetted changes make it to production. Branch-based promotions also facilitate team collaboration by clearly delineating stages of the deployment pipeline.

What are the benefits of maintaining separate repositories for each environment?

Maintaining separate repositories for each environment provides isolation and independent management, allowing for more controlled and secure deployments. This setup ensures that changes in one environment do not inadvertently affect another, providing a clear separation of concerns. Additionally, it simplifies compliance and auditing by keeping environment-specific configurations and histories distinct and traceable. This approach can also improve security by restricting access to sensitive production environments.

How can pull request workflows facilitate change management in GitOps?

Pull request (PR) workflows enable teams to propose, review, and approve changes before merging them into the main branch. This process ensures that all changes are subjected to peer review, improving code quality and reducing the likelihood of errors. In a GitOps setup, PR workflows also provide an opportunity to run automated tests and validations on proposed changes, catching issues early in the deployment pipeline. This not only enhances collaboration but also promotes accountability and transparency in the deployment process.

How do automated deployments improve the efficiency of GitOps workflows?

Automated deployments streamline the GitOps workflow by ensuring that changes are applied to the infrastructure as soon as they are merged into the main branch. This reduces the time and effort required for manual deployments, minimizing human error and accelerating the deployment process. Automated deployments also enable continuous delivery, ensuring that the infrastructure is always up to date with the latest changes defined in Git. This leads to more consistent and reliable deployments, enhancing overall system stability.

What are canary releases and progressive delivery, and how do they fit into GitOps?

Canary releases and progressive delivery strategies involve gradually rolling out changes to a subset of users or environments to reduce risk and ensure stability before full deployment. In a GitOps context, these strategies can be implemented using automated deployment pipelines that control the rollout process based on predefined criteria. This allows teams to monitor the impact of changes and quickly roll back if issues are detected, providing a safer and more controlled way to introduce updates. Integrating these strategies with GitOps allows teams to use version control and automated reconciliation to manage gradual rollouts effectively.

> **Interview tip**
>
> **Question:** *How do you implement canary with Argo Rollouts and Argo CD?*
>
> **Answer:** Define a Rollout resource with canary steps, traffic routing via service mesh/ Ingress/Gateway; use AnalysisTemplates referencing Prometheus or other metrics; Argo CD treats Rollouts like any CRD and syncs desired state; rollback is automatic if analysis fails.

How do you handle secrets management with GitOps?

Managing secrets is one of the biggest challenges in GitOps. The core issue lies in Git repositories, designed for version control and collaboration, making them unsuitable for storing sensitive information. Storing secrets in Git exposes them to potential unauthorized access, as anyone with access to the repository could view or modify these secrets. Additionally, once secrets are committed to a Git repository, they become part of the version history, making it difficult to completely remove them if they are inadvertently exposed.

Given these challenges, you must implement robust solutions for secrets management in GitOps. The following sections cover effective strategies by exploring questions often encountered when discussing advanced Kubernetes topics, where having strong answers provides a significant advantage.

How can you use external secret management tools?

External secret management tools such as HashiCorp Vault, AWS Secrets Manager, and Azure Key Vault provide robust security and access controls for managing secrets. These tools store secrets outside of Git and provide APIs to retrieve them securely at runtime. Integrating these tools with your GitOps workflow ensures sensitive information is never exposed in your repositories, which maintains the confidentiality and integrity of your secrets.

For a more Kubernetes-native approach, many teams adopt the **External Secrets Operator** (**ESO**). This powerful operator extends the Kubernetes API with a custom resource called `ExternalSecret`. Instead of storing any encrypted data in Git, you commit a simple `ExternalSecret` manifest. This manifest acts as a pointer, defining which secret to fetch from an external provider such as HashiCorp Vault, AWS Secrets Manager, or Azure Key Vault, and what to name the resulting native Kubernetes Secret.

The ESO runs within your cluster, watches for these `ExternalSecret` resources, and automatically performs the following workflow:

- It authenticates with the external secret management tool.
- It securely fetches the specified secret data.
- It creates a standard Kubernetes Secret in the cluster with the retrieved data.

This pattern is highly effective because your Git repository—the single source of truth—contains no sensitive information whatsoever, not even in encrypted form. Your application Pods can then mount the synchronized, native Kubernetes Secret as they normally would, completely unaware of the underlying mechanism. This provides a clean separation of concerns and aligns with the strictest security postures while remaining fully compatible with GitOps principles.

How do sealed secrets work and why are they beneficial?

Sealed Secrets, a solution provided by Bitnami, allows you to encrypt secrets before committing them to Git. These sealed secrets can only be decrypted by the controller running in your Kubernetes cluster. This ensures that even if the encrypted secrets are stored in a public repository, they cannot be decrypted without the proper keys. Using Sealed Secrets provides a balance between GitOps principles and security, allowing you to manage secrets as code while keeping them protected.

For an interview, demonstrating that you understand the trade-offs between these two popular approaches is crucial. Here is a direct comparison:

Criteria	Sealed Secrets	External Secrets Operator (ESO)
Setup Complexity	Simpler. Requires installing a controller and using the kubeseal CLI.	More complex. Requires installing the operator and connecting it to an external secret store (such as Vault or a cloud provider's manager).
Secret Storage	Secrets are encrypted and stored in Git along with other manifests.	Only a pointer to the secret is stored in Git. The actual secret data remains in a separate, secure system.
Developer Workflow	Developers use a CLI (kubeseal) to encrypt secrets before committing to Git.	Developers commit a manifest that references the external secret. No special encryption CLI is needed.
Separation of Concerns	Lower. Encrypted secrets live in the same repository as application code.	Higher. A clean separation where Git contains no sensitive data, not even encrypted.
Best For...	Teams wanting a straightforward, self-contained solution with everything in Git.	Teams needing to integrate with existing secret managers or enforce very strict security policies.

Table 11.1 – Sealed Secrets versus External Secrets Operator

How can environment variables and ConfigMaps be used for non-sensitive configuration data?

For non-sensitive configuration data, you can use Kubernetes ConfigMaps and environment variables. ConfigMaps allow you to decouple configuration artifacts from image content, making it easier to manage configuration updates. By storing non-sensitive data separately, you reduce the risk of exposing critical information. Environment variables can also be used to inject configuration data at runtime, providing a flexible way to manage application settings without hardcoding them into your Git repositories.

What access controls should be implemented for Git repositories and CI/CD pipelines?

Implementing strict access controls for your Git repositories and CI/CD pipelines is essential to ensure that only authorized personnel can view or modify secrets. Use **role-based access control (RBAC)** to define who can access, modify, or deploy configurations. Regularly audit access logs and monitor for any unauthorized attempts to access your secrets. By enforcing strong access controls, you can minimize the risk of unauthorized access and maintain the security of your GitOps workflows.

Why is regular audit and monitoring important for secret management?

Regular audits and monitoring help detect and prevent unauthorized access to your secrets. Implement logging and monitoring tools to track access and changes to your secrets. Continuous monitoring allows you to quickly identify and respond to potential security breaches, ensuring that your secrets remain protected. By maintaining a vigilant approach to audit and monitoring, you can enhance the overall security of your GitOps practices.

Implementing these strategies allows you to effectively manage secrets in a GitOps environment, ensuring your sensitive information remains secure while you benefit from the automation and efficiency of GitOps.

After understanding the intricacies of setting up GitOps workflows, structuring repositories, and managing secrets, it's essential to follow the tools that facilitate these processes. One of the most powerful and popular tools in the GitOps ecosystem is Argo CD.

As we delve into the next section, we will examine what Argo CD is and its vital role in enhancing GitOps practices. Leveraging Argo CD helps teams streamline their continuous delivery pipelines and ensures their Kubernetes clusters are always in sync with the desired state in their Git repositories. This section will provide an in-depth look at Argo CD's features, benefits, and how it integrates seamlessly into the GitOps workflow.

What is Argo CD and what is its role in the GitOps ecosystem?

While **Argo CD** is one of the most popular tools for implementing GitOps, it's not the only one. Other tools, such as Flux, Jenkins X, and Weave GitOps also provide robust solutions for GitOps practices. However, Argo CD stands out due to its extensive feature set and strong community support. This chapter focuses on Argo CD, addressing the most common questions about its architecture, concepts, and functionalities. Let's dive into what makes Argo CD a preferred choice for many Kubernetes practitioners.

What is Argo CD architecture?

Argo CD consists of three main components that work together to ensure your applications remain in sync with the desired state defined in your Git repositories:

1. **Application controller**: This component continuously monitors applications, comparing their live state against the desired state as specified in the Git repository. When discrepancies are detected, the application controller can take corrective actions to reconcile the two states.

2. **Repository server**: Repository Server maintains a local cache of your Git repositories and is responsible for generating Kubernetes manifests. This caching mechanism helps optimize performance by reducing the need for frequent `git fetch` operations.

3. **API server**: The API server provides endpoints for the Argo CD web UI, CLI, and external systems, facilitating deployment management and enhancing security. It allows users to interact with Argo CD through a RESTful API, making it easier to automate and integrate with other tools.

Let's look at the high-level picture representing how Argo CD works, with all important components listed:

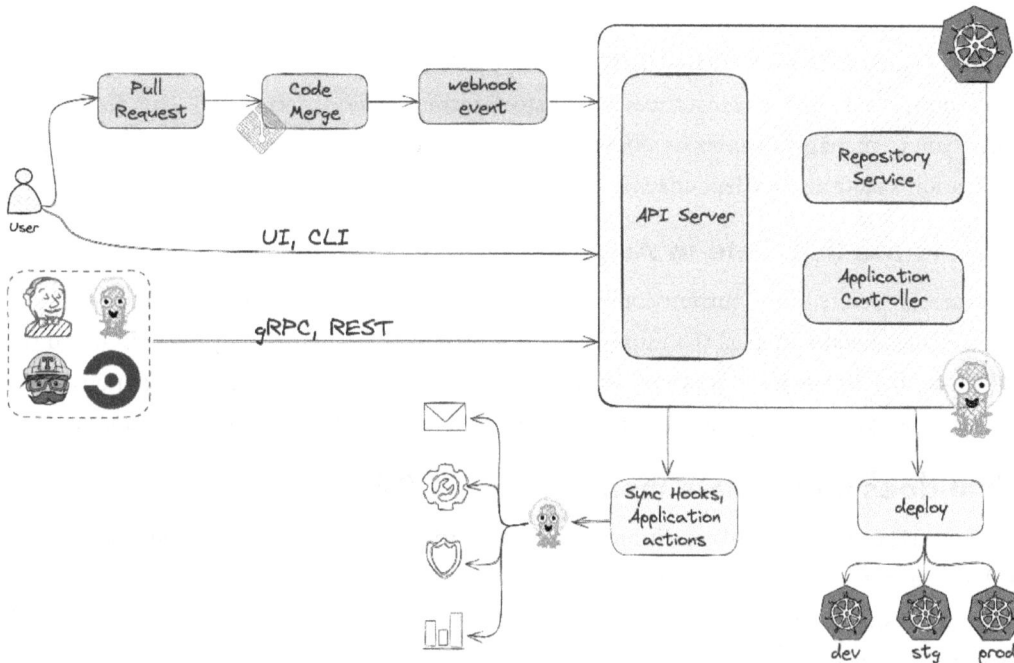

Figure 11.2 – Argo CD architecture

These components work in unison to automate and manage the deployment of applications, ensuring that your live infrastructure always reflects the desired state defined in your Git repositories.

What are the key concepts in Argo CD?

Understanding the basic concepts of Argo CD is crucial for effectively using the tool. Let's explore some key terms you should be familiar with by answering the questions that follow.

What role does the Argo CD Controller play?

The application controller is the heart of Argo CD, installed in your Kubernetes cluster. It implements the Kubernetes controller pattern to continuously monitor and reconcile applications. By comparing the live state of your applications against the desired state specified in the Git repository, the application controller ensures that your infrastructure remains consistent and aligned with your defined configurations. If discrepancies are found, the controller takes corrective actions to bring the live state in sync with the target state.

How does Argo CD define an application?

In Argo CD, an application is a collection of Kubernetes resources that collectively deploy and manage your workload. This is more than just a single deployment or service; it's an organized group of resources that are treated as a single entity. Argo CD stores the details of these applications within your cluster as instances of a **custom resource definition (CRD)**. This abstraction allows you to manage complex deployments more efficiently, providing a holistic view of your application's state and its dependencies.

What is the live state in Argo CD?

The live state refers to the current condition of your application within the Kubernetes cluster. This includes details such as the number of Pods running, the images they are using, and the current configuration of services and deployments. The live state is dynamic and changes as the application runs, reflecting real-time data about the operational environment of your applications.

What does target state mean in Argo CD?

The target state is the desired condition of your application as defined in your Git repository. This declarative state specifies how your application should be configured and operated, including the exact versions of images, the desired number of replicas, and specific configurations for each resource. When you make changes to your application's configuration in the Git repository, the target state is updated. Argo CD then works to align the live state with this target state through automated synchronization processes.

What happens during a refresh in Argo CD?

During a refresh, Argo CD fetches the latest target state from your Git repository and compares it against the current live state in the Kubernetes cluster. This process helps identify any differences between the desired configuration and the actual running state of the application. A refresh does not necessarily apply changes but serves as a crucial step to detect deviations and prepare for synchronization. This comparison ensures that any drift from the target state is promptly identified.

What is the sync process in Argo CD?

Syncing is the process by which Argo CD applies the changes identified during a refresh to bring the live state in line with the target state. Each sync operation methodically updates the live state to match the configurations specified in the Git repository. This might involve deploying new versions of applications, adjusting resource configurations, or scaling services. The sync process ensures that your Kubernetes cluster is always running the precise configurations you've defined, maintaining consistency and reducing the risk of configuration drift.

By understanding and leveraging these key concepts, you can effectively implement and manage GitOps workflows using Argo CD. The clear separation between live state and target state, coupled with automated monitoring and synchronization, ensures that your deployments are reliable and consistent. This approach not only simplifies managing complex Kubernetes applications but also enhances collaboration, as changes are tracked and managed through a version-controlled system.

What are the key features of Argo CD?

Argo CD has become a highly popular tool in the GitOps ecosystem, and this is largely due to its extensive feature set, which addresses the core needs of modern Kubernetes application management. Let's explore why Argo CD stands out and what functionalities make it such a powerful tool.

Why is Argo CD so popular?

Argo CD's popularity stems from its ability to automate and streamline the deployment process while maintaining a high degree of reliability and consistency. By integrating deeply with GitOps principles, Argo CD ensures that application deployments are not only automated but also version-controlled and auditable. Its support for multiple configuration management tools, robust security features, and user-friendly interfaces make it a versatile choice for teams of all sizes.

How does Argo CD automate deployments?

Argo CD automates the deployment of applications to specified target environments, significantly reducing the need for manual intervention and the likelihood of errors. Once the desired state is defined in a Git repository, Argo CD continuously monitors the repository for changes. When a change is detected, it automatically updates the live state of the application to match the desired state. This automation ensures that deployments are consistent and reliable, adhering to the configurations specified in Git.

How does Argo CD ensure GitOps-style deployments?

Argo CD ensures GitOps-style deployments by syncing the application state with the desired state declared in Git. This means that any changes to the application's configuration in the Git repository are automatically applied to the Kubernetes cluster. The continuous synchronization between the repository and the cluster maintains consistency, ensuring that the live state always matches the target state. This automated syncing process simplifies deployments and reduces configuration drift.

Which configuration management tools does Argo CD support?

Argo CD supports a wide range of configuration management and templating tools, providing flexibility in managing Kubernetes manifests. Some of the key tools supported include the following:

- **Kustomize**: Allows the customization of Kubernetes configurations
- **Helm**: Facilitates packaging and deploying Kubernetes applications
- **Jsonnet**: Provides a flexible way to generate Kubernetes manifests
- **Plain YAML**: Supports straightforward YAML configuration files

This support for multiple tools allows teams to choose the best fit for their workflows and easily integrate Argo CD into their existing setup.

What SSO integrations does Argo CD offer?

Argo CD enhances security and user management through **Single Sign-On** (**SSO**) integration with various identity providers, including the following:

- OpenID Connect (OIDC)
- OAuth2
- LDAP
- SAML 2.0

- GitHub
- GitLab
- Microsoft
- LinkedIn

These integrations allow users to authenticate using their existing credentials, simplifying access management and improving security.

How does Argo CD handle multi-tenancy and authorization?

Argo CD handles multi-tenancy and authorization through RBAC and multi-tenancy features. RBAC allows administrators to define fine-grained permissions, ensuring that users have access only to the resources they need. Multi-tenancy features enable the isolation of different teams or projects within the same Argo CD instance, providing a secure and organized way to manage multiple environments.

> **Interview tip**
>
> **Question:** *What is an AppProject and how does it enforce multi-tenancy?*
>
> **Answer:** The AppProject is an Argo CD CRD that scopes allowed source repos, destinations (clusters/namespaces), cluster-scoped kinds, resource quotas/limits, sync windows, and RBAC roles. It prevents apps from deploying to unauthorized clusters/namespaces or reading from unapproved repos.

Security best practice: When configuring Argo CD, always follow the principle of least privilege. An Argo CD instance should only have permissions to manage the specific namespaces defined in its target destination(s). Avoid giving it cluster-wide `cluster-admin` privileges in production. Use Argo CD projects to enforce stricter RBAC on who can deploy what and where.

What rollback capabilities does Argo CD provide?

Argo CD provides robust rollback capabilities, enabling quick recovery from errors. Users can easily roll back to any previously committed application configuration stored in the Git repository. This feature is particularly useful in case of deployment failures or unexpected issues, as it allows for immediate reversion to a known good state, minimizing downtime and disruption.

How does Argo CD analyze application health status?

Argo CD includes a comprehensive health status analysis of application resources. It monitors the health of various Kubernetes objects such as Pods, Services, and Deployments, providing real-time insights into the state of your applications. Health checks and status assessments help in maintaining the stability of deployments, allowing for proactive management and troubleshooting.

What interfaces does Argo CD offer for managing applications?

Argo CD provides both a web UI and a CLI for managing applications, offering flexibility in how users interact with the tool:

- **Web UI**: An intuitive, user-friendly interface that provides real-time views of application activity, deployment statuses, and sync operations. The web UI makes it easy to visualize the state of your applications and perform administrative tasks.
- **CLI**: A powerful command-line interface that offers comprehensive control over Argo CD operations. The CLI is ideal for scripting, automation, and integration with other tools, providing a robust way to manage deployments programmatically.

Argo CD's extensive feature set, including automated deployments, support for multiple configuration tools, SSO integration, RBAC, rollback capabilities, health status analysis, and versatile interfaces, makes it a standout choice for implementing GitOps in Kubernetes environments. These features collectively enhance the efficiency, security, and reliability of application deployments, solidifying Argo CD's place as a leading tool in the GitOps ecosystem.

In the next section, we will explore practical use cases and scenarios with Argo CD in GitOps. This will include real-world examples of how Argo CD can be leveraged to streamline deployments and manage complex Kubernetes environments. We'll also look at how Argo CD's features can be applied to maximize efficiency and security in your GitOps workflows.

Practical use cases and scenarios with Argo CD in GitOps

One common use case for Argo CD is deploying and managing cluster add-ons and performing cluster bootstrapping. In this scenario, a platform or infrastructure team is responsible for provisioning add-ons such as the Prometheus Operator or Argo Workflows controller to multiple Kubernetes clusters.

Here are the related key points:

- **Automation across many clusters**: Argo CD allows automating add-on deployment across many clusters, ranging from tens to thousands. This ensures that all clusters are consistently configured with the necessary add-ons.

- **Targeting specific clusters**: You can target specific subsets of clusters using labels and selectors. This is useful when different clusters need different configurations or add-ons.

- **Git-managed manifests**: Add-on manifests are stored in Git, and Argo CD syncs them to the clusters. This ensures that the desired state is version-controlled and auditable.

- **Flexible generators**: Argo CD supports different generators (list, cluster, git) to define target clusters. This flexibility allows for more dynamic and scalable management of clusters.

This approach provides a scalable way to manage the lifecycle of cluster add-ons in a GitOps manner, ensuring consistency and reliability across all environments.

How can Argo CD enable self-service for applications on multi-tenant clusters?

Another powerful use case is enabling developer self-service for applications on multi-tenant Kubernetes clusters. The goal is to allow developers to deploy their own applications to one or more clusters in an automated way using Argo CD, without needing administrator involvement for each deployment.

The key aspects of this use case are as follows:

- **Developer-defined manifests**: Developers define application manifests in their own Git repositories. This empowers them to control their application configurations and deployments.

- **Argo CD project and RBAC rules**: Argo CD projects and RBAC rules govern which clusters and namespaces developers can deploy to. This ensures that developers have the autonomy they need while maintaining control and isolation.

- **Automated provisioning**: Argo CD automates the provisioning of developer applications, reducing the need for manual intervention and accelerating the deployment process.

This self-service model empowers developers with more autonomy while still adhering to the organization's governance policies, fostering innovation and agility.

How does Argo CD manage the promotion of applications across environments?

Argo CD is also used to manage the promotion of applications across different environments, such as development, staging, and production.

A typical workflow includes the following:

1. **Feature branch changes**: Developers make changes to application code and manifests in a feature branch.

2. **Merge after testing**: Changes are merged to the main branch after thorough testing and review.

3. **Automatic deployment to dev**: Argo CD automatically deploys the new version to the development environment.

4. **Promotion to staging and production**: After further testing, the change is promoted to staging and then production by updating the Argo CD application configuration to point to the new version.

5. **Branching/tagging support**: Utilizes Argo CD's Git branching and tagging support for smooth promotion workflows.

6. **Consistent deployment**: Ensures that the desired version is deployed in each environment.

7. **Easy rollback**: Rollback is straightforward by reverting the Argo CD application configuration to the previous version.

8. **CI/CD integration**: Integrates seamlessly with CI/CD pipelines to automate the workflow.

This entire flow can be visualized as follows:

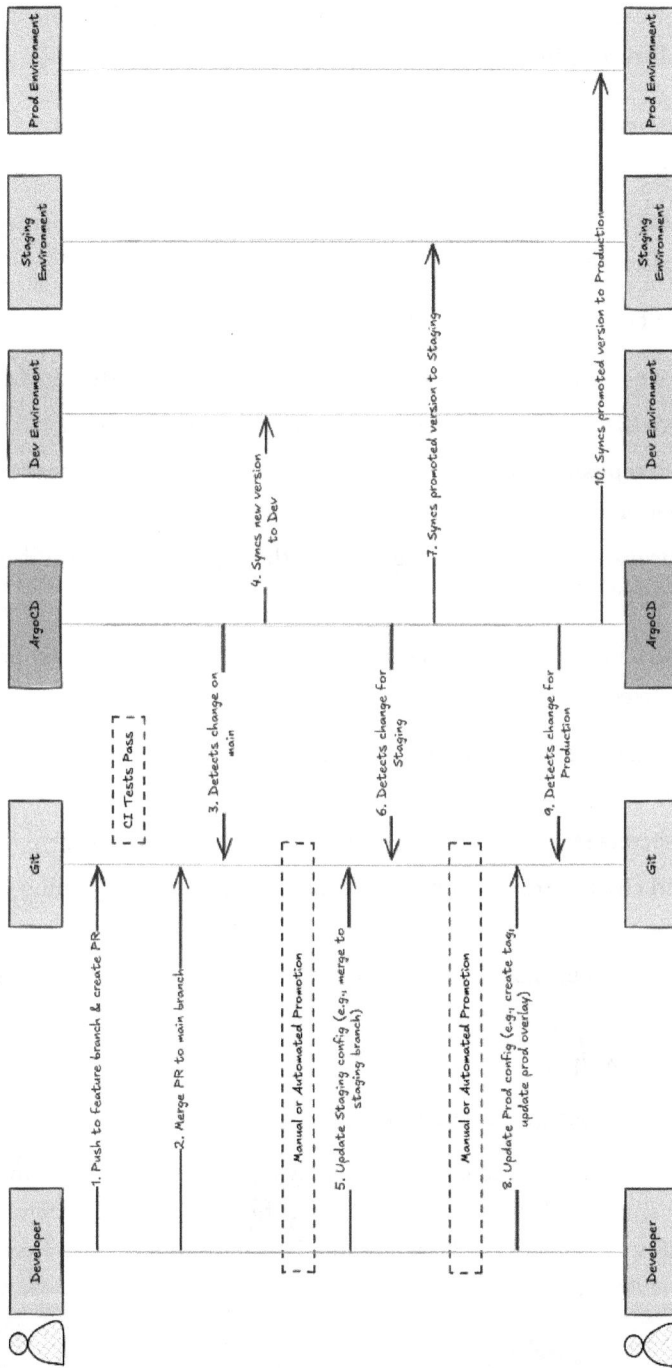

Figure 11.3 – Application promotion: the process of moving a version across environments

This use case showcases how Argo CD enables repeatable, auditable deployments across the software delivery lifecycle, enhancing efficiency and reliability.

How can Argo CD help with disaster recovery and cluster rebuilding?

GitOps with Argo CD is invaluable for disaster recovery scenarios where Kubernetes clusters need to be rebuilt from scratch.

Here are the steps of the recovery process:

1. **Provision a new cluster**: Start by provisioning a new Kubernetes cluster.

2. **Install Argo CD**: Install Argo CD on the newly provisioned cluster.

3. **Point to Git repositories**: Configure Argo CD to point to the Git repositories that contain the application manifests.

4. **Sync applications**: Argo CD will then sync all the applications and add-ons to the cluster based on the Git state.

There are more considerations you should know about the disaster recovery process and other components connected with Argo CD itself:

- **Highly available Git repositories**: Ensure the Git repository is highly available and backed up

- **External secrets store**: Use an external secrets store to persist secrets outside of Git

- **Automated cluster provisioning**: Automate the cluster provisioning process to speed up recovery

- **Regular testing**: Regularly test the disaster recovery procedure to verify its effectiveness

> **Interview tip**
>
> **Question:** *Outline a GitOps-based DR plan for an EKS cluster.*
>
> **Answer:** IaC to recreate VPC/EKS; bootstrap Argo CD; point to infra/addons/app repos; use ESO for secrets; restore PV data from snapshots or external DB backups; verify with runbooks and regular game days. Ensure Git is HA and keys are available (SOPS/ESO).

Implementing GitOps with Argo CD provides a reliable way to recover Kubernetes environments in the face of disasters, reducing downtime and complexity.

How does Argo CD support deploying applications to multiple clusters?

Argo CD supports deploying applications to multiple Kubernetes clusters from a single Argo CD instance, which is useful for several scenarios.

Let's have a look at some scenarios:

- **Multi-cluster components**: An application that has components deployed to multiple clusters
- **Regional deployments**: Deploying the same application to many clusters in different regions
- **Centralized management**: Centralizing the management of applications across clusters

Argo CD supports the deployment in the preceding scenarios in the following ways:

- **Git-managed manifests**: Application manifests are stored in Git as usual
- **Multi-cluster spec**: The Argo CD application spec defines multiple target clusters and namespaces
- **Syncing across clusters**: Argo CD handles syncing the manifests to the various clusters, ensuring consistent deployments

This multi-cluster support is a key feature that enables complex multi-cluster deployments with Argo CD, providing centralized control and efficiency.

These use cases demonstrate how Argo CD can be applied to solve real-world challenges around deploying and managing applications in Kubernetes environments. Its GitOps architecture, multi-cluster support, and rich feature set make it a valuable tool for various scenarios. By automating deployments, enabling self-service, managing promotions across environments, supporting disaster recovery, and facilitating multi-cluster deployments, Argo CD proves to be an essential component in modern Kubernetes management.

In the next section, we will explore advanced Argo CD patterns such as the "App-of-Apps" pattern and ApplicationSets. These patterns help manage complex Kubernetes environments more effectively. Additionally, we will cover best practices for implementing these patterns to maximize efficiency and security in your deployments.

Delving deeper — Advanced topics and patterns in Argo CD

In this section, we will explore advanced patterns in Argo CD, specifically the *App-of-Apps* pattern and *ApplicationSets*. These patterns are essential for managing complex Kubernetes environments more effectively and enhancing your GitOps practices. They are often discussed in interviews to assess your advanced knowledge of Kubernetes and Argo CD. Understanding and being able to implement these patterns can significantly improve your ability to manage and scale Kubernetes deployments. Let's dive into how these patterns work, their benefits, and when to use them.

What is the App-of-Apps pattern?

The **App-of-Apps pattern** solves a common problem: how do you manage your Argo CD applications themselves using GitOps? Simple. You create a single "root" Argo CD application that doesn't point to your app's code (like a Deployment manifest). Instead, it points to a Git directory full of *other* Argo CD application manifests. When you sync the root app, Argo CD creates all the "child" applications, which then go on to deploy your actual microservices. It's a powerful way to bootstrap an entire environment from a single source.

How it works

1. **Create a root application:** You start by creating a root application that points to a Git directory containing application manifests for child apps

2. **Define child applications:** Each child application manifest then points to a directory containing the actual Kubernetes manifests for that app, such as deployments and services

3. **Monitor and sync:** Argo CD will monitor and sync the root application, which in turn creates the child applications based on the manifests

4. **Deploy child applications:** Child applications then sync and deploy the actual app's Kubernetes manifests to the cluster

Benefits

- **Centralized management:** Enables managing multiple apps via a single root application resource

- **Logical grouping:** Allows the grouping of logically related apps composed of Helm charts and Kubernetes YAML

- **Efficient monitoring:** Provides a single *watcher* app to monitor and sync multiple child apps

- **GitOps management**: Enables *GitOps* style management of the application resources themselves

Here is how it looks in a high-level picture depicting everything in one place:

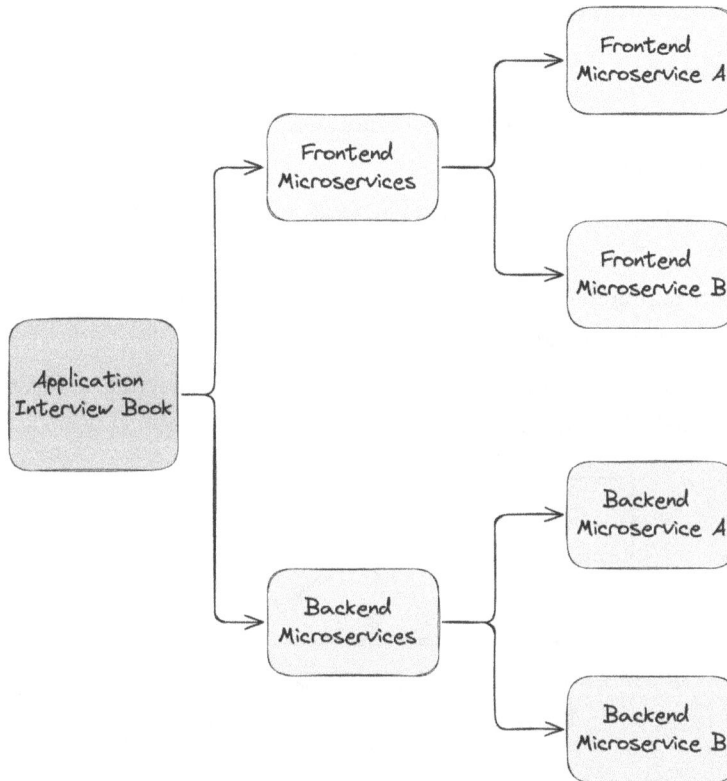

Figure 11.4 – The "App-of-Apps" pattern

When to use

- **Bootstrapping new clusters**: When setting up a new cluster with multiple applications
- **Managing related apps**: When grouping related apps into a single management unit
- **GitOps for application resources**: When implementing GitOps for the Argo CD application resources themselves

Now let's talk about another Argo CD object, called ApplicationSet, which brings us further in implementing more complex solutions using the GitOps approach.

What is ApplicationSet?

ApplicationSet builds on the App-of-Apps concept to provide a more flexible way to automate the generation of Argo CD applications. It allows you to define templates for applications and generate them dynamically based on various parameters.

How it works

1. **Define an ApplicationSet resource**: Create an ApplicationSet resource that defines how to generate application manifests.

2. **Use generators**: ApplicationSet uses generators (list, cluster, git, etc.) to generate parameters.

3. **Substitute parameters**: Parameters are then substituted into an application template to generate application manifests.

4. **Monitor and sync**: Argo CD will monitor and sync the generated applications based on the ApplicationSet definition.

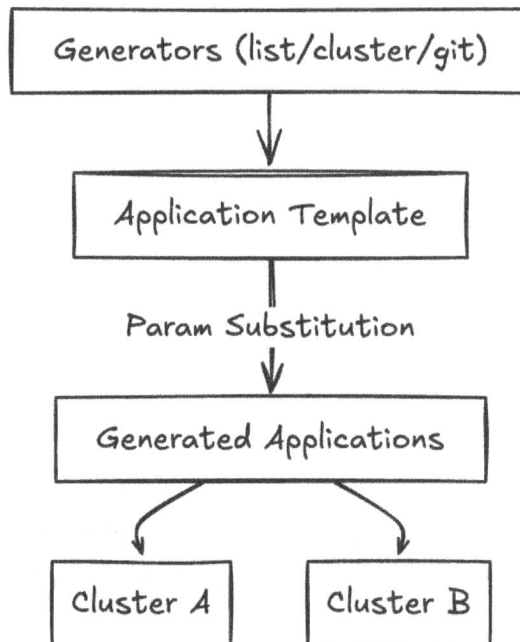

Figure 11.5 – ApplicationSet generators and templating flow

As shown in *Figure 11.5*, generators feed parameters into a template to produce per-destination applications that Argo CD then reconciles.

Benefits

- **Templating for multiple clusters/environments**: Enables templating applications for **multiple clusters/environments** from a single ApplicationSet

- **Automated generation**: Automates application generation based on Git or Argo CD settings (e.g., clusters)

- **Advanced use cases**: Supports more advanced use cases such as deploying from multiple Git repos

- **Consistency and efficiency**: Reduces manual effort and ensures consistency in application configuration

When to use

- **Multi-cluster deployments**: When deploying an app to multiple clusters or environments

- **Automated application generation**: When automating application generation based on Git repo structure (e.g., monorepo pattern)

- **Self-service deployment**: When enabling self-service app deployment for different teams using a single Argo CD instance.

Now let's compare both patterns (approaches) to be able to answer questions about the pros and cons of them.

How do these two patterns compare?

Both the App-of-Apps pattern and ApplicationSet enable key GitOps benefits such as automation, consistency, and scalability. However, they cater to different levels of complexity and use cases:

- **App-of-Apps**: Provides a straightforward way to group and manage multiple applications. Ideal for simpler scenarios where you need a centralized management point.

- **ApplicationSet**: Offers more advanced capabilities and automation. Suitable for complex environments requiring dynamic application generation across multiple clusters and teams.

Think of it this way: **App-of-Apps** is for when you have a known, finite set of applications to manage. **ApplicationSet** is for when you need to dynamically generate applications from a template, such as for multi-cluster deployments or creating ephemeral preview environments for every pull request.

Example: Implementing the App-of-Apps pattern

Let's look at a practical example of implementing the App-of-Apps pattern:

1. **Step 1: Create the root application**

    ```yaml
    apiVersion: argoproj.io/v1alpha1
    kind: Application
    metadata:
      name: root-app
      namespace: Argo CD
    spec:
      project: default
      source:
        repoURL: 'https://github.com/your-org/your-repo.git'
        targetRevision: HEAD
        path: root-apps
      destination:
        server: 'https://kubernetes.default.svc'
        namespace: Argo CD
      syncPolicy:
        automated:
          prune: true
          selfHeal: true
    ```

💡 **Quick tip**: Enhance your coding experience with the **AI Code Explainer** and **Quick Copy** features. Open this book in the next-gen Packt Reader. Click the **Copy** button

(1) to quickly copy code into your coding environment, or click the **Explain** button

(2) to get the AI assistant to explain a block of code to you.

Copy   Explain
 ①   ②

```
function calculate(a, b) {
  return {sum: a + b};
};
```

🔒 **The next-gen Packt Reader** is included for free with the purchase of this book. Scan the QR code OR go to https://packtpub.com/unlock, then use the search bar to find this book by name. Double-check the edition shown to make sure you get the right one.

Note

While **v1alpha1** may seem like a pre-release version, it is the long-standing, stable API version for Argo CD's core Custom Resources. The Argo CD project has maintained this for backward compatibility. Mentioning this nuance can demonstrate a deeper, practical understanding of the tool.

1. **Step 2: Define child applications**

   In the root-apps directory, create individual application manifests for each child application.

   ```yaml
   apiVersion: argoproj.io/v1alpha1
   kind: Application
   metadata:
     name: child-app1
     namespace: Argo CD
   spec:
     project: default
     source:
       repoURL: 'https://github.com/your-org/your-repo.git'
       targetRevision: HEAD
       path: apps/child-app1
     destination:
       server: 'https://kubernetes.default.svc'
       namespace: default
     syncPolicy:
       automated:
         prune: true
         selfHeal: true
   ```

   Repeat the preceding manifest for additional child applications.

2. **Step 3: Monitor and sync**

   Argo CD will automatically monitor the root application and create the child applications as defined.

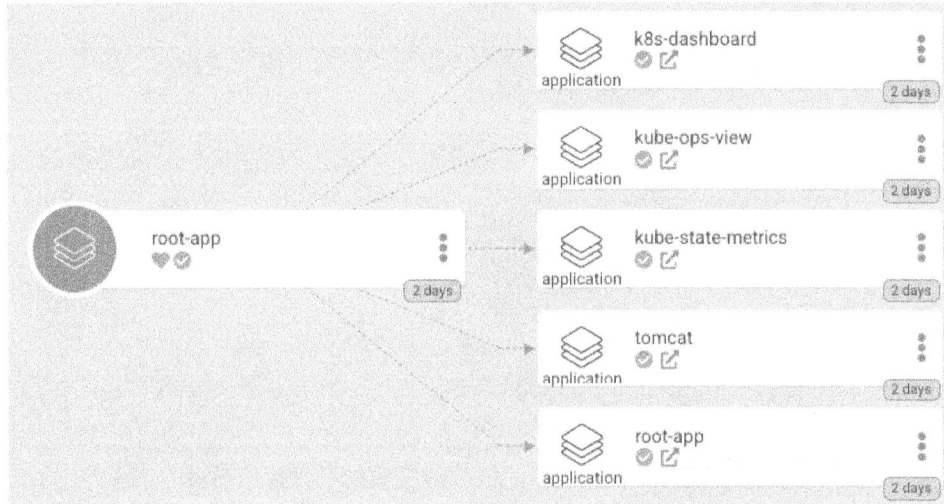

Figure 11.6 – App-of-Apps implementation

Example: Implementing ApplicationSet

Now, let's see how to implement ApplicationSet for more dynamic application management:

1. **Step 1: Define an ApplicationSet resource**

```
apiVersion: argoproj.io/v1alpha1
kind: ApplicationSet
metadata:
  name: apps
  namespace: Argo CD
spec:
  generators:
  - list:
      elements:
      - cluster: cluster-a
        url: 'https://cluster-a.example.com'
      - cluster: cluster-b
        url: 'https://cluster-b.example.com'
  template:
    metadata:
      name: '{{cluster}}-app'
    spec:
      project: default
```

```
source:
  repoURL: 'https://github.com/your-org/your-repo.git'
  targetRevision: HEAD
  path: apps/{{cluster}}
destination:
  server: '{{url}}'
  namespace: default
syncPolicy:
  automated:
    prune: true
    selfHeal: true
```

2. **Step 2: Monitor and sync**

   Argo CD will dynamically generate and sync applications for each cluster defined in the list generator.

   Both the App-of-Apps pattern and ApplicationSet provide robust solutions for managing Kubernetes applications with Argo CD. The App-of-Apps pattern is ideal for simpler scenarios where centralized management is needed, while ApplicationSet offers advanced automation and flexibility for complex multi-cluster and multi-environment deployments. By understanding and implementing these patterns, you can enhance your GitOps workflows, achieving greater automation, consistency, and scalability.

Summary

In this chapter, we explored GitOps and its implementation using Argo CD. We started by understanding the core principles of GitOps, including declarative infrastructure, version control, automated deployments, and continuous reconciliation. These principles improve the predictability, security, and efficiency of managing Kubernetes environments.

Argo CD plays a crucial role in integrating GitOps practices with Kubernetes. We examined its architecture, focusing on the application controller, Repository Server, and API server, and how they work together to maintain the desired state of applications as defined in Git repositories.

Key concepts such as live state, target state, refresh, and sync processes were discussed, providing a foundation for effectively utilizing Argo CD. We also highlighted Argo CD's features, including support for multiple configuration management tools, SSO integration, RBAC, and multi-cluster deployments.

Practical use cases demonstrated Argo CD's application in real-world scenarios, from automating cluster add-ons and enabling developer self-service to managing application promotion and facilitating disaster recovery. We also covered the advanced *App-of-Apps* pattern and ApplicationSets, which offer sophisticated management and automation of applications.

As we conclude our discussion on GitOps and Argo CD, it's essential to recognize that this entire automated, declarative framework, from Argo CD's Application CRD to the App-of-Apps pattern, is built upon the ability to extend the Kubernetes API. Understanding this core mechanism is the next step in your journey. In the next chapter, we will dive into the **Custom Resource Definitions (CRDs)** and operators that make tools such as Argo CD possible.

Unlock this book's exclusive benefits now

UNLOCK NOW

Scan this QR code or go to `https://packtpub.com/unlock`, then search for this book by name.

Note: Keep your purchase invoice ready before you start.

Part 5

Reliability, Monitoring, and Maintenance

This part will help you keep your Kubernetes clusters healthy and running smoothly. You'll learn how to spot issues before they become problems, monitor what's happening inside your system, and carry out updates and maintenance without downtime. We'll also cover how to apply these best practices to custom resources, so your entire setup—built-in or custom—stays reliable and efficient.

This part of the book includes the following chapters:

- *Chapter 12, Custom Resource Definitions and Operators*
- *Chapter 13, Ensuring High Availability and Reliability*
- *Chapter 14, Monitoring Best Practices*
- *Chapter 15, Backup, Maintenance, and Disaster Recovery in Kubernetes*

12

Custom Resource Definitions and Operators

In Kubernetes, the ability to extend the core functionalities to suit specific application requirements is vital. **Custom resource definitions (CRDs)** and **Operators** are two powerful tools that allow you to do that, providing greater flexibility and control over your Kubernetes environment.

CRDs enable you to create resource types within Kubernetes. These custom resources function just like the standard, built-in resources such as Pods and Services. By defining CRDs, you can tailor Kubernetes to understand and manage custom resources specific to your application needs. This is particularly useful when the default Kubernetes objects must fully address your requirements.

Operators take the concept of CRDs a step further. While CRDs allow you to define custom resources, Operators enable you to automate the management of these resources. An Operator is a controller that uses CRDs to manage the lifecycle of complex applications.

Operators encode operational knowledge into software, allowing Kubernetes to manage applications automatically. This includes deploying, scaling, healing, and backing up applications. By using Operators, you can ensure that applications are handled consistently and efficiently, reducing the operational burden.

In this chapter, we will discuss the most critical questions that can be asked during technical interviews with CRDs and Operators.

We will cover the following key topics in this chapter:

- How can the basic API of Kubernetes be extended?
- What is a CRD?
- What is a Kubernetes Operator?
- How can you develop an Operator?
- What are some examples of Operators you know?

So, let's get started!

How can the basic API of Kubernetes be extended?

Kubernetes is a powerful orchestration platform that provides a robust and extensible API, allowing users and components to interact with and manage the cluster. Understanding how to extend this API is crucial for tailoring Kubernetes to specific needs and enhancing its capabilities. This chapter will examine the Kubernetes API, including its structure, storage, and various methods for extending its functionality.

How does the Kubernetes API separate different resources?

The Kubernetes API serves as the core interface for managing all operations within the cluster. It exposes endpoints for various resources, allowing users to **create, read, update, and delete** (**CRUD**) these resources. The API is organized into different groups and versions, ensuring a clear and structured approach to managing the diverse components of Kubernetes. Let's take a look at them:

- **API groups**: The Kubernetes API is divided into multiple groups to categorize resources logically. For example, the core group includes essential resources such as Pods and Services, while the apps group includes higher-level resources such as Deployments and StatefulSets.

- **API versions**: Each API group can have multiple versions (e.g., v1, v1beta1, etc.). These versions allow for the evolution and improvement of the API while maintaining backward compatibility. This versioning system ensures that changes and new features can be introduced without disrupting existing deployments.

API groups and versions are the foundation for the API server's functionality. But how does it work in real clusters? Let's move forward and learn about components such as CRDs and Operators.

How do you list all available API groups?

kubectl (and the API in general) provides several ways to list all CRDs in general and specific API groups:

```
> kubectl crds
alertmanagers.monitoring.coreos.com
podmonitors.monitoring.coreos.com

…

> kubectl api-resources
> kubectl api-resources --api-group= monitoring.coreos.com
NAME        SHORTNAMES    APIVERSION      NAMESPACED    KIND
alertmanagerconfigs  amcfg            monitoring.coreos.com/v1alpha1    true
AlertmanagerConfig
alertmanagers      am              monitoring.coreos.com/v1          true
Alertmanager
```

Using those two commands, you can check the support of the API objects in your cluster and use the command samples as your response to this question, which you may be asked in the interview.

What is a CRD?

CRDs are a powerful Kubernetes feature that allows users to create custom resources. These custom resources extend the Kubernetes API to support new types of objects beyond the built-in ones, such as Pods, Services, and Deployments. Using CRDs, you can define and manage resources specific to your application or operational needs, enabling a higher degree of customization and flexibility within your Kubernetes environment. CRDs will allow you to add Kubernetes functionality specific to your applications. For instance, you can create custom resources for managing complex application configurations, operational workflows, or third-party services. To fully leverage custom resources, you often pair them with custom controllers. These controllers watch for changes to custom resources and perform necessary actions, effectively automating the management of your custom resources. Typically, these controllers are a part of the operator, which we will discuss later.

A CRD is a blueprint for a custom resource. It defines the schema, validation rules, and other characteristics of the custom resource. Custom resources can be namespaced or cluster-scoped. This is described in the CRD specification and determines whether the resource is available within a specific namespace or across the entire cluster. To create a CRD, write a YAML file specifying the custom resource's schema, including its metadata, specifications, and validation rules. Let's prepare a CRD for the packt.com book object, which contains two fields in the spec: book (which represents the name) and year. It will look like the following:

```yaml
---
apiVersion: apiextensions.k8s.io/v1
kind: CustomResourceDefinition
metadata:
  name: books.packt.com
spec:
  group: packt.com
  names:
    kind: Book
    listKind: BookList
    plural: books
    singular: book
  scope: Namespaced
  versions:
  - name: v1
    schema:
      openAPIV3Schema:
        properties:
          apiVersion:
            type: string
          kind:
            type: string
          metadata:
            type: object
          spec:
            properties:
              book:
                type: string
              year:
                type: integer
            type: object
          status:
            type: object
        type: object
```

Once the YAML file is ready, apply it to your Kubernetes cluster using the `kubectl apply -f <crd-file>.yaml` command. This registers the CRD with the Kubernetes API server, making the new custom resource type available.

After a CRD is registered, you can create, read, update, and delete instances of your custom resource using standard Kubernetes commands. For example, to create a new instance of a custom resource, you would write a YAML file for the resource and apply it using `kubectl apply -f <resource-file>.yaml`.

Here is a resource file example for our CRD managing book objects:

```
---
apiVersion: packt.com/v1
kind: Book
metadata:
  name: k8s-interview-guide
spec:
  book: "K8S interviewing guide"
  year: 2024
```

This knowledge is enough to answer questions related to the topic of CRDs. Now, we can move on and discuss webhooks and Operators.

What is a Kubernetes Operator?

A **Kubernetes Operator** is a method of packaging, deploying, and managing a Kubernetes application. An Operator extends the Kubernetes API with custom resources and controllers, automating the management of applications and resources. Operators simplify the deployment and lifecycle management of complex applications on Kubernetes by encoding operational knowledge into software.

Operators leverage CRDs to define new types of resources that represent an application's desired state. A custom controller, a vital operator component, manages these custom resources. The controller continuously monitors the state of the custom resource and performs necessary actions to reconcile the actual state with the desired state.

The concept of Operators was introduced to address the challenge of managing stateful applications on Kubernetes. Stateless applications, such as web servers, are relatively simple to operate using standard Kubernetes primitives. However, stateful applications, such as databases, require more complex operations such as backups, restores, scaling, and upgrades. Operators automate these tasks, ensuring consistency and reducing the manual effort to manage these applications.

Critical components of a Kubernetes Operator and its roles

First, a Kubernetes Operator almost always includes CRDs (as we discussed) together with appropriate **custom resources (CRs)** that it uses to manage resources in the cluster.

It also includes the following components:

- **Controller**: This is the core component of a Kubernetes Operator. It contains the logic to manage the application lifecycle and ensure that the actual state matches the desired state specified in the CR. The controller continuously watches for changes to the CRs and takes appropriate actions to reconcile differences. This process is known as the **reconciliation loop**. In other words, it ensures that the application is correctly deployed and configured, adjusts the number of instances based on specified criteria or workload demands, manages application upgrades while ensuring minimal downtime and preserving data integrity, detects and recovers from failures to maintain application availability, and collects metrics and health information to make informed decisions about the application's state.

  The reconciliation loop is not really a component; it's a fundamental pattern used by the controller. It operates continuously, checking the desired state specified in the CR against the application's actual state. If discrepancies are found, the controller takes action to align the actual state with the desired state. This loop ensures that the application remains in the desired configuration and can respond dynamically to changes.

- **Event handlers**: These are mechanisms within the controller that respond to changes in the Kubernetes cluster. They watch for events such as creating, modifying, or deleting CRs. When such an event occurs, the handler triggers the reconciliation loop to process the change and update the application's state accordingly.

- **Client libraries**: These are used by the controller to interact with the Kubernetes API. An example is the Kubernetes `client-go` library. These libraries provide the necessary functions to list, watch, create, update, and delete Kubernetes resources. The controller can perform the operations required to manage the application and its components by leveraging client libraries.

- **Operator Lifecycle Manager (OLM)**: This is an optional but valuable component for managing the lifecycle of Operators. OLM simplifies the deployment, management, and upgrade of Operators within a Kubernetes cluster. It provides a standardized way to package, deploy, and maintain Operators, ensuring they are consistently managed and updated.

Operators also leverage other Kubernetes features, such as RBAC (please refer back to *Chapter 9* if you don't remember what this is), jobs, and so on, to make all the changes as smooth as possible. However, it's mostly up to the Operator developers to design and implement this logic.

On a high level, the Operator logic and workflow look like the following:

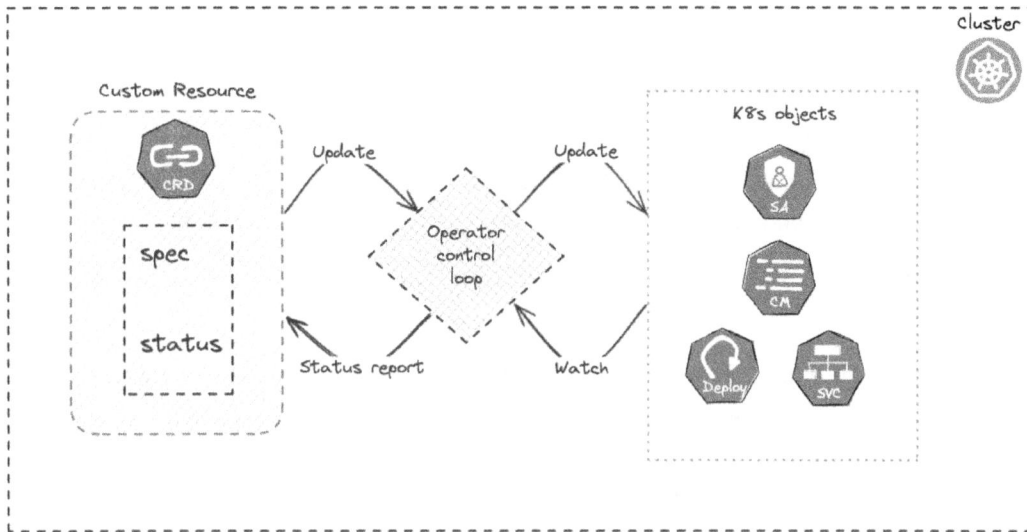

Figure 12.1 – Simplified Operator lifecycle

Figure 12.1 illustrates the control loop of a Kubernetes operator, which monitors and manages CRs defined by CRDs. The Operator observes changes in the CR's specification (spec), updates the status as needed, and manages related Kubernetes objects such as the **service account (SA)**, **ConfigMap (CM)**, Deployments, and Services to maintain the desired state of the application in the cluster.

What are Kubernetes webhooks?

This question is also related to CRDs and Operators because they were created to make using CRDs easier and more predictable using webhooks.

Kubernetes webhooks are HTTP callbacks that receive and process requests to customize and extend Kubernetes operations. They allow external services to interact with the Kubernetes API, enabling custom logic during the request processing lifecycle. Webhooks enforce policies, validate resource configurations, and mutate resource specifications, providing a flexible way to extend Kubernetes without modifying its core code base.

There are several types of webhooks in Kubernetes:

	Mutating Admission	Validating Admission	Conversion
Purpose	Modify objects before they are persisted in `etcd`	Validate objects before they are persisted	Convert CR objects between API versions
Use cases	Inject default values, modify configurations, or add fields	Enforce compliance, security policies, or validate configurations	Handle custom logic for converting resource definitions
Example	Automatically adding a sidecar container to Pods	Ensuring all pods have resource limits defined	Converting a `v1alpha1` CR to `v1beta1` during an upgrade

Table 12.1 – Various Kubernetes webhooks

Now that we know what the Operator does and how it works, let's try to better understand its internals to learn the answers to more real, experience-oriented questions about Operators.

How can you develop an Operator?

The process is straightforward, and we have already covered some parts of this question. In general, to develop your Operator, you must follow these steps:

1. **Prepare the architecture**: You must define all requirements (functional and non-functional), understand how your Operator will behave, and determine what exactly it should be responsible for. Here are the requirements for a sample Kubernetes Operator:

   - **Functional**: The Operator should create, update, and delete Kubernetes resources (e.g., Deployments, Services, and CMs) based on the CR's spec, ensuring that the application maintains the desired state. The Operator should update the CR's `status` field to reflect the current state of the application (e.g., number of running Pods, readiness state, etc.) and provide feedback for debugging and monitoring.

   - **Non-functional**: The Operator must handle a large number of CRs and manage them efficiently, even in high-demand clusters, without causing performance issues. The Operator should be resilient to failures, automatically recovering from errors and ensuring that managed resources reach the desired state even in the face of transient issues or node restarts.

2. **Define your custom resource**: At this stage, your team should define the CR your Operator will manage. This involves creating CRDs that specify the schema and validation rules for your CR.

3. **Set up your development environment**: This step is required before the actual development of the Operators. You need to select the framework (the most popular is the Operator SDK, which you can find at `https://github.com/operator-framework/operator-sdk`), define it, and install all required dependencies.

4. **Initiate the Operator project**: At this stage, you must create the bootstrap using your chosen framework. The following is an example command for the Operator SDK: `operator-sdk init`.

5. **Controller logic implementation**: This takes time and requires appropriate software development skills (in Golang, in most cases). The controller is the core component of the Operator that contains the logic to manage the CR (including the reconciliation logic to ensure the actual state matches the desired state specified in the CR).

6. **Implement resource creation and update handling logic**: This is the next step in using the Kubernetes client libraries to create, update, and delete Kubernetes resources based on the state of the CR.

7. **Build, test, and distribute the Operator as a package**: Follow DevOps best practices and ship your Operator as a Helm package for your clients.

We prepared a simple Operator using the Operator SDK (mentioned as an example earlier in the third point), implementing the CRD for the book we used before. This is for demonstration purposes only. It does the following: if it notices any book object in the cluster, it creates the Pod, which prints the book's information (name and year). You can find the source code in the book's accompanying GitHub repository at:

`https://github.com/PacktPublishing/Cracking-the-Kubernetes-Interview/tree/main/chapter-12`

What are some examples of Operators you know?

On this type of question, the interviewer can ask about the examples you've used before. Here is the list of the most used and well-known operators:

- **Prometheus Operator** simplifies the deployment and management of Prometheus monitoring instances. It abstracts the complex configuration required to deploy Prometheus and its associated components.

It can be found here: `https://github.com/prometheus-operator/prometheus-operator`.

These are the key features:

- Automates the creation and management of Prometheus instances
- Manages Prometheus configurations and rules
- Supports CRDs for Prometheus, Alertmanager, and related components

- **Elastic Cloud on Kubernetes** (**ECK**) provides a Kubernetes Operator to manage Elasticsearch, Kibana, and other Elastic Stack components. It ensures that these components are deployed, configured, and maintained correctly.

It can be found here: `https://github.com/elastic/cloud-on-k8s`.

These are the key features:

- Automates the deployment and management of Elasticsearch and Kibana
- Handles upgrades and scaling of Elastic Stack components
- Supports secure communication between Elastic Stack components
- Provides built-in monitoring and logging for Elastic Stack deployments

- **Kafka Operator (Strimzi)** provides a Kubernetes Operator to deploy and manage Apache Kafka clusters. It simplifies the complexity of running Kafka on Kubernetes.

It can be found here: `https://github.com/strimzi/strimzi-kafka-operator`.

These are the key features:

- Automates the deployment and configuration of Kafka clusters
- Manages Kafka topics and user configurations
- Supports rolling updates and scaling of Kafka brokers
- Provides monitoring and alerting for Kafka clusters

- **MySQL Operator** automates MySQL clusters' deployment, management, and operation on Kubernetes. It ensures high availability and simplifies database management.

It can be found here: `https://github.com/mysql/mysql-operator`.

These are the key features:

- Automates the creation and management of MySQL InnoDB clusters
- Supports automatic failover and recovery

- Provides easy scaling of MySQL instances
- Integrates with Kubernetes Secrets for secure credential management

- **MongoDB Operator** (**MongoDB Community Kubernetes Operator**) enables the management of MongoDB clusters on Kubernetes. It automates the deployment, scaling, and maintenance of MongoDB.

  It can be found here: `https://github.com/mongodb/mongodb-kubernetes-operator`.

  These are the key features:

  - Simplifies the deployment of MongoDB replica sets and sharded clusters
  - Supports automatic backups and restores
  - Provides monitoring and alerting for MongoDB instances
  - Integrates with Kubernetes Secrets for managing database credentials

Please keep in mind these Operators as examples because it will be a real advantage if you can not only answer the questions about Operators in general but also provide real examples that IT specialists across the world are using every day.

Summary

In this chapter, we delved into the concepts of CRDs and Kubernetes Operators, two pivotal elements that enhance Kubernetes' extensibility and automation capabilities. We began by understanding CRDs, which allow the creation of CR types tailored to specific application needs. This included a detailed look at how to define and manage CRDs and their role in extending the Kubernetes API to support new resource types.

Next, we explored Kubernetes Operators, which leverage CRDs to automate the management of complex applications. Operators encapsulate operational knowledge, enabling automatic application deployment, scaling, and maintenance. We discussed the critical components of Operators, including CRs, controllers, and the reconciliation loop, and walked through developing and deploying an Operator.

The chapter also covered various types of webhooks—mutating, validating, conversion, and authentication webhooks—and their use in conjunction with CRDs to enforce policies, validate configurations, and handle custom logic during API request processing.

By the end of the chapter, you gained a comprehensive understanding of how to extend Kubernetes using CRDs and Operators, how to implement CR management and automation, and how to integrate webhooks to enhance the functionality and security of your Kubernetes environment. This knowledge is crucial for anyone looking to manage and automate Kubernetes applications effectively, ensuring efficiency, consistency, and reliability.

In the next chapter, we're going to talk about Kubernetes clusters and the high-availability and reliability of applications, to be able to answer more complicated and production-related questions in interviews.

13

Ensuring High Availability and Reliability

In modern IT, constant uptime isn't a feature—it's a requirement. When users can't access a website, app, or service, it leads to frustration, a loss of trust, and financial damage. This is why high availability and reliability are crucial, both for the infrastructure and the applications running on top of it.

But what do these terms mean for your Kubernetes cluster and the apps it runs? In this chapter, we'll break down the key concepts of high availability and reliability, focusing on how Kubernetes ensures these at the cluster level, and how you can extend this to your applications running within the cluster.

We'll also provide practical tips to help you build a reliable, highly available Kubernetes environment, both for the platform itself and the apps it manages, and we'll dive into some interview-style questions to help you confidently explain these topics when you're asked about them in a Kubernetes interview.

This chapter will explore the core principles of high availability and how they apply within Kubernetes environments. It will guide you through designing highly available Kubernetes clusters, ensuring resilience at the infrastructure level. Additionally, you'll learn how to implement high availability across worker nodes and at the application layer to minimize downtime and maintain consistent performance under varying conditions.

We will cover the following main headings:

- The three pillars of a robust system: HA, reliability, and resiliency
- Securing the brain: control plane high availability
- Building a resilient workforce: worker node and application availability

The three pillars of a robust system: HA, reliability, and resiliency

Before we get into the details of how Kubernetes helps with high availability, reliability, and resiliency, it's important to understand what these terms mean. We'll start by defining what high availability means, how it differs from reliability and resiliency, and why these concepts are critical for any modern application running in a Kubernetes cluster.

What is high availability?

High availability (**HA**) means designing your system to stay operational even when parts of it fail. We measure it as a percentage of uptime per year. For example, a system with 99.9% availability has an expected downtime of just a few hours per year. The higher the availability, the more complex and resilient the system needs to be.

Here's a table showing how much downtime is allowed per year depending on the percentage of availability:

Availability (%)	Downtime per year
90% ("one nine")	36.5 days
99% ("two nines")	3.65 days
99.9% ("three nines")	8.77 hours
99.99% ("four nines")	52.56 minutes
99.999% ("five nines")	5.26 minutes

Table 13.1 – The "nines" of availability: permitted annual downtime

Notice how downtime shrinks dramatically with each "nine" you add. For example, moving from 99% (3.65 days of downtime) to 99.9% (8.77 hours of downtime) isn't just a 1% improvement—it's a 10x jump in the level of availability your system needs to achieve. This is because moving from 99% to 99.9% reduces downtime from 1% (of total time) to 0.1%, which is a tenfold increase in system complexity.

Example — HA in practice

Let's say you have an *online shopping application* running on Kubernetes. HA for this app means that it remains accessible to users even if something in the infrastructure fails. Here's how that works:

- You run **multiple replicas** of your app (e.g., 3 replicas of your shopping service) across different nodes
- If one of the nodes goes down, Kubernetes automatically shifts the load to the other nodes, keeping the app up and running without users noticing the failure

In short, Kubernetes keeps your app online by shifting work away from the failed node. This is essential for maintaining availability during failures.

What is reliability?

While high availability ensures that your application stays up and running, **reliability** focuses on how well your app performs over time. Even if your app is always available, it may not always function correctly. Reliability is about ensuring **consistent performance** and avoiding crashes, slowdowns, and errors.

For example, imagine your *online shopping application* is highly available, but sometimes during peak traffic (such as Black Friday), the app becomes slow, or certain features fail to load properly. The app is still technically "up," but if users experience frequent issues or slow performance, it isn't considered reliable.

Here's what might happen:

- Your app may experience slow response times or crashes during high traffic due to poor configuration or underlying infrastructure issues.
- Kubernetes may ensure the app remains running (HA), but if these performance issues occur regularly, your app is not reliable from the users' perspective.

Example — Reliability in practice

Let's go back to our *shopping application* example. Let's say it's Black Friday, and your app is experiencing a huge spike in traffic. Even though Kubernetes keeps your app running, customers are complaining about slow load times during checkout, or worse, the checkout page crashes occasionally.

- **HA:** Your app is always running and accessible (HA is achieved).
- **Reliability:** Despite being up, your app isn't performing well—it's slow or buggy. The system isn't consistently delivering the quality your users expect, which means it's not reliable.

Key point

Reliability is about *how well your app works over time*. To be reliable, your app needs to provide consistent performance, free from frequent slowdowns, crashes, or other issues. Simply being available isn't enough.

What is resiliency?

Resiliency is about how fast your application recovers from failure. It's not just about staying available but about bouncing back **quickly and effectively** after encountering issues. A resilient system can absorb failures, adapt, and recover while minimizing the impact on users.

For example, consider the **database** behind your shopping application. If one of the database nodes goes down, this might cause errors in your application. If your system is resilient, it can handle the failure and recover quickly, ensuring minimal downtime and impact on users. Here's how it could work:

- Kubernetes might automatically restart the affected Pods to recover from the failure
- Your system might have fallback mechanisms, such as a replicated database or a cached version of your app, which takes over until the database is back online

In this case, even though there was a failure, the system recovered fast enough that users experienced minimal disruption.

Example – Resiliency in practice

Now, let's imagine one of the **database nodes** for your shopping application crashes during a flash sale. Without resiliency, this would cause significant downtime, and users would be unable to complete their transactions. However, in a resilient system, the following would occur:

- Kubernetes automatically detects the issue and restarts the affected Pods
- A **replica of the database or a cached version of the app** steps in, allowing the app to continue functioning
- Once the database is back online, Kubernetes resumes normal operation

Key point

Resiliency is about *how fast your app can recover* from an issue and continue functioning. Even if something breaks, a resilient system can quickly recover and maintain service with minimal disruption to users.

Bringing it all together — HA, reliability, and resiliency

To see how these concepts work together, let's use a real-world scenario: an **e-commerce app** during a major flash sale. Here's how each of these concepts plays out during the sale:

1. **HA**: During the flash sale, your app is running across multiple servers, ensuring that if one server fails, the others keep your app available. Users can continue browsing and shopping without any noticeable disruption. Even if part of your infrastructure goes down, your system remains accessible to customers.

    Result: Your app stays **up and running**, meeting the high availability goal.

2. **Reliability**: Although your app is available, users are starting to experience slow response times during checkout. The app is struggling under the pressure of increased traffic, and some users are even encountering checkout failures. This indicates that while your app is available, it isn't **performing reliably** under the heavy load.

    Result: Your app **is highly available** but **not reliable** because it can't handle the load effectively.

3. **Resiliency**: Now, imagine that the overloaded database crashes completely. However, your system is resilient because you have a **replicated database** ready to take over. Kubernetes automatically redirects traffic to the backup, and users can continue with their purchases without significant downtime. The system bounces back quickly, and the impact on your users is minimal.

    Result: Your app **recovers quickly** from the database failure, demonstrating **resiliency**.

Here's a summary:

*   HA ensures your app stays up and running even when part of the infrastructure fails
*   Reliability ensures that your app functions correctly and consistently under normal and peak conditions
*   Resiliency ensures your app can recover quickly after a failure, minimizing user impact

Now that we understand the importance of HA, reliability, and resiliency, it's time to explore how Kubernetes can help you achieve these goals in practice. In the next section, we'll dive into the practical implementation of HA and resiliency in Kubernetes, including how to configure the control plane, worker nodes, and underlying infrastructure to ensure your system stays robust, even in the face of failure.

Securing the brain: Control plane high availability

This section dives deep into designing highly available, reliable, and resilient Kubernetes clusters. We will cover strategies for cluster-level HA, node-level HA, and ensuring reliable networking in Kubernetes environments. These strategies are critical for both the infrastructure and the applications running within the cluster.

By the end of this part, you'll be ready to implement HA features and explain them clearly during a Kubernetes interview. Let's start by exploring cluster-level HA, which includes setting up multiple control plane nodes, managing etcd clusters, and load balancing.

Cluster-level HA

Ensuring high availability at the cluster level is foundational for any Kubernetes environment. If the control plane is down, your cluster is effectively dead. This section focuses on **multi-control-plane setups**, **etcd clustering**, and **load balancing** for API servers. These are essential components to ensure your cluster stays operational even if part of the infrastructure fails.

What is a multi-control-plane setup in Kubernetes?

So, why is a multi-control-plane setup important for Kubernetes HA? In Kubernetes, the control plane (which includes the API server, etcd, controller manager, and scheduler) is responsible for managing the cluster's state and scheduling workloads. If the control plane fails, the entire cluster can be affected. A **multi-control-plane setup** ensures that if one control plane node goes down, others can take over, keeping your cluster operational.

A typical HA setup involves deploying **at least three control plane nodes** to ensure fault tolerance and quorum. Quorum ensures that distributed systems such as etcd can make safe decisions. An odd number of nodes (such as three or five) is crucial to tolerate failures without causing data corruption.

Example – Setting up a multi-control-plane cluster

Here's an example of a **kubeadm configuration** for a multi-control-plane setup:

```
apiVersion: kubeadm.k8s.io/v1beta4
kind: ClusterConfiguration
kubernetesVersion: stable
controlPlaneEndpoint: "LOAD_BALANCER_DNS:LOAD_BALANCER_PORT"
```

Let's take a look at the multi-control-plane architecture, as follows:

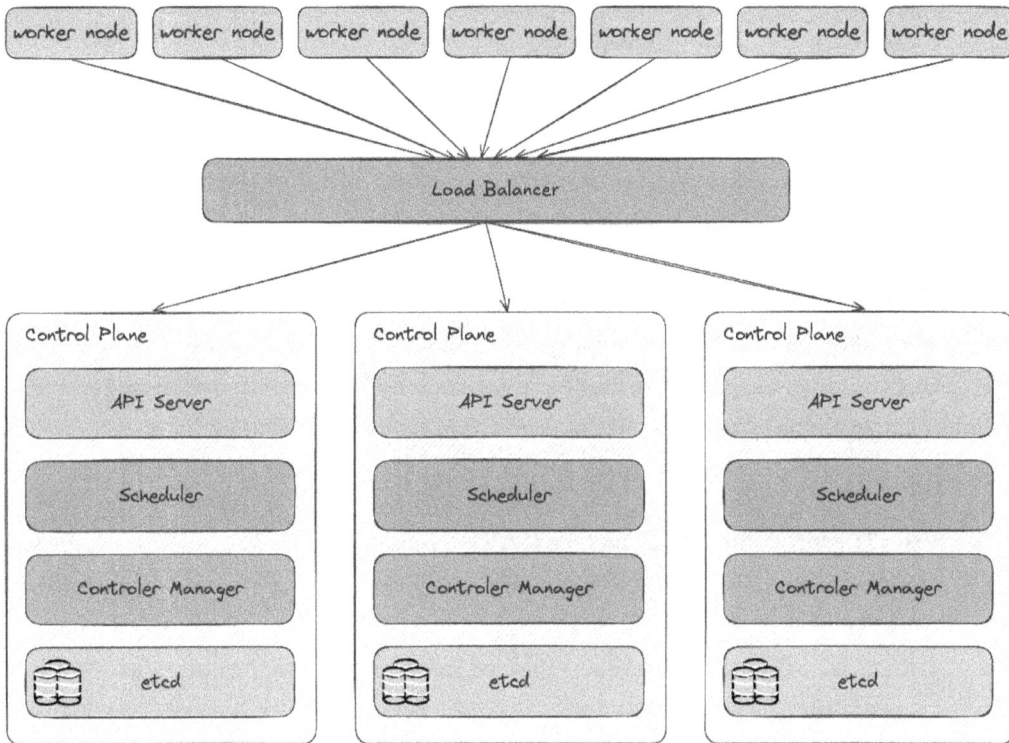

Figure 13.1 – Multi-control-plane architecture

In the configuration shown in *Figure 13.1*, we define a load balancer endpoint that will route traffic to the multiple API servers running across your control plane nodes. This ensures that if one API server fails, the load balancer redirects traffic to the remaining active API servers.

> **Interview tip**
>
> **Question**: *How do you achieve control plane HA in Kubernetes?*
>
> **Answer**: To achieve control plane HA, we set up a multi-control-plane cluster with at least three control plane nodes. We also use an external load balancer to distribute traffic across the API servers to prevent downtime if one of the API servers goes down.

Now that we've explored the importance of a multi-control-plane setup for achieving HA in Kubernetes, we must ensure that traffic to the control plane is efficiently distributed across these multiple control-plane nodes. This is where a load balancer becomes critical.

In a multi-control-plane configuration, you have multiple instances of the API server running across different nodes. This redundancy is great for uptime, but it creates a new problem: how do you know which API server to talk to?

A load balancer solves this problem by distributing traffic across all healthy API servers. It continually monitors the health of each API server through checks on port 6443 and redirects traffic away from any API server that becomes unhealthy. Without a load balancer, your users or systems could end up sending requests to an unavailable or overloaded API server, leading to downtime.

Load balancing for API servers

How do you load balance API servers in a Kubernetes cluster? In a multi-control-plane setup, you need to distribute incoming traffic to the API servers running on your control plane nodes. A **load balancer** achieves this by routing traffic to healthy API servers and avoiding any that are down.

Key strategies for load-balancing API servers include the following:

- **Use a TCP forwarding load balancer**: Services such as **AWS Elastic Load Balancing** (**ELB**) or Google Cloud Load Balancing are commonly used to handle traffic for Kubernetes control planes. These load balancers use TCP forwarding to route traffic to API servers.
- **Configure health checks**: Make sure the load balancer checks the health of each API server by performing health checks on port 6443 (the default `kube-apiserver` port). If an API server fails a health check, the load balancer will stop sending traffic to it.

Example – Load balancer configuration

Here's how you might configure a load balancer on AWS to handle traffic for your API servers:

- **Target group**: Create a TCP target group and add the control plane nodes as targets on port 6443.
- **Health check**: Configure a health check on the target group to verify the health of the API servers. The health check should be a TCP check on port 6443.

By using a load balancer, you ensure that API traffic is always routed to healthy API servers, improving the availability and reliability of the control plane.

Interview tip

Question: *Why do you need a load balancer for the API servers in a Kubernetes multi-control-plane setup?*

Answer: A load balancer is essential in a multi-control-plane setup because it distributes traffic across the API servers running on different control plane nodes. This ensures that if one API server goes down, the load balancer can redirect traffic to the remaining healthy API servers, preventing downtime.

While the load balancer ensures that traffic is properly routed to healthy API servers in a multi-control-plane setup, just as important, you must safeguard the control plane's data. This is where the etcd cluster comes into play.

Etcd is the central data store for Kubernetes, holding the state of the entire cluster. Ensuring that etcd is highly available and reliable is critical because if etcd fails or loses quorum, the cluster's ability to manage workloads can be severely impacted, even if the API servers are reachable through the load balancer.

Etcd clustering and backup strategies

Etcd is a critical component of the Kubernetes control plane, as it stores the entire cluster's state. Ensuring HA for etcd is essential. If etcd fails, you risk losing important data about your cluster, which could result in downtime or even cluster failure.

How do you ensure etcd HA?

What strategies can be used to ensure the HA of the etcd cluster in Kubernetes? To achieve high availability for etcd, you need to focus on two critical aspects: quorum and fault tolerance. Quorum is essential for the reliability of any distributed system such as etcd, which manages the state of your Kubernetes cluster.

What is quorum in etcd?

Quorum refers to the minimum number of etcd nodes that must agree on changes to the cluster state before they are committed. For an etcd cluster to function properly, more than half of the nodes (a majority) must be available and in agreement. This ensures that the system can tolerate failures without risking data corruption or inconsistencies.

For example, as we can see in the following diagram, in a three-node etcd cluster, a quorum would require at least two nodes to be available and in agreement. This means the cluster can tolerate the failure of one node but will stop functioning if two nodes go down.

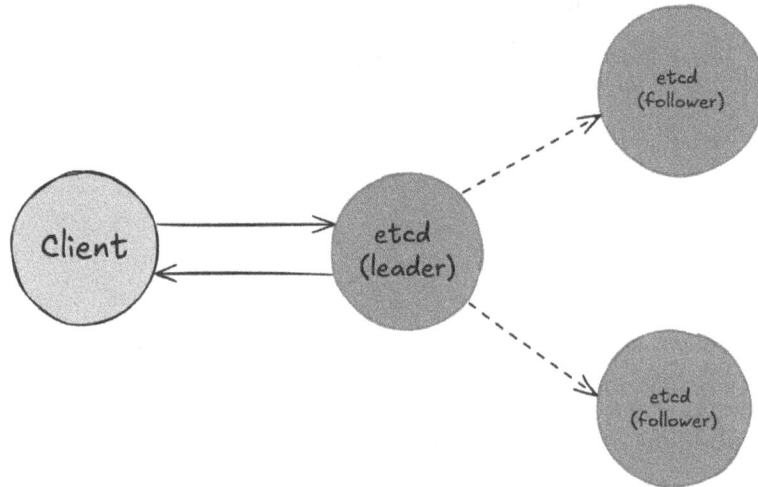

Figure 13.2 – Etcd quorum

When etcd loses quorum, it cannot make decisions or write new data to the cluster, leading to a loss of availability.

The following table illustrates how quorum works based on the number of etcd instances:

Number of instances	Quorum (nodes required)	Fault tolerance (nodes that can fail)
1	1	1
3	2	1
5	3	2
7	4	3

Table 13.2 – Etcd quorum and fault tolerance requirements

The following can be seen in *Table 13.2*:

- In a three-node etcd cluster, a quorum requires two nodes, allowing one node to fail without affecting the cluster's operation
- In a five-node etcd cluster, a quorum requires three nodes, and two nodes can fail while the cluster remains operational

- A seven-node etcd cluster increases the fault tolerance to three nodes but comes with added complexity and higher resource costs

> **Important note**
>
> While adding more nodes increases fault tolerance, it also introduces greater over-head in terms of performance and network traffic. It's generally recommended to start with a three-node etcd cluster unless you need more fault tolerance.

Strategies to ensure etcd HA

To achieve HA for etcd, you should do the following:

1. **Deploy etcd as a cluster**: A highly available etcd cluster should consist of at least three nodes to ensure quorum and fault tolerance. This allows etcd to continue operating even if one node fails.

2. **Use an external etcd cluster**: By deploying etcd as an external cluster, separate from the Kubernetes control plane, you improve both scalability and fault tolerance. This setup isolates etcd from any potential failures in the control plane, ensuring that your cluster state remains intact even if control plane components experience issues.

3. **Implement regular backups**: Backups are critical for recovery in case of etcd failure. Using etcdctl, you can automate etcd snapshots.

Here's an example command to back up etcd:

```
ETCDCTL_API=3 etcdctl snapshot save /path/to/backup.db \
  --endpoints=https://etcd1.example.com:2379, https://etcd2.example.
com:2379,https://etcd3.example.com:2379 \
  --cacert=/etc/etcd/pki/ca.pem \
  --cert=/etc/etcd/pki/etcd.pem \
  --key=/etc/etcd/pki/etcd-key.pem
```

Let's look at the explanation of this:

- `ETCDCTL_API=3`: Specifies the etcd API version (version 3 is the latest).
- `etcdctl snapshot save /path/to/backup.db`: Takes a snapshot and saves it to the specified path (`/path/to/backup.db`).
- `--endpoints`: Points to the etcd server URL. Here it's running locally (`https://127.0.0.1:2379`).
- `--cacert`, `--cert`, `--key`: These flags provide the necessary certificates and keys to authenticate with the etcd server securely.

The following figure shows a highly available Kubernetes architecture with a load balancer distributing traffic across multiple control plane nodes. Each control plane node runs key Kubernetes components such as the API server, scheduler, and controller manager. The etcd cluster is deployed externally with three nodes, ensuring HA and resilience against failures.

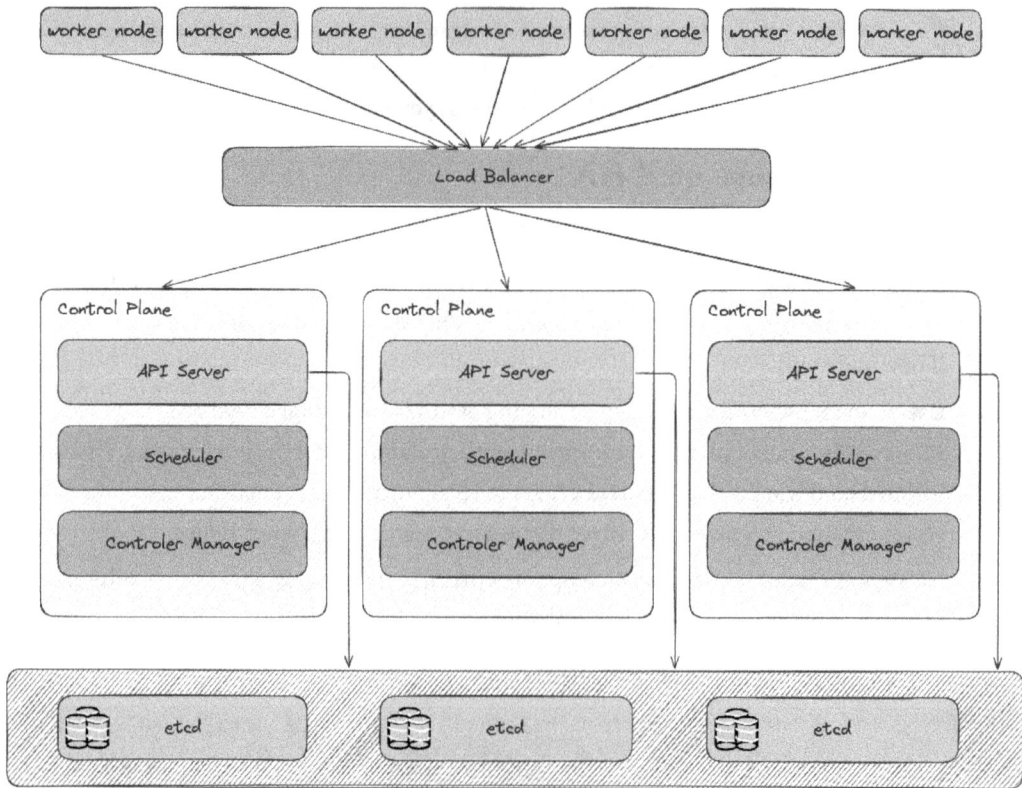

Figure 13.3 – K8S architecture with etcd HA configuration

In this section, we focused on ensuring HA for the control plane through a multi-control-plane setup and load balancing for API servers. Now, we'll shift our focus to worker nodes and applications, ensuring that they remain highly available through strategies such as node pools, auto-scaling, taints and tolerations, and handling node failures.

Building a resilient workforce: worker node and application availability

The next layer of resilience lies in the **worker nodes** and **applications** themselves. In this section, we'll focus on strategies that ensure workloads continue to run smoothly, even when individual nodes encounter issues or traffic surges. Key approaches include **node pools**, **autoscaling**, and more advanced workload distribution mechanisms.

Node pools and autoscaling for efficient resource management

> **Interview tip**
>
> **Question:** *What are node pools, and how do they contribute to HA in Kubernetes?*
>
> **Answer:** Think of node pools as specialized teams in your workforce. You wouldn't ask your data scientists (CPU-intensive nodes) to also handle the company's caching servers (memory-intensive nodes). Node pools let you group nodes with specific hardware (such as GPUs or extra RAM) and assign the right workloads to them, preventing resource conflicts and improving stability.

Why is this important?

Mixing different types of workloads on the same node pool can lead to resource contention, negatively impacting performance. For instance, a compute-heavy application sharing resources with a memory-intensive one could degrade the performance of both. By isolating these workloads into different node pools, you ensure each application gets the resources it needs without interference.

Example – Creating node pools for different workloads

Let's say your cluster hosts two applications: one requires high CPU for data processing, and the other needs more memory for caching. To optimize their performance and maintain HA, you can create separate node pools for each type of workload. Here's an example:

```
kubectl label nodes node1 compute-intensive=true
kubectl label nodes node2 memory-intensive=true
```

Once you've labeled the nodes, you can configure your deployments to target specific node pools based on the resource requirements of your workloads. This helps in assigning the right workloads to the appropriate nodes and ensures that each workload gets the resources it needs without interference.

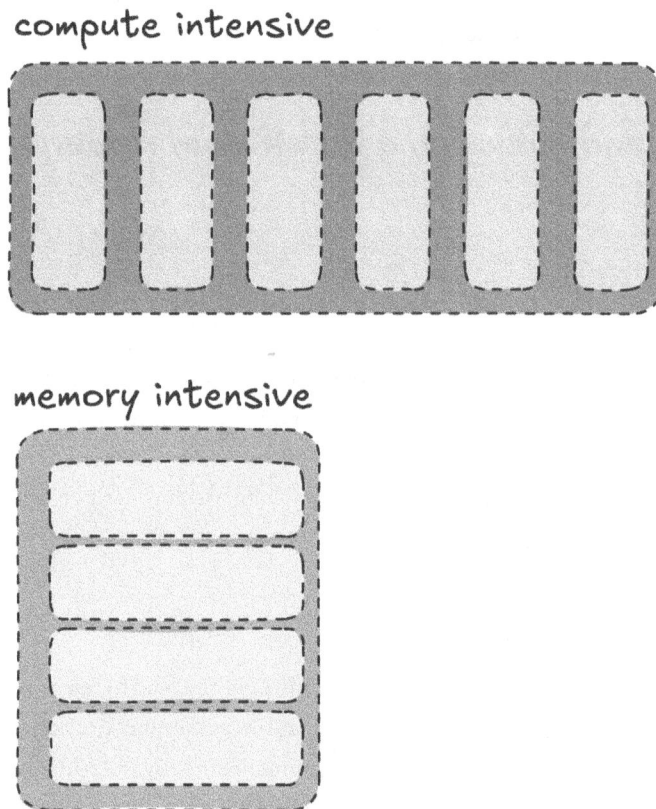

Figure 13.4 – Node pools for different workloads

Once labeled, you can configure your deployments to schedule Pods on the appropriate nodes based on their resource requirements.

Autoscaling for HA

In a resilient Kubernetes cluster, running multiple instances of nodes and applications is key to avoiding disruptions. The more nodes and application instances you have, the better you can distribute traffic and workloads, preventing failures from impacting your entire system. Within the cluster, the **Horizontal Pod Autoscaler (HPA)** plays a significant role in scaling your applications based on metrics such as CPU and memory usage, improving both availability and resilience.

We've already covered the detailed implementation of autoscaling in *Chapter 5*, and the comparison between horizontal and vertical scaling in *Chapter 4*. Here, we'll briefly review autoscaling from a resilience perspective.

Cluster Autoscaler and Karpenter for node pool resilience

There are a couple of options for scaling a Kubernetes cluster: you can either use the **Cluster Autoscaler** or configure an alternative such as **Karpenter**. Both tools ensure that your node pools can automatically scale based on changing resource demands. When traffic spikes occur, the autoscaler adds new nodes to handle the load. Conversely, when demand decreases, it scales down, optimizing resource usage and reducing costs.

Why is autoscaling important for HA?

Without autoscaling, your cluster might run out of resources during unexpected traffic surges, leading to application failures or degraded performance. Autoscaling helps by dynamically adjusting the number of nodes in your cluster, ensuring that your applications always have enough resources to meet current demands.

> **Interview tip**
>
> **Question:** *How does Kubernetes autoscaling contribute to HA?*
>
> **Answer:** Kubernetes autoscaling helps ensure HA by automatically adjusting the number of worker nodes or Pod replicas in response to traffic or resource demands. When demand increases, the Cluster Autoscaler adds new nodes to prevent service degradation. Similarly, the HPA scales up application Pods to maintain performance, further enhancing the resilience and availability of the application.

Scaling applications across multiple nodes improves availability, but Kubernetes' default scheduling might place multiple Pods on the same node, as shown in *Figure 13.5*:

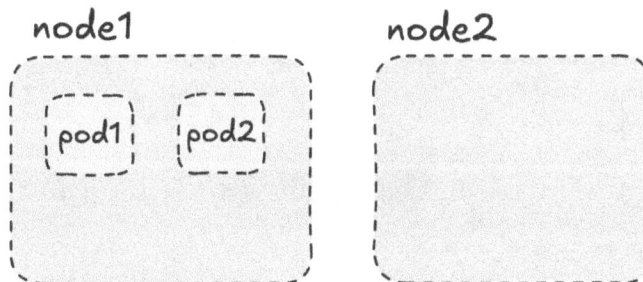

Figure 13.5 – All Pods on one node

When multiple Pods are placed on the same node, it can lead to resource contention or even single-node failures that affect your application. To avoid this, we need to define additional scheduling constraints, such as **taints**, **tolerations**, and so on. These mechanisms allow us to control how Pods are distributed across nodes, ensuring they either spread out evenly or target specific nodes (for instance, GPU nodes for machine learning tasks).

Spreading workloads in Kubernetes

Controlling where Pods land is crucial for performance and reliability. Kubernetes provides several mechanisms to help with Pod placement, including **node affinity**, **inter-pod affinity** and **anti-affinity**, **taints** and **tolerations**, and the more advanced **topology spread constraints**. These tools give you flexibility in spreading workloads to meet the needs of different applications and environments.

What is node affinity?

How does node affinity help in scheduling workloads in Kubernetes? **Node affinity** lets you specify rules to guide the placement of Pods on certain nodes based on labels. This is especially useful when specific workloads require certain types of hardware or configurations.

There are two types of node affinity:

- **Required node affinity**: These are hard constraints. If a node doesn't meet these criteria, the Pod won't be scheduled there.

- **Preferred node affinity**: These are preferences rather than strict requirements. Kubernetes will try to place the Pod on a matching node, but it's not guaranteed.

Example — Node affinity for specific hardware

Imagine you need to ensure that a Pod only runs on nodes equipped with SSD storage. You can define the following node affinity rule in your Pod's specification:

```
affinity:
  nodeAffinity:
    requiredDuringSchedulingIgnoredDuringExecution:
      nodeSelectorTerms:
      - matchExpressions:
        - key: disktype
          operator: In
          values:
          - ssd
```

This configuration makes sure the Pod is scheduled on a node labeled with `disktype = ssd`. If no such node is available, the Pod won't be scheduled.

What are inter-Pod affinity and anti-affinity?

How do inter-Pod affinity and anti-affinity improve workload placement in Kubernetes? **Inter-Pod affinity** and **anti-affinity** are mechanisms that allow you to control how Pods are scheduled based on the labels of other Pods running in your cluster. These features help ensure that related services are placed either **together** (affinity) or **apart** (anti-affinity), depending on your application's requirements.

- **Pod affinity**: This attracts a Pod to nodes where other Pods with specific labels are already running. It's useful when you want related services to be co-located for low-latency communication or shared dependencies. For example, a web application Pod might benefit from being scheduled on the same node as a Redis cache to minimize network latency.

- **Pod anti-affinity**: This ensures that certain Pods are not placed on the same node. It's commonly used to distribute replicas of a service across different nodes for HA, preventing a single point of failure. If one node goes down, having Pods spread across different nodes ensures that other replicas remain available.

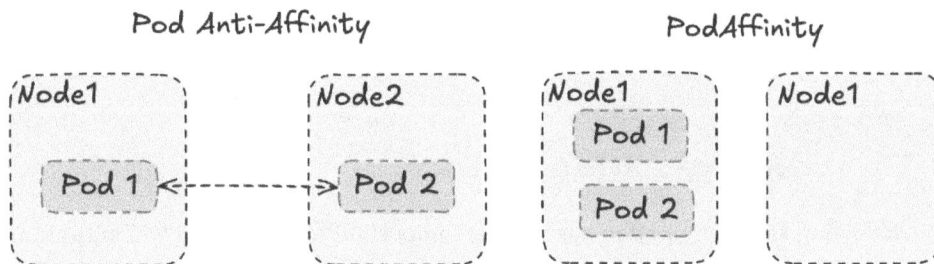

Figure 13.6 – Pod affinity and anti-affinity

By effectively using Pod affinity and anti-affinity rules, you can optimize the placement of your workloads, ensuring both performance and HA are maintained across your Kubernetes cluster.

How do inter-Pod affinity and anti-affinity work?

Kubernetes uses **labels** on Pods and nodes to implement affinity and anti-affinity. By setting up **affinity rules** or **anti-affinity rules** in your Pod specifications, the Kubernetes scheduler will either try to co-locate Pods with certain labels (affinity) or prevent them from being placed on the same node (anti-affinity).

Both affinity and anti-affinity can be defined in two ways:

- **Required during scheduling (hard constraints)**: Pods must follow the specified rules. If the requirements aren't met, the Pod won't be scheduled.

- **Preferred during scheduling (soft constraints)**: Pods will be scheduled according to the rules, but the scheduler can override them if necessary.

Example — Pod anti-affinity for HA

Consider a situation where you have a web store application with multiple replicas. You want to ensure that each replica runs on a different node to avoid downtime if a node fails. This is a typical use case for Pod anti-affinity.

Here's an example configuration of Pod anti-affinity, ensuring that Pods labeled app = web-store are spread across different nodes:

```
affinity:
  podAntiAffinity:
    requiredDuringSchedulingIgnoredDuringExecution:
      - labelSelector:
          matchExpressions:
          - key: app
            operator: In
            values:
            - web-store
        topologyKey: "kubernetes.io/hostname"
```

The following key configuration elements are important for setting up Pod anti-affinity to ensure HA.

- labelSelector: Specifies which Pods this rule applies to (in this case, Pods with the label app = web-store)

- topologyKey: Specifies that Pods with the app = web-store label must be placed on different nodes (based on the hostname key)

This configuration ensures that no two web-store Pods are scheduled on the same node, improving fault tolerance and HA.

Example: Pod Affinity for low-latency communication

Now, imagine you have a web server application that frequently communicates with a Redis cache. You want to ensure that the web server and Redis Pods are co-located on the same node to minimize network latency.

Here's how you can define Pod affinity to co-locate the two services:

```
affinity:
  podAffinity:
    requiredDuringSchedulingIgnoredDuringExecution:
      - labelSelector:
          matchExpressions:
          - key: app
            operator: In
            values:
            - redis
        topologyKey: "kubernetes.io/hostname"
```

This configuration ensures that Pods labeled app = web-server will be scheduled on nodes where Pods with the label app = redis are already running. This can greatly reduce network latency between services that need to interact frequently.

Why use inter-Pod affinity and anti-affinity?

Here's why inter-Pod affinity and anti-affinity are critical for Kubernetes deployments:

- **Low-latency communication:** For applications that require real-time interaction, such as a web server and a caching service, co-locating Pods on the same node reduces network overhead.

- **Improved fault tolerance:** By spreading Pod replicas across nodes (using anti-affinity), you ensure that the failure of a single node doesn't take down all replicas, improving the overall availability of your service.

- **Enhanced resource utilization:** Affinity and anti-affinity rules can help you balance workloads across your cluster, ensuring efficient use of resources.

Interview tip

Question #1: *How do inter-Pod affinity and anti-affinity contribute to workload placement?*

Answer: Inter-Pod affinity attracts Pods to nodes where other related Pods are already running, which is useful for improving communication between services. Anti-affinity, on the other hand, repels Pods from being scheduled on the same node, ensuring HA by spreading replicas across different nodes.

Question #2: *When would you use Pod anti-affinity in a Kubernetes cluster?*

Answer: Pod anti-affinity is used when you want to spread Pod replicas across multiple nodes to ensure HA. This is especially useful for stateful applications or services with multiple replicas, as it ensures that a node failure doesn't take down all replicas, maintaining service uptime.

By properly implementing inter-Pod affinity and anti-affinity rules, you can optimize both performance and resilience in your Kubernetes cluster, ensuring that Pods are strategically placed to meet your application's needs.

Best practices for using affinity and anti-affinity

Here are some best practices to consider when using affinity and anti-affinity rules to optimize your Kubernetes workloads.

- **Use Pod affinity for related services:** Co-locate services that need to communicate frequently, such as web servers and databases, to reduce latency and improve performance.

- **Use Pod anti-affinity for replicas:** Spread replicas of critical services across nodes to prevent downtime due to node failure. This is especially important for stateful applications that rely on multiple replicas.

- **Combine affinity and anti-affinity:** Use a combination of both to balance service interaction and resilience, ensuring that related services are co-located while also maintaining fault tolerance.

By understanding and properly implementing Pod affinity and anti-affinity, you can greatly improve the reliability and performance of your Kubernetes workloads. These mechanisms offer fine-grained control over Pod placement, ensuring your applications are both **resilient** and **optimized** for their specific requirements.

What are taints and tolerations?

How do taints and tolerations work together in Kubernetes? **Taints and tolerations** are mechanisms that Kubernetes uses to control how Pods are scheduled on nodes. **Taints** are applied to nodes to "repel" certain Pods, ensuring that only specific workloads are scheduled on those nodes. Conversely, **tolerations** are applied to Pods to allow them to be scheduled on tainted nodes. This combination gives you precise control over workload distribution, allowing you to dedicate nodes for specialized purposes or prevent certain types of workloads from running on inappropriate nodes.

Why are taints and tolerations necessary?

In large Kubernetes clusters, not all nodes are the same. Some nodes may have specialized hardware, such as **GPUs**, or may be dedicated to particular workloads. Without taints and tolerations, Kubernetes could schedule any Pod on any available node, which might lead to inefficient resource use or performance issues. For example, you don't want general-purpose workloads consuming resources on GPU nodes if they don't require GPU processing.

Here are common scenarios where taints and tolerations are essential:

- **Dedicating nodes for specific workloads:** For instance, you may have nodes with GPUs that should only run machine learning workloads. You can taint these nodes so that only Pods with GPU requirements (and matching tolerations) are scheduled there.

- **Isolating nodes for maintenance or troubleshooting:** You can taint a node undergoing maintenance to prevent new Pods from being scheduled on it while tolerating only critical workloads that must continue running.

- **Evicting Pods from problematic nodes:** If a node is experiencing issues, you can use taints to stop Pods from being scheduled on it until the issue is resolved, allowing the rest of the cluster to function normally.

How do taints and tolerations work?

A taint is applied to a node to specify that only Pods with the corresponding toleration can be scheduled there. Taints use key-value pairs and an "effect" to describe their behavior. The most common effect is `NoSchedule`, which prevents any Pod from being scheduled on the node unless it has a matching toleration.

Tolerations are applied to Pods, allowing them to bypass taints that have been applied to nodes. This ensures that only certain Pods are allowed to run on those nodes, based on the specified toleration.

Example — Applying a taint and toleration

Let's say you have a node that you want to dedicate to GPU workloads. First, you would taint the node to prevent non-GPU workloads from being scheduled there:

```
kubectl taint nodes node1 gpu=true:NoSchedule
```

This `NoSchedule` taint ensures that only Pods with matching toleration can be scheduled on `node1`. Next, you would add a corresponding toleration to the GPU workload Pod:

```
tolerations:
- key: "gpu"
  operator: "Equal"
  value: "true"
  effect: "NoSchedule"
```

This configuration allows the Pod to be scheduled on `node1`, ensuring that only GPU-dependent workloads run on nodes with GPU resources.

> **Interview tip**
>
> **Question:** *Can you explain a scenario where taints and tolerations are critical for workload isolation?*
>
> **Answer:** Taints and tolerations are critical when you need to isolate workloads on specific nodes. For example, if you have nodes with GPUs, you can taint those nodes so that only GPU-dependent workloads are scheduled there. Non-GPU workloads will be repelled from those nodes unless they have the appropriate toleration, ensuring efficient use of the GPU resources.

Best practices for using taints and tolerations

To get the most out of taints and tolerations, it's important to follow best practices to maintain cluster efficiency and prevent unnecessary complexity.

- **Dedicating nodes for specialized hardware**: If you have nodes with special hardware (such as GPUs, FPGAs, or SSDs), use taints to dedicate those nodes to specific workloads. This ensures that only appropriate workloads are scheduled on those nodes, optimizing hardware utilization.

- **Simplify taints and tolerations**: Overcomplicating taint and toleration configurations can lead to management headaches. Use clear and concise keys and values for taints to ensure readability and ease of maintenance.

- **Using node affinity with taints**: Combining node affinity with taints ensures that workloads are scheduled on the correct nodes based on both Pod requirements and node capabilities. This is especially useful for nodes with specific hardware or special configurations.

- **Isolating nodes for maintenance or issues**: When a node is undergoing maintenance or experiencing issues, taint the node with `NoSchedule` to prevent new workloads from being scheduled, but use tolerations for critical Pods that must keep running.

- **Monitor cluster efficiency**: Overusing taints and tolerations can lead to inefficient resource utilization, driving up cluster costs. Use tools such as Kubecost to monitor and optimize your resource allocation.

Advanced use case – Handling node maintenance

Let's say you need to perform maintenance on a node, but you want to ensure that only essential services remain running while preventing new Pods from being scheduled.

You can apply a taint with the `NoSchedule` effect, and then apply tolerations to critical Pods as shown here:

```
kubectl taint nodes node1 maintenance=true:NoSchedule
```

Figure 13.7 illustrates how applying a taint with the `NoSchedule` effect on `node1` prevents new Pods from being scheduled on that node. Only Pods with a matching toleration are allowed, ensuring that essential workloads can continue while others are kept off the node during maintenance.

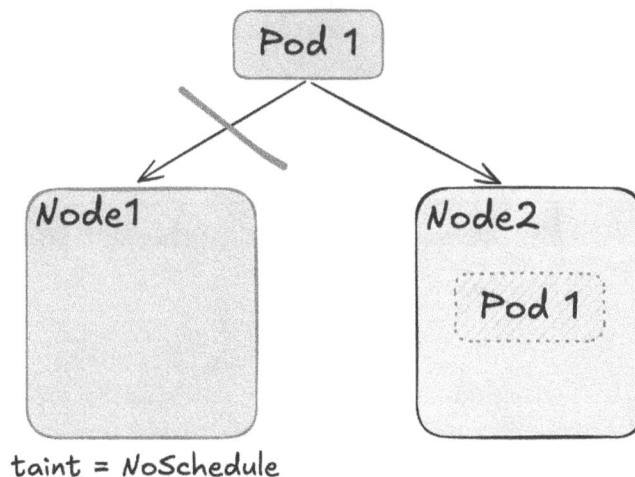

Figure 13.7 – Pod affinity and anti-affinity

Now, the node won't accept any new Pods unless they have a matching toleration:

```
tolerations:
- key: "maintenance"
  operator: "Equal"
  value: "true"
  effect: "NoSchedule"
```

This setup ensures that only Pods essential for the maintenance process (or those that must keep running during maintenance) are allowed on the node, while other non-essential workloads are evicted or prevented from being scheduled.

Interview tip

Question: *How do taints and tolerations contribute to HA in Kubernetes?*

Answer: Taints and tolerations ensure HA by allowing you to control where Pods can be scheduled. By tainting nodes with specific requirements or hardware, you can dedicate those nodes to particular workloads, ensuring that Pods are only placed on appropriate nodes. This prevents overloading critical nodes and ensures that workloads remain resilient in case of node failures.

Additional example – Combining taints and affinity

Imagine you have nodes that are equipped with GPUs, and you want to ensure that only machine learning workloads can access these nodes. You could use both taints and node affinity to achieve this:

1. **Tainting the GPU nodes:**

    ```
    kubectl taint nodes node-gpu gpu=true:NoSchedule
    ```

2. **Applying node affinity in the Pod spec:**

```
affinity:
  nodeAffinity:
    requiredDuringSchedulingIgnoredDuringExecution:
      nodeSelectorTerms:
      - matchExpressions:
        - key: gpu
          operator: In
          values:
          - "true"
tolerations:
- key: "gpu"
  operator: "Equal"
  value: "true"
  effect: "NoSchedule"
```

This ensures that machine learning Pods with GPU requirements are scheduled only on nodes with GPU resources, leveraging both taints and node affinity to control workload placement effectively.

Taints and tolerations provide fine-grained control over Pod scheduling in Kubernetes. They help you manage complex scenarios where certain nodes need to be reserved for specific workloads, or where workloads need to avoid certain nodes entirely. By understanding how to use these tools effectively, you can ensure that your cluster remains highly available, resilient, and optimized for performance.

Spreading Pods evenly with topology spread constraints

Mentioning topology spread constraints in an interview signals that your knowledge is current. While Pod anti-affinity can prevent Pods from landing on the same node, it's a blunt instrument. Topology spread constraints provide a much more sophisticated way to distribute Pods evenly across failure domains such as availability zones, regions, or nodes. Interviewers want to see if you can articulate why this even distribution is critical for building truly highly available applications.

This feature directly addresses a core challenge in distributed systems: preventing a single infrastructure failure (such as a rack or zonal outage) from taking down your entire application. Being able to explain how to configure it demonstrates a mature understanding of production-grade Kubernetes deployments.

Core explanation

Topology spread constraints control how Pods are spread across different groups of nodes, defined by a topology key. The goal is to achieve a balanced distribution of your application's Pods to improve HA and resource utilization.

> **Interview tip**
>
> **Question:** *What are topology spread constraints and why are they important for HA?*
>
> **Answer:** They are a powerful scheduling feature that ensures Pods are distributed evenly across different failure domains, such as cloud provider availability zones or physical racks. This is critical for HA because it prevents a single point of failure—such as a zone outage—from taking down all of an application's replicas.

The key parameters are as follows:

- `maxSkew`: Describes the maximum allowed difference between the number of Pods in any two topology domains. A `maxSkew` parameter of 1 means the Pods must be distributed as evenly as possible.

- `topologyKey`: The node label used to identify the topology domain. Common keys are `topology.kubernetes.io/zone` for availability zones and `kubernetes.ioio/hostname` for individual nodes.

- `whenUnsatisfiable`: Defines what to do if a Pod can't satisfy the spread constraint. It can be `DoNotSchedule` (the default) or `ScheduleAnyway`.

> **Interview tip**
>
> **Question:** *When would you use topology spread constraints instead of Pod anti-affinity?*
>
> **Answer:** You should prefer topology spread constraints to achieve an even spread of replicas for HA. Pod anti-affinity is more of a binary rule—it only ensures that certain Pods don't run on the same node. Topology spread constraints give you more nuanced control by defining an acceptable "skew," ensuring a balanced distribution across many nodes or zones, which is generally what you want for a stateless, replicated service.

For example, if you have three nodes in a zone and six replicas of your application, a constraint with `topologyKey: kubernetes.io/hostname` and `maxSkew: 1` would ensure that each node gets exactly two replicas.

This deployment ensures that its six replicas are spread evenly across both availability zones and the nodes within those zones.

```yaml
apiVersion: apps/v1
kind: Deployment
metadata:
  name: my-app-deployment
spec:
  replicas: 6
  selector:
    matchLabels:
      app: my-app
  template:
    metadata:
      labels:
        app: my-app
    spec:
      topologySpreadConstraints:
      - maxSkew: 1
        # why it matters: Prevents all pods from landing in one
        # availability zone.
        topologyKey: "topology.kubernetes.io/zone"
        whenUnsatisfiable: DoNotSchedule
        labelSelector:
          matchLabels:
            app: my-app
      - maxSkew: 1
        # why it matters: Ensures pods are also
spread across nodes within        # each zone.
        topologyKey: "kubernetes.io/hostname"
        whenUnsatisfiable: DoNotSchedule
        labelSelector:
          matchLabels:
            app: my-app
      containers:
      - name: my-app-container
        image: nginx
```

While affinity rules and spread constraints allow you to define where Pods *should* be scheduled, there's another crucial scheduling mechanism that works in reverse: allowing nodes to repel Pods. This powerful feature, known as taints and tolerations, gives you control over which workloads are allowed to run on specific nodes. It's essential for tasks such as dedicating nodes with special hardware or safely performing node maintenance, which we'll explore next.

Pod disruption budgets for HA

In a Kubernetes cluster, **pod disruption budgets (PDBs)** are essential for ensuring that your applications remain available during voluntary disruptions such as **node drains, cluster maintenance**, or **Pod evictions**. These disruptions can be planned operations, such as upgrading the nodes or scaling the cluster, or triggered events such as applying changes that require Pods to be rescheduled.

By using PDBs, you ensure that Kubernetes does not evict too many Pods at once, keeping your application resilient and minimizing downtime during maintenance activities.

Why are PDBs necessary?

Why should you implement PDBs in Kubernetes? Without PDBs, Kubernetes may evict multiple Pods during maintenance activities such as node drains or upgrades, leaving your service under-provisioned or even unavailable. This is especially critical for **stateful applications** or **highly available workloads** that require a minimum number of replicas to function effectively. By defining a PDB, you prevent the system from evicting more than a certain number of Pods, ensuring that the remaining replicas are enough to keep the service running.

The following figure shows how PDBs work during a node drain. While **pod-1** is being terminated on **node-1**, **pod-2** is protected from termination on **node-2** due to the PDB, and **pod-3** remains pending on **node-3**. This ensures that disruptions do not impact more Pods than allowed by the PDB, maintaining service availability.

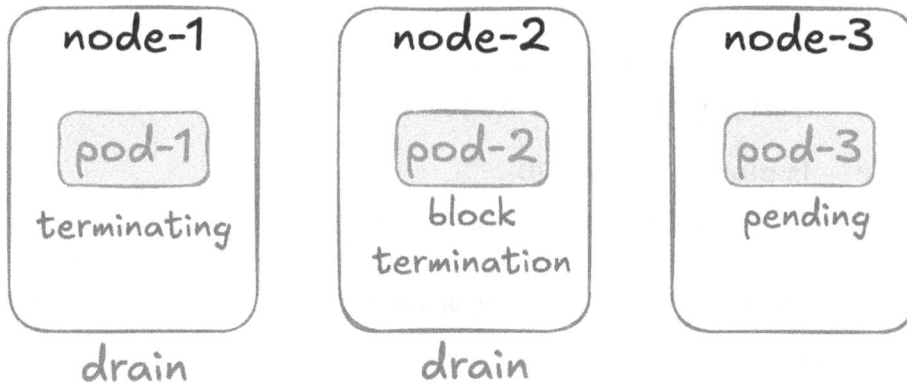

Figure 13.8 – Pod disruption budget

The key benefits of PDBs include the following:

- **Ensuring application availability**: PDBs guarantee that a specified number of Pod replicas remain available during voluntary disruptions, preventing service outages
- **Controlling Pod evictions**: When performing cluster maintenance, such as draining nodes or applying updates, PDBs ensure that the process is gradual and doesn't overwhelm your application
- **Improving resilience during scaling**: If your cluster autoscaler adjusts the number of nodes, PDBs prevent the cluster from scaling down too aggressively, ensuring that your critical services remain running

How does a PDB work?

PDBs work by setting a **minimum number of Pods** that must remain available or a **maximum number of Pods** that can be disrupted at any given time. When a voluntary disruption occurs, Kubernetes checks the PDB to ensure the disruption won't reduce the number of available Pods below the defined threshold. If the threshold is violated, Kubernetes postpones the disruption until the system can maintain the specified availability.

There are two main properties you can configure in a PDB:

- minAvailable: This property ensures that at least a specific number of Pods are always running. For example, if you have 5 replicas of a critical service, you can set minAvailable to 3, which means at least 3 Pods must remain running even during disruptions.

- maxUnavailable: This property defines the maximum number of Pods that can be unavailable during a disruption. For example, if you set maxUnavailable to 1 in a deployment with 5 replicas, only 1 Pod can be evicted at a time.

Example — Implementing a PDB

Let's walk through the implementation of a PDB for a critical application. Suppose you have a deployment running 5 replicas of your application, and you want to ensure that at least 2 Pods are always available, even during voluntary disruptions such as node upgrades.

Here's how you would define a PDB:

```
apiVersion: policy/v1
kind: PodDisruptionBudget
metadata:
  name: my-app-pdb
spec:
  minAvailable: 2
  selector:
    matchLabels:
      app: my-app
```

In this example, we note the following:

- minAvailable: 2 ensures that at least 2 Pods remain available during node maintenance or scaling events

- The selector uses the app:my-app label to apply this PDB to all Pods labeled with my-app

With this configuration, if you initiate a node drain, Kubernetes will make sure that at least 2 Pods are running before evicting any additional Pods, ensuring your application remains functional during the operation.

Benefits of using PDBs

The following are key benefits of implementing PDBs in your Kubernetes cluster:

1. **Ensures a minimum level of availability**: By setting a PDB, you can ensure that a minimum number of Pod replicas remain available at all times. This is especially important for applications that cannot tolerate downtime, such as web servers, databases, or other critical services.

2. **Prevents disruptions during cluster maintenance**: During cluster maintenance (such as upgrading nodes, scaling nodes, or applying patches), Kubernetes might need to evict Pods from certain nodes. PDBs prevent Kubernetes from evicting too many Pods at once, which would otherwise reduce your application's availability.

3. **Improves cluster stability during autoscaling**: When autoscaling up or down, you want to ensure that the system doesn't terminate too many Pods at once. A PDB helps the autoscaler respect the needs of your application, preventing aggressive scale-downs that could impact performance or availability.

4. **Enhances application resilience**: By ensuring that a minimum number of Pods are always available, PDBs protect your application from disruptions that could otherwise cause service degradation or outages.

Best practices for using PDBs

The following are best practices for effectively using PDBs to maintain application availability and resilience.

1. **Use PDBs for critical workloads**: Always define PDBs for mission-critical applications that cannot tolerate downtime. This includes databases, web servers, and any services with strict uptime requirements.

2. **Balance between minAvailable and maxUnavailable**: Choose the right balance between `minAvailable` and `maxUnavailable` depending on your application's needs. For example, highly resilient, stateless services may tolerate a more aggressive disruption policy (`maxUnavailable`), while stateful applications with tight uptime requirements should have a stricter policy (`minAvailable`).

3. **Monitor PDBs during maintenance**: During planned maintenance, always ensure that PDBs are properly enforced to avoid application disruptions. This can be especially important during node upgrades or rolling updates.

4. **Combine PDBs with HPA:** When using HPA, make sure to adjust your PDBs to reflect the number of replicas available at any given time. For example, if your application is set to scale between 3 and 10 replicas, your PDB should account for this variation to avoid conflicts during scaling events.

Real-world use case – Managing disruptions during node drains

Imagine you need to upgrade several nodes in your cluster. Without a PDB, Kubernetes could drain a node and evict multiple Pods, leading to a significant reduction in your application's availability. By implementing a PDB, you can ensure that the number of available Pods never falls below the critical threshold.

For example, if you have a service with 6 replicas and you set `minAvailable: 4`, Kubernetes will ensure that at least 4 Pods remain running at all times. During the node drain, the system will evict Pods gradually, only when enough replicas are available on other nodes. This guarantees that your service remains operational throughout the entire maintenance process.

> **Interview tip**
>
> **Question #1:** *Why are PDBs important for HA in Kubernetes?*
>
> **Answer:** PDBs ensure that a minimum number of Pod replicas remain available during voluntary disruptions such as node drains or maintenance. By setting a PDB, you prevent Kubernetes from evicting too many Pods at once, protecting your application from service outages.
>
> **Question #2:** *When would you use a PDB in a Kubernetes environment?*
>
> **Answer:** You would use a PDB when you want to ensure that your application remains available during voluntary disruptions such as node upgrades, scaling events, or Pod evictions. PDBs are especially useful for critical applications that require HA.

PDBs are an essential tool for ensuring that your applications remain available and resilient during planned or voluntary disruptions. By setting `minAvailable` or `maxUnavailable` parameters, you can control how many Pods are allowed to be evicted during node maintenance or scaling events. When used correctly, PDBs help maintain HA, improve resilience, and ensure that your services remain functional, even during critical operations such as node drains or cluster upgrades.

By integrating PDBs into your Kubernetes strategy, you can protect your workloads from disruptions and ensure a smooth, resilient experience for your users and applications.

Summary

In today's IT landscape, HA and reliability are critical for keeping systems operational. In this chapter, we explored how Kubernetes ensures HA, reliability, and resiliency at both the infrastructure and application levels.

HA ensures your system remains up even when parts of the infrastructure fail. Techniques such as using multi-control-plane control planes, etcd clustering, and load balancing ensure continuous operation. Reliability, on the other hand, focuses on consistent performance over time, ensuring that applications avoid slowdowns or errors under load. Resiliency is about recovering quickly from failures using self-healing mechanisms such as automatic Pod restarts and fallback systems.

We also covered node pools, autoscaling, Pod affinity/anti-affinity, taints and tolerations, and PDBs to ensure efficient resource distribution, avoid disruptions, and maintain high performance during maintenance and scaling events.

However, none of these strategies can succeed without *effective monitoring*. Monitoring allows you to detect issues early, track performance, and ensure that your HA and resiliency patterns are functioning as intended.

In the next chapter, we'll dive into monitoring in Kubernetes and explore how it serves as the foundation for maintaining a reliable and highly available system. Without proper monitoring, it's difficult to implement any HA pattern or guarantee application resilience.

14

Monitoring Best Practices

Monitoring is critical to managing a Kubernetes cluster as it provides the necessary visibility to ensure the health, performance, and reliability of the infrastructure and applications running within it. Effective monitoring helps identify and resolve issues before they impact end users, optimizing resource usage and maintaining system performance. In a dynamic environment such as Kubernetes, where applications and workloads constantly change, robust monitoring becomes even more crucial.

This chapter will guide you through the basics of Kubernetes monitoring, highlighting why it is essential and what key metrics should be tracked. We'll delve into various strategies and explore a range of tools that can help you implement an effective monitoring system. From open source solutions such as Prometheus and Grafana to comprehensive logging stacks such as the **Elastic Stack (ELK)**, we will cover each tool's features, benefits, and use cases. By the end of this chapter, you will have a solid understanding of how to monitor your Kubernetes cluster effectively and the best practices to follow to ensure your system remains healthy and performant.

Specifically, this chapter will cover the following key topics:

- What is monitoring in general?
- Which monitoring tools and frameworks are essential for Kubernetes?
- How can effective monitoring, visualization, and alerting be set up?

What is monitoring in general?

Monitoring involves collecting various metrics that offer insights into the health, performance, and reliability of both the infrastructure and applications running within the cluster. In Kubernetes, this means tracking resource usage (CPU, memory, and network), Pod and node health, and application-specific performance indicators. Effective monitoring is essential for ensuring system stability, detecting issues early, and optimizing resource allocation in dynamic, containerized environments.

> **Interview tip**
>
> **Question:** *Why is monitoring essential in a Kubernetes environment?*
>
> **Answer:** Monitoring helps with tracking resource usage, detecting issues before they impact users, and optimizing system performance. Since Kubernetes is dynamic, workloads change constantly, making real-time visibility crucial for stability and efficiency.

What is a metric?

A **metric** is a numerical representation of data collected at regular intervals to monitor a system's performance and behavior. In the context of Kubernetes, metrics can include data points such as CPU usage, memory consumption, network throughput, and the number of active Pods. These metrics help administrators understand how their applications and infrastructure perform and identify potential issues before they escalate.

Collecting metrics is crucial for several reasons:

- **Proactive issue detection**: Kubernetes administrators can identify and address potential problems before they impact users by monitoring key metrics
- **Resource optimization**: Metrics provide insights into resource usage, helping with optimizing resource allocation to improve efficiency and reduce costs
- **Performance tuning**: Regularly analyzing metrics allows application and system performance to be fine-tuned, ensuring the system runs smoothly
- **Compliance and auditing**: Tracking metrics helps maintain compliance with regulatory requirements and provides a historical record for auditing purposes

In general, you can separate all metrics (and monitoring based on them) into two groups:

Whitebox monitoring: This involves collecting internal metrics from applications and infrastructure components. These metrics provide detailed insights into the inner workings of the system. Whitebox monitoring offers granular visibility into the system, making diagnosing and troubleshooting issues easier. It provides a deep understanding of the system's operation, which is essential for performance tuning and optimization. Examples include CPU usage, memory consumption, application-specific metrics such as request latency, error rates, and internal state information.

Blackbox monitoring: This involves testing a system's external behavior without knowledge of its internal workings. It focuses on the end user experience and the availability and performance of services. Blackbox monitoring helps ensure the system meets user expectations by validating that services are available and functioning correctly. It provides a high-level overview of the system's health from the user's perspective. Examples include HTTP checks, ping tests, and synthetic transactions that simulate user interactions.

> **Interview tip**
>
> **Question:** *What is the difference between whitebox and blackbox monitoring?*
>
> **Answer:** Whitebox monitoring collects internal system metrics, such as CPU usage, memory consumption, and request latency, providing detailed visibility into the application's behavior. Blackbox monitoring, on the other hand, tests external system behavior, focusing on availability and performance from the end user's perspective by using methods such as HTTP checks and synthetic transactions.

Both whitebox and blackbox monitoring are essential in a well-rounded monitoring strategy. Whitebox monitoring provides the detailed internal metrics needed to optimize and maintain the system, while blackbox monitoring ensures that the system meets external performance and availability standards.

Figure 14.1 summarizes the difference between these two metrics.

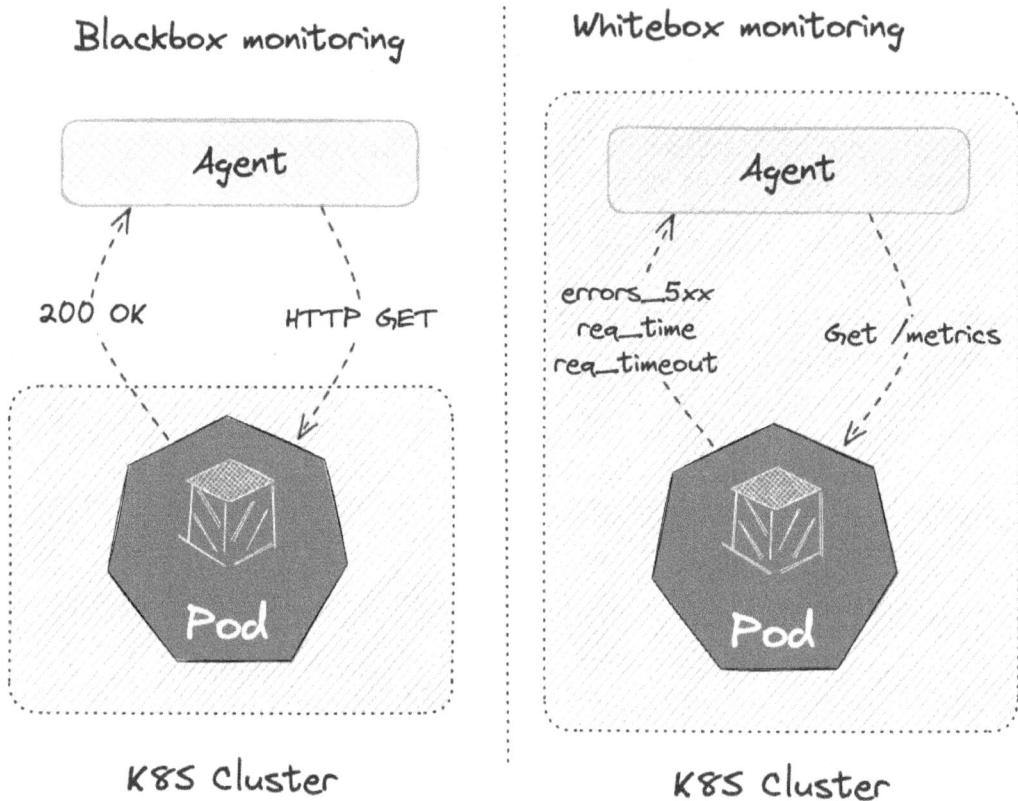

Figure 14.1 – Blackbox versus whitebox monitoring at a glance

Both whitebox and blackbox monitoring complement each other, creating a comprehensive observability strategy. By combining detailed internal insights with high-level external checks, administrators can ensure their Kubernetes environments remain both efficient and reliable, proactively addressing issues before they impact users.

What are log aggregation solutions, and how do they work?

Log aggregation solutions are essential for collecting, centralizing, and analyzing log data from various sources within a Kubernetes cluster. They enable administrators and developers to gain insights into the behavior and performance of their applications and infrastructure. By centralizing logs, these solutions simplify troubleshooting, enhance visibility, and support compliance and auditing requirements.

Log aggregation solutions collect log data from multiple sources, such as application containers, system components, and network devices, and store it in a centralized location. This centralized approach allows for efficient searching, filtering, and analysis of log data. Let's look at some of the critical features of log aggregation solutions:

- **Centralized storage**: Aggregates logs from various sources into a single, searchable repository

- **Real-time processing**: Processes and analyzes logs as they are generated to provide timely insights

- **Search and filtering**: Enables users to search, filter, and query logs based on various criteria

- **Visualization and dashboards**: Provides tools for visualizing log data and creating dashboards for monitoring and analysis

- **Alerting and notifications**: Generates alerts based on log patterns and anomalies to notify administrators of potential issues

Log aggregation solutions typically follow a three-step process:

1. **Collection:**

    - Agents or daemons are deployed on each node within the Kubernetes cluster to collect logs from various sources. Popular log forwarders include *Fluentd, Filebeat, Promtail,* and *Logstash.*

    - In a Kubernetes environment, container logs are stored in each node's/var/log/ containers directory. Log forwarders collect these logs and send them to the central aggregation system.

    - Logs from system components, such as the kubelet and API servers, are also collected by log forwarders.

2. **Centralization:**

    - The collected logs are sent to a central log aggregator, which stores them in a centralized database or storage system. Elasticsearch (OpenSearch), Loki, and Splunk are popular choices for log aggregation.

    - The log aggregator processes incoming log data, parsing and transforming it as needed before storing it. This step may involve removing sensitive information, standardizing log formats, and enriching logs with additional metadata.

3. **Analysis:**

- Users can search and query the centralized log repository using tools such as Kibana, Grafana, or the Splunk interface. These tools provide powerful search capabilities, allowing users to filter logs based on various criteria, such as time range, log level, and specific keywords.

- Log aggregation solutions offer visualization tools for creating dashboards and charts, making it easier to analyze trends and patterns in log data. These visualizations help with understanding the system's behavior and identifying anomalies.

- The system can generate alerts when specific conditions are met based on predefined rules and patterns. For example, an alert could be triggered if a particular error message appears frequently in the logs or if there is a sudden spike in log volume.

Figure 14.2 illustrates a typical log aggregation system in a Kubernetes environment, showing how logs are collected from application Pods, processed centrally, and then made accessible for querying and visualization by users.

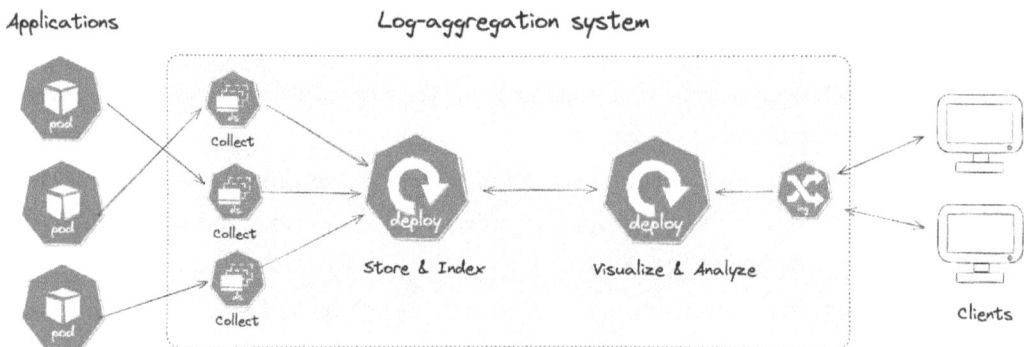

Figure 14.2 – Centralized logging solution at a glance

Log aggregation solutions play a vital role in managing and maintaining Kubernetes clusters by providing centralized log collection, processing, and analysis. These tools enable administrators to gain insights into the system's behavior, troubleshoot issues, and ensure the health and performance of their applications and infrastructure. Implementing a robust log aggregation strategy can enhance visibility, improve operational efficiency, and maintain a reliable and secure Kubernetes environment.

However, you should never forget that extracting application-related metrics from the logs is expensive because you should only store the full-text log for one metric. Instead, it's always recommended that you implement as many metrics as possible using your application code. You can collect metrics using your monitoring system and perform further analysis. In most cases, log-based metrics are 200% more expensive than metric-based ones (for long-term storage, it can be even more).

> **Interview tip**
>
> **Question:** *Why is log aggregation important in Kubernetes?*
>
> **Answer:** Log aggregation centralizes logs from containers, system components, and network devices, making it easier to search, filter, and analyze logs in real time. This improves troubleshooting, enhances visibility into system behavior, and helps with compliance and auditing by ensuring all logs are stored in a structured and accessible manner.

Later in this chapter, we will review some solutions on the market that you can use to build a production-ready log aggregation for your systems.

What is tracing?

Tracing is a method that's used to monitor and analyze the execution of requests as they flow through the various services and components in a distributed system. Tracing helps provide a detailed view of how requests are processed, where delays might occur, and how services interact in the context of Kubernetes and microservices architectures. Let's look at the key concepts regarding tracing:

- **Span:** This is a single operation within a trace. It represents a unit of work and contains details such as the operation's name, start time, duration, and any associated metadata (tags). Spans can have child spans, representing sub-operations within a more extensive operation, helping to build a hierarchy of operations.

- **Traces:** These represent a request's complete journey as the request moves through various services and components. They consist of multiple spans, each representing a step in the request's life cycle. Traces provide a comprehensive view of the entire request path, making it easier to identify performance bottlenecks and failures.

- **Context propagation:** This involves passing trace context (such as the trace ID and span ID) along with requests as they move through different services. This ensures that all spans within a trace are linked, providing a coherent view of the request flow.

Implementing tracing can give the project a significant understanding of how the system behaves in general and even for some concrete transactions of your microservices to troubleshoot performance issues that cannot be identified by looking at logs or the monitoring system.

This means that the project can do the following, though it's not limited to these aspects:

- **Identify performance bottlenecks**: Tracing helps pinpoint where delays are occurring in the request flow. By analyzing spans and their durations, you can identify and optimize slow components to ensure better performance.

- **Understand service interactions**: Tracing provides visibility into how services interact. This is particularly important in microservices architectures, where requests often traverse multiple services before completion.

- **Diagnose failures**: When an error occurs, tracing can help identify the root cause by showing which component or service failed and what the system's state was at the time.

- **Optimize resource usage**: This can be done by understanding the flow of requests and identifying bottlenecks. This will allow you to optimize resource allocation and improve your system's overall efficiency.

Tracing is a powerful technique for monitoring and analyzing distributed systems, providing detailed insights into request flows, service interactions, and performance bottlenecks. By implementing tracking in your Kubernetes environment, you can improve the reliability and performance of your applications, quickly diagnose and resolve issues, and gain a deeper understanding of how your services operate. Tools such as Jaeger, Zipkin, and OpenTelemetry offer robust solutions for collecting, storing, and analyzing trace data, helping you maintain a healthy and efficient system.

Interview tip

Question: *How does tracing help with troubleshooting microservices in Kubernetes?*

Answer: Tracing provides a detailed view of request flows across services, helping to pinpoint performance bottlenecks, diagnose failures, and optimize resource usage. By linking spans together, tracing tools such as Jaeger, Zipkin, and OpenTelemetry allow teams to track requests from end to end, making it easier to debug complex interactions that logs and metrics alone may not reveal.

What is observability, and how does it differ from monitoring?

The terms observability and monitoring are often used interchangeably, but they refer to different concepts in managing and maintaining systems, mainly distributed systems such as those running on Kubernetes. Understanding the distinction between the two is crucial for building robust and reliable systems.

Observability is a property of a system that reflects how well you can understand its internal state based on the data it produces. It is a holistic approach that combines different types of telemetry data—logs, metrics, and traces—to provide a comprehensive view of the system's behavior and performance.

Let's take a closer look at the critical components of observability:

- **Metrics**: Quantitative data that measures the performance and health of various components in the system.
- **Logs**: These are detailed, timestamped records of events within the system. They provide context and insights into what happened at specific points in time.
- **Traces**: These are pieces of data that capture the flow of requests as they traverse different services and components in a distributed system. They help identify bottlenecks and latency issues.

Here are the goals of observability:

- **Understanding system behavior**: Observability helps us understand how a system operates under different conditions and how its components interact
- **Proactive problem detection**: By providing deep insights into the system's internal state, observability enables early detection of potential issues before they escalate and become critical problems
- **Performance optimization**: Detailed visibility into the system's behavior allows for more effective performance tuning and optimization

Figure 14.3 is an easy-to-remember visualization of the difference between monitoring and observability.

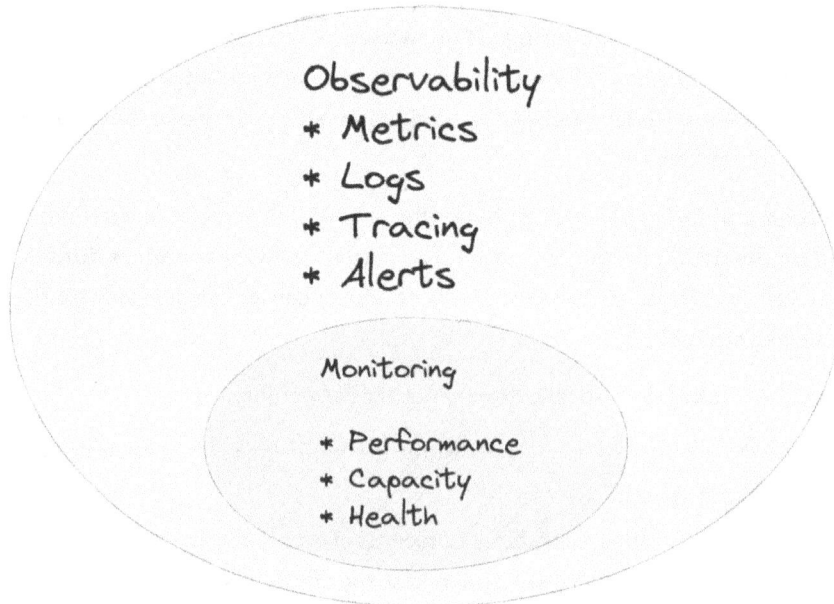

Figure 14.3 – Observability versus monitoring at a glance

So far, we have bridged the potential gap in your knowledge regarding the basics of monitoring and observability in general. Next, we'll look at concrete implementations and tools in Kubernetes environments.

Which monitoring tools and frameworks are essential for Kubernetes?

Effective monitoring is crucial for maintaining the health, performance, and reliability of Kubernetes clusters and their applications. In this section, we'll cover some essential monitoring tools and frameworks that are widely used in Kubernetes environments. These tools help collect, store, visualize, and analyze metrics, logs, and traces, providing comprehensive observability of your Kubernetes infrastructure.

What is the Metrics Server, and why do we need it?

We mentioned this component in previous chapters (when we discussed the HPA and scaling in general) because it's the key component not only for monitoring but also for scaling the applications inside the cluster.

The **Kubernetes Metrics Server** is a cluster-wide aggregator of resource usage data. It provides CPU and memory usage metrics for nodes and Pods, which Kubernetes components use to make decisions for tasks such as autoscaling.

We always recommend installing this component right after cluster creation because it's weighted to be concerned about resource consumption. The potential value it can give you in the first few seconds after it's installed is huge.

For more information on this, please see `https://kubernetes-sigs.github.io/metrics-server`.

> **Interview tip**
>
> **Question:** *Why is the Metrics Server important for scaling applications?*
>
> **Answer:** The Metrics Server collects real-time CPU and memory usage data from nodes and Pods, enabling Kubernetes to make scaling decisions. It is essential for HPA and the Kubernetes **Vertical Pod Autoscaler (VPA)**, allowing them to adjust resources dynamically based on actual workload demand.

What monitoring systems can be used for Kubernetes?

Answering this type of question should be based on your experience. However, knowing more about monitoring systems will also be helpful.

In addition to the tools mentioned here, there are other tools available, such as InfluxDB, Zabbix, Nagios, cloud-specific solutions (CloudWatch, Stackdriver, etc.), and others. Still, they aren't used as much in real projects and aren't as recommended based on my experience.

Prometheus

Prometheus is an open source monitoring and alerting toolkit designed for reliability and scalability. It collects and stores metrics as time series data, providing powerful querying capabilities. Here are some of its significant features:

- A multi-dimensional model with time series data identified by metric name and key/value pairs
- **Prometheus Query Language (PromQL)** for querying metrics in real time
- A built-in alert manager to handle and route alerts based on metric thresholds
- A robust ecosystem with integrations for various data sources and exporters

Prometheus (`https://prometheus.io`) has become the de facto standard for monitoring Kubernetes environments, and for good reason. Its widespread adoption is attributed to several key features and benefits that make it an ideal fit for Kubernetes's dynamic, containerized world. It's easy to deploy and manage, and it's Kubernetes-native, so it works well there.

For a highly available Prometheus installation, you can use Thanos to make monitoring stable and production-ready (`https://thanos.io`).

What is the Prometheus exporter?

Sometimes, even in the Kubernetes interview, you may be asked questions about an exporter in Prometheus. The **Prometheus exporter** is a component that collects metrics from a given system, service, or application and exposes them in a format that Prometheus can scrape. Exporters play a crucial role in integrating Prometheus with various systems, allowing Prometheus to collect metrics from a wide range of sources. If something does not expose metrics for Prometheus, you can find or write your own exporter to make it happen.

Prometheus exporters are essential components for integrating Prometheus with various systems and services. They enable Prometheus to collect multiple metrics, providing valuable insights into system performance and health. Using exporters, you can extend Prometheus's monitoring capabilities so that they cover a broad spectrum of use cases, ensuring comprehensive observability for your applications and infrastructure.

VictoriaMetrics

VictoriaMetrics is an open source time series database and monitoring solution designed to handle large-scale metrics data effectively. It is known for its high performance, scalability, and cost-effectiveness, making it a popular choice for monitoring large and complex environments, including Kubernetes clusters.

The following are the key features of VictoriaMetrics:

- VictoriaMetrics is optimized for **high performance** and can ingest millions of data points per second with low resource consumption. It achieves this through efficient data structures and algorithms that minimize the overhead of data storage and retrieval.
- VictoriaMetrics **can scale vertically and horizontally**. It supports single-node deployments for simplicity and ease of use and cluster deployments for high availability and horizontal scaling. This flexibility makes it suitable for environments of all sizes, from small setups to large-scale, distributed systems.

- One of VictoriaMetrics's standout features is its **cost-effective storage**. It uses advanced compression techniques to significantly reduce the storage footprint of time series data, lowering the overall cost of storing large volumes of metrics data.

- VictoriaMetrics is **fully compatible with the Prometheus ecosystem**. It supports PromQL and can act as a drop-in replacement for Prometheus in many scenarios. It also supports remote storage, allowing Prometheus servers to offload data to VictoriaMetrics.

- In cluster mode, VictoriaMetrics is **highly available and durable**. It replicates data across multiple nodes to ensure the system remains operational, even if some fail. This replication also ensures data durability, protecting against data loss.

- VictoriaMetrics is designed to deliver **fast query performance**, even with large datasets. Its optimized query engine can handle complex queries efficiently, making it suitable for real-time analytics and monitoring.

- VictoriaMetrics offers a **simple setup process and user-friendly operation**. It provides pre-built binaries, Docker images, and Helm charts for easy deployment in various environments, including Kubernetes.

- VictoriaMetrics includes **built-in downsampling capabilities**, allowing it to reduce the resolution of older data while retaining its overall trends and patterns. This feature helps with managing storage costs and improves query performance over long periods.

VictoriaMetrics is a powerful and efficient time series database and monitoring solution that handles large-scale metrics data in Kubernetes and other environments. Its high performance, scalability, cost-effective storage, and compatibility with Prometheus make it a compelling choice for organizations looking to implement or enhance their monitoring infrastructure. Whether you need to monitor a small Kubernetes cluster or manage a vast amount of metrics data across an extensive, distributed system, VictoriaMetrics offers the capabilities and flexibility required to meet your needs (`https://victoriametrics.com`).

DataDog and New Relic

While open source solutions such as Prometheus and VictoriaMetrics are popular for Kubernetes monitoring, several paid solutions offer advanced features, comprehensive support, and ease of use. These solutions often provide a unified metrics, logs, and traces platform, offering a more integrated observability experience.

If your company has a big budget, you should consider evaluating and adopting paid solutions such as Datadog and New Relic.

Datadog

Datadog (`https://www.datadoghq.com/`) is a comprehensive monitoring and analytics platform that provides end-to-end visibility into your applications and infrastructure. It integrates seamlessly with Kubernetes and offers robust features for monitoring, logging, and tracing within a single platform.

Its key features are as follows:

- **Unified monitoring**: Datadog provides a single pane of glass for monitoring metrics, traces, and logs. This unified approach simplifies observability and helps correlate data from different sources.
- **Kubernetes integration**: Datadog offers deep integration with Kubernetes, including out-of-the-box dashboards for nodes, Pods, and cluster metrics. It supports the automatic discovery of Kubernetes components and workloads.
- **Advanced analytics**: Datadog's analytics capabilities include anomaly detection, predictive monitoring, and machine-learning-based insights. These features help identify performance issues before they impact users.
- **Alerting and notifications**: Datadog provides robust alerting capabilities, allowing users to set thresholds and create alerts for various conditions. Notifications can be sent via email, Slack, PagerDuty, and other channels.
- **Security monitoring**: In addition to performance monitoring, Datadog includes features for security monitoring, such as detecting anomalous behavior and potential threats.

New Relic

New Relic (`https://newrelic.com/`) is a comprehensive observability platform that offers full-stack monitoring, including infrastructure, application performance, and digital customer experience. It provides a wide range of tools for monitoring Kubernetes environments.

Its key features are as follows:

- **Full-stack observability**: New Relic provides visibility into the entire stack, from infrastructure and Kubernetes clusters to application performance and user experience. This holistic view helps identify and resolve issues faster.
- **Distributed tracing**: New Relic's distributed tracing capabilities allow users to trace requests across microservices and understand the performance of complex, distributed applications.

- **Custom instrumentation**: Users can add custom instrumentation to their applications using New Relic's SDKs and APIs, allowing for granular monitoring of specific business metrics.

- **AI-powered insights**: New Relic leverages AI to provide insights and recommendations based on historical data and detected anomalies. This helps proactively address performance issues and optimize the system.

- **Integration with DevOps tools**: New Relic integrates with various DevOps tools and platforms, including CI/CD pipelines, incident management systems, and cloud providers, to streamline workflows and improve operational efficiency.

How do you visualize your metrics to clarify them for the whole company?

To ensure that metrics are useful for the entire company, they must be presented in a clear, accessible, and meaningful way. This means using tools that allow teams across different departments—such as engineering, operations, and business stakeholders—to easily interpret data, track trends, and respond to potential issues. A well-structured visualization system helps bridge the gap between technical insights and business impact, ensuring that performance and reliability concerns are addressed proactively.

One of the most widely used and standardized solutions for metric visualization is **Grafana**. While paid solutions such as DataDog and New Relic offer built-in dashboards, Grafana stands out as the industry-standard open source platform for monitoring and observability. It enables teams to consolidate data from multiple sources into interactive dashboards, making it easier to communicate complex system metrics to both technical and non-technical audiences.

Grafana

Grafana (`https://grafana.com`) is a powerful open source platform for monitoring and observability, known for its extensive dashboard capabilities. It integrates seamlessly with various data sources, such as Prometheus, InfluxDB, Elasticsearch, and others, allowing users to visualize and analyze multiple metrics. Grafana dashboards are highly customizable, enabling users to create interactive and dynamic visualizations tailored to their needs.

One of Grafana's critical features is its ability to create and manage dashboards composed of panels. Each panel can display data in various forms, including graphs, charts, tables, and heat maps. These panels can be arranged and resized to create a comprehensive and intuitive view of your data. Grafana also supports a wide array of visualization types, such as line charts, bar charts, pie charts, and single stat panels, which help present data effectively.

Grafana dashboards are interactive, allowing users to analyze data for more detailed analysis. Features such as templating enable the creation of dynamic dashboards that can adapt to different variables and data sources, making it easier to explore various data dimensions. Time range controls and data filtering options further enhance the usability of dashboards, providing flexibility in how data is viewed and analyzed.

Another significant capability of Grafana dashboards is the alerting feature. Users can define alert rules on specific panels, triggering notifications through various channels such as email, Slack, or PagerDuty when certain conditions are met. This helps in proactive monitoring and ensures that critical issues are addressed promptly.

Grafana also supports annotations, which allow users to mark specific events on graphs to provide context to the data. This is particularly useful for correlating events with changes in metrics. Additionally, dashboards can be shared easily within teams or publicly, facilitating collaboration and broader access to insights.

In summary, Grafana's dashboard capabilities provide a robust and flexible platform for visualizing and monitoring data. Its extensive customization options, interactive features, and integration with various data sources make it an invaluable tool for gaining insights and maintaining the health and performance of your systems.

What log aggregation solutions do you know about for Kubernetes?

Besides the paid solutions we already mentioned (DataDog and New Relic), which also have built-in log aggregation features, there are three more strong players in the logs-related field today.

Elasticsearch (OpenSearch)-based solutions (aka ELK)

ELK (`https://www.elastic.co/elastic-stack`) is a powerful open source log management and analysis platform. It consists of Elasticsearch (OpenSearch: `https://opensearch.org`) for storage and search, Logstash (or another shipper) for log ingestion and processing, and Kibana (OpenSearch dashboards) for visualization. In the Kubernetes clusters for collecting logs, you can select Fluentd, Fluent Bit, or Filebeat as a solution. All of them have their pros and cons, but they are outside the scope of this book.

Its key features are as follows:

- **Elasticsearch (OpenSearch)**: A distributed search and analytics engine that stores log data and provides powerful search and query capabilities.

- **Logstash:** It is a server-side data processing pipeline that ingests logs from various sources, processes them, and sends them to Elasticsearch (OpenSearch). It can be used alone or with the shippers to process complicated logs.

- **Kibana (OpenSearch dashboards):** It is a visualization tool that provides an intuitive interface for exploring, analyzing, and visualizing log data.

- **Scalability:** Designed to scale horizontally, it is suitable for large-scale deployments.

- **Plugins and integrations:** An extensive ecosystem of plugins for various data sources and destinations.

Loki

Loki (`https://grafana.com/oss/loki`) is a cost-effective and easy-to-operate log aggregation system. It is part of the Grafana ecosystem and integrates seamlessly with Grafana for visualization.

Its key features are as follows:

- **Scalable and efficient storage:** Optimized for storing and querying log data efficiently

- **Integration with Grafana:** Provides a consistent user experience for metrics and logs within Grafana

- **LogQL query language:** A powerful query language for filtering and analyzing log data

- **Multi-tenancy:** Supports multi-tenancy for isolating log data between different users or teams

Splunk

Splunk (`https://www.splunk.com`) is a paid solution. It is used by enterprise companies (mostly) to build a natural, comprehensive log management and analysis platform that provides advanced features for collecting, indexing, and analyzing log data from various sources.

Its features include the following:

- **Advanced analytics:** Powerful search and analysis capabilities for log data

- **Machine learning:** Built-in machine learning tools for anomaly detection and predictive analytics

- **Customizable dashboards:** Rich visualization options for creating interactive dashboards

- **Enterprise-grade features:** Robust security, compliance, and scalability features for large organizations

What options can you use to implement tracing for Kubernetes apps?

Tracing is essential for understanding the performance and behavior of microservices in a Kubernetes environment. It helps track requests as they move through different services, providing insights into latencies, errors, and bottlenecks. The paid solutions we discussed previously, such as New Relic and DataDog, have their own implementations for **application performance monitoring (APM)** and tracing in general. Let's look at some other popular options for implementing tracing in Kubernetes applications.

Jaeger

Jaeger (`https://www.jaegertracing.io`) is an open source end-to-end distributed tracing tool developed by Uber Technologies. It is designed to monitor and troubleshoot microservices-based distribution systems.

Its key features include the following:

- Distributed context propagation
- Storage and retrieval of trace data
- Query and visualization capabilities
- Integration with multiple frameworks and libraries
- Support for various storage backends (e.g., Cassandra, Elasticsearch, Kafka)

OpenTelemetry

OpenTelemetry (`https://opentelemetry.io/`) is an open source observability framework that provides APIs and tools to collect and export traces, metrics, and logs. It is a merger of the OpenTracing and OpenCensus projects.

Its key features are as follows:

- Unified instrumentation for tracing, metrics, and logs
- Comprehensive support for various programming languages
- Compatibility with multiple backends (e.g., Jaeger, Zipkin, Prometheus)
- Flexible and extensible architecture

Grafana Tempo

Tempo is an open source, high-volume distributed tracing backend developed by Grafana Labs. It is designed to handle large amounts of trace data with minimal dependencies efficiently, leveraging object storage for cost-effective, long-term retention.

Its key features are as follows:

- **High-volume ingestion**: Capable of ingesting large volumes of trace data efficiently, making it suitable for high-throughput environments

- **Minimal dependencies**: Simple to deploy with minimal dependencies, reducing the complexity of setup

- **Cost-effective storage**: Uses object storage (e.g., AWS S3, Google Cloud Storage) to store trace data, lowering storage costs

- **Seamless Grafana integration**: Integrates seamlessly with Grafana, providing a unified experience for visualizing traces alongside metrics and logs

- **Compatibility with OpenTelemetry and Jaeger**: Supports standard tracing protocols, making it easy to instrument applications using widely used libraries

- **Multi-tenancy**: Supports multi-tenancy, allowing data isolation to be used for different teams or applications

There are more tools available, such as Zipkin or cloud-specific tools (e.g., AWS X-Ray), but we want to give you the bare minimum to help you pass the interview.

Now, let's review the best practices for implementing monitoring and observability platforms in real projects.

How can effective monitoring, visualization, and alerting be set up?

Setting up effective monitoring, visualization, and alerting for your Kubernetes environment ensures you can quickly detect, diagnose, and resolve issues, maintain system performance, and optimize resource usage. But how do you separate which alerts you should be notified of as soon as possible (critical severity) and which you can treat as warnings and read about once a week? We will start by looking at the four golden signals and how they can be used in the actual implementation, as well as their best practices.

What are the four golden signals?

The **four golden signals** concept provides a robust framework for monitoring distributed systems such as Kubernetes. These signals are crucial metrics that offer a comprehensive view of the system's health and performance. The four golden signals are *latency, traffic, errors*, and *saturation*. Understanding and measuring these signals can help you identify issues and optimize the performance of your applications and infrastructure. It's created for web applications, which are still around 90% of all production systems worldwide. This definition was prepared and tested in natural production systems by the Google SRE teams, and later, they made it public in their SRE materials.

Let's review all four signals one by one:

- **Latency** measures the time it takes to service a request. It includes the time taken for a request to travel from the client to the server, the processing time on the server, and the time taken for the response to travel back to the client. There are two types of latency:

    - **Request latency**: The time taken to process a single request
    - **End-to-End latency**: The total time a request takes to complete, including network delays

    You can use monitoring tools such as Prometheus to collect and record latency metrics.

    High latency can indicate performance issues that affect the user experience. By monitoring latency, you can identify slow components in your system and optimize them to improve overall performance. Keeping latency low is crucial for maintaining a responsive and reliable service.

- **Traffic** measures the amount of demand being placed on your system. It can be measured in various units, such as the number of **requests per second** (RPS), transactions per second, or the volume of data being processed.

    Understanding traffic patterns helps with capacity planning and scaling your infrastructure to handle varying loads. Monitoring traffic allows you to detect spikes or drops in usage, indicating issues or changes in user behavior. Properly managing traffic ensures that your system can handle the load without performance degradation occurring.

- **Errors** measure the rate of failed requests or transactions in your system. This includes HTTP 5xx errors, database errors, timeouts, and other failures.

  High error rates can indicate critical issues that impact the reliability and availability of your services. Monitoring errors helps you quickly detect and resolve problems, ensuring your system remains robust and dependable. Reducing the error rate improves user satisfaction and trust in your service.

- **Saturation** measures the utilization of your system's resources, such as CPU, memory, disk I/O, and network bandwidth. It indicates how much of your system's capacity is being used and how close it is to its limits.

  Use monitoring tools to track CPU, memory, disk I/O, and network usage.

  High saturation levels can lead to resource contention, degraded performance, and instability. By monitoring saturation, you can identify when your system is reaching its capacity and take proactive measures to scale resources or optimize performance. Keeping saturation in check ensures your system can handle the workload efficiently and maintain high performance.

To monitor the four golden signals in a Kubernetes environment effectively, you can use a combination of tools, such as Prometheus, Grafana, and some logging aggregation solutions, as discussed previously. Here's a brief overview of how these tools are used:

- **Prometheus**: Collects and stores metrics, including latency, traffic, errors, and saturation
- **Grafana**: Visualizes the metrics collected by Prometheus, allowing you to create dashboards and set up alerts
- **Fluentd**: In conjunction with Elasticsearch/OpenSearch, this tool collects logs that can be used to analyze errors and understand system behavior

Focusing on the four golden signals can help you gain a comprehensive understanding of your system's health and performance. This approach helps you quickly identify and address issues, optimize resource usage, and ensure a reliable and responsive service for your users.

What must be monitored in the Kubernetes cluster?

Monitoring systems, such as Prometheus, typically include metrics and alerts that they collect and process. The number of predefined metrics can reach the thousands, so you must know what you should process in order. Here are the crucial metrics you should monitor in a Kubernetes cluster:

1. Collect and analyze node metrics from the control and data plane nodes. Here is a list of the most important metrics to collect and analyze:

    - **CPU usage**: This metric tracks CPU utilization and load average, helping to identify resource contention and potential performance bottlenecks

    - **Memory usage**: This metric measures memory utilization and swap usage to detect memory exhaustion, which can lead to Pod eviction and system instability

    - **Disk I/O**: This metric monitors **Input/Output per Second (IOPS)** and I/O time to detect storage performance issues that may slow down applications

    - **Network I/O**: This metric captures the amount of data transmitted and received over the network to help identify congestion and potential bottlenecks

2. Pod metrics allow you to check the state of the workloads you run inside the cluster and be able to track the performance issues your application can have:

    - **CPU and memory usage**: This metric analyzes CPU and memory requests, limits, and actual usage to detect inefficient resource allocation that may impact application performance

    - **Restart count**: This metric tracks the number of times a Pod has been restarted, which may indicate crashes, misconfigurations, or resource exhaustion

    - **Persistent disk usage**: This metric measures the available disk space for stateful applications to ensure continuous operation without storage-related failures occurring

3. Cluster metrics represent the actual status of the cluster and its health in general:

    - **Cluster resource usage**: This metric aggregates node and Pod resource usage to support capacity planning and efficient resource allocation

    - **Scheduler performance**: This metric tracks the number of scheduling attempts that have occurred and their duration to ensure that workloads are assigned to nodes efficiently

    - **API server metrics**: This metric measures the number of API requests that have occurred, as well as their response times, to detect latency issues and failures in the Kubernetes control plane

4. Application metrics can be exported from the workloads we run inside the cluster or externally (via some exporters, such as Blackbox Exporter) so that we can check and track how our applications behave for our end users. They're based on custom metrics

that are exposed by applications and include metrics such as request latency, error rates, and throughput. Monitoring these metrics helps ensure application performance and reliability.

5. Ingress and egress traffic metrics from ingress controllers and the service mesh (e.g., Nginx) track traffic entering and leaving the cluster. This helps with managing application performance and security.

6. Security metrics provide some additions to cluster monitoring, but focus on security. There are two groups of metrics:

   - Audit logs, which record all requests that are sent to the Kubernetes API server, providing a trail for security, auditing, and compliance

   - Metrics from policy engines such as OPA/Gatekeeper, which track policy violations within the cluster and help ensure compliance with security and governance policies

By focusing on these essential metrics, you can proactively manage your Kubernetes environment, optimize resource usage, and maintain system stability. Now that we understand what metrics are, let's discuss the important topic of **alerting**, which allows Kubernetes administrators to react to any issues with and within clusters they are responsible for.

How do we configure alerting for Kubernetes workloads?

How alerting is implemented can vary depending on the monitoring system you use. For Prometheus-based solutions, there is a powerful component called **Alertmanager**. Grafana also supports built-in alerting and notification features that you can use.

When answering this question, you can suggest the following approach and share your personal experience on real projects (if any):

- You must prepare the alerting rules and configure notification channels with escalation policies based on the metrics you have chosen as the most important for your team, application, and business.

- Alerts should be configured based on their severity, and you shouldn't send everything in one place. People sleep on those channels or emails and don't track the state.

- Alerts should be grouped, if possible, by some condition (alert or group of resources).

- Your escalation policies should include at least two people (or a group of people) in every policy tree. This will give you additional confidence that important alerts won't be missed or ignored.

Following this simple and easy-to-remember list of recommendations, you and your team will always be ready to create a production-ready notification system to resolve issues before the end users face them.

> **Interview tip**
>
> **Question:** *What are the key best practices for configuring alerting in Kubernetes?*
>
> **Answer:** Alerts should be prioritized by severity and sent to the appropriate channels to avoid noise and alert fatigue. Grouping alerts by related conditions improves clarity, and escalation policies should always involve at least two people to ensure critical issues are addressed promptly.

Summary

In this chapter, we explored the essentials of monitoring Kubernetes clusters, highlighting the importance of tracking key metrics such as CPU usage, memory usage, and Pod status to ensure the health and performance of your environment. We discussed Prometheus for metrics collection and Grafana for visualization, emphasizing the need for clear and accessible dashboards that help identify trends and potential issues.

Effective alerting was another focus. There, we covered the importance of having a comprehensive alerting system that includes real-time monitoring, clear and actionable alerts, and multiple notification channels. An ideal system also incorporates severity levels, silencing rules, and integration with incident management tools to streamline responses.

Following these best practices, you can maintain a robust and reliable Kubernetes environment, proactively addressing issues and optimizing resource usage to ensure high performance and availability. However, even with the best monitoring strategies, failures, data loss, or infrastructure outages can still occur. In the next chapter, we will dive into backup, maintenance, and disaster recovery in Kubernetes, exploring how to protect critical data, ensure cluster stability, and recover from unexpected failures effectively.

15

Backup, Maintenance, and Disaster Recovery in Kubernetes

In *Chapter 13*, we explored strategies for ensuring high availability in Kubernetes to keep your applications running smoothly, even when components fail. *Chapter 14* built on this foundation by focusing on monitoring and providing insights into the health and performance of your clusters. But keeping a cluster online is only part of the story. What happens if a datastore fails, an upgrade goes wrong, or an entire region goes offline? To keep your services resilient, you need solid backup strategies, a well-maintained cluster, and a clear plan for recovering from disasters.

In this chapter, we'll focus on three key areas. First, we'll explore Kubernetes backup strategies for disaster recovery, looking at the different types of backups, what needs protection beyond etcd, and the tools that make the process reliable and efficient. Next, we'll examine Kubernetes maintenance best practices, including how to perform smooth upgrades, manage resources effectively, and keep a cluster healthy over time. Finally, we'll discuss how to develop disaster recovery plans by designing, testing, and refining procedures that enable quick recovery after failures while minimizing downtime.

We will be covering the following main headings:

- What are the key Kubernetes backup strategies for disaster recovery?
- Kubernetes maintenance
- Developing disaster recovery plans

By the end of this chapter, you'll know how to protect both your data and your cluster, keep it running smoothly, and recover fast when things go wrong.

What are the key Kubernetes backup strategies for disaster recovery?

Ensuring that you can restore your Kubernetes cluster and applications to a known good state after a failure is critical. This involves understanding what a backup is, the types of backups available, and why you need to back up more than just etcd. By choosing the right methods and tools and following best practices, you can ensure that your backups are reliable and secure.

Understanding backups in Kubernetes

A **backup** is a copy of data taken at a specific point in time that can be used to restore and recover data after a loss or corruption event. In Kubernetes, backups are essential for the following reasons:

- **Disaster recovery**: Recovering from catastrophic failures such as hardware malfunctions or data center outages
- **Data protection**: Guarding against data corruption, accidental deletions, or malicious activities
- **Migration**: Moving applications and data between clusters or environments

Kubernetes's dynamic, ephemeral workloads complicate traditional backup approaches. Containers and Pods can be created and destroyed rapidly, and applications can scale up or down based on demand. Traditional backup methods may not capture the transient state of these resources effectively.

Types of backups

There are various backup options in Kubernetes:

- **Full backups**: Full backups allow you to restore your entire cluster to its exact state at the time of the backup. This is especially useful in scenarios where a complete recovery is necessary, such as catastrophic failures or total data loss. By having a full backup, you ensure that every component—including applications, configurations, and data—is preserved, providing a reliable foundation for disaster recovery. This type of backup allows you to capture all the data and configurations in your cluster at a specific point in time. They provide a complete snapshot but can be time-consuming and storage-intensive.

- **Incremental backups**: Incremental backups enable efficient use of storage and network resources by only capturing the differences since the last backup (whether full or incremental). This allows for more frequent backups with minimal overhead, reducing the potential for data loss between backups. However, restoring from incremental backups requires all previous backup data in the sequence, which can complicate the recovery process. They only back up data that has changed since the last backup. These types of backups are faster and use less storage, but require a chain of backups for full recovery.

- **Differential backups**: Differential backups allow you to restore data more quickly than incremental backups because they only require the last full backup and the most recent differential backup. This type of backup reduces the amount of data to be restored compared to a full backup, while simplifying the restoration process compared to incremental backups. It provides a middle ground in terms of storage requirements and recovery speed. It backs up all data changes since the last full backup. They strike a balance between full and incremental backups.

- **Application-level backups**: Application-level backups let you target specific applications or namespaces within your cluster. This granularity enables you to restore individual applications without affecting the entire cluster, which is ideal for scenarios where only certain components fail or when you need to roll back a particular application to a previous state. It also reduces backup sizes and speeds up both backup and recovery times for those specific applications. This type of backup focuses on backing up individual applications and their data, allowing for more granular recovery options.

To better understand how each type of backup works in Kubernetes, take a look at *Figure 15.1*. It visually breaks down the differences between full backups, incremental backups, and differential backups. Here, you can see how each method handles data changes over time and what this means for storage use and recovery complexity.

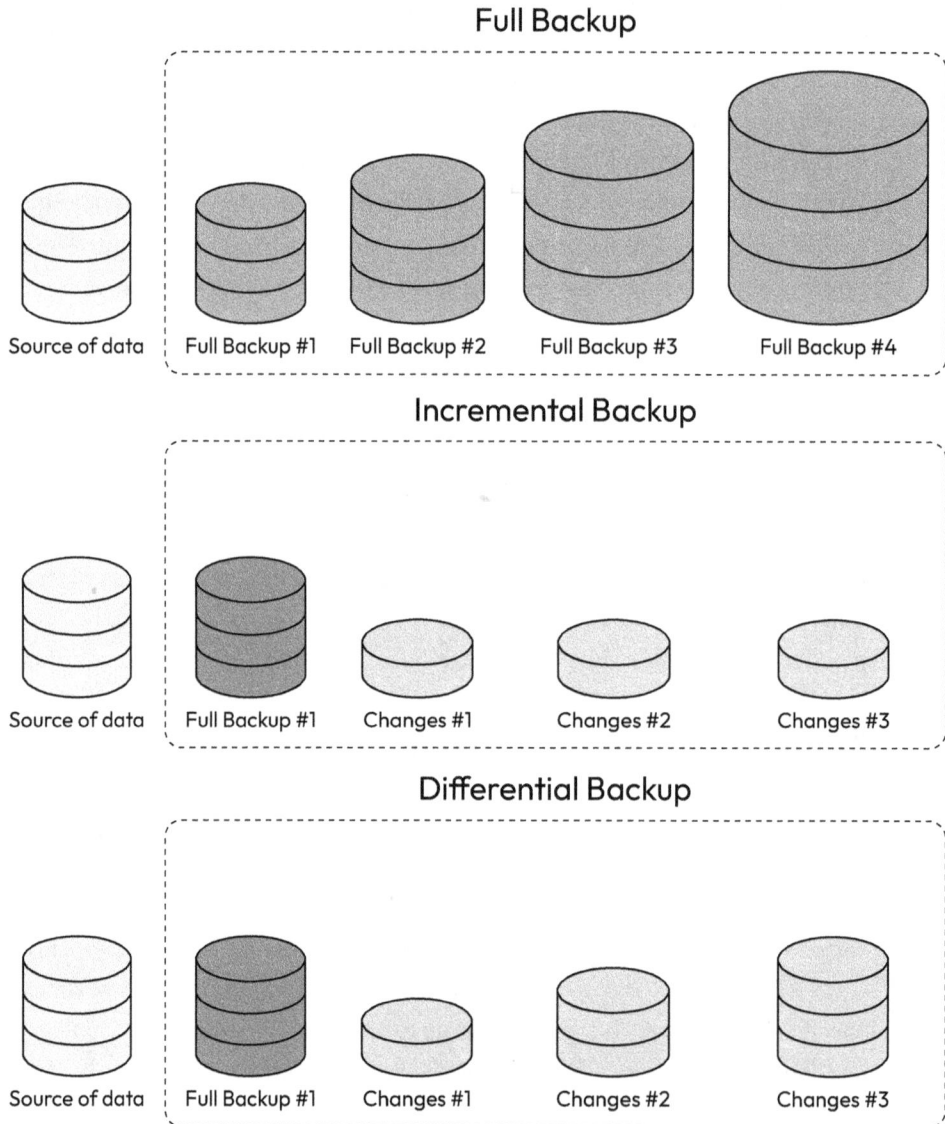

Figure 15.1 – What to back up

> **Interview tip**
>
> **Question:** *How do different types of backups in Kubernetes help in optimizing storage and recovery time?*
>
> **Answer:**
>
> - **Full backups:** Simple but storage-heavy, these allow single-file cluster restoration
>
> - **Incremental backups:** Efficient in terms of storage, only capturing changes since the last backup, though recovery is slower since all backups are required
>
> - **Differential backups:** Balance storage and recovery speed by capturing changes since the last full backup, needing only the latest full and differential backups to restore
>
> - **Application-level backups:** Back up specific applications, reducing data volume and speeding up recovery for individual applications

Knowing about these types of backups will help you design an efficient backup strategy for data protection and resource use.

Why must you back up more than etcd?

While etcd is the central datastore for Kubernetes, relying solely on etcd backups may not be sufficient for complete recovery. Here's why:

- **etcd stores cluster state, not application data**: etcd holds the desired state of the cluster, including configurations for Kubernetes objects such as Deployments, Services, ConfigMaps, and Secrets. However, it does not store the actual data used by your applications, especially the data within **PersistentVolumes (PVs)**.

- **PVs contain stateful data:** Applications such as databases store their data on PVs. Backing up etcd does not capture the data stored in these volumes. Losing PV data can result in significant data loss for stateful applications.

- **ConfigMaps and Secrets need protection**: ConfigMaps and Secrets are API objects stored in etcd, and an etcd snapshot includes their full contents (Secret values are Base64-encoded, not encrypted by default). The risk isn't that Secrets are missing from the snapshot—it's how you protect the snapshot and any exported data. Encrypt backups at rest, lock down access, and prefer a KMS-backed setup for Secret encryption at rest in the cluster.

- **Custom resource definitions (CRDs)**: CRDs extend Kubernetes functionality, and their definitions are stored in etcd. Backing up etcd will capture these definitions, but it may not include any associated data that resides outside of etcd—for example, external databases or storage systems that the custom resources manage. If this external data isn't backed up, a full restoration of the CRD's functionality may not be possible.

- **Application manifests and configurations**: Your deployment manifests, Helm charts, and other configuration files define how your applications run. Backing up these files ensures you can redeploy your applications accurately.

A comprehensive backup strategy must include more than just etcd. It should cover all aspects of your cluster and applications to ensure a full recovery in any disaster scenario. The following diagram summarizes the key Kubernetes components and resources that should be included in a comprehensive backup strategy.

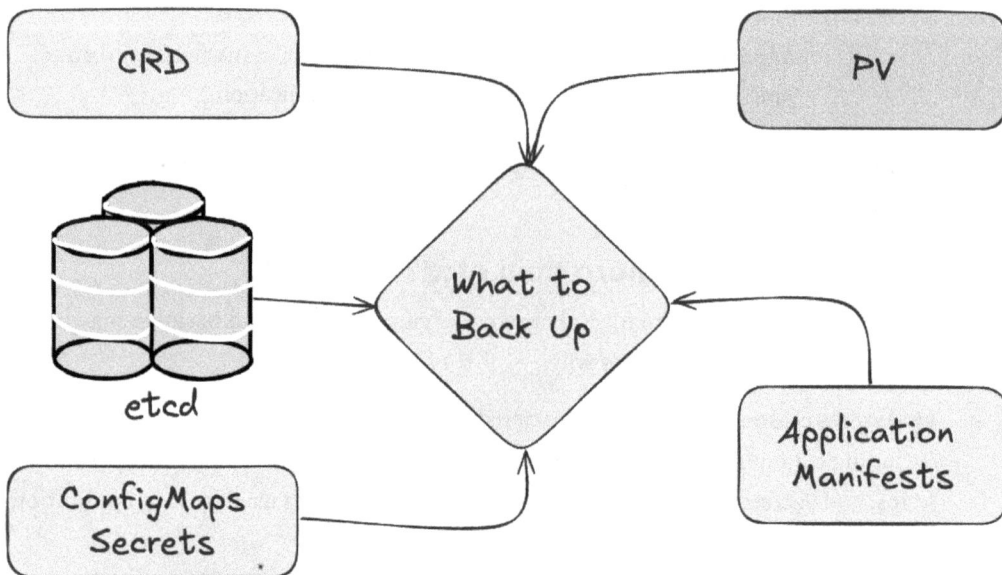

Figure 15.2 – What every comprehensive backup must cover

In this diagram, each box represents a critical category of Kubernetes data that should be included in your backup plan. etcd holds the cluster's state and configuration, PVs store application data, ConfigMaps and Secrets contain essential configuration and credentials, CRDs define extended Kubernetes functionality, and application manifests describe how your workloads are deployed. Backing up all these components ensures that you can fully restore both the cluster's control plane and the workloads it runs.

Now that we understand why it is necessary to back up more than just etcd, let's see what needs to be backed up.

What to back up

An effective backup strategy starts with identifying all the components that need protection. We will take a look at them in this section.

etcd data

The etcd key-value store is the backbone of the Kubernetes cluster, holding all cluster state and configuration data. Backing up etcd is crucial because losing it can render the cluster inoperative.

Example: If etcd data is corrupted or lost, you might lose information about Deployments, Services, and other critical configurations, making cluster recovery nearly impossible without backups.

How to back up etcd

You can use the etcdctl command-line tool to back up etcd data:

```
ETCDCTL_API=3 etcdctl snapshot save snapshot.db \
    --endpoints=https://127.0.0.1:2379 \
    --cacert=/path/to/ca.crt \
    --cert=/path/to/etcd-client.crt \
    --key=/path/to/etcd-client.key
```

This command creates a point-in-time snapshot of the etcd datastore and saves it as snapshot.db on the local machine. You can later use this snapshot to restore the cluster's state to the moment the backup was taken.

> **Interview tip**
>
> **Question:** *What's the difference between restoring etcd and restoring applications? When would you choose each?*
>
> **Answer:** An etcd restore reconstitutes **cluster state** (API objects) and is usually used for control plane recovery after catastrophic failure. It won't restore **application data** stored in PVs. Application restores target a namespace/application and include data (via CSI snapshots or database-native backups). Choose etcd restore when the control plane is corrupt/unavailable; choose application restore when a single application is broken or when you're migrating between clusters where full cluster restoration isn't desired. Mention that the desired ordering is infrastructure (CRDs/cluster-scoped) → namespaces → application resources → data restore → validations.

PVs

PVs store the data for stateful applications such as databases. Without backups of PVs, you risk losing important application data.

Example: A MySQL database running in Kubernetes stores its data on a PV. If the underlying storage fails and you haven't backed up the PV, you could lose all your database records.

How to back up PVs

Implement one of two common approaches:

- **Volume snapshots**: Use Kubernetes `VolumeSnapshot` resources if your storage provider supports it:

```
apiVersion: snapshot.storage.k8s.io/v1
kind: VolumeSnapshot
metadata:
  name: mysql-data-snapshot
  namespace: database
spec:
  volumeSnapshotClassName: csi-snapshot-class
  source:
    persistentVolumeClaimName: mysql-pvc
```

  Applying this manifest creates a snapshot of the PersistentVolumeClaim (`mysql-pvc`) using the specified snapshot class. This snapshot can later be used to restore the volume to the exact state it was in when the snapshot was taken.

- **Application-level tools**: Use database-specific backup tools, such as those for MySQL:

```
mysqldump -u <user> -p<password> --all-databases > backup.sql
```

  Alternatively, you can use pg_dump for PostgreSQL:

```
pg_dump -U -F c > backup.dump
```

ConfigMaps and Secrets

ConfigMaps store non-sensitive configuration data, while Secrets store sensitive information such as passwords and API keys. Both are essential for application functionality.

Example: An application might use a ConfigMap for environment variables and a Secret for database credentials. Losing these would prevent the application from running correctly.

How to back up ConfigMaps and Secrets (safely)

You can export ConfigMaps and Secrets using `kubectl`:

- **ConfigMaps**: It's safe to export ConfigMaps, either for documentation purposes or for managing them declaratively through GitOps:

```
kubectl get configmaps --all-namespaces -o yaml > configmaps.yaml
```

- **Secrets**: Avoid dumping raw Secrets to disk. They are already included in etcd snapshots. If you must store Secrets outside the cluster, encrypt them (for example, SOPS with Cloud KMS) or use sealed Secrets/external Secrets so that plaintext values never live in Git or on disk.

> **Security note**
>
> Treat etcd snapshots and any exported Secret material as highly sensitive. Store off-site, encrypt at rest, and restrict access to a minimal set of operators.

The following diagram illustrates the importance of securing backups for both ConfigMaps and Secrets. The top row shows a ConfigMap being backed up without special handling, as it contains non-sensitive configuration data. The bottom row shows a Secret being backed up with encryption (indicated by the lock icon), highlighting that sensitive information should always be encrypted during backup to prevent unauthorized access.

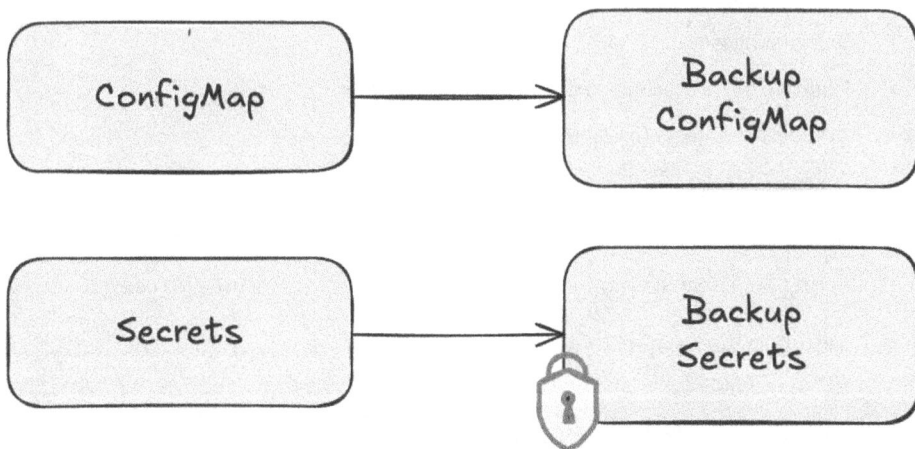

Figure 15.3 – Encrypting sensitive data

CRDs

CRDs allow you to define custom resources, extending Kubernetes functionalities. Backing them up ensures that custom behaviors and configurations are preserved.

Example: If you have CRDs for a custom controller or operator, losing them would break the functionality of those custom resources.

How to back up CRDs

Export CRDs using kubectl:

```
kubectl get crds -o yaml > crds-backup.yaml
```

This command retrieves all CRDs in the cluster and outputs them in YAML format to a file named crds-backup.yaml. You can later use this file to restore the CRDs in another cluster or after a disaster.

Cluster-scoped and foundational resources (don't skip these)

Beyond CRDs themselves, a reliable restore depends on a set of cluster-level and foundational objects that many workloads assume exist. Back them up regularly and restore them before namespaced workloads.

The following is a checklist (cluster-level or global in effect):

- ClusterRoles and ClusterRoleBindings (RBAC)
- StorageClasses
- PriorityClasses
- (Validating/Mutating) WebhookConfigurations
- APIService objects (for aggregated APIs)
- IngressClasses
- Namespaces (definitions and labels/annotations such as Pod Security Admission)

The following is a checklist (namespaced but foundational—include for completeness):

- ResourceQuotas and LimitRanges
- NetworkPolicies
- **PodDisruptionBudgets (PDBs)**

The following are some examples of quick exports:

```
# Cluster-scoped resources
kubectl get
clusterroles,clusterrolebindings,storageclasses,priorityclasses,
validatingwebhookconfigurations,mutatingwebhookconfigurations,apiservices,
ingressclasses -o yaml > cluster-scoped.yaml
# Namespace definitions (with labels/annotations) and key namespace-level
baselines
kubectl get namespaces -o yaml > namespaces.yaml
kubectl get resourcequotas,limitranges,networkpolicies -A -o yaml >
namespace-baselines.yaml
```

CR instances (not just CRDs):

Backing up CRDs alone isn't enough. You should also export the CustomResource objects that use them. A simple approach is to iterate over CRDs and dump their instances:

```
# Example approach: export all CRs for every CRD
for crd in $(kubectl get crd -o name | cut -d/ -f2); do
    kubectl get "$crd" -A -o yaml >> custom-resources.yaml || true
done
```

Note

The recommended restore order is: CRDs → cluster-scoped (RBAC, StorageClasses, WebhookConfigurations, APIService, IngressClasses, PriorityClasses) → namespaces → namespaced baselines (ResourceQuotas/LimitRanges/NetworkPolicies/PDBs) → workloads → data (PVs/DBs).

Application-specific data

This includes deployment manifests, service definitions, Helm charts, and other resources that define how your applications run in the cluster.

Example: Your CI/CD pipeline uses Helm charts to deploy applications. Backing up these charts ensures you can redeploy the applications with the same configurations.

How to back up application data

There are a couple of ways to do this:

- Store manifests and configurations in a version-controlled repository such as Git
- Use tools such as Helm or Kustomize to manage application configurations declaratively

> **Interview tip**
>
> **Question:** *Why is it important to back up PVs separately from etcd in Kubernetes?*
>
> **Answer:** etcd stores the cluster's state and configurations, but does not include the actual data within PVs. PVs contain the data for stateful applications such as databases, which is critical for data integrity and business operations. Backing up etcd alone won't capture this application data. Therefore, you need to back up PVs separately to ensure that you can restore both the cluster's state and the application's data in the event of a failure.

With the core backup requirements in mind, we can now explore the tools that simplify and automate these processes.

Backup tools and solutions

Backing up a Kubernetes cluster can be a complex task due to the platform's dynamic nature and the variety of components involved. Manually managing backups for etcd, PVs, ConfigMaps, Secrets, and other resources can be time-consuming and error-prone. Fortunately, there are multiple tools designed specifically to simplify Kubernetes backups. These tools automate the backup and restoration processes, ensuring consistency and reducing the risk of human error.

> **Interview tip**
>
> **Question:** *Explain the pitfalls of using database logical dumps versus CSI snapshots.*
>
> **Answer:** Logical dumps (`mysqldump`, `pg_dump`) are portable and schema-aware but can be slow and produce inconsistent backups without proper locking/transaction settings. CSI snapshots are instantaneous and consistent at the volume layer, but portability across storage backends/clouds can be limited; you may need a data export step for cross-cloud disaster recovery. Mature setups often do both: frequent snapshots for fast rollback and periodic logical backups for portability.

In this section, we will review some of the most popular Kubernetes backup tools. Each tool offers a unique set of features, benefits, and considerations. By exploring these options, you can choose a solution that best fits your cluster's needs, aligns with your operational practices, and supports your disaster recovery objectives.

Understanding the capabilities of these tools will help you do the following:

- **Automate backup processes**: Schedule regular backups without manual intervention
- **Simplify restorations**: Quickly restore resources and data in the event of a failure
- **Ensure consistency**: Maintain a consistent state across backups, reducing configuration drift
- **Integrate with existing workflows**: Seamlessly incorporate backups into your CI/CD pipelines and operational routines
- **Enhance security**: Leverage built-in features for encrypting data and securing backups

Now, let's look at a few popular Kubernetes backup tools:

- Velero (formerly Heptio Ark)
- Kasten K10
- Stash
- Native Kubernetes tools (`kubectl`, `etcdctl`)

Each of these tools addresses different aspects of Kubernetes backups, from cluster-level snapshots to application-specific data protection. Here, we'll delve into their key features, use cases, and how they can be implemented in your environment.

Interview tip

Question: *Why is it important to use specialized backup tools for Kubernetes rather than traditional backup solutions?*

Answer: Kubernetes is a highly dynamic and distributed system with components such as Pods, Services, ConfigMaps, Secrets, and PVs that can change frequently. Traditional backup solutions may not understand Kubernetes-specific resources and relationships, leading to incomplete or inconsistent backups. Specialized Kubernetes backup tools are designed to interact with the Kubernetes API, understand the cluster's state, and handle the complexities of backing up and restoring Kubernetes resources effectively. They can capture the entire application stack, including configurations and stateful data, ensuring a consistent and reliable backup process.

Considerations when choosing a backup tool

Before diving into the tools themselves, it's essential to consider several factors that will influence your choice:

- **Cluster size and complexity**: Larger clusters with many resources may require more robust tools that can scale accordingly

- **Application requirements**: Statefulness, data consistency needs, and specific application architectures may dictate certain backup approaches

- **Regulatory compliance**: Industries with strict compliance requirements may need tools that offer encryption, auditing, and retention policies

- **Infrastructure environment**: On-premises, cloud, or hybrid environments may influence tool compatibility and storage backend options

- **Ease of use and learning curve**: Tools with intuitive interfaces and good documentation can reduce implementation time

- **Community and support**: Active development communities and available support channels can be crucial for troubleshooting and updates

- **Cost**: Budget constraints may affect whether you opt for open source solutions or commercial offerings

Based on the factors we've just discussed, here's a quick comparison of popular Kubernetes backup tools, their core capabilities, and the situations where they are most effective:

Tool	Key Features	Best For
Velero	Open source, scheduled backups, migration	General-purpose backups, cluster migrations
Kasten K10	Enterprise features, policy automation	Enterprises needing advanced data management
Stash	Operator-based, database support	Application-specific backups, GitOps workflows
Native tools	Manual backups with kubectl and etcdctl	Small clusters, learning, custom automation

Table 15.1 – A comparison of popular Kubernetes backup tools, their key features, and best-use scenarios

Each tool offers unique features and focuses on different backup aspects. When choosing a tool, consider the complexity of your cluster, data protection needs, regulatory requirements, and your team's familiarity with the tool.

Once you've selected the right backup tool for your environment, the next step is to follow proven best practices to ensure your backups are reliable, secure, and easy to restore.

Best practices for Kubernetes backups

Implementing effective backup strategies in Kubernetes requires more than just picking the right tool. Here are some best practices to follow:

- **Automate backups:** Use a tool that allows you to schedule backups regularly, reducing the risk of human error and ensuring up-to-date data recovery points.

- **Test restorations regularly**: Regularly test backup restoration processes to confirm that your backups are reliable and to identify any potential issues before a disaster occurs.

- **Encrypt sensitive data:** Ensure that backups, especially those containing Secrets or sensitive application data, are encrypted both in transit and at rest to prevent unauthorized access.

- **Consider application-level backups:** For critical applications, consider backing up at the application level (e.g., using `mysqldump` for MySQL) in addition to implementing cluster-wide backups. This allows for more granular control and faster recovery.

- **Maintain backup retention policies:** Define a clear retention policy for your backups. Retain backups based on your organization's needs and compliance requirements, but avoid storing excess data, which can increase costs.

- **Use volume snapshots where possible:** If your storage provider supports it, leverage Kubernetes VolumeSnapshot resources to back up PVs; this can simplify the restoration of stateful applications.

- **Document the process:** Create and maintain clear documentation for your backup and restoration processes. This documentation should be easily accessible to all relevant team members and updated regularly.

- **Enable Secrets encryption at rest:** Use an EncryptionConfiguration with a KMS provider so that Secret values are encrypted before they're written to etcd. This reduces the blast radius if etcd or a snapshot is exposed.

By following these best practices, you'll enhance the resilience of your Kubernetes environment, making sure that data protection and disaster recovery processes are both effective and reliable.

With a solid backup and recovery plan in place, the next critical component of managing a resilient Kubernetes environment is **ongoing maintenance**. Proper maintenance ensures that your cluster operates efficiently, remains secure, and minimizes downtime. From performing upgrades to managing resources effectively, regular maintenance practices help prevent issues before they arise.

In the next section, we'll dive into best practices for Kubernetes maintenance, including the following aspects:

- **Smooth upgrade processes**: Ensuring seamless upgrades to newer Kubernetes versions and cluster components
- **Resource management**: Managing resource quotas, limits, and requests to maintain optimal performance
- **Routine health checks**: Implementing checks and alerts to monitor cluster health

By implementing these maintenance strategies, you'll keep your Kubernetes clusters stable and efficient, preparing them to handle the challenges of production environments with minimal disruptions. Let's explore these essential maintenance practices in detail.

Kubernetes maintenance

Maintenance is a critical aspect of managing any Kubernetes environment, whether in development, testing, or production. In a Kubernetes tech interview, you'll often need to explain how to maintain a cluster, handle upgrades, manage nodes, and follow best practices. Mastering these concepts not only improves your knowledge but also prepares you to respond effectively to complex interview questions.

Version policy and safe upgrade order

Keeping versions within supported skew prevents subtle API and scheduling issues during upgrades:

- **Order matters**: Upgrade the control plane first, then the node kubelet and `kubectl`
- **Version skew**: Keep a kubelet within *N* or *N-1* of the API server to avoid incompatibilities
- **One node at a time**: For each node, use the same sequence: cordon → drain (respect PDBs) → upgrade → uncordon
- **Practice in staging first**: Rehearse the plan against a staging cluster to surface add-on or admission-webhook issues early

Choose your maintenance path first:

- **Managed control planes (EKS/GKE/AKS):**
  - The provider upgrades the **control plane**.
  - You plan **node group** updates (new image/AMI, new kubelet), test add-ons, and handle surge/batch behavior.

- **kubeadm/self-managed:** You own **everything**—first use `kubeadm upgrade plan` and `kubeadm upgrade apply` to update the control plane, then upgrade each node individually.. You also own etcd care, certificates, and add-on compatibility.

> **Rule of thumb**
>
> Managed control planes means fewer moving parts, but they still need node and add-on diligence. Using kubeadm means full control, but also full responsibility.

This policy frames the steps you'll follow in the next subsections and keeps the cluster stable during rolling upgrades.

Cluster upgrades

Kubernetes regularly releases new versions to improve security, performance, and features. Keeping your cluster up to date is essential for stability and to leverage the latest Kubernetes capabilities. Cluster upgrades involve updating different components, including control plane components, worker nodes, applications, and dependencies.

How do you upgrade Kubernetes components?

The upgrade process typically starts with the control plane components such as `kube-apiserver`, `kube-controller-manager`, and `kube-scheduler`. Control plane upgrades ensure the cluster can orchestrate workloads effectively.

Here's an example of how you might approach a Kubernetes upgrade, starting with safeguarding your cluster's critical data:

1. **Back up your etcd datastore**: As etcd stores the entire state of the cluster, a backup ensures you can restore the cluster if anything goes wrong during the upgrade:

    ```
    ETCDCTL_API=3 etcdctl snapshot save snapshot.db \
        --endpoints=https://127.0.0.1:2379 \
        --cacert=/path/to/ca.crt \
        --cert=/path/to/etcd-client.crt \
        --key=/path/to/etcd-client.key
    ```

2. **Upgrade control plane components**: Most managed Kubernetes services provide auto-mated upgrade options. For self-managed clusters, you can use kubeadm to upgrade the control plane:

    ```
    sudo kubeadm upgrade apply v1.32.0
    ```

3. **Upgrade kubelet and kubectl**: After upgrading the control plane, update the kubelet and kubectl binaries on each node so that they match the control plane version:

    ```
    sudo apt-get update && sudo apt-get install -y kubelet kubectl
    sudo systemctl restart kubelet
    ```

> **Interview tip**
>
> **Question:** *Why is it important to upgrade control plane components first?*
>
> **Answer:** The control plane manages the cluster, including scheduling, scaling, and monitoring workloads. Upgrading it first ensures that it can handle newer API ver-sions and changes before worker nodes, reducing the chance of compatibility issues.

In summary, upgrading Kubernetes starts with taking an etcd backup to safeguard the cluster state. Next, you update the control plane components to the desired version, followed by upgrading kubelet and kubectl on each node to ensure version compatibility. This sequence minimizes downtime and reduces the risk of version mismatches.

With the control plane updated and stable, the next step is to upgrade the worker nodes so that they remain compatible with the control plane and continue running workloads reliably.

How do you upgrade worker nodes?

Upgrading worker nodes comes after the control plane to ensure compatibility and stability across the cluster. The control plane manages core services (e.g., scheduling and monitoring) and the Kubernetes API, so it needs to be upgraded first so that it can handle any changes in API versions, resource definitions, or security protocols. Once the control plane is stable, you can move on and upgrade worker nodes one by one to minimize downtime.

Once the control plane is stable, you can proceed with upgrading the worker nodes. The following process ensures workloads are redirected safely and nodes are prepared for the upgrade:

1. **Cordon the node**: This prevents new Pods from being scheduled on the node, maintaining stability by redirecting new workloads to other nodes:

    ```
    kubectl cordon <node-name>
    ```

    See the left-hand side of *Figure 15.4*—this visually demonstrates the effect of cordoning a node, marking it as `SchedulingDisabled` so that new Pods aren't placed there.

2. **Drain the node**: Draining safely evicts all running Pods, moving them to other available nodes in the cluster. Use `--ignore-daemonsets` to keep DaemonSets running:

    ```
    kubectl drain <node-name> --ignore-daemonsets
    ```

    See the right-hand side of *Figure 15.4*—here, you can see that all Pods have been moved off the outdated node, preparing it for the upgrade.

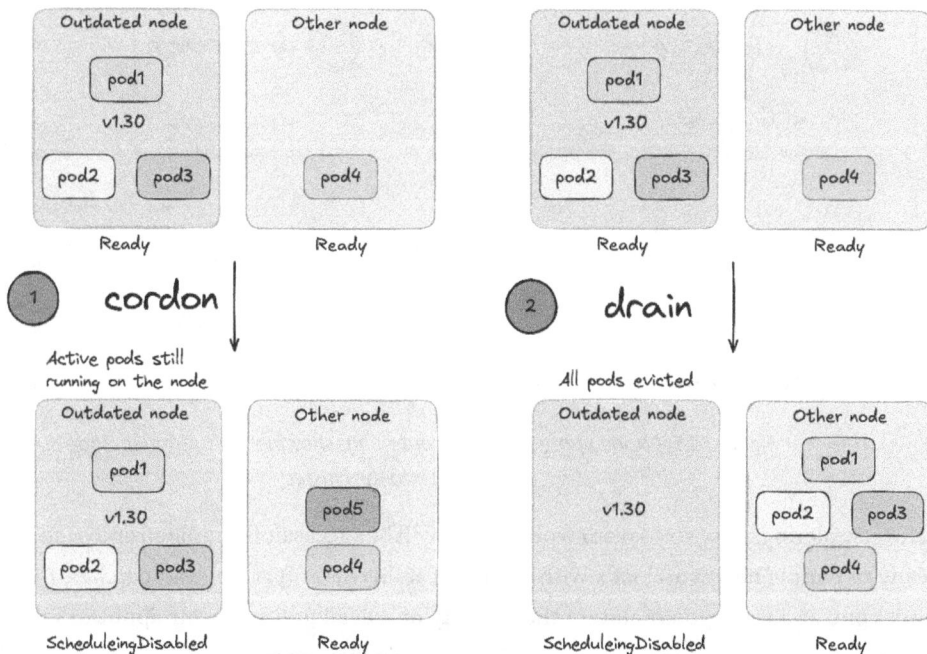

Figure 15.4 – Node cordoning and draining sequence, visualizing the safe relocation of Pods

3. **Upgrade the node software**: Update the kubelet and other node-related software. This upgrade might require a reboot for changes to be applied.

    See the left-hand side of *Figure 15.5*—here, the node's version updates from an outdated version (e.g., v1.30) to a current version (e.g., v1.31) while marked as `SchedulingDisabled`.

4. **Uncordon the node**: Allow new workloads to be scheduled on the upgraded node, restoring it to full operation:

```
kubectl uncordon <node-name>
```

See the right-hand side of *Figure 15.5*—this shows the node back in rotation, ready to accept new Pods with updated software.

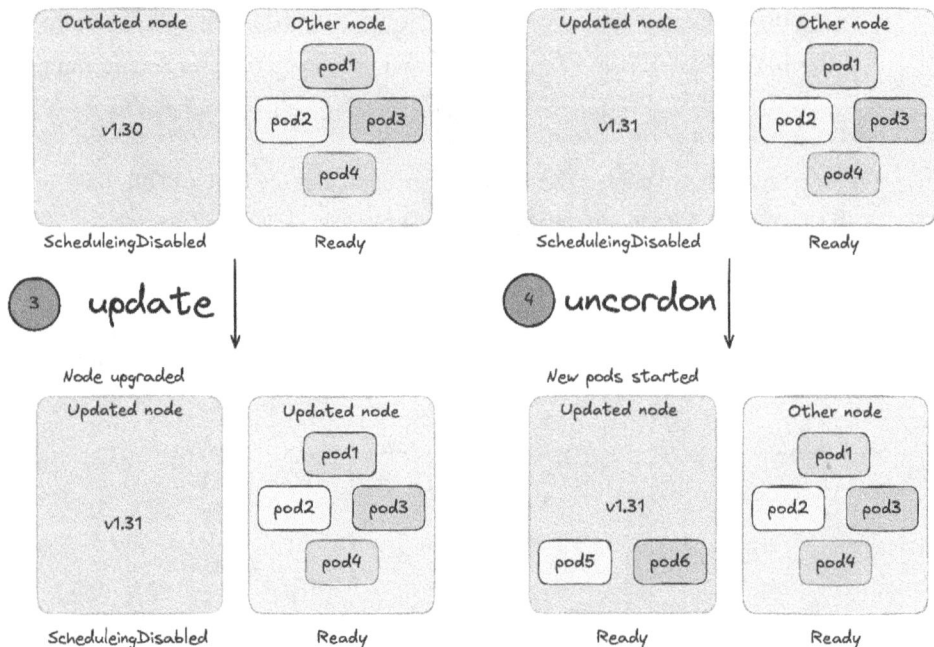

Figure 15.5 – Node upgrade and uncordoning, showing the upgraded node reintegrated into the cluster

After completing these steps, your worker node will be successfully updated and back in rotation, ready to handle new workloads with the latest Kubernetes features and patches. By updating nodes one at a time, you maintain the stability and availability of your applications, avoiding service interruptions during the process. This incremental approach is essential for minimizing risk, especially in production environments.

In summary: cordon, drain, upgrade, uncordon. Repeat this cycle for each node to maintain high availability while keeping your cluster up to date.

Protecting availability with PDBs

Node drains and autoscaling can evict too many replicas at once. A PDB prevents voluntary disruptions from dropping service below a safe floor:

```
apiVersion: policy/v1
kind: PodDisruptionBudget
metadata:
  name: api-pdb
spec:
  minAvailable: 2
  selector:
    matchLabels:
      app: api
```

> **Why it matters**
>
> During maintenance, a PDB ensures at least two replicas of app=api remain available while nodes are drained or updated.

With your cluster's nodes fully upgraded and stable, the next step is to ensure that the applications and their dependencies are also updated so that they match the new environment. This helps maintain compatibility, security, and performance across the entire stack.

How do you upgrade applications and dependencies?

Upgrading application dependencies in Kubernetes involves carefully managing each component and ensuring compatibility with updated Kubernetes versions. Here's a detailed approach to handling these upgrades:

- **Rolling updates for deployments**: Use Kubernetes rolling updates to update applications without downtime. This process gradually replaces older Pod versions with new ones:

```
kubectl set image deployment/my-app my-container=my-app:v2
```

- **Testing in staging**: Always test application upgrades in a staging environment. Deploy the new version, monitor it for stability, and identify any issues before moving to production.

- **Updating ConfigMaps and Secrets**: If applications depend on specific configurations or secrets, update these resources carefully. Rolling out new ConfigMaps or Secrets versions may require redeploying Pods to reflect changes.

- **Dependency management**: Ensure your applications' dependencies, such as database versions, APIs, or third-party services, are compatible with the new Kubernetes version. Incompatible dependencies can lead to runtime errors or degraded performance.

> **Interview tip**
>
> **Question:** *How do rolling updates help maintain application availability during upgrades?*
>
> **Answer:** Rolling updates replace older Pods one by one, allowing the new version to be tested in real time without disrupting the service. This ensures minimal downtime and seamless deployment for users.

Now that we've covered individual upgrade procedures for components, nodes, and applications, let's put it all together in a complete, step-by-step production scenario. This will show how the different upgrade stages fit into a cohesive process for minimizing downtime and maintaining cluster stability.

Complete Kubernetes cluster upgrade steps (production scenario)

Upgrading a Kubernetes cluster in production demands a careful, step-by-step approach. Each stage helps manage the complexities of a production-grade upgrade, minimizing downtime and ensuring stability. Let's understand this better:

1. **Preparation: Backups and staging environment**

    The first phase of a production-grade Kubernetes upgrade is all about preparation. Before making any changes to the live cluster, it's critical to secure reliable backups and validate the upgrade process in a safe, controlled staging environment:

    - **Automated backups**: Use tools such as Velero to back up critical components, especially etcd. This provides a safety net if anything goes wrong.

    - **Staging environment**: Make sure your staging environment mirrors production exactly, including any incremental upgrades. If production was upgraded from v1.18 to v1.31 incrementally, replicate this path in staging. Testing only the latest version upgrade in a clean environment may overlook compatibility issues present in production.

Interview tip

Question: *Why should staging mirror production during an upgrade?*

Answer: Matching production in staging helps catch issues that may only emerge with specific configurations, workloads, or incremental upgrades. It ensures that the upgrade process and potential impacts are fully understood before they're applied to production.

2. **API resources check: Validate compatibility**

Verify that all API resources are compatible with the target Kubernetes version. Each Kubernetes version deprecates certain APIs, so outdated resources can break during an upgrade.

Also, check for deprecated APIs. You should run checks on resources such as PodSecurityPolicies, NetworkPolicies, and Ingresses. Updating deprecated APIs in advance prevents unexpected downtime or broken workloads.

Interview tip

Question: *Why is it crucial to address deprecated APIs before an upgrade?*

Answer: Deprecated APIs may no longer be supported in the upgraded version, leading to service disruptions if they aren't updated. Addressing these issues in advance ensures that the upgrade doesn't introduce compatibility issues.

3. **Upgrade the control plane (one minor version at a time)**

Begin with the control plane upgrade to the next minor version (e.g., from v1.30 to v1.31). Upgrading the control plane first enables the cluster to manage workloads effectively with new API changes.

Upgrading one minor version at a time avoids risks associated with skipping multiple versions, such as incompatibilities and configuration issues.

Here are some pitfalls to avoid:

- Skipping versions risks API compatibility problems and may require extensive manual fixes
- Overloading the cluster with multiple upgrades simultaneously can lead to complex failures that are difficult to troubleshoot

4. **Upgrade worker nodes (one minor version at a time)**

    Upgrade worker nodes individually to minimize downtime. Use the cordon, drain, and uncordon process for each node to ensure workloads are rescheduled gracefully.

    Post-upgrade, monitor each node's logs and workload performance for any inconsistencies or issues.

5. **Update add-ons: Ensure compatibility with the new version**

    Cluster add-ons, such as CNI plugins, Ingress controllers, and DNS plugins, should be compatible with the upgraded version of Kubernetes. Neglecting this step can lead to vulnerabilities or compatibility problems.

    Once the core cluster components are upgraded, it's equally important to verify that all add-ons—such as CNI plugins, Ingress controllers, and DNS plugins—are compatible with the new Kubernetes version. The following steps outline how to update and validate these add-ons to prevent compatibility issues:

    - **Upgrade Helm charts for applications first**: Start with application Helm charts to make sure applications are compatible with the cluster's new capabilities.
    - **Update core add-ons**: Update each add-on to the recommended version for the new Kubernetes release. Validate all updates in staging before deploying to production.

    Warning

    If add-ons are incompatible with the new version, network issues or service routing failures can arise, leading to application downtime.

6. **Monitor cluster health**

    After each stage, monitor cluster health metrics, logs, and application performance for at least a week to ensure stability. Use monitoring tools such as Prometheus, Grafana, or CloudWatch to track cluster health and catch any hidden issues.

    You should focus on network and application-level monitoring: add-ons, especially network-related ones such as CNIs, can introduce subtle issues. Ensure you have robust monitoring and alerting in place.

7. **Repeat in production after validation in staging**

    Once the upgrade process is validated in staging, apply it to the production environment. Upgrading in phases—one environment at a time—helps ensure stability across multiple clusters.

    If your organization has multiple environments (e.g., dev, test, prod), consider upgrading non-production clusters first and monitoring stability before upgrading production.

8. **Iterate for the next version**

    Cluster upgrades should be an ongoing process. Plan to upgrade to the next minor version (e.g., from v1.31 to v1.32) once your cluster is stable. Regular, incremental upgrades prevent technical debt and improve security.

Following these steps ensures a smooth and reliable upgrade path. This methodical approach minimizes risks and keeps your Kubernetes cluster up to date with the latest best practices.

Developing disaster recovery plans

Backups are essential, but they're only half of the story. Having a copy of your data is one thing; knowing how to use it effectively when disaster strikes is another. A disaster recovery plan is the bridge between a backup sitting in storage and a fully restored, functional Kubernetes environment. Without a plan, even the best backups can leave you scrambling in the middle of an outage.

Kubernetes adds its own complexity to disaster recovery planning. It's a distributed system, often running across multiple nodes and using a mix of stateless and stateful workloads. Recovery isn't just about putting files back—it's about restoring cluster state, re-deploying workloads, reconnecting storage, and getting services running in the right order, all under pressure.

Setting objectives: RTO and RPO

Two key metrics guide disaster recovery planning:

*   **Recovery Time Objective (RTO)**: The maximum acceptable time your services can be down
*   **Recovery Point Objective (RPO)**: The maximum acceptable amount of data loss, measured in time

For example, if your RTO is 30 minutes and your RPO is 5 minutes, your disaster recovery approach must ensure the cluster is back online in under half an hour and that you lose no more than 5 minutes of data.

Interview tip

Question: *How do you set and meet RPO/RTO targets for a multi-tenant cluster?*

Answer: Define business RPO/RTO per tenant; map to schedules (e.g., hourly incrementals and nightly fulls; CSI snapshots every 15 minutes for Tier 1). Use storage-level snapshots for fast RTO; off-site copies for DR. Enforce per-namespace policies (labels/annotations) that are consumed by your backup operator. Continuously test restores and report achieved RTO/RPO. Tie failures to alerts and SLOs.

These numbers should not be picked by the engineering team in isolation—they need to be agreed upon with business stakeholders. A disaster recovery plan that restores in 4 hours when the business needs 30 minutes is a failure, even if the backups work perfectly.

Mapping the RPO/RTO to backup strategies

Targets are only useful when they drive concrete schedules and architectures. Use the following table as a starting point; tune the ranges with real restore tests in your environment.

Typical ranges

Assume healthy storage with medium clusters. Always validate with drills.

As shown in *Table 15.2*, faster recovery (lower RTO) and lower data loss (lower RPO) generally cost more—in terms of either storage, compute, or operational complexity. Start with the strategy that meets your targets on paper, then run restore drills and adjust frequency, tooling, or topology until your measured RPO/RTO meets the goal consistently.

Strategy	Example Schedule	Typical RPO	Typical RTO	Notes
Full only	Nightly full	≤24 h	1–3 h	Simple and cheapest; slowest recovery; not for Tier 1.
Full and differential	Weekly full and daily differential	≤24 h	1–2 h	Faster restore than incrementals; moderate cost.
Full and incremental	Weekly full and hourly incremental	≤60 mins	2–4 h	Efficient storage; longer restore chain.

Strategy	Example Schedule	Typical RPO	Typical RTO	Notes
CSI volume snapshots	Every 15 minutes and daily off-site copy	≤15 mins	5–30 mins	Fast rollback in-region; cross-region needs copy.
Application-level logical backups	Hourly dumps and nightly full	≤60 mins	30–90 mins	Portable; slower on large databases without tuning.
Continuous database replication	Streaming WAL/ binlog and periodic snapshots	≤1–5 mins	10–30 mins	Low RPO; ensure replica consistency and cutover steps.
Active/active multi-region	Synchronous replication and periodic snapshots	≈0	1–5 mins	Highest cost/complexity; best RTO/RPO for Tier 0.

Table 15.2 – Mapping backup/disaster recovery strategies to achievable RPO/RTO (typical ranges)

Choosing schedules to meet targets

Here's how you should go about this:

- Start from the business targets (e.g., RTO 30 minutes, RPO 5 minutes).
- Pick the data path that can achieve the RPO (e.g., snapshots every 5–15 minutes, or streaming replication).
- Ensure there's an off-site copy aligned with the same RPO for regional failures.
- Run a restore drill and record actual RTO/RPO; adjust the frequency, tooling, or topology until you meet the goal.
- Document the cost trade-offs (storage, egress, extra clusters) and get stakeholder sign-off.

Common disaster scenarios in Kubernetes

Your disaster recovery plan should be built around realistic failure modes, such as the following:

- **Cluster-level failures**: Control plane outage, etcd corruption, or complete cluster loss
- **Storage failures**: Loss of PVs or cloud storage service disruption
- **Application-level failures**: A bad deployment or configuration push that takes down services
- **Regional outages**: Entire cloud regions going offline due to provider or infrastructure issues

> **Tip**
>
> When listing scenarios, include both technical and operational disasters—for example, accidental data deletion by a team member or security incidents such as ransomware attacks.

Building an effective Kubernetes disaster recovery plan

A strong disaster recovery plan is not a single document but a set of *tested, repeatable processes*:

1. **Document recovery procedures:**
   - Spell out, step by step, how to restore workloads, configurations, and data.
   - Store this document in version control and in an offline location.

2. **Automate cluster recreation:**
   - Use **Infrastructure as Code (IaC)** (Terraform, Pulumi) to provision new clusters.
   - Use GitOps tools (Argo CD, Flux) to redeploy workloads from a known-good state.

3. **Data recovery playbooks:**
   - Define how to restore etcd, PVs, and application-level data (e.g., database restores).
   - Include commands, storage locations, and access details.

4. **Failover and redundancy:**
   - Consider multi-cluster or multi-region strategies.
   - Use DNS-based failover (e.g., ExternalDNS with Route 53 or Cloud DNS) to shift traffic automatically.

5. **Test, test, test:**
   - Run disaster recovery drills at least quarterly.
   - Simulate failures and measure actual RTO/RPO against targets.

Example: Recovering from a regional outage

Imagine you're running a production workload in AWS eu-central-1 and the entire region experiences an outage. Your disaster recovery plan could include the following aspects:

- A second Kubernetes cluster in eu-west-1 with essential services pre-deployed but scaled to zero
- Nightly backups of etcd and PV snapshots that are replicated to eu-west-1 S3 storage
- A Route 53 DNS failover policy that automatically switches traffic to the standby cluster when health checks fail
- An IaC pipeline that can scale workloads to production levels within minutes

If executed correctly, your team could restore full service in under 20 minutes with minimal data loss.

> **Interview tip**
>
> **Question:** *In Kubernetes, how would you design a disaster recovery plan for a production cluster?*
>
> **Answer:** I'd start by defining the RTO and RPO with stakeholders. Then, I'd implement regular backups for etcd, PVs, and application configurations, stored in multiple regions. I'd use IaC and GitOps for rapid redeployment. I'd also test restores regularly to confirm they meet our RTO/RPO, and include a communication plan so that everyone knows their role during recovery.

Summary

In this chapter, we delved into key strategies for ensuring the resilience of Kubernetes clusters. We covered the following topics:

- **Backup strategies**: First, we explored full, incremental, differential, and application-level backups, each designed to optimize storage and recovery speed. We also emphasized the importance of backing up resources beyond etcd, including PVs, ConfigMaps, Secrets, CRDs, and application configurations.

- **Backup tools and best practices**: Then, we introduced tools such as Velero, Kasten K10, and Stash, which streamline Kubernetes-specific backup processes. Best practices for effective backup management include automation, encryption, regular testing, retention policies, and documentation to ensure data protection and recovery efficiency.

- **Cluster maintenance**: Next, we highlighted best practices for ongoing maintenance, such as using namespaces for resource organization, implementing health checks, and adhering to the principle of least privilege for enhanced security. Automation of routine tasks, such as backups and monitoring, was also emphasized as a way to minimize human error and enhance reliability.

- **Upgrading the cluster**: Finally, we examined the step-by-step upgrade process, covering control plane and worker node upgrades, dependency management, and add-on updates. This chapter stressed the importance of performing upgrades incrementally (one minor version at a time) to avoid compatibility issues, testing thoroughly in a mirrored staging environment, and carefully monitoring the cluster after each phase.

By mastering these backup and maintenance strategies, you can ensure your Kubernetes clusters remain robust, resilient, and prepared for unforeseen events.

Now that you've learned how to maintain and protect your Kubernetes environment, the next step is understanding how to troubleshoot when things go wrong. In *Chapter 16*, we'll explore common issues you may encounter, such as applications failing to run correctly, nodes becoming unresponsive, or network communication errors. This chapter will provide a practical guide to diagnosing and resolving these challenges, equipping you with essential troubleshooting skills for effective Kubernetes management.

Unlock this book's exclusive benefits now

UNLOCK NOW

Scan this QR code or go to `https://packtpub.com/unlock`, then search for this book by name.

Note: Keep your purchase invoice ready before you start.

Part 6

Troubleshooting and Best Practices

This part offers practical tips for troubleshooting and keeping your Kubernetes environment stable—even when things go wrong. You'll learn how to quickly identify and fix common issues, along with proven strategies for regaining control during live production incidents. It's all about staying calm under pressure and keeping your systems running smoothly when it matters most.

This part of the book includes the following chapters:

- *Chapter 16, Real-world Troubleshooting Scenarios*
- *Chapter 17, Common Mistakes and How to Avoid Them*
- *Chapter 18, Interview Stories from Authors*

16

Real-World Troubleshooting Scenarios

In Kubernetes environments, things break—and often when you least expect them to. Pods get stuck in a `Pending` state, containers fail to start, applications behave unpredictably, or traffic mysteriously stops routing. These issues don't just affect system stability—they directly impact customer experience and **business continuity (BC)**. Whether you're operating production-grade clusters or preparing for a senior DevOps or SRE interview, being able to troubleshoot effectively is a must-have skill.

In this chapter, we shift from theory to the practical skills that define a top-tier engineer. When a system as complex as Kubernetes fails, your value is measured by how effectively you can restore service. We will equip you with a powerful, systematic framework for diagnosing any issue you'll face in a production environment.

We'll begin by establishing the foundational mental models for structured troubleshooting. Then, we'll apply these models to dissect the most common and critical failure domains:

- **Mastering the Pod lifecycle**: From `Pending` pods that won't schedule to containers stuck in a `CrashLoopBackOff` state, we'll cover every stage
- **Untangling network issues**: We'll trace the path from external requests through Ingress and Services, troubleshoot DNS failures, and debug `NetworkPolicy` conflicts
- **Resolving performance bottlenecks**: You'll learn how to diagnose CPU throttling, memory limits, and `OOMKilled` events, and how to fine-tune autoscaling

We will be covering the following main headings:

- Establishing a troubleshooter's mindset
- Mastering pod lifecycle troubleshooting
- Network troubleshooting
- Performance optimization and troubleshooting

By the end of the chapter, you'll not only know how to fix these problems but also how to clearly explain your process during a high-stakes interview.

Establishing a troubleshooter's mindset

In a complex distributed system such as Kubernetes, a chaotic, reactive approach to troubleshooting leads to extended downtime and unresolved issues. Before we dive into specific failure scenarios, it's crucial to establish the correct mindset. The difference between a junior and a senior engineer isn't knowing more commands; it's applying a structured, repeatable methodology to get to the root cause faster. The models discussed in this section provide that essential framework.

Why this matters in interviews

In a Kubernetes interview, especially for a senior role, simply listing `kubectl` commands is not enough. Interviewers want to evaluate your *thought process*. They're evaluating your ability to handle a crisis methodically rather than chaotically. A vague alert such as "Application X is down" is a common prompt designed to test whether you can apply a structured, repeatable methodology to isolate a root cause under pressure.

You distinguish yourself by explaining *how* you think, not just *what* you do. Articulating a clear mental model shows you can navigate the complexity of a distributed system without getting lost chasing misleading symptoms. This chapter gives you three powerful, interconnected models that will form the backbone of your troubleshooting narrative, helping you to structure your answers and impress your interviewers.

The foundational models of troubleshooting

An expert troubleshooter doesn't guess; they use a system. You can solve almost any Kubernetes problem by combining three mental models. An observability flow helps you detect the symptom, a layered model helps you locate *where* the problem is, and a tactical triage strategy helps you fix the most common issues quickly.

The layered debugging model

The most effective way to approach an unknown failure is to think of Kubernetes as a stack of layers. Each layer depends on the one below it. A problem in the storage layer will eventually bubble up and manifest as an application error. By examining the layers systematically, you can efficiently isolate the true root cause.

The canonical layers for troubleshooting are the following:

- **Application layer:** Your actual code. Is it throwing exceptions? Is there a performance bottleneck?
- **Pod and configuration layer:** The pod lifecycle. Is it crash looping? Are its ConfigMaps or Secrets incorrect? Are probes failing?
- **Node layer:** The worker machine. Is it out of CPU, memory, or disk? Is the kubelet healthy?
- **Networking layer:** How services talk. Is CoreDNS failing? Is a NetworkPolicy blocking traffic? Is the Ingress routing correctly?
- **Storage layer:** Persistent data. Can your **PersistentVolumeClaim (PVC)** bind to a **PersistentVolume (PV)**? Is the underlying storage system healthy?
- **Cluster infrastructure layer:** The control plane. Is the API server responsive? Is etcd healthy?

The "bottom-up" triage strategy

For the most common failure—an application that you can't access from outside—you need a quick, tactical playbook. The "bottom-up" strategy follows the flow of traffic in reverse, starting from the closest point to the application. It is described as follows:

1. **Troubleshoot the Pods:** Are they running and ready? If the pods aren't healthy, nothing else matters.
2. **Troubleshoot the Service:** Is the Service selecting the ready pods? Check your labels, selectors, and endpoints.
3. **Troubleshoot the Ingress:** Is the Ingress resource correctly configured to route external traffic to the Service?

This simple three-step process resolves the vast majority of day-to-day deployment failures.

The observability-driven flow

A modern SRE-driven approach uses tooling to guide the troubleshooting process. This flow moves you from a high-level symptom to a specific root cause in three phases:

1. **Lightly identify**: Start with your dashboards (e.g., Grafana). What's the high-level symptom? Is latency spiking? Are HTTP 5xx errors increasing? The goal is to form a hypothesis and identify a suspicious area (e.g., "The issue seems to be in the `checkout-service` namespace").

2. **Closely identify**: Use the three pillars of observability—**metrics**, **logs**, and **traces**—to zoom in. Check detailed metrics for suspicious pods. Analyze logs for specific error messages. Use distributed tracing to see which microservice call is failing. The goal is to find a specific component (e.g., "Pod `checkout-service-xyz` is `OOMKilled`").

3. **Thoroughly identify**: Go deep on the specific component. Analyze its YAML (`kubectl get pod -o yaml`), inspect its configuration, or debug the application code. This is the final step to find and confirm the root cause.

These models are not mutually exclusive; you'll use them together. The observability flow might help you "lightly identify" a spike in 503 errors. This points you to the networking layer. Within that layer, you apply the "bottom-up" triage to check that the Ingress, Service, and Pods are correctly configured. This entire process, showing how a symptom guides you through the different models, is visualized in *Figure 16.1*.

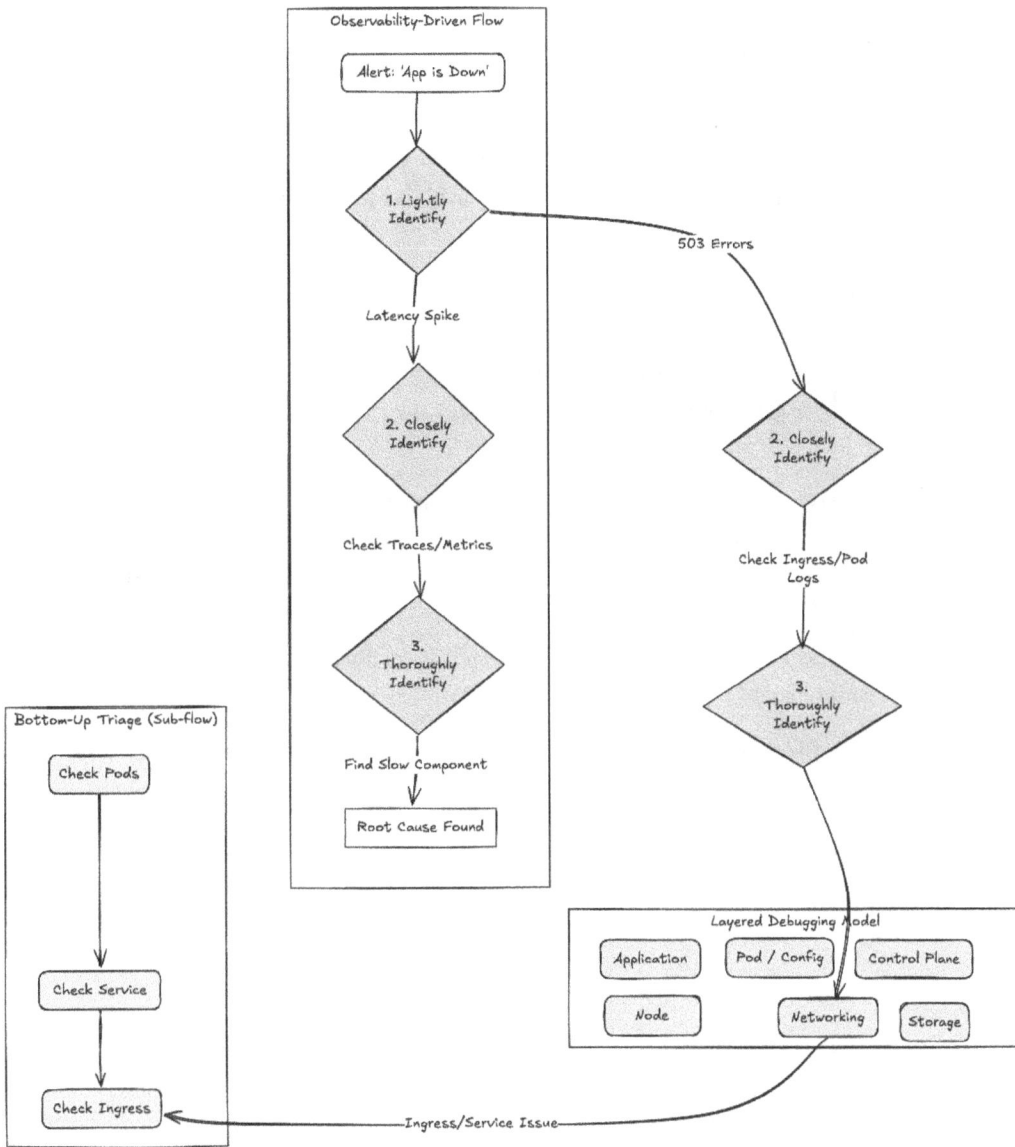

Observability-Driven Flow

Alert: 'App is Down'

1. Lightly Identify

503 Errors

Latency Spike

2. Closely Identify

2. Closely Identify

Check Traces/Metrics

Check Ingress/Pod Logs

3. Thoroughly Identify

3. Thoroughly Identify

Find Slow Component

Root Cause Found

Bottom-Up Triage (Sub-flow)

Check Pods

Check Service

Check Ingress

Layered Debugging Model

Application | Pod / Config | Control Plane

Node | Networking | Storage

Ingress/Service Issue

Figure 16.1 – A unified troubleshooting workflow

Interview tip

Question: *You've just been paged for a critical production outage. The alert is vague: "Application X is down." Walk me through your first five minutes.*

Answer: My priority is to understand the blast radius and the nature of the failure. I wouldn't immediately SSH into a box.

First minute (lightly identify): I'll go straight to our primary Grafana dashboard for the service. I'm looking for high-level symptoms: Is this affecting all users or just some? Are HTTP 500s spiking, or is it latency, or are requests not getting through at all? I'm forming a quick hypothesis. For example, a spike in 503s suggests a connectivity or availability problem.

Next two minutes (closely identify): Based on the dashboard, I'll dive into the relevant pillar of observability. If it's 503s, I'll check the logs for my Ingress controller and the application pods for connection errors. If it's latency, I'll look at a distributed trace in Jaeger to see which downstream service is slow. My goal is to move from a general symptom ("app is down") to a specific, actionable problem ("`auth-service` is timing out").

Final two minutes (thoroughly identify): Once I've identified a component—say, the `auth-service` pods—I'll start my targeted `kubectl` commands. I'll check with `kubectl get pods` to see whether they're running and ready. If not, I'll run `kubectl describe pod` to check for events such as OOM kills or probe failures. If they are running, I'll check their logs with `kubectl logs`. This structured flow prevents guessing and quickly narrows the scope of the problem.

You now have the essential mental framework that separates a senior engineer from a junior one. Before we apply this framework to specific problems, let's solidify the core principles.

Remember that in any troubleshooting scenario, your goal is to demonstrate a *structured thought process*, not just recite commands. You'll achieve this by combining the three models we discussed:

- The observability-driven flow, to guide your investigation from symptom to cause
- The layered model, to pinpoint where in the stack the problem lies
- The bottom-up triage, as your go-to playbook for common application access issues

Always start with high-level observability to form a hypothesis before diving deep, and be ready to articulate how metrics, logs, and traces each play a unique role in finding the root cause.

With this framework firmly in mind, let's put it into practice. We'll begin with the most fundamental and frequent point of failure: the pod lifecycle.

Mastering pod lifecycle troubleshooting

The pod is the atomic unit of Kubernetes, the smallest and most fundamental building block. If you can't get a pod to run, your application is dead on arrival. This makes pod lifecycle issues the most common and critical problems you'll face. In this section, we will walk through the entire lifecycle of a pod, from its creation to its termination, and cover the systematic steps to diagnose failures at each stage. We begin with the very first hurdle: getting a pod scheduled onto a node.

Pod scheduling failures: The stuck Pending pod

A Pending pod is a fundamental "Day 1" problem in Kubernetes. If you can't get a pod to schedule, nothing else can happen. Interviewers use this scenario to test your core diagnostic skills. They want to see whether you can systematically determine *why* the scheduler, the component responsible for placing pods onto nodes, has rejected your workload. Your ability to calmly use kubectl describe to read scheduler events is a crucial first impression.

Diagnosing the Pending state

When a pod's status is Pending, it means the cluster has accepted the pod object, but it cannot be placed onto a node. The Kubernetes scheduler acts as a gatekeeper, and it has found no node that satisfies the pod's requirements. Your job is to ask the scheduler why.

Your first and most important command is kubectl describe pod <pod-name>. The output is verbose, but your focus should be on the Events section at the bottom. This is where the scheduler leaves you a message explaining its decision. The scheduler runs the pod through a series of filters, and if any check fails, the pod remains in a Pending state, as illustrated in the following workflow (*Figure 16.2*).

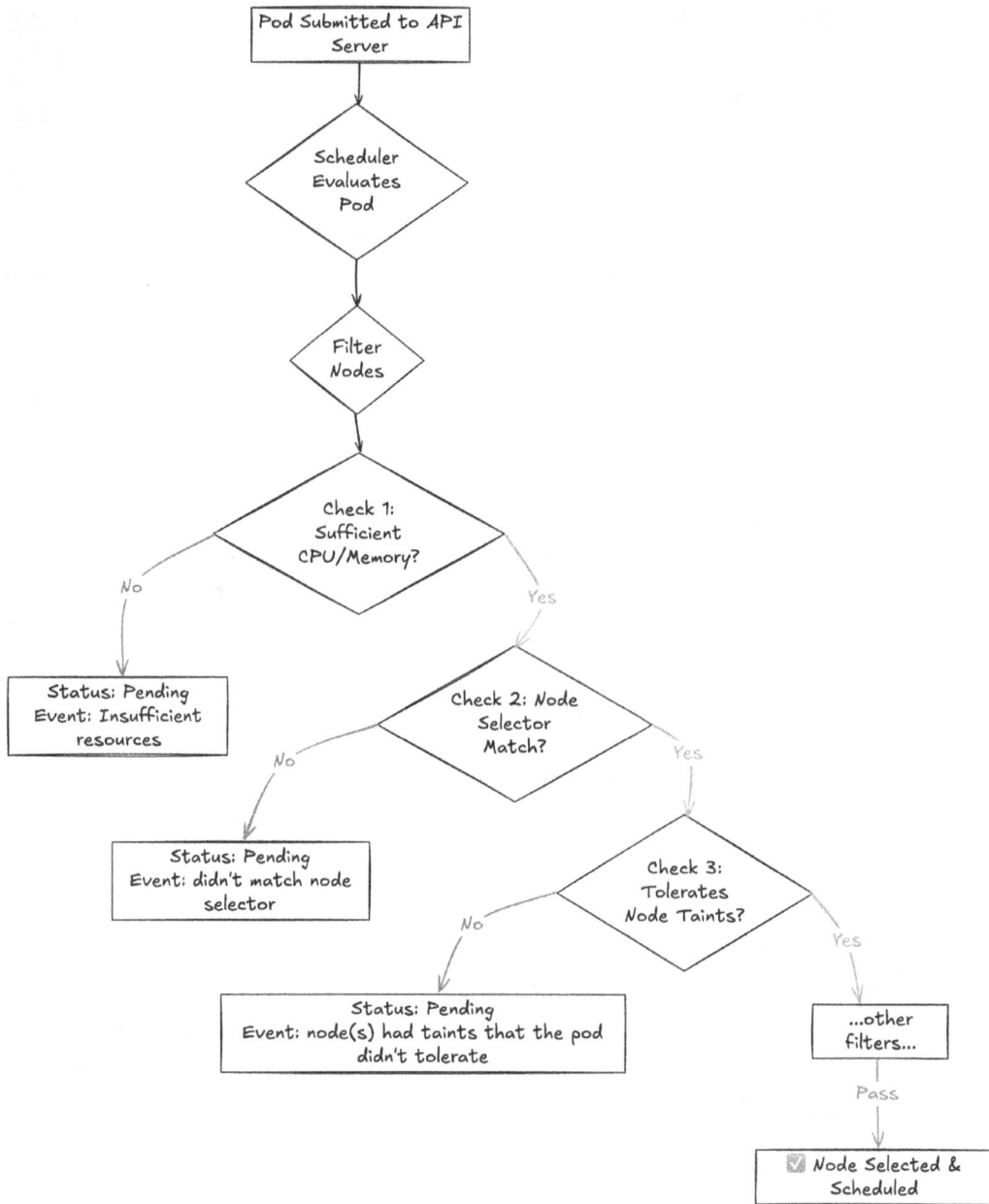

Figure 16.2 – The Kubernetes scheduler's filtering process

Common reasons a pod remains in a `Pending` state include the following:

- **Insufficient resources**: The most common cause. The scheduler checks whether any node has enough free CPU and memory to meet the pod's `spec.resources.requests`. If no single node has enough, the pod will wait. The event will clearly state something like this:

  ```
  0/3 nodes are available: 3 Insufficient memory.
  ```

- **Node selector mismatch**: If your pod spec includes a `nodeSelector` label, the scheduler will only consider nodes with those exact labels. If no nodes have the required labels, the event will say the following:

  ```
  0/3 nodes are available: 3 node(s) didn't match node selector.
  ```

- **Taints and tolerations**: Taints are labels placed on nodes to repel pods. A pod can only be scheduled on a tainted node if it has a matching `toleration` label. If a pod doesn't tolerate the taints on available nodes, it will remain `Pending`.

- **Volume mounting issues**: If a pod requests a PVC, it will remain `Pending` until that PVC is bound to a PV. This can be delayed if no suitable PV is available.

- **hostPort conflicts**: Using `hostPort` directly binds a pod to a port on the node's network interface. Since a port can only be used once per node, this severely restricts scheduling. If another pod (or a process on the host) is already using that port on every available node, the pod will remain `Pending`. It's a best practice to avoid `hostPort` and use a `Service` resource for exposure instead.

> **Interview tip**
>
> **Question:** *What could cause a Pod to remain in a Pending state, and how would you resolve it?*
>
> **Answer:** Pending pods usually indicate scheduling issues. I would run `kubectl describe` pod to check events. Common causes are a lack of resources (CPU/memory) on any node, missing PV (for PVCs), or constraints such as node selectors, taints, or `hostPort` conflicts. Depending on the cause, I'd free up resources or add nodes, fix the node selector/taint mismatch, ensure volumes are bound, or remove the `hostPort` requirement as appropriate.

Mini-case study: The over-requested pod

A development team deploys a new microservice with a memory request of 4 Gi. The cluster has three worker nodes, but after running `kubectl top nodes`, the team sees that each node only has 2 Gi of allocatable memory available and takes a closer look at the situation:

- **Symptom**: The pod remains `Pending` indefinitely.

- **Diagnosis**: Running `kubectl describe` pod on the new pod shows the event:

  ```
  FailedScheduling: 0/3 nodes are available: 3 Insufficient memory.
  ```

- **Resolution**: The team edits the deployment manifest, reducing the memory request to a more realistic 1 Gi. Upon applying the change, the scheduler immediately finds a suitable node, and the pod moves to the `ContainerCreating` state.

Image pull errors and container startup issues

After a pod is scheduled to a node, the first thing the node's kubelet must do is pull the container image. If this step fails, your application is dead in the water. Troubleshooting `ImagePullBackOff` is a test of your attention to detail and your understanding of how Kubernetes interacts with external systems such as container registries. Interviewers expect you to quickly diagnose common issues such as typos, authentication failures with private registries, and registry connectivity.

Diagnosing image pull failures

An `ImagePullBackOff` status is not an error itself, but rather a waiting state. It means Kubernetes tried to pull an image, failed, and is now "backing off" for a progressively longer period before retrying. The actual error happened earlier. Your task is to find that initial error event.

As with `Pending` pods, your primary tool is the following:

```
kubectl describe pod <pod-name>
```

The specific reason for the failure will be in the `Events` section. Common causes for image pull failures include the following:

- **Incorrect image name or tag**: This is the most frequent culprit. A simple typo in the image name or a tag that doesn't exist in the repository (such as using `:latest` when only `:v1.0` exists) will cause a "not found" error. Always double-check your deployment manifest against the image registry.

- **Private registry authentication failure**: If the image is in a private registry, the cluster needs credentials to access it. This is handled by creating a `Secret` resource of type `kubernetes.io/dockerconfigjson` and referencing it in your pod spec with the `imagePullSecrets` field. If the secret is missing, incorrect, or not referenced, you'll see an authentication error event.

- **Registry unreachable**: Less commonly, the node itself may not be able to reach the container registry due to network issues, a firewall rule, or a registry outage.

To confirm the problem, you can try to pull the image manually. If you have access to the node, you can use a runtime-specific command such as the following to see whether the node can fetch the image:

```
crictl pull my-registry/my-app:v1.0
```

> **Interview tip**
>
> **Question**: *What's the difference between* `ErrImagePull` *and* `ImagePullBackOff`?
>
> **Answer**: `ErrImagePull` is the actual error state. It means a single attempt to pull the image has failed. `ImagePullBackOff` is a waiting state. After Kubernetes encounters an `ErrImagePull` status, it waits for a calculated back-off period and then tries again. So, you'll often see the status cycling between `ErrImagePull` as it fails and `ImagePullBackOff` as it waits to retry. Essentially, `ErrImagePull` is the immediate problem, and `ImagePullBackOff` is the resulting loop.

Mini-case study: The missing tag

A team deploys an update to their application, referencing the `myapp:latest` image in their manifest. They assume this tag exists because it's the default. However, they then encounter the following:

- **Symptom**: The new pods are stuck in an `ImagePullBackOff` state.
- **Diagnosis**: The `kubectl describe` pod command reveals an event with the following message:

```
Failed to pull image "myapp:latest": rpc error: code = NotFound desc
= failed to pull and unpack image "docker.io/library/myapp:latest":
failed to resolve reference "docker.io/library/myapp:latest":
myapp:latest not found.
```

- A quick check of their container registry shows that their CI/CD pipeline tags images with specific versions (e.g., myapp:v1.2.0), not :latest.

- **Resolution**: The team updates the Deployment to use the correct image tag, myapp:v1.2.0. The kubelet successfully pulls the image on its next attempt, and the pod starts correctly.

Once the container image is successfully pulled onto the node, the kubelet's next job is to start the container. This is the moment of truth where your application code finally runs, and it's also where the most notorious of all Kubernetes pod issues can appear.

CrashLoopBackOff and container crash diagnostics

The CrashLoopBackOff status is arguably the most common pod-level problem you will encounter. An interviewer will almost certainly ask you about it. This question tests your ability to debug issues *inside* your container. A successful answer demonstrates that you can connect a Kubernetes status to an underlying application failure, a misconfiguration, or a resource constraint, and that you know the precise commands to find the evidence you need.

Diagnosing a CrashLoopBackOff scenario

Like ImagePullBackOff, CrashLoopBackOff is a waiting state, not a direct error. It signifies that a container is starting, crashing, and being restarted by Kubernetes in a loop. To prevent a faulty container from overwhelming the system, Kubernetes enforces an increasing back-off delay between each restart attempt.

Your mission is to find out why the container is crashing. This requires a multi-step investigation:

1. **Inspect the pod's state**: Start with the following:

   ```
   kubectl describe pod <pod-name>
   ```

   In the State field, you'll see Waiting, with the Reason value as CrashLoopBackOff.

   More importantly, look at the Last State field for the previously terminated container. It will often show an exit code.

   An exit code of 1 typically indicates an application error, while an exit code of 137 specifically means the container was killed for exceeding its memory limit (OOMKilled).

2. **Fetch the logs**: This is the most critical step. Since the current container may have just restarted and has no logs, you need the logs from the *previous* crashed instance. Use the --previous flag to get them:

   ```
   kubectl logs <pod-name> --previous
   ```

Look for stack traces, exceptions, "file not found" errors, or any other message that indicates why the application terminated.

3. **Investigate the cause**: The logs and exit code will point you to one of several common culprits:

   - **Application error**: A bug in the code, such as an uncaught exception on startup, is a very common cause.

   - **Configuration error**: The application might be crashing because it can't find a configuration file. This often happens due to a typo in a VolumeMount path or a missing ConfigMap/Secret.

   - **Out of memory (OOMKilled)**: If you see Reason: OOMKilled and Exit Code: 137 in the describe output, the container was killed by the kernel for using more memory than its limit.

   - **Failing liveness probe**: If a liveness probe fails repeatedly, the kubelet assumes the application is hung and kills the container to restart it. If the application is slow to start or the probe is misconfigured, this can cause a permanent crash loop.

If the container crashes too quickly to generate logs, kubectl debug is a modern, powerful tool that lets you create a copy of the pod with a different command, allowing you to poke around its filesystem and environment. Let's walk through a common scenario. A pod named broken-app is in a CrashLoopBackOff state, but kubectl logs broken-app --previous shows nothing. This suggests the application is failing before it can even write to standard output, so the following actions are required:

4. **Launch a debug pod**: First, create an interactive copy of the pod. This command creates a new pod named broken-app-debug from the original, but overrides the entrypoint to give you a shell instead of running the crashing application:

```
kubectl debug -it broken-app --copy-to=broken-app-debug -- /bin/sh
```

5. **Investigate inside the container**: You will now have a shell prompt (#) inside the broken-app-debug container's environment. The application is not running, but you have access to its exact filesystem and environment variables. You can now do the following:

   - Check for a missing configuration file: ls /etc/config/

   - Verify that environment variables are set correctly: env | grep API_KEY

   - Try to run the application binary manually to see the crash error directly in your terminal: ./app-binary

6. **Clean up**: The debug pod (broken-app-debug) is a real pod running in your cluster and won't be deleted automatically. Once you are finished with your investigation, exit the shell and be sure to clean it up:

```
kubectl delete pod broken-app-debug
```

The entire restart loop and the points where you can intervene to diagnose it are visualized in *Figure 16.3*.

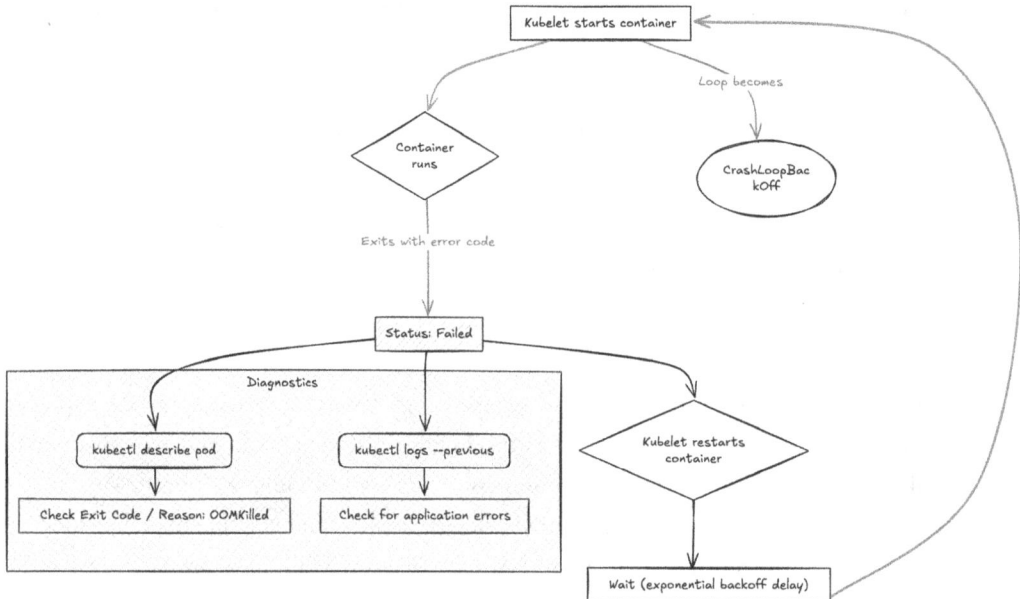

Figure 16.3 – The CrashLoopBackOff restart cycle

Interview tip

Question: *A pod is restarting. How can you tell if it's due to a liveness probe failure versus the application crashing on its own?*

Answer: I would look at the Events section in the output of kubectl describe pod. If a liveness probe is failing, Kubernetes will generate a specific event that says something such as Liveness probe failed. This indicates the kubelet is the one killing the container. If I don't see that event and the container's Last State field shows a nonzero exit code, it's more likely that the application process itself is crashing due to an internal error.

Mini-case studies

Theory provides the roadmap, but seeing it in action solidifies your understanding. To make these diagnostic steps concrete, let's walk through a few common real-world scenarios. Each case study will present a symptom, the exact commands used to investigate it, and the final resolution. These examples are designed to mirror the problems you will face both in production and during a technical interview.

Missing config file

A microservice pod enters CrashLoopBackOff. The team runs the following:

```
kubectl logs --previous
```

They see an Error: "FileNotFound: /etc/config/config.yaml" error, so they inspect the pod's manifest with the following:

```
kubectl get pod -o yaml
```

After running the previous command, they discover a typo in the volumeMounts path. After correcting the path in their Deployment and reapplying it, the container finds the file and starts successfully.

OOMKilled Java application

A Java service pod keeps restarting, so the team runs the following command:

```
kubectl describe pod
```

This shows the previous container's Reason value as OOMKilled and Exit Code as 137. The team sees the pod has a memory limit of only 256 Mi. They increase the memory limit in the Deployment to 1 Gi, and the pod runs without crashing. For a long-term fix, they investigate the application for memory leaks.

Sometimes, a pod keeps restarting even when its application logs are clean and there are no obvious errors. In these cases, the culprit isn't your application crashing on its own, but rather Kubernetes itself proactively killing the container. This often points to a problem with one of Kubernetes' health-checking mechanisms: the liveness probe.

Health check failures: Liveness and readiness probes

Probes are the heart of Kubernetes' self-healing capabilities. Understanding the critical difference between a liveness and a readiness probe is non-negotiable in an interview. Confusing the two can lead to poorly designed applications that either cause unnecessary restarts or black-hole user traffic. Interviewers will test your ability to not only define them but also explain how to configure them properly to create robust, resilient services.

Diagnosing probe failures

Kubernetes uses probes to ask your application about its health. There are two main types, and their purposes are distinct and crucial:

- **Liveness probe**: Answers the question, "Is the application still alive?" It's designed to catch true deadlocks or hung processes where the application is running but completely unresponsive. If a liveness probe fails, the kubelet's only remedy is to kill and restart the container.

- **Readiness probe**: Answers the question, "Is the application ready to serve traffic?" It's used to signal when your application is busy, still starting up, or temporarily unable to handle requests. If a readiness probe fails, the pod's IP is removed from the associated Service's endpoints, effectively taking it out of the load balancer's rotation. The pod is not restarted.

The critical difference in these outcomes is visualized in *Figure 16.4*.

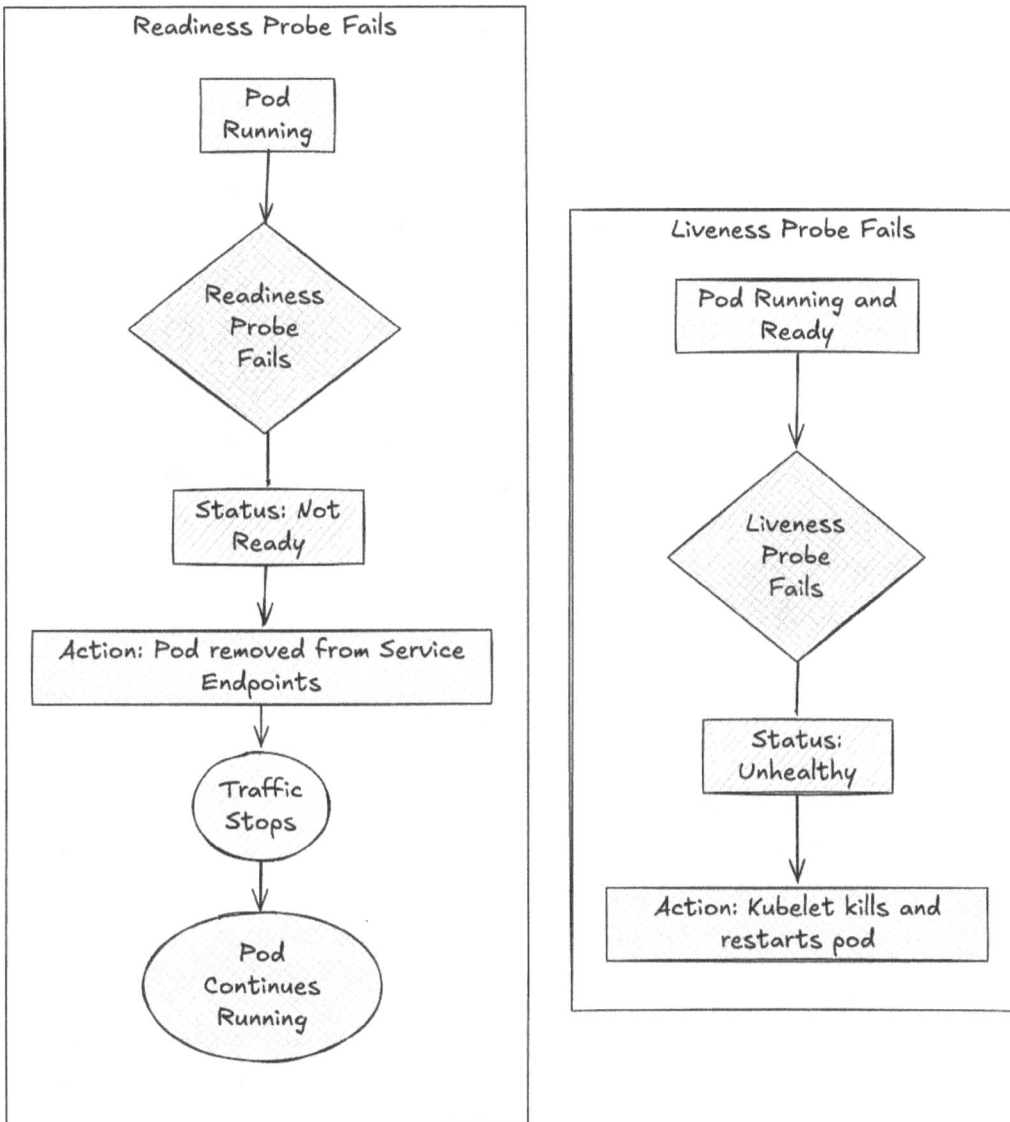

Figure 16.4 – Liveness versus readiness probe failure outcomes

This distinction explains the two primary symptoms of probe failures:

- A **failing liveness probe** causes periodic restarts, even if the app isn't crashing on its own

- A **failing readiness probe** results in a pod that is in a Running state but not a Ready state (e.g., the READY column shows 0/1), and it won't receive any traffic

To troubleshoot a probe failure, follow these steps:

1. **Check the events**: As always, the following is your starting point:

```
kubectl describe pod <pod-name>
```

The Events section will contain explicit messages such as `Liveness probe failed with statuscode: 503` or `Readiness probe failed: Get "http://:8080/health": connection refused`. This confirms that a probe is the issue.

2. **Verify the endpoint manually**: The probe's configuration might be wrong, or your app might not be listening correctly. The best way to check is to test the endpoint from inside the container itself:

```
kubectl exec <pod-name> -- curl http://localhost:8080/health
```

If this command fails, you have an application or configuration problem (wrong port, wrong path, etc.).

3. **Review probe timing**: Probes are highly sensitive to timing. Check these fields in your pod spec:

   - `initialDelaySeconds`: How long to wait after the container starts before firing the first probe. If your app takes 30 seconds to start, this must be at least 30.
   - `periodSeconds`: How often to probe.
   - `timeoutSeconds`: How long to wait for a response. A high-load app might need more than the default one-second timeout.
   - `failureThreshold`: How many consecutive failures are needed to mark the probe as failed.

A common best practice is to set a generous `initialDelaySeconds` value on your readiness probe to let the application start up gracefully and only use a liveness probe to recover from conditions where a restart is the only solution.

Interview tip

Question: *Explain the difference between a liveness and a readiness probe. When would you use one, the other, or both?*

Answer: They serve two distinct purposes for self-healing. A liveness probe is for catastrophic failure; it asks, "Is the app alive?" If it fails, Kubernetes restarts the container. You'd use it to recover from a deadlock. A readiness probe is for temporary states; it asks, "Is the app ready for traffic?" If it fails, Kubernetes just stops sending it traffic. You'd use it to manage startup sequences or when an app needs to load a large cache. You almost always want a readiness probe to ensure smooth startups and deployments. You should only add a liveness probe if your application has a tendency to enter a hung state where a restart is the only known fix. Using a liveness probe too aggressively can cause more problems than it solves.

Mini-case study: The overly aggressive liveness probe

A team notices their web server pods are restarting every few minutes during peak traffic. The application logs show no errors, so they investigate further:

- **Symptom**: Pods are periodically killed and restarted.
- **Diagnosis**: Running `kubectl describe pod` on a restarting pod shows events for `Liveness probe failed`. The probe is configured with a `timeoutSeconds` value of 1. Under heavy load, the application sometimes takes longer than one second to respond to the `/health` check, causing the probe to fail.
- **Resolution**: The team increases the `timeoutSeconds` value to 5 and the `failureThreshold` value to 3 in their Deployment manifest. This makes the probe more tolerant of transient slowdowns, and the pods stop restarting unnecessarily.

We've now covered how pods are created, how they start, and how they are kept healthy. But what about the end of their lifecycle? Deleting a pod should be simple, but sometimes, they refuse to disappear, getting stuck in a `Terminating` state. This final lifecycle problem often points to a powerful but sometimes problematic Kubernetes feature: finalizers.

The final stage: Stuck terminating pods and finalizers

When a pod's status is Terminating, it means the deletion process has begun, but something is preventing it from completing. The pod object will not be removed from the API server until all cleanup tasks are finished. More often than not, the culprit is a **finalizer**.

A finalizer is a list of keys in a resource's metadata that signals to Kubernetes that it must wait for a specific controller to perform cleanup actions *before* the resource can be fully deleted. Think of it as a pre-delete checklist. If the controller responsible for an item on that checklist is broken or misconfigured, it will never give the "all clear," and the pod will be stuck in Terminating forever.

Common causes include the following:

- **Orphaned finalizer**: This is the most frequent cause. A controller, often from a third-party operator or tool, adds a finalizer to a pod. If that controller crashes or has a bug, it may never remove the finalizer, leaving the pod in limbo. Your first step is to inspect the pod's YAML for this checklist:

```
kubectl get pod <pod-name> -o yaml
```

  Look for a metadata.finalizers array.

- **Underlying infrastructure issues**: The pod might be waiting for an external resource to be cleaned up. For example, the kubelet might be unable to unmount a PV because the underlying storage system (such as AWS EBS or a SAN) is unresponsive. These issues are harder to spot and may require checking the kubelet logs on the node.

- **Application ignoring SIGTERM**: When you delete a pod, its containers receive a SIGTERM signal, giving them a chance to shut down gracefully (default: 30 seconds). If your application ignores this signal, it won't shut down. Kubernetes will wait for the grace period to expire and then forcibly kill it with SIGKILL. If a pod is stuck for much longer than its grace period, the issue is likely a finalizer or infrastructure problem, not the application itself.

If you've identified a finalizer from a broken controller as the cause, you can manually remove it as a last resort.

> **Warning**
>
> This can be a dangerous operation. Only do this if you are certain that no cleanup is required or that you can perform it manually:
>
> ```
> kubectl patch pod <pod-name> -p
> '{"metadata":{"finalizers":null}}'
> ```

Pod lifecycle summary

We've now walked through the entire lifecycle of a pod, from scheduling failures to termination blocks. Each state presents unique challenges, but a systematic approach using kubectl describe and kubectl logs and inspecting the object's YAML will almost always lead you to the root cause.

The flowchart in *Figure 16.5* provides a complete mental map for diagnosing any pod-related issue, guiding you from the symptom to the correct command.

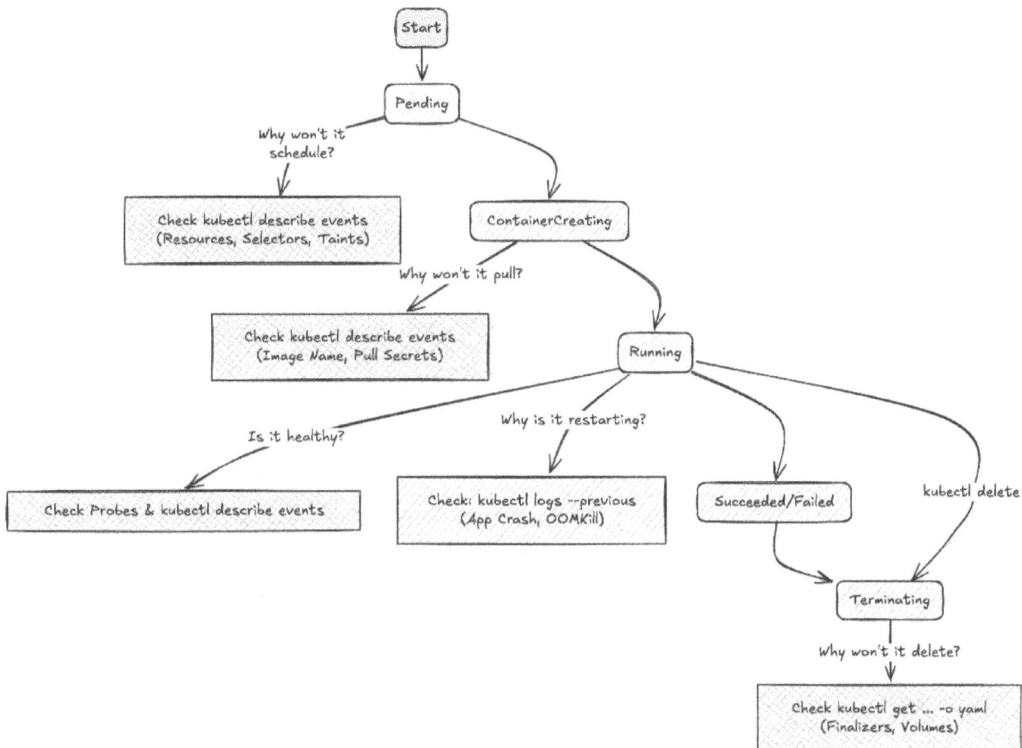

Figure 16.5 – A diagnostic flowchart for the pod lifecycle

Mastering these states is the first and most critical step in becoming a proficient Kubernetes troubleshooter. By learning how to systematically read a pod's status, events, and logs, you have built the foundational skills needed to solve the majority of common problems.

But a healthy, running pod is useless if it can't communicate. This brings us to the next layer of complexity. Once your pods are running successfully, you need to make them accessible—both to each other and to the outside world. A perfectly healthy pod that can't be reached by its users is still a failing application.

In the following sections, we will apply our structured troubleshooting models to the intricate world of Kubernetes networking. We'll untangle issues with Service connectivity, DNS resolution, Network Policies, and Ingress routing to ensure your applications can communicate reliably.

Network troubleshooting

We've established how to get your pods up and running. Now, we'll tackle the next crucial step: making them talk to each other and the outside world. This is where Kubernetes networking comes in, with the Service object at its core. A Service provides a stable IP address and DNS name for a group of pods, but simple misconfigurations can easily break this vital link. This section will guide you through diagnosing these common networking problems.

Service connectivity: Missing endpoints

The connection between a Service and its pods is the most fundamental concept in Kubernetes networking. An interviewer will expect you to know that a Service doesn't connect to pods directly, but rather through a label-selector mechanism. A Service with no endpoints is a classic problem that tests this core knowledge. Your ability to quickly diagnose a label mismatch demonstrates a solid understanding of how Kubernetes service discovery works.

A Kubernetes **Service** acts as a stable network endpoint for a fluctuating group of pods. It finds which pods to send traffic to by using a **selector**, which is a query for pods with matching **labels**. When this match is successful, Kubernetes creates an Endpoints or EndpointSlice object that lists the IP addresses and ports of healthy, matching pods. This fundamental relationship is illustrated in *Figure 16.6*.

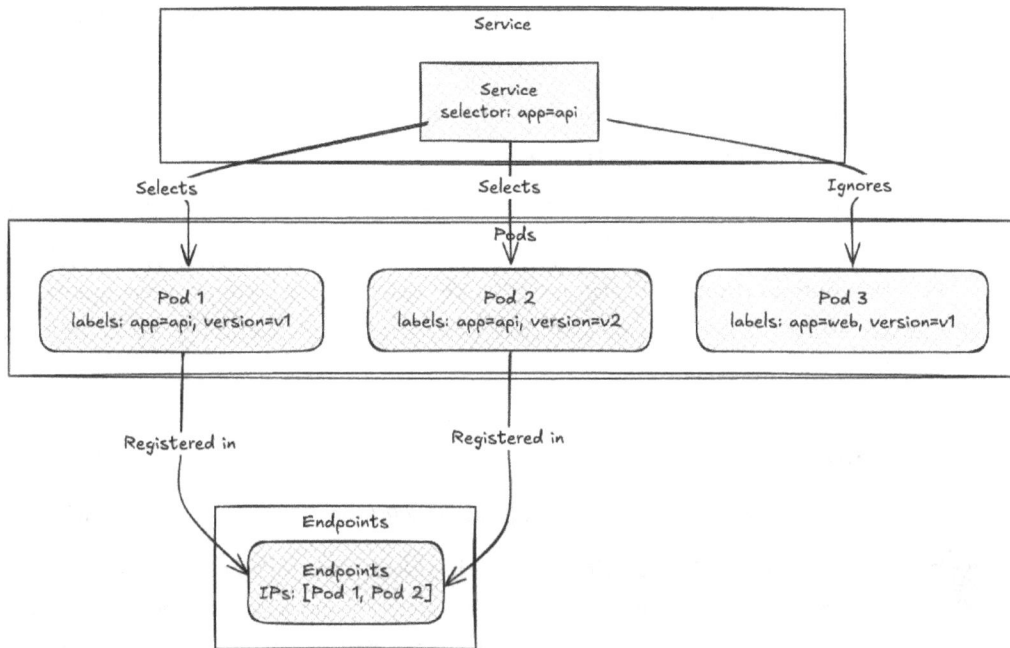

Figure 16.6 – The Service, selector, and label mechanism

The most common symptom of a problem here is a Service that receives requests but leads no-where, often resulting in connection timeouts. A tell-tale sign is when a Service has no associated endpoints.

Your primary diagnostic tool is the following:

```
kubectl describe service <service-name>
```

Pay close attention to two fields:

- `Selector`: This shows the key-value pairs the Service is looking for (e.g., app=frontend)
- `Endpoints`: This shows a list of `IP:Port` combinations the Service is currently directing traffic to

If the `Endpoints` field is `<none>`, you have a problem. It means the selector did not find any match-ing pods. To confirm this, you can use the Service's selector to manually search for pods:

```
kubectl get pods --selector=app=frontend
```

If this command returns no pods, you've found the root cause. This usually happens for one of three reasons:

- **Label mismatch:** The labels on your pods (e.g., app=web-frontend) do not exactly match the Service's selector (e.g., app=frontend).

- **Pods not ready:** A pod will only be added to the endpoint list if it is in the Ready state. If your pods are running but failing their readiness probes, they will not receive traffic.

- **Port misconfiguration:** The targetPort value in the Service manifest must match the containerPort value on the pods. If they don't align, traffic won't be correctly routed even if the endpoints are listed.

> **Interview tip**
>
> **Question:** *Does a pod need to be in a Running state to be in a Service's endpoint list?*
>
> **Answer:** Not just Running; it needs to be in a Ready state. A pod's IP is only added to an Endpoints object after it has started successfully and passed its readiness probe (if one is defined). This is a crucial feature that prevents traffic from being sent to pods that are still initializing or are temporarily overloaded.

Mini-case study: The typo in the label

A team deploys a new payments microservice. They create a Service to expose it, but other microservices are unable to reach it, reporting connection timeouts:

- **Symptom:** Calls to the payments Service fail.

- **Diagnosis:** The team runs the following command:

    kubectl describe service payments

    They see that the Endpoints field is <none>. They check the Service's selector and see that it's looking for app: payments. However, when they inspect their Deployment, they realize the pod template has a typo in its label: app: pay.

- **Resolution:** They correct the label in the Deployment manifest to app: payments and apply the change. A moment later, they run kubectl describe service payments again and see the pods' IP addresses correctly listed in the Endpoints field. The service immediately starts working.

Once a Service is correctly linked to its pods via endpoints, the next question is: How do other pods find the Service? While they could use its ClusterIP, the best practice is to use its DNS name. This is where Kubernetes' internal DNS system, **CoreDNS**, comes into play. If DNS fails, the entire service discovery mechanism breaks down, even if all your Services and pods are perfectly healthy.

DNS failures: The "Could Not Resolve Host" error

DNS is a critical, cluster-wide dependency. A DNS outage can bring down every application that communicates over the network. An interviewer will ask about DNS to verify that you can troubleshoot not just your own application, but also the shared cluster infrastructure it relies on. Your ability to systematically debug DNS shows you can handle problems that have a broad impact.

Diagnosing DNS resolution failures

By default, Kubernetes provides cluster-wide DNS using CoreDNS. It's responsible for resolving two types of names:

- **Internal service names,** such as `payments-api.default.svc.cluster.local`, which resolves to the Service's ClusterIP
- **External hostnames,** such as `google.com`, which it forwards to an upstream DNS server

A failure in this system typically appears in your application logs as `Could not resolve host"` or `Temporary failure in name resolution`. Your troubleshooting process should follow the path of a DNS query:

1. **Confirm from a client pod:** First, verify that DNS is actually the problem. The best tool for this is `nslookup`. You can run it from an existing pod or launch a dedicated debug pod:

   ```
   kubectl run dns-test --image=busybox:stable -it --rm -- nslookup
   payments-api
   ```

   If this command times out or returns an error such as the following, you have a confirmed DNS issue:

   ```
   server can't find ...
   ```

2. **Check the DNS server (CoreDNS):** If lookups are failing, your next step is to inspect the health of the CoreDNS pods themselves. They live in the `kube-system` namespace:

   ```
   kubectl get pods -n kube-system -l k8s-app=kube-dns
   ```

Ensure these pods are in a Running state, not in a CrashLoopBackOff state. If they are failing, check their logs for errors, which can often point to a misconfigured CoreDNS ConfigMap:

```
kubectl logs -n kube-system -l k8s-app=kube-dns
```

3. **Check the kube-dns Service**: The CoreDNS pods are exposed by a Service, usually named kube-dns. Every pod in the cluster is configured to send its DNS queries to this Service's IP address. Verify that this Service exists and has a ClusterIP:

```
kubectl get svc -n kube-system kube-dns
```

4. **Check for blockages**: If CoreDNS is running but unreachable, a NetworkPolicy might be the culprit. A misconfigured policy could be blocking Egress traffic on UDP port 53 from your application pods to the kube-system namespace, preventing the query from ever reaching the server. This entire query path, from the client pod to the CoreDNS server and back, along with these common failure points, is visualized in *Figure 16.7*.

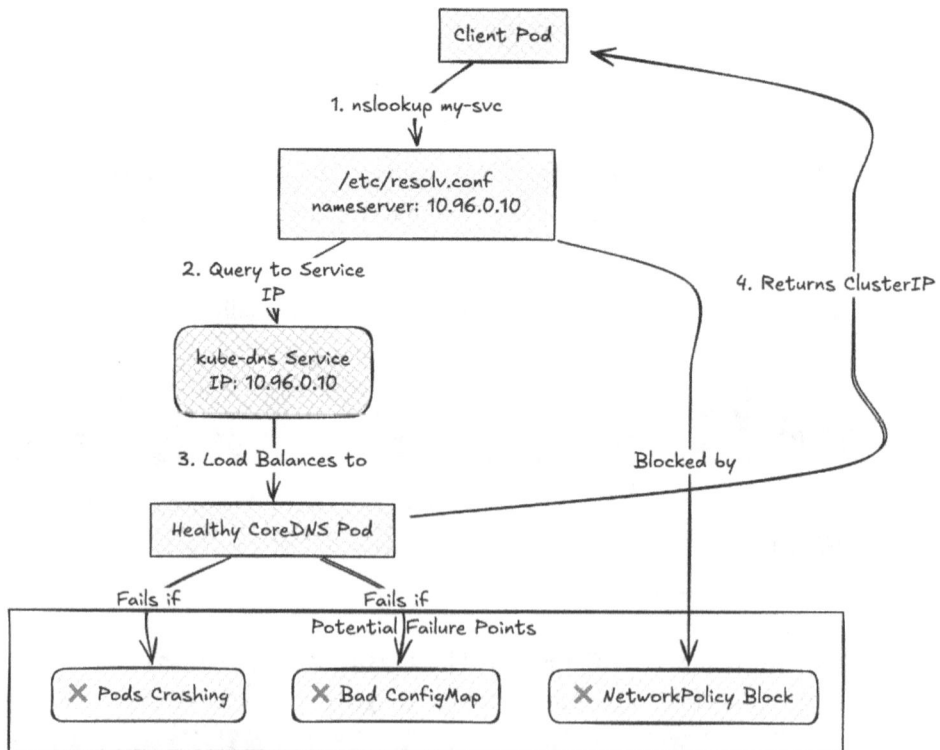

Figure 16.7 – The DNS lookup path and common failure points

> **Interview tip**
>
> **Question:** *A pod cannot resolve a Service's hostname. Walk me through your trouble-shooting steps.*
>
> **Answer:** First, I'd confirm it's a DNS issue by exec-ing into the pod and using nslookup on the service name. If that fails, my suspicion shifts to CoreDNS. I'd then check the status of the CoreDNS pods in the kube-system namespace to ensure they are running and not crashing. I'd also check their logs for any obvious errors. If the pods are healthy, I'd verify that the kube-dns Service exists and has a ClusterIP. Finally, I'd consider whether a NetworkPolicy could be blocking DNS queries from my application pod to the CoreDNS service, which happens over UDP port 53.

Mini-case study: The overreaching network policy

After a security hardening initiative, multiple applications in the cluster suddenly lose connectivity to their databases:

- **Symptom**: Application logs are filled with DNS resolution errors. The team runs the following command from an application pod:

```
nslookup database-svc
```

This results in the following output:

```
;; connection timed out; no servers could be reached
```

- **Diagnosis**: The team checks CoreDNS and finds the pods are running perfectly. However, they discover that a new, restrictive NetworkPolicy was applied to the application namespaces. This policy forgot to include an Egress rule to allow traffic to the kube-system namespace on UDP port 53.

- **Resolution**: They update the NetworkPolicy to explicitly allow DNS queries. Immediately, nslookup succeeds, and the applications reconnect to their databases.

With a functioning DNS, your pods can now resolve service names to IP addresses. But just because you have the right address, doesn't mean you're allowed through the door. By default, Kubernetes networking is a wide-open plain where any pod can talk to any other pod. For security, we introduce Network Policies to act as a firewall. This crucial security feature, however, is a common source of "mystery" connectivity issues where traffic is silently dropped.

Firewall rules: Debugging Network Policies

Network Policies are a key security feature in Kubernetes. Questions about them test your understanding of zero-trust networking principles. An interviewer wants to see that you can balance security with functionality and, most importantly, that you know how to debug policy rules when they inevitably block legitimate traffic. This shows you can think about the system as a whole, not just a single application.

Diagnosing Network Policy blocks

The most important concept to understand is this: by default, all pods in a cluster can communicate with each other. However, the moment you apply a Network Policy that selects a pod, that pod becomes **deny-by-default**. It will reject all traffic unless a rule in the policy explicitly allows it.

The classic symptom of a Network Policy issue is a `connection timed out` error between pods, even when you've confirmed that Services and DNS are working correctly.

To troubleshoot a suspected policy block, follow this workflow:

1. **Check whether a policy applies**: First, determine whether any policies are selecting your source or destination pod. Check the relevant namespace:

    ```
    kubectl get networkpolicy -n <namespace>
    ```

    If this returns nothing, a Network Policy is not your problem.

2. **Analyze the policy rules**: If policies exist, you must read them carefully with the following:

    ```
    kubectl describe networkpolicy <policy-name>
    ```

    Pay close attention to the following:

    *   `podSelector`: This determines which pods this policy applies to. If your pod's labels match, it is being firewalled.

    *   `ingress rules`: These define what incoming traffic is allowed. If this section is empty, no traffic is allowed in.

    *   `egress rules`: These define what outgoing traffic is allowed. If this section is empty, the pod cannot initiate any connections.

3. **Verify labels:** Ingress rules often allow traffic based on the labels of the source pod (using podSelector within the from field). A common error is deploying a new service whose pods lack the label required by the policy on the destination pod. *Figure 16.8* provides a clear example, showing how a policy on a database pod allows traffic from a correctly labeled API pod while blocking traffic from a frontend pod.

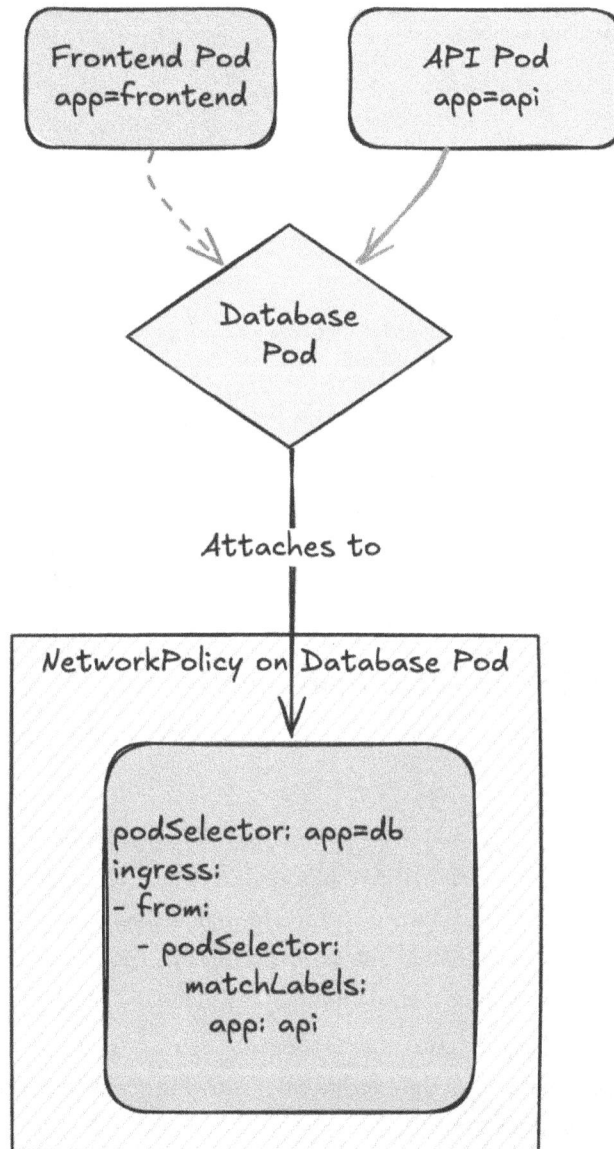

Figure 16.8 – An Ingress Network Policy in action

4. **Use a debug tool**: The best way to confirm a network block is to use a network trouble-shooting tool such as the `nicolaka/netshoot` container. Launch it in the source namespace and try to connect to the destination pod's IP and port:

```
kubectl run tmp-netshoot --rm -it --image nicolaka/netshoot -- bash
```

Inside the container, a command such as the following will hang and time out if a policy is blocking the connection:

```
telnet <destination-pod-ip> <port>
```

A common best practice is to always include an Egress rule that allows DNS traffic when creating restrictive policies. Otherwise, your firewalled pods won't even be able to resolve hostnames.

> **Interview tip**
>
> **Question:** *You're creating a Network Policy to lock down a pod, only allowing it to talk to a specific database service. What other critical rule should you almost always include?*
>
> **Answer:** You should almost always include an *Egress rule to allow DNS traffic*. The policy will block all outgoing traffic by default, including DNS queries to CoreDNS. Without this rule, your application won't be able to resolve the hostname of the database service, or any other hostname, for that matter. The rule should allow Egress traffic to the `kube-system` namespace on UDP port 53.

Mini-case study: The blocked internal call

In a multi-tier application, `payment-service` suddenly cannot connect to `user-service`, causing transactions to fail:

- **Symptom**: Calls from `payment-service` to `user-service` are timing out.
- **Diagnosis**: The team confirms DNS resolution is working. They run `kubectl get netpol -n user-namespace` and find a policy applied to `user-service`. Describing the policy reveals it has an Ingress rule that only allows traffic from pods with the `role: frontend` label. The `payment-service` pods do not have this label.
- **Resolution**: The team updates the `NetworkPolicy` for `user-service` to add another `podSelector` instance to the Ingress rule, allowing traffic from pods with the `app: payment-service` label. Connectivity is immediately restored.

We've now secured the communication paths inside our cluster with Network Policies. The final piece of the networking puzzle is allowing external users to access our applications. This is the job of an Ingress, which acts as the front door to your cluster, directing outside traffic to the correct internal services. This multilayered path, from the user's browser all the way to your pod, introduces several new potential points of failure.

External access: Debugging the Ingress path

Ingress is how your application is exposed to the world and generates value. If external traffic can't get in, the application is effectively down for your users. Interviewers will test your ability to troubleshoot this entire request path systematically—from DNS and cloud load balancers down to the Kubernetes services and pods. A strong answer demonstrates a holistic understanding of a production web stack.

Diagnosing the Ingress path

An Ingress isn't a single thing, but a chain of components that must all work together. A request from a user must successfully navigate this path:

External DNS → Cloud load balancer → Ingress Controller → Service → Pod

This entire path, along with the key commands and checks for each stage, is visualized in *Figure 16.9*.

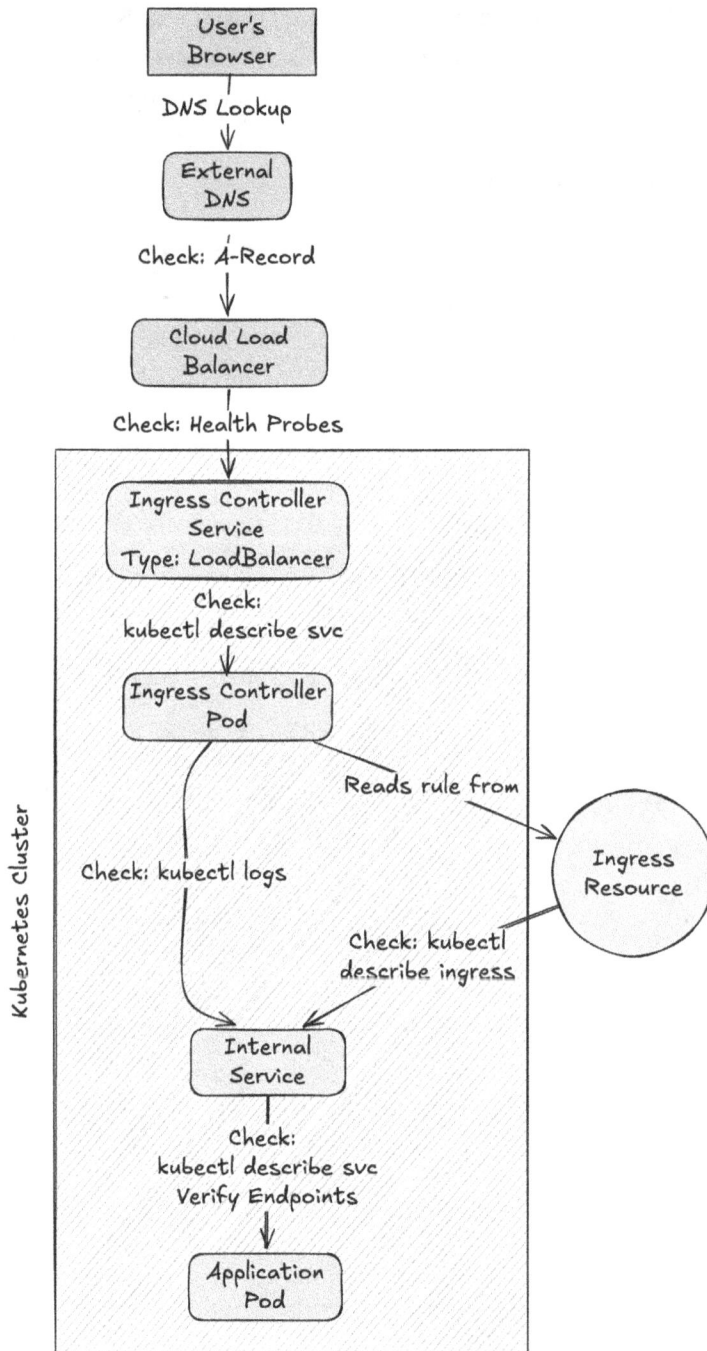

Figure 16.9 – The Ingress traffic path and diagnostic checks

Troubleshooting Ingress means methodically checking each link in this chain. If you get a 404 Not Found or 502 Bad Gateway error, start from the outside and work your way in. The process is listed as follows:

1. **Check the external path (DNS and LoadBalancer)**: First, ensure your domain's DNS A-record points to the correct IP address. You can get this IP from the ADDRESS field of the Ingress Controller's Service, which is typically of type LoadBalancer:

   ```
   kubectl get service -n ingress-nginx
   ```

   If the EXTERNAL-IP value is <pending>, there's an issue with your cloud provider provisioning the load balancer.

2. **Check the Ingress resource**: This is your "map" for routing. Use the following command to verify that the host, path, and backend services are all correctly defined:

   ```
   kubectl describe ingress <ingress-name>
   ```

   A simple typo here is a very common error.

3. **Check the Ingress Controller**: This is the "traffic cop" that reads the Ingress resource and applies routing rules. Check the following:

   - Run the following command to see whether the controller pods are running:

     ```
     kubectl get pods -n <ingress-namespace>
     ```

   - Find out whether there are any errors in their logs by running the following:

     ```
     kubectl logs <ingress-controller-pod>
     ```

   This can reveal issues such as not being able to find the backend Service or errors with reloading its configuration.

4. **Check the final link (Controller → Service → Pod)**: You must confirm that the Ingress Controller can reach the final destination Service. The most definitive test is to exec into the controller pod and try to curl the Service directly:

   ```
   kubectl exec -it <ingress-controller-pod> -n <ingress-namespace> --
   curl http://<service-name>.<service-namespace>.svc.cluster.local
   ```

   If this fails, the problem lies with the Service itself (e.g., it has no endpoints), which you can debug using the steps from section 2. If it succeeds, you know the internal routing is correct, and the problem is further upstream.

> **Interview tip**
>
> **Question:** *What is the difference between an Ingress and an Ingress Controller?*
>
> **Answer:** They are two distinct but related components. The Ingress is just a Kubernetes resource—a YAML file where you declare routing rules, such as "requests for `host: foo.com` should go to `service: foo-svc`." It's just a piece of configuration. The Ingress Controller is the actual application (such as NGINX or Traefik) running in pods in your cluster that reads all the Ingress resources and actually implements those rules by configuring itself as a reverse proxy. Without an Ingress Controller, an Ingress resource does nothing.

Mini-case study: The multilayered failure

A team deploys a new service at `api.example.com/v1`, but clients are getting a 404 Not Found page from the default NGINX backend:

- **Symptom**: Ingress is not routing to the correct backend service.
- **Diagnosis 1**: The team runs the following command:

```
kubectl describe ingress
```

  They find no issues. The rules look correct.

- **Diagnosis 2**: They check the NGINX Ingress Controller logs. The logs show requests coming in for `api.example.com`, but there is no mention of the `/v1` path. The team realizes the Ingress resource was created in the `default` namespace, but the `api-v1` Service it was pointing to was in the `api` namespace. The controller couldn't find the Service, so it fell back to the default backend.

- **Resolution**: They updated the Ingress manifest to specify the correct backend service namespace (`service: { name: 'api-v1', port: { number: 80 }, namespace: 'api' }`). After applying the change, traffic began flowing correctly.

Mastering Kubernetes networking

We've now traced the path of a network packet from start to finish—from internal service discovery and DNS resolution to the complex routing of external traffic through an Ingress. The key to network troubleshooting is to *think like a packet*, methodically checking each link in the communication chain. If you can do that, you can solve nearly any connectivity issue you'll face.

But getting packets to the right place is only half the battle.

Performance optimization and troubleshooting

A running, connected application can still fail under load if it doesn't have the resources it needs to perform well. This brings us to our final, and often most complex, area of troubleshooting: performance. Here, we move from asking "Is it working?" to "Is it working *efficiently*?" We'll investigate what happens when your application runs out of memory or CPU and how to ensure it scales to meet demand.

Memory pressure: The OOMKilled pod

This is a critical SRE and DevOps topic. Questions about resource management test your understanding of how to build stable, predictable systems. An interviewer wants to know that you can configure appropriate resource limits to prevent a single memory-hungry application from destabilizing an entire node. Your ability to diagnose an OOMKilled event shows you can connect the dots between Kubernetes-level metrics and application-level behavior.

Diagnosing OOMKilled events

When a container tries to use more memory than its defined **limit**, the Linux kernel on the node steps in and kills the offending process. Kubernetes reports this event with the OOMKilled status (which stands for "out of memory killed"). This is not a gentle request; it's an immediate termination.

This is fundamentally different from CPU limits. If a container exceeds its CPU limit, it is simply **throttled** (slowed down). If it exceeds its memory limit, it is **killed**.

Your troubleshooting workflow should be as follows:

1. **Confirm the OOM kill:** The evidence is found in the output of the following command:

   ```
   kubectl describe pod <pod-name>
   ```

   Look at the Last State field of the terminated container. You are looking for two key pieces of evidence:

   - Reason: OOMKilled
   - Exit Code: 137

   If you see these, you have a confirmed OOM kill.

2. **Check usage versus limits:** Now that you know that the pod was killed for using too much memory, find out what the limit was. The `describe` output shows the configured `Limits` values for the container. You can compare this to the actual usage at the time of the crash by using monitoring tools such as Prometheus or by checking the output of `kubectl top pod <pod-name>` (if the Metrics Server is installed).

3. **Analyze application behavior:** The final thing to look at is why the application used so much memory. Was it a sudden spike due to a large request, or was it a gradual memory leak over time? This is where you need to look at application-level metrics or logs, or even use a memory profiler to diagnose the root cause in the code.

It's also important to distinguish this from a node-level **eviction**. If the *node* itself runs out of memory, Kubernetes will start evicting pods (often starting with lower-priority ones) to reclaim resources. An evicted pod will have the `Evicted` status, not `OOMKilled`.

The detailed interaction between the pod, the Linux kernel, and the kubelet during this process is visualized in *Figure 16.10*.

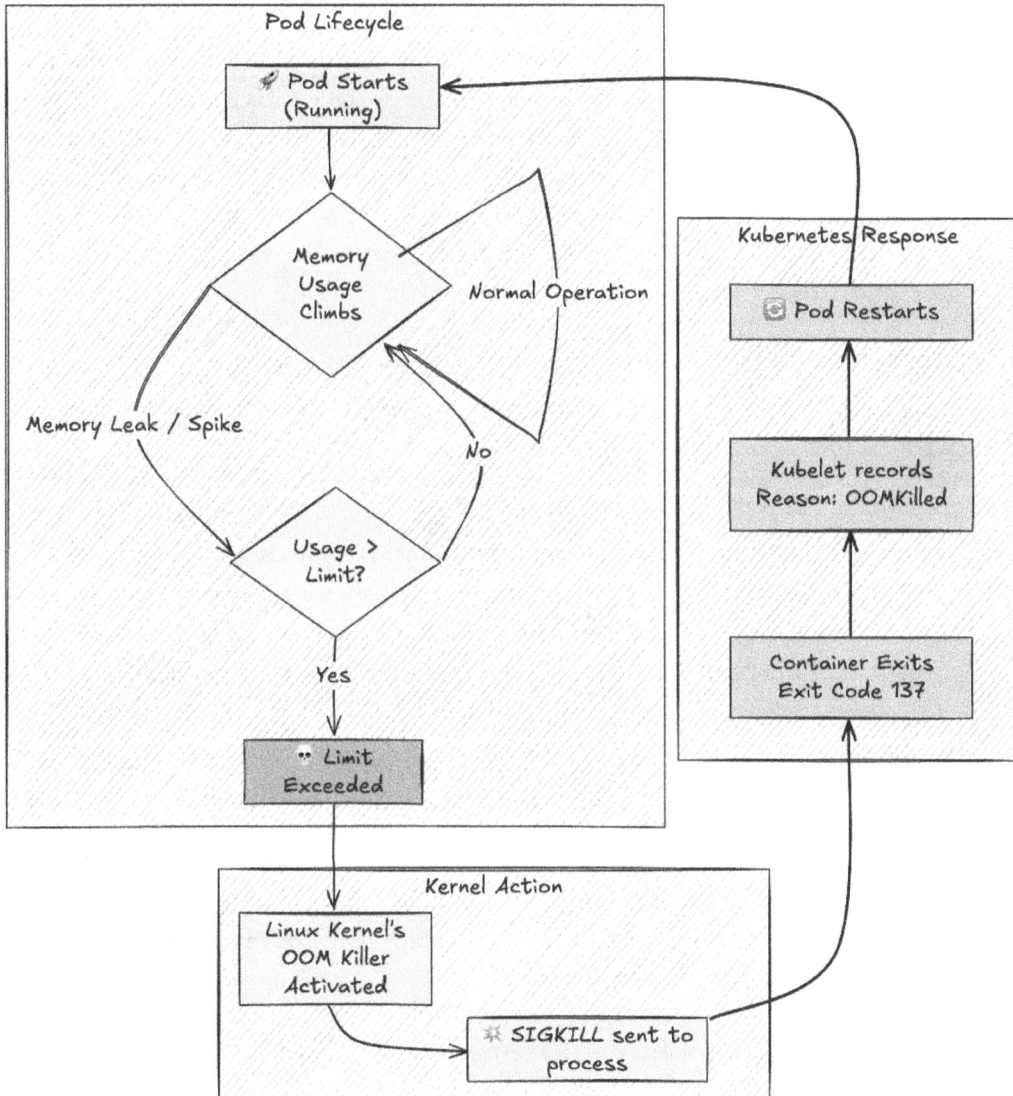

Figure 16.10 – The detailed OOMKilled process

Interview tip

Question: *What happens when a container exceeds its memory limit in Kubernetes?*

Answer: If a container tries to use more memory than its specified limit, the kubelet directs the underlying Linux kernel to terminate the process immediately. This is called an OOM kill. The pod's container will be killed, and Kubernetes will report its last state with the reason OOMKilled and an exit code of 137. Unlike CPU limits, which just throttle the process, memory limits are a hard ceiling, and exceeding them results in termination. Kubernetes will then restart the container according to its restart policy.

Mini-case study: The memory-hungry Java service

A team deploys a new Java microservice with a memory limit of 256 Mi. The pod starts but enters a CrashLoopBackOff state after a few minutes of use:

- **Symptom**: The pod is repeatedly restarting.
- **Diagnosis**: The kubectl describe pod command shows the Last State field has Reason: OOMKilled and Exit Code: 137. The team realizes that while the container limit was 256 Mi, the **Java Virtual Machine (JVM)** inside it was not configured with a maximum heap size (-Xmx). By default, the JVM was trying to allocate more memory than the container was allowed, triggering the OOM killer.
- **Resolution**: They update their Dockerfile to launch the application with -Xmx200m, ensuring the JVM's heap stays well within the container's 256 Mi limit. The pod now runs stably.

While an OOMKilled event is a loud and obvious failure, not all resource problems are so dramatic. The other critical resource, CPU, is managed very differently. Exceeding a CPU limit won't kill your pod, but it can lead to a silent, insidious performance degradation that is often much harder to diagnose. This is the world of CPU throttling.

CPU throttling: The silent performance killer

This topic tests your understanding of nuanced performance tuning. It shows you know the crucial difference between "hard" limits (memory) and "soft" limits (CPU). An interviewer wants to see that you can use monitoring and metrics to find and fix "slow" applications, which is often a more advanced skill than just fixing crashed ones. Discussing CPU throttling signals that you think about application performance, not just availability.

Diagnosing CPU throttling

When a container has a CPU limit, Kubernetes uses the Linux **Completely Fair Scheduler (CFS)** to enforce it. If your application tries to use more CPU than its limit allows, it isn't killed; it's **throttled**. This means the scheduler forces the process to wait, effectively capping its CPU usage. This core difference in enforcement—a hard kill for memory versus a soft cap for CPU—is visualized in *Figure 16.11*.

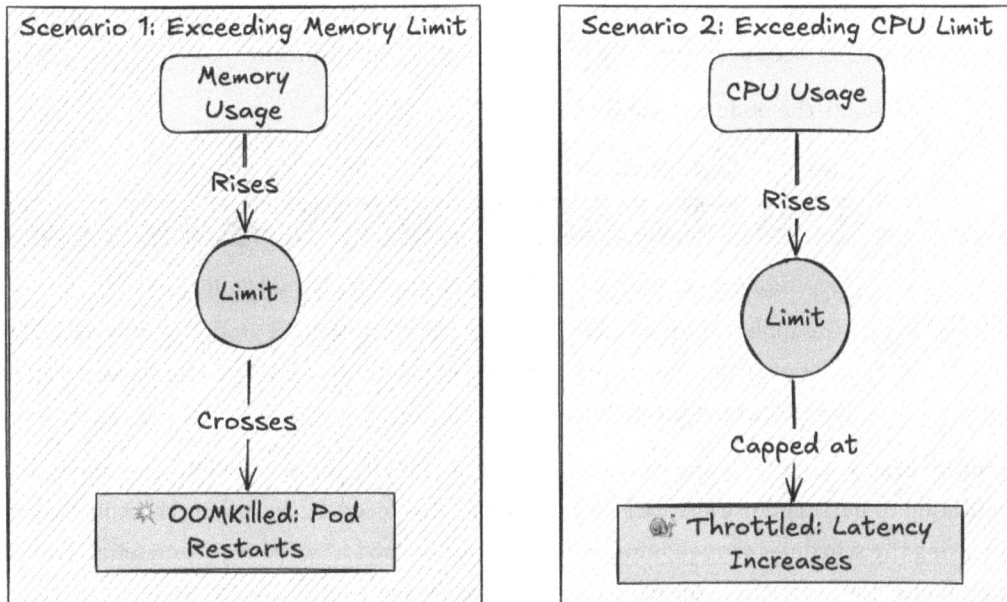

Figure 16.11 – Contrasting memory and CPU limit enforcement

The primary symptom is poor application performance—high latency, slow response times, or timeouts under load. The tricky part is that if you run the following command, you might simply see the CPU usage flatlining exactly at its limit, which doesn't look like an error. The application is slow because it *wants* more CPU but isn't allowed to get it:

```
kubectl top pod
```

To find the root cause, follow this workflow:

1. **Find the throttling evidence**: Unlike OOMKilled, there's no obvious Kubernetes event for throttling. The definitive proof is found in monitoring metrics. If you are using Prometheus, the key metric to look for is container_cpu_cfs_throttled_periods_total. If this metric is consistently increasing for your container, it is being throttled.

2. **Compare usage and limits:** Check the pod's configured CPU limit with the following command:

```
kubectl describe pod
```

Compare this to its real-time usage with the following:

```
kubectl top pod
```

Or, even better, look at a graph in your monitoring system. If the usage graph looks like a flat line pressed against the limit, it's a strong sign of throttling.

3. **Investigate the node and application:**

   - Is the entire node out of CPU? Check with the following command:

     ```
     kubectl top node
     ```

   - If so, adding more pods won't help; you need to scale up your cluster.

   - Is the application inefficient? Use an application-specific profiler to see where CPU cycles are being spent. Optimizing the code is often a better long-term solution than just giving the pod more CPU.

A modern best practice for many workloads is to set a CPU request but no limit. This allows the application to burst and use spare CPU on the node when needed, preventing throttling while still giving the scheduler enough information to place the pod intelligently. For latency-critical applications, however, setting the request and limit to the same value (Guaranteed QoS) provides the most predictable performance.

Interview tip

Question: *What happens when a container hits its CPU limit? How is this different from hitting a memory limit?*

Answer: When a container hits its CPU limit, it gets throttled. The scheduler enforces the limit by making the process wait, so it never uses more than its allotted share of CPU time over a given period. This makes the application slower. It's very different from a memory limit. If a container hits its memory limit, it gets killed immediately with an OOMKilled error. So, the CPU limit is a "soft" cap that degrades performance, while the memory limit is a "hard" cap that causes a crash.

Mini-case study: The throttled API

A team's web API service experiences a dramatic spike in response time during load testing:

- **Symptom**: API latency increases from 50 ms to over 2,000 ms under load.

- **Diagnosis**: The pod was configured with a CPU limit of 500 m (half a core). The team inspects their Grafana dashboard and sees two things: the pod's CPU usage is flatlined at exactly 500 m, and the `container_cpu_cfs_throttled_periods_total` metric is increasing rapidly. This confirms the application needs more CPU but is being capped.

- **Resolution**: They update the Deployment to remove the CPU limit while keeping the request at 500 m. In the next load test, the pod is able to burst its CPU usage up to 1.5 cores, and the latency remains low. This buys them time to profile and optimize a CPU-intensive function in the application code.

Manually adjusting resource limits is a reactive solution to performance problems. A truly robust system, however, should adapt to load automatically. Instead of giving one pod more CPU, what if we could just add more pods when traffic increases? This is the principle of horizontal scaling, and in Kubernetes, it's managed by the **Horizontal Pod Autoscaler (HPA)**. But what happens when the autoscaler itself doesn't work as expected?

Autoscaling failures: The inactive HPA

The HPA is a cornerstone of building scalable, cost-effective applications on Kubernetes. An interviewer will ask about it to see whether you understand the entire mechanism—from the metrics pipeline that feeds it data to the pod configurations required to make it work. Troubleshooting the HPA is a system-level problem that shows you can debug interactions between monitoring, application load, and Kubernetes automation.

Diagnosing HPA issues

The HPA is a control loop that watches a metric, such as average CPU utilization, for a set of pods. If the current value deviates from the target you've set, it automatically changes the number of replicas in the Deployment or ReplicaSet.

When the HPA isn't scaling as you expect, it's almost always because of a breakdown in this information pipeline. This entire control loop and its critical dependencies are visualized in *Figure 16.12*.

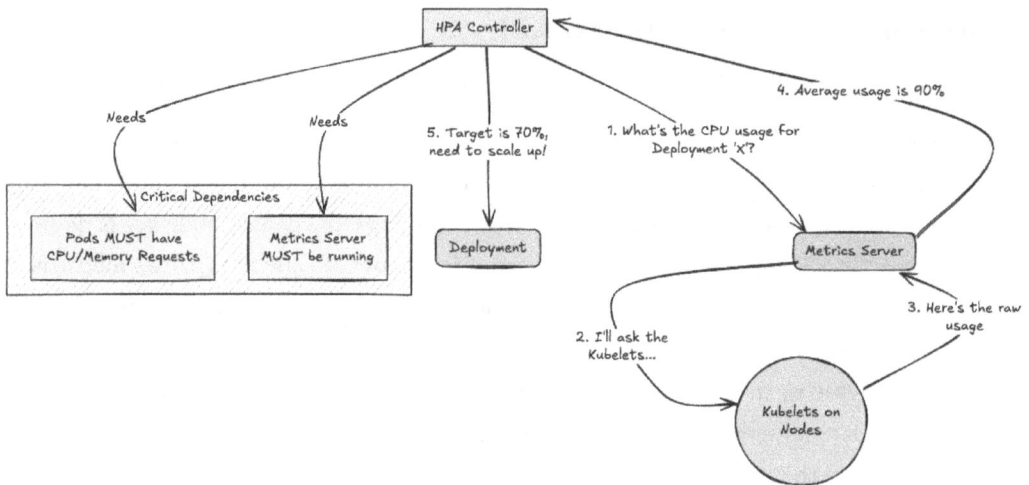

Figure 16.12 – The HPA control loop and dependencies

Your troubleshooting should follow the flow just shown:

1. **Check the HPA object itself:** This is your starting point. Use the following command:

    ```
    kubectl describe hpa <hpa-name>
    ```

    Look at the Metrics section. A common sign of failure is seeing <unknown> for the current usage (e.g., Metrics: (current / target) <unknown> / 70%). This means the HPA is not receiving data. Also, check the Events section for any errors.

2. **Check the metrics pipeline:** The HPA gets its data from the cluster's metrics aggregation API. This API is typically provided by a component called metrics-server. You must have a working metrics-server component in your cluster for HPA to function on CPU or memory. An easy way to test it is to run the following:

    ```
    kubectl top pods
    ```

    If this command fails or returns no data, your metrics-server component is broken or not installed, and that's the root cause of your HPA issue.

3. **Check the pod specification:** This is the most common "gotcha." To calculate a CPU or memory utilization percentage, the HPA needs a baseline to compare against. That baseline is the request resource set on the container. If your containers do not have resources. requests.cpu defined in their manifest, the HPA cannot calculate the utilization percentage and will fail to scale.

4. **Check the logic and capacity:**

- Is the current metric (50%) actually above the target (70%)?

- Have you hit the `maxReplicas` limit defined in the HPA?

- If the HPA is trying to scale up (check its events), are the new pods stuck in a `Pending` state because the cluster is out of nodes? If so, the problem isn't the HPA; it's cluster capacity.

> **Interview tip**
>
> **Question:** *Why might an HPA not scale up a deployment even if the pods are very busy?*
>
> **Answer:** There are a few key reasons. I'd check them in this order:
>
> First, I'd run `kubectl describe hpa` to see what it's reporting. If the metrics show as `<unknown>`, it means the data pipeline is broken.
>
> This usually points to one of two things: either `metrics-server` isn't running correctly in the cluster, or the pods in the deployment are missing resource requests. The HPA needs a request value to calculate a utilization percentage.
>
> If the metrics are appearing correctly, I'd then check the HPA's own configuration. Maybe the current usage hasn't actually crossed the target threshold, or perhaps it has already scaled up to its configured `maxReplicas` value.
>
> Finally, I'd check the ReplicaSet events to see if the HPA did try to scale, but the new pods are stuck in `Pending` due to a lack of cluster resources.

Mini-case study: HPA not scaling due to missing requests

An e-commerce site has an HPA configured to scale its frontend deployment when CPU usage exceeds 70%. During a flash sale, the existing pods are overwhelmed, but the HPA does not add any new replicas:

- **Symptom:** Pods are overloaded, but the HPA isn't scaling the deployment.

- **Diagnosis:** The team runs the following command:

```
kubectl describe hpa frontend-hpa
```

They see the metric status is <unknown> / 70%. This tells them the HPA isn't getting data. They confirm the metrics-server component is running because the following command works:

```
kubectl top pods
```

They then inspect the frontend Deployment's manifest and discover the pod spec has resource limits but no requests.

- **Resolution**: They add a resources.requests.cpu field to the container spec and redeploy. The HPA immediately starts reporting the correct CPU utilization and scales the deployment out to handle the traffic spike.

The HPA is a powerful example of how monitoring data can be used to automate performance management. But reactive scaling is just one part of the story. A truly mature engineering practice involves using a rich toolkit of observability and profiling tools to proactively understand and optimize application performance *before* it triggers an autoscaler or causes an outage. This final section explores essential tools that complete your performance troubleshooting arsenal.

The proactive toolkit: Monitoring and observability

This is a high-level, architectural topic. An interviewer will ask about your preferred toolset to gauge your practical experience with modern SRE and observability practices. Your ability to articulate the roles of different tools—and especially to explain the "three pillars of observability" (metrics, logs, and traces)—shows that you don't just fix problems, but you build systems to prevent and quickly diagnose them.

Building your performance toolkit

Effective performance management goes beyond reactive troubleshooting. It requires a comprehensive observability strategy. While Kubernetes provides basic events and metrics, a professional-grade setup integrates several specialized tools:

- **Metrics (Prometheus and Grafana)**: This is the de facto foundation for Kubernetes monitoring. Prometheus is a time-series database that scrapes numerical metrics from your cluster and applications (via exporters such as kube-state-metrics and node-exporter). Grafana is a visualization tool that turns raw data into powerful dashboards. With Grafana, you can correlate events; for example, visualizing a spike in API latency happening at the exact same time as an increase in CPU throttling, instantly pointing you to the cause.

- **Logs (Loki or EFK Stack)**: While metrics tell you what happened (e.g., "error rate increased"), logs tell you why. A centralized logging stack, such as the classic **EFK** (which stands for **Elasticsearch, Fluentd, Kibana**) stack or the more modern Loki, allows you to search and analyze logs from all your pods in one place to find specific error messages or warnings.

- **Traces (OpenTelemetry (OTel) and Jaeger/Zipkin)**: In a microservices architecture, a single user request can travel through dozens of services. If that request is slow, how do you know which service is the bottleneck? This is where distributed tracing is indispensable. The modern industry standard for this is **OTEL**, a CNCF-backed observability framework. You instrument your application code using OTel's SDKs to generate trace data. This data is then sent to a backend collector and visualizer such as **Jaeger** or **Zipkin**. By looking at a trace, you can see a request's entire journey as a single waterfall diagram, showing exactly how long it spent in each service and database call. This makes it possible to instantly pinpoint latency bottlenecks.

- **Profiling and application performance monitoring (APM)**: When you've identified a specific pod or container that is using too much CPU or memory, you need to go deeper. A language-specific profiler (such as pprof for Go or JProfiler for Java) can tell you exactly which function or line of code is responsible. APM tools such as Datadog and New Relic often bundle these capabilities together.

- **Capacity planning and advanced autoscaling**: Beyond observability, a mature practice involves proactive capacity planning and more sophisticated autoscaling. The **Vertical Pod Autoscaler (VPA)** analyzes a workload's past usage and can recommend—or even automatically apply—the optimal CPU and memory requests and limits, helping you to "right-size" your pods. For applications that don't scale on CPU or memory, the **Kubernetes Event-Driven Autoscaler (KEDA)** is essential. It extends the HPA to allow scaling based on hundreds of event sources, such as the number of messages in a Kafka topic or the length of a queue in RabbitMQ, which is perfect for **event-driven architectures (EDAs)**.

Interview tip

Question: *How would you debug a high-latency issue for a request that involves five different microservices?*

Answer: This is the perfect use case for **distributed tracing**. Trying to correlate logs from five different services would be extremely difficult. With a tracing tool such as Jaeger, I can look up the trace ID for a slow request and see a single, unified view of its entire journey. I can see exactly how much time was spent in each of the five services, as well as any database or external API calls they made. This would immediately show me if, for example, the third service in the chain is taking 2 seconds while all the others are taking 50 milliseconds, instantly identifying it as the bottleneck.

Real-world example: Hunting a memory leak

A team notices that one of their key microservices periodically slows down and restarts every few days:

- **Symptom**: Gradual performance degradation followed by an OOMKilled restart.
- **Diagnosis**: Using their Grafana dashboard, they look at the pod's memory usage graph from Prometheus. They see a "sawtooth" pattern: the memory usage climbs steadily over 48 hours, then sharply drops to 0 (the restart). This is a classic sign of a memory leak.
- **Resolution**: They enable a memory profiler in the application. The next time the memory usage gets high, they take a heap dump. The analysis reveals that a cache object is growing without bound and is never being cleared. They fix the bug in the caching logic, and the memory usage stabilizes. They also add a Prometheus alert to notify them if memory usage grows abnormally in the future.

Summary

We began this chapter by establishing a core principle: effective troubleshooting is not about knowing every command, but about having a **structured mental model**. We applied this principle across the three most common failure domains you will face.

First, we mastered the **pod lifecycle**, learning to diagnose everything from a Pending pod that won't schedule to a Terminating pod that won't disappear. Next, we navigated the complexities of **Kubernetes networking**, tracing the path of a request from external DNS all the way through Ingress, Services, and Network Policies. Finally, we tackled **performance**, learning to identify and resolve resource bottlenecks such as OOMKilled pods and CPU throttling.

Armed with these frameworks and practical techniques, you are now well equipped to confidently diagnose real-world production issues and, just as importantly, to articulate your sophisticated thought process in any Kubernetes interview.

Having the technical skills to debug a `CrashLoopBackOff` scenario or trace a network request is essential, but it's only half the equation in a senior-level interview. The other half is communicating that knowledge effectively under pressure. How do you turn a complex war story into a concise, compelling answer? How do you avoid common traps that make even experienced engineers seem junior?

The next chapter moves beyond the terminal and into the interview room itself. We'll explore the most common mistakes candidates make and provide frameworks to help you showcase your technical depth with the clarity and confidence that will land you the job.

Unlock this book's exclusive benefits now

UNLOCK NOW

Scan this QR code or go to `https://packtpub.com/unlock`, then search for this book by name.

Note: Keep your purchase invoice ready before you start.

17

Common Mistakes and How to Avoid Them

Congratulations! You have managed production clusters, automated deployments, and wrangled distributed systems. But as you prepare for staff-level interviews, you quickly realize that mastery of the terminal alone isn't a ticket to success. The real world of Kubernetes interviewing is as much about how you communicate and reason as it is about what you know.

Kubernetes interviews for senior and staff roles are specifically designed to mirror production complexity. You'll face scenarios where you must not only demonstrate technical depth but do so with clarity, humility, and business awareness. Interviewers expect you to turn your experience into concise stories that show your judgment: how you handle cascading failures, difficult trade-offs, and teamwork in the storm.

This chapter is your actionable roadmap to interview preparation—not with flashcards, but with frameworks, real-world stories, and professional presence.

We will be covering the following main headings:

- The behavioral framework
- Kubernetes problem-solving frameworks
- Technical communication mastery

The behavioral framework

Let's understand why the story structure wins in interviews. A rambling, technical monologue will lose your interviewers. Don't just list your skills; tell a story. Senior engineers stand out by framing their experience in concise narratives. The best tool for this is the **STAR method** (short for **situation, task, action, result**), which turns a rambling technical answer into a powerful, memorable story.

Your secret weapon: the STAR method for engineering stories

To make this practical, here's what a STAR-based answer actually sounds like for a Kubernetes interview question. Notice how each part is clear, specific, and tied to measurable outcomes:

- **Situation:** "Last quarter, our Kubernetes cluster had frequent etcd leader election failures, leading to sporadic deployment delays and developer escalations."
- **Task:** "As a staff SRE, I had to diagnose the root cause and restore normal operations—without causing downtime for external services."
- **Action:** "I analyzed etcd health, identified a network partition issue via Prometheus metrics, coordinated with network ops to find a misconfigured MTU on one rack, and tuned heartbeat intervals to stabilize the consensus algorithm."
- **Result:** "Leader election timeouts dropped from 60 seconds to under 30, API error rates fell to zero, and we created a new playbook for distributed partition troubleshooting."

This structure turns a technical story into a clear narrative that your interviewers can actually follow. Let's explore why STAR stories are so powerful in making your expertise stand out.

What makes STAR stories so powerful?

A well-told STAR story does three transformative things in your interview:

- **Anchors attention:** With each phase, your interviewers know where they are in your story. No background detail gets lost, and no achievement stands unsupported.
- **Highlights impact:** Results—including metrics, downtime avoided, dollars saved, or even organizational improvements—make clear not just what happened, but why it mattered.
- **Demonstrates growth:** By ending with lessons learned and process improvements, you're signaling that you're always evolving, key at senior levels.

But perhaps best of all, STAR isn't just a *trick* for the interview room. Great engineering teams already use this structure for postmortems and architectural documents. *"Here's what went wrong, here's who tackled it and how, here's what worked, and here's how we'll do better next time."* If you practice STAR for interviews, you're also practicing better postmortems and more effective leadership communication—a true career multiplier.

> **Interview tip**
>
> **Question:** *Interviewers often ask you to "Tell me about a time when...". How does the STAR method help you structure a compelling answer for these behavioral questions?*
>
> **Answer:** The STAR method provides a narrative framework that prevents rambling and focuses your answer on impact. It stands for *situation, task, action, and result.* You start by setting the context (*situation*) and explaining your specific responsibility (*task*). Then, you detail the concrete steps you took (*action*), and crucially, you conclude with the measurable outcome (*result*). This structure turns a simple anecdote into a powerful story that showcases your problem-solving skills, your ability to handle pressure, and the tangible value you delivered.

Now that you understand why STAR stories can transform your interviews and your career, it's time to learn how to craft your own, making them interview-ready and genuinely reflective of your experience.

Making your own STAR stories interview-ready

When you're headed into a big interview—especially at the staff or senior level—you don't want to scramble to recall details from a past incident. The secret? Treat your experience the way great authors treat their most powerful anecdotes: prepare them, polish them, keep them at your fingertips.

One proven, practical method is to create a *living deck* of STAR stories—almost like sticky notes, but far more purposeful. Spend some quiet, focused time before the interview to reflect on a handful of key Kubernetes moments from your career. Don't just reach for the legendary outages or high-drama fire drills. Some of the best stories come from those everyday puzzles: maybe you fine-tuned an HPA to stop runaway costs, or orchestrated a seamless migration so that your end users barely noticed.

As you build each story, write it out STAR-style, but do it as if you're jotting a post-it note to your future self:

- What was truly at stake? (The *situation*—what made this moment matter?)

- What was the mission? (The *task*—what needed to be solved, and why were you the one responsible?)

- What did you actually do? (The *action*—what steps, tools, and negotiations or quick thinking pushed it across the finish line?)

- What changed? What was tangibly better after? (The *result*—including not just operational metrics, but how you leveled up the team or the system overall.)

Once you've got your mini-library of STAR stories, make them part of your active preparation. Review them before the interview, just like you'd check your slides before a conference talk. When a panel throws you a curveball—*"When was the last time you mitigated a production issue?"*—you'll simply reach for the story that fits, with the confidence and precision of someone who's already mapped the territory. To make this even more concrete, here's a visual that maps how the STAR framework overlays onto real Kubernetes architecture and workflows:

Control Plane

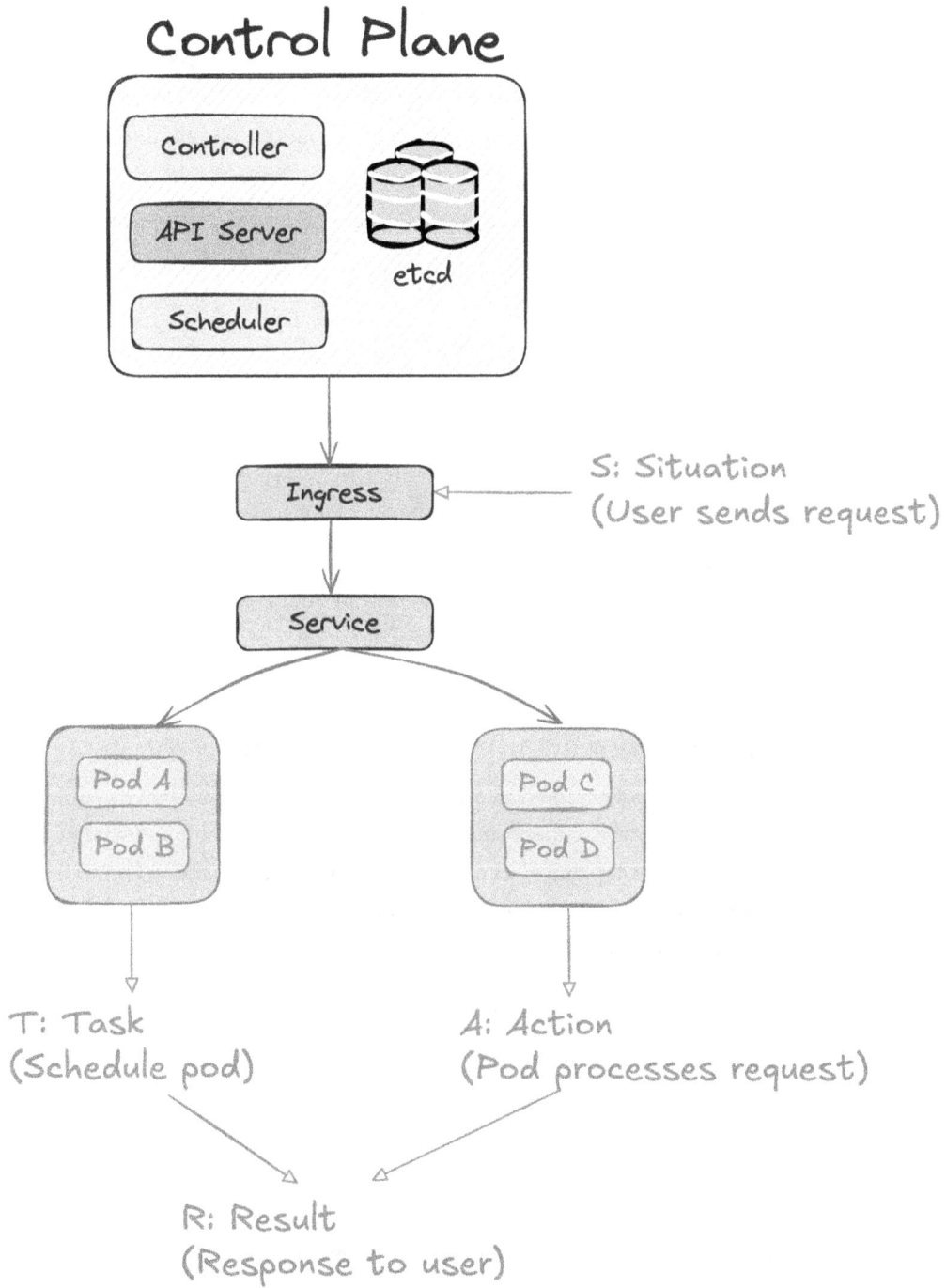

Figure 17.1 – STAR workflow overlay on Kubernetes architecture diagram

Figure 17.1 visually connects the STAR framework with the flow of a Kubernetes request through the cluster. It shows how a user request (*situation*) enters via Ingress, leading to scheduling decisions (*task*), processing within Pods (*action*), and finally, returning a response to the user (*result*). By mapping STAR onto Kubernetes internals, you can see how your troubleshooting stories align directly with the system's architecture.

Think of these STAR stories not as a script you're locked to, but as anchors. They free up your mental bandwidth to handle surprises, connect dots, and even turn follow-ups into deeper conversations. It's a strategy that transforms your career history from a jumble of memories into a professional edge you can count on—every single time.

> **Tip**
>
> Most postmortems and retrospectives written by high-performing SREs follow a STAR-like narrative, so building this habit pays off long after the interview.

Now that you've seen how STAR stories help you communicate your experience clearly, let's shift to the frameworks that will help you systematically solve Kubernetes problems during interviews and on the job.

Kubernetes problem-solving frameworks

Welcome to the hot seat. By this point in your interview journey, you've demonstrated your foundational knowledge. Now, the hiring manager wants to see how you handle things when they break. This chapter isn't just about memorizing error codes; it's about building a mental framework to diagnose and solve real-world Kubernetes problems under pressure. We'll tackle the common, tricky, and advanced scenarios that separate a good engineer from a great one. Let's dive in.

Foundational diagnostics

In this section, we'll break down the Kubernetes issues you're almost certain to face, both in interviews and in real-world on-call. We'll cover why Pods get stuck in the Pending state, how to approach CrashLoopBackOff issues systematically, and what to check when your application can't pull its container image. By mastering these scenarios, you'll build confidence in your diagnostics while demonstrating to interviewers that you can keep systems stable under pressure. These are the scenarios you are almost guaranteed to encounter. Mastering them shows you have a solid operational footing.

Why are my Pods stuck in a Pending state?

This is often one of the first troubleshooting questions you'll face. It's a classic because it tests your core understanding of the scheduler.

What the interviewer is really asking: They're testing your understanding of the **Pod scheduling lifecycle**. Do you know the sequence of events that must happen for a Pod to run on a node? Can you systematically identify the bottleneck? This question probes your grasp of resource management and the scheduler's role.

> **Interview tip**
>
> **Question:** *A Pod is stuck in a Pending state. What does this status fundamentally mean, and what is the first command you would run to begin your investigation?*
>
> **Answer:** A Pending state means the Pod has been accepted by the Kubernetes API server, but the scheduler cannot place it onto a valid node. The issue lies within the scheduling process, not the application itself. The first and most effective command is `kubectl describe pod <pod-name>`. The Events section in the output is invaluable because it almost always contains a specific message from the scheduler explaining why it failed, such as `Insufficient cpu` or a failure to match affinity rules.

Your strategy: Start by defining the Pending state simply: "A Pod is Pending when the API has accepted it, but the scheduler can't assign it to a node. This usually happens for one of a few key reasons."

Then, walk through the diagnostic process.

"My first step is always to run `kubectl describe pod <pod-name>`. The Events section in the output is your first stop; it usually tells you exactly why the scheduler failed. The most common culprits are the following:

- **Resource starvation:** The Pod is requesting more CPU or memory than any single node can provide. The scheduler can't find a home for it.
- **No available nodes:** All nodes in the cluster might be fully utilized, or the cluster might have scaled down to zero nodes if using a cluster autoscaler.
- **Taints and tolerations:** The Pod might not have the necessary *toleration* to be scheduled on a node that has a *taint*. For example, control plane nodes are often tainted to prevent regular workloads from running on them.

- **Affinity/anti-affinity rules**: The Pod's scheduling rules (e.g., nodeSelector or nodeAffinity) might be too restrictive, preventing it from being placed on any available node.

- **Persistent volume claims (PVCs)**: If the Pod depends on a PVC, it will remain Pending until that volume can be successfully bound and mounted. Issues with the StorageClass or available persistent volumes can cause this.

I'd start by checking the resource requests in the describe output and comparing them to the capacity of the nodes. If that looks fine, I'd check for taints and any affinity rules."

Code/YAML example: Here's how you'd use kubectl describe to diagnose the issue:

```
kubectl describe pod my-pending-pod
Name:          my-pending-pod
Namespace:     default
Priority:      0
Node:          <none>
Status:        Pending
...
Events:
  Type      Reason            Age    From              Message
  ----      ------            ----   ----              -------
  Warning   FailedScheduling  2m     default-scheduler  0/3 nodes are
available: 3 Insufficient cpu.
```

"As you can see in this example, the Events section clearly states that the scheduler failed because of insufficient CPU. This tells me immediately to look at the Pod's CPU requests and the available CPU on my nodes."

Real-world example: "In a previous role, we had a new service that was consistently stuck in Pending. The developer had copied a manifest from another high-performance service without adjusting the resource requests. The pod was requesting eight CPU cores, but our standard cluster nodes only had four cores available. The scheduler was doing its job perfectly, but no node could satisfy the request. By running kubectl describe and seeing the Insufficient cpu message, we were able to identify the misconfiguration in under a minute, adjust the request down to a more reasonable 250m (a quarter of a core), and the Pod scheduled instantly. It was a simple fix, but it highlights the importance of starting with the basics."

The following diagram presents a simplified decision process for this:

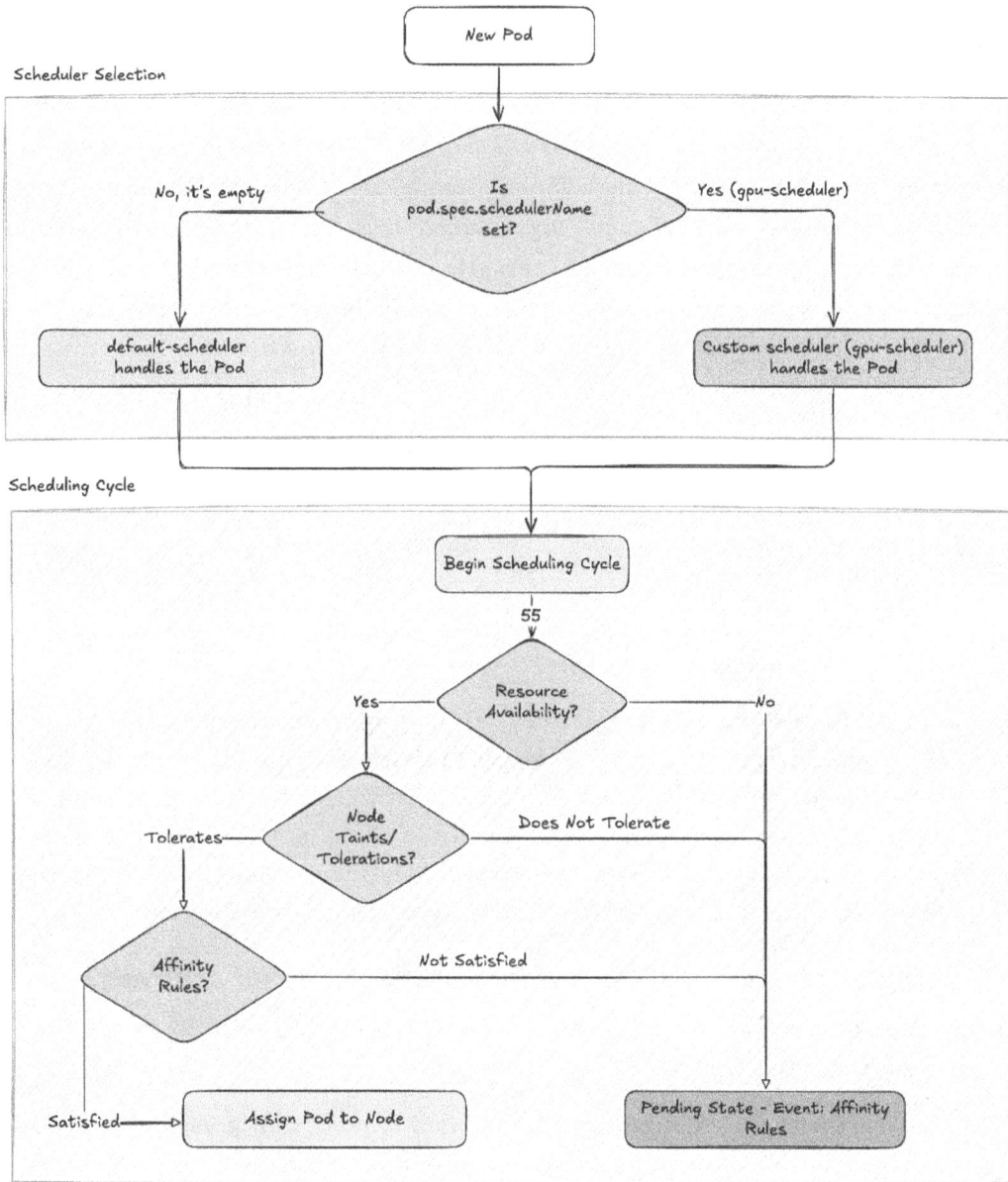

Figure 17.2 – Kubernetes scheduler's decision process

This diagram illustrates the Kubernetes scheduler's decision-making process, highlighting a key feature: the ability to run multiple schedulers in a cluster. The first stage, *scheduler selection*, shows how a Pod is assigned to a scheduler. If a Pod's `spec.schedulerName` field is set, the designated scheduler handles it; otherwise, the cluster's default scheduler picks it up.

Once a scheduler takes charge, it begins the *scheduling cycle*. It walks through the critical checks for placing a new Pod: verifying whether sufficient resources are available, evaluating node taints and the Pod's tolerations, and finally, applying any affinity or anti-affinity rules. If all constraints are satisfied, the Pod is assigned to a node. Otherwise, it remains in the `Pending` state, with the failed condition—such as missing tolerations or unsatisfiable affinity rules—logged in the `Events` section. This visual reinforces why understanding each stage of the scheduling flow is essential for diagnosing why a Pod won't start.

With scheduling issues covered, let's move on to a different but equally common challenge: how to troubleshoot a Pod that keeps crashing after it starts.

Interview tip

Question: *Beyond insufficient CPU or memory, what are two other common reasons a Pod might be stuck in the Pending state?*

Answer: Two very common reasons are issues with taints and tolerations, and PVCs. A node might have a taint—for example, to reserve it for specific workloads—and the Pod will not be scheduled on it unless it has a matching toleration. Secondly, if a Pod's definition includes a PVC, it will remain `Pending` until that volume can be successfully bound and mounted. Problems with the underlying `StorageClass` or a lack of available persistent volumes can block this process indefinitely.

My application can't pull its container image. What's wrong?

The dreaded `ImagePullBackOff` or `ErrImagePull` status means the kubelet on a node cannot fetch the container image from the registry.

What the interviewer is really asking: This probes your knowledge of the image registry interaction. Do you understand public versus private registries, authentication (`imagePullSecrets`), and how kubelet resolves image tags?

Your strategy: "An `ImagePullBackOff` error means the container never even started. The problem is purely about fetching the image from a registry. My checklist includes the following:

1. **Check the image name:** The most common cause is a simple typo. I'd run `kubectl describe pod <pod-name>` and carefully check the image URL in the container spec. Is the registry name correct? Is the image name spelled correctly? Is the tag correct?

2. **Verify the secret:** If the image is in a private registry, it needs `imagePullSecrets`. I'd check that the secret exists in the same namespace as the Pod (`kubectl get secret <secret-name> -n <namespace>`). Then, I'd verify that the Deployment or Pod spec correctly references this secret.

3. **Test the secret:** I would then decode the secret (`kubectl get secret <secret-name> -o yaml`) to ensure the credentials inside are valid and have not expired. I might even use `docker login` on a machine to test the credentials against the private registry directly.

4. **Check network connectivity:** In rare cases, the node itself might not have network connectivity to the image registry (e.g., a firewall rule blocking access to Docker Hub, GCR, or a private registry). I'd try to SSH into the node and manually run `docker pull <image-name>` to confirm."

Code/YAML example: Here's how `imagePullSecret` is referenced in a Deployment. A mistake here is very common:

```yaml
# deployment.yaml
apiVersion: apps/v1
kind: Deployment
metadata:
  name: private-app
  namespace: secure
spec:
  template:
    spec:
      containers:
      - name: main
        image: my-private-registry.io/apps/super-secret-app:1.0
      # This is the crucial link to the secret
      imagePullSecrets:
      - name: my-registry-creds
---
```

```
# The secret must also exist in the 'secure' namespace
apiVersion: v1
kind: Secret
metadata:
  name: my-registry-creds
  namespace: secure
type: kubernetes.io/dockerconfigjson
data:
  .dockerconfigjson: ewoJImF1dGhzIjogewoJCSJteS1wcml2YXRlLXJlZ2lzdHJ5Lmlv
IjogewoJCQkJImF1dGGgiOiAiAiZEhWcFpEeHZjM1JvWTI5c2IySmhiR052Ym5NPSIKCQkJfQoJfX0=
```

ewoJImF1dGhzIjogewoJCSJteS1wcml2YXRlLXJlZ2lzdHJ5Lmlv
IjogewoJCQkJImF1dGGgiOiAiAiZEhWcFpEeHZjM1JvWTI5c2IySmhiR052Ym5NPSIKCQkJfQoJfX0=

"A frequent error is creating the secret in the `default` namespace but deploying the Pod into a different one, such as `secure`. Since secrets are namespaced, the Pod can't find it, and the image pull fails."

Interview tip

Question: *What does an ImagePullBackOff or ErrImagePull status mean, and what is a common namespace-related mistake that causes it?*

Answer: These statuses indicate that the kubelet on a node cannot fetch the container image from the specified registry. This is a pre-startup failure. A very common mistake when using a private registry is a mismatch in namespaces. You might create the `imagePullSecret` with the registry credentials in the `default` namespace, but then deploy the Pod into a different namespace, such as `secure`. Since secrets are namespaced, the Pod cannot find the secret and fails authentication, resulting in an `ImagePullBackOff` status.

Real-world example: "We had an `ImagePullBackOff` error for a critical service in our staging environment. We checked the image name, and it was correct. We confirmed the `imagePullSecret` was attached to the service account the Pod was using. Everything looked perfect. After two hours of debugging, we found the issue was a CNI network policy that was applied to the `kube-system` namespace. It inadvertently blocked egress traffic from the nodes themselves to the internet on port 443. The kubelet, running on the node, couldn't reach our cloud provider's container registry. It was a subtle issue that required looking beyond the Pod and into the cluster's fundamental network setup."

With the foundational diagnostics covered, it's time to level up. Let's move into the more intricate world of Kubernetes networking and state management, where problems often span multiple layers of the system.

Intermediate networking and state

In this section, we move beyond single-Pod issues to focus on how different components communicate within the cluster and how that communication can break down. These questions reflect a more advanced tier of operational knowledge, where you're expected to diagnose connectivity and access problems that span Pods, services, namespaces, and even Ingress configurations. We'll cover what to check when your application is deployed but unreachable from outside the cluster, and how to methodically debug inter-Pod communication issues across namespaces. Mastery here shows that you understand not just how Kubernetes schedules workloads, but how it enables, and sometimes blocks, critical network flows between them.

I've deployed my app, but I can't access it from outside the cluster. What should I check?

This is a classic networking problem: your application is running, but it's unreachable from the outside.

What the interviewer is really asking: Do you understand the difference between a Pod, a Service, and an Ingress? Can you trace the path of a request from the internet to your container?

Your strategy: This requires tracing the traffic flow from outside in. My process is as follows:

1. **Check the Service**: First, is there a Service object pointing to the pods? I'd run `kubectl get svc <service-name>`:

    -   What is its type? If it's `ClusterIP` (the default), it's only reachable from *inside* the cluster. This is a very common mistake. To expose it externally, it needs to be `NodePort` or `LoadBalancer`.

    -   Does the Service's `selector` match the labels on the Pods? I'd check `kubectl describe svc <service-name>` and look at the `Endpoints` field. If it's empty, the selector isn't matching any running Pods.

2. **Check the Ingress:** If they are using an Ingress, I'd check that next:

   - Does the Ingress service name and service port correctly point to the Service from *Step 1*?

   - Is the Ingress controller running? An Ingress object does nothing on its own; it requires a controller (such as NGINX, Traefik, or one from a cloud provider) to be running in the cluster to fulfill the rules. I'd check for the Ingress controller Pods in `kube-system` or a dedicated namespace:

   - Are the DNS records for the host in the Ingress rule pointing to the load balancer created by the Ingress controller?

3. **Check network policies:** Just like with Pod-to-Pod communication, a `NetworkPolicy` could be blocking traffic from the Ingress controller to the application Pods. I'd check for any policies in the application's namespace.

Code/YAML example: Here is an Ingress manifest showing the link between the host, the Ingress object, and the backend Service:

```
apiVersion: networking.k8s.io/v1
kind: Ingress
metadata:
  name: my-app-ingress
  annotations:
    kubernetes.io/ingress.class: "nginx"
spec:
  rules:
  - host: "myapp.example.com" # Is DNS pointing here?
    http:
      paths:
      - path: /
        pathType: Prefix
        backend:
          service:
            name: my-app-service # Does this Service exist?
            port:
              number: 80 # Does the service expose this port?
```

```
---
apiVersion: v1
kind: Service
metadata:
  name: my-app-service
spec:
  selector:
    app: my-app # Do the pods have this label?
  ports:
    - protocol: TCP
      port: 80
      targetPort: 8080 # Does the container listen on 8080?
  type: ClusterIP # Ingress can route to a ClusterIP service, this is
fine.
```

"In this setup, a request to myapp.example.com hits the NGINX Ingress controller's load balancer. The controller sees the host header, finds this Ingress rule, and forwards the traffic to the my-app-service on port 80, which then sends it to a backend Pod on targetPort 8080. A mistake in any part of this chain will break connectivity."

Real-world example: "A team deployed a new version of their service and reported it was unreachable. They swore up and down that the Service and Ingress YAMLs were identical to the previous, working version. We checked, and they were. The Pods were running and healthy. The Service endpoints were populated correctly. After 30 minutes, we discovered the issue: in their CI pipeline, they had updated the Pod's label from app: my-app to app: my-app-v2 but had forgotten to update the Service's selector to match. The Service was looking for Pods that no longer existed. It was a classic selector mismatch. We updated the selector, and traffic started flowing immediately."

To visualize this end-to-end flow, here's a breakdown of how an external request reaches a Kubernetes application—and where things can go wrong along the way:

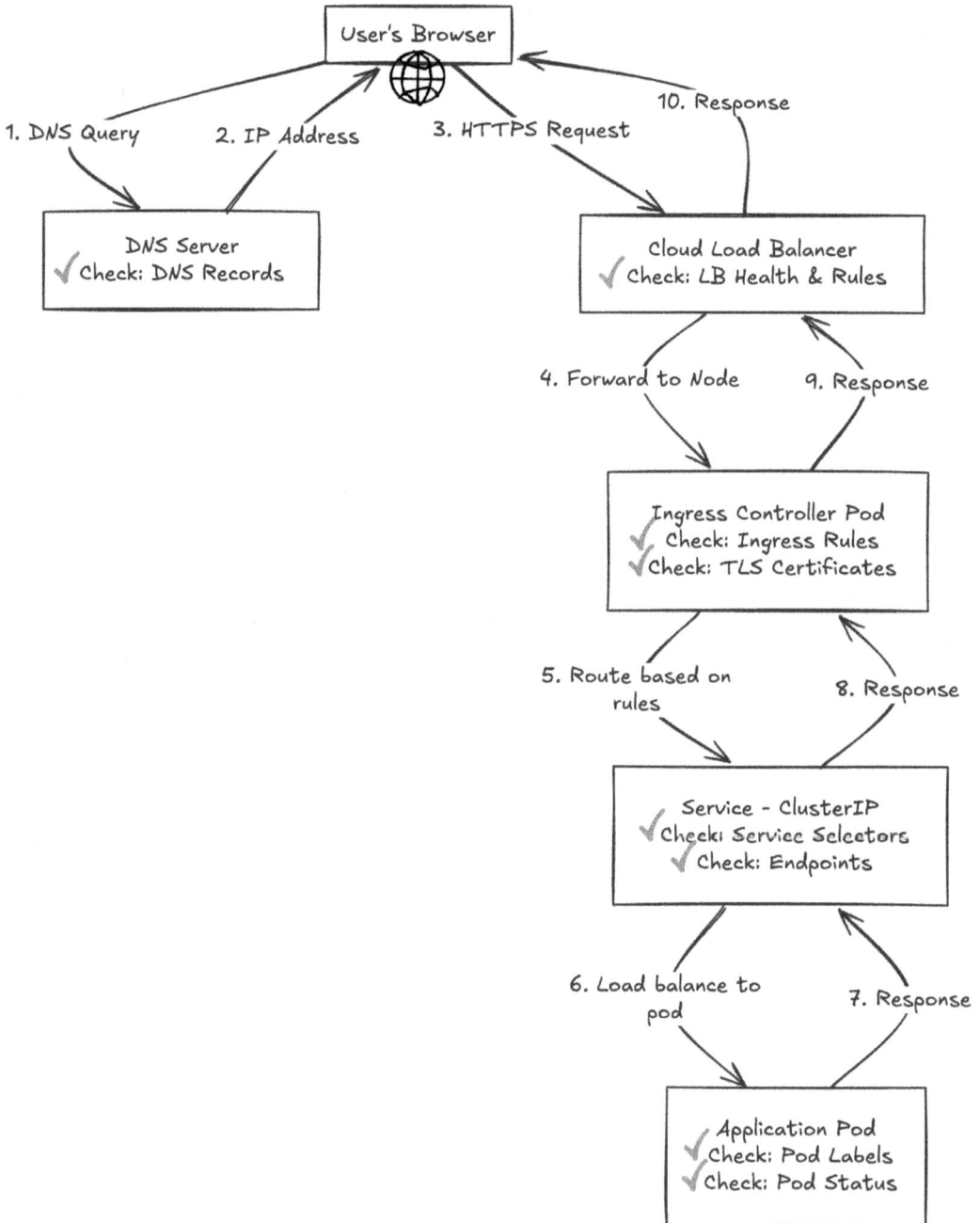

Figure 17.3 – Path of an external request

This diagram traces the full lifecycle of an external HTTPS request as it travels through a Kubernetes cluster. It begins with a DNS lookup, proceeds through a cloud load balancer, and reaches the Ingress controller Pod, which uses defined rules to match hostnames and forward traffic to a backend Service. That Service uses label selectors to route requests to the appropriate Pods. Along the way, the diagram highlights critical checkpoints—such as verifying DNS records, Ingress rules, TLS certificates, and Pod health—that help isolate where a connectivity issue might occur. This visual reinforces the importance of methodically checking each link in the chain when an application is unreachable from outside the cluster.

> **Interview tip**
>
> **Question:** *You've deployed an application, but it's not accessible from the outside. What is the role of a Service's selector in this scenario, and what's the quickest way to verify it's working?*
>
> **Answer:** A Service's selector creates the crucial link between the Service and the Pods it's supposed to manage. It's a set of labels that the Service uses to find all the Pods that are part of its backend group. If there's a typo in the labels or the selector, the Service won't find any Pods. The quickest way to verify this is to run `kubectl describe svc <service-name>` and check the `Endpoints` field. If it's empty or `<none>`, it's a clear sign of a selector mismatch, and the Service has no Pods to send traffic to.

Let's now shift our attention from external access to internal communication, specifically, how to diagnose inter-Pod connectivity issues that occur across namespaces.

Debug inter-Pod communication failures across namespaces

This question moves beyond a single pod and into the realm of cluster networking.

What the interviewer is really asking: They want to know whether you understand Kubernetes networking concepts, specifically **Network Policies** and the role of the **container network interface (CNI)**. Can you diagnose connectivity issues that aren't a simple *is the service down* problem?

Your strategy: Acknowledge the layers involved. "If Pods in different namespaces can't communicate, your first suspect should almost always be a `NetworkPolicy`. My process is to verify the connectivity layer by layer as follows:

1. **Confirm DNS resolution**: First, I'd exec into the source Pod and use `nslookup` or `dig` to ensure the service in the other namespace is resolvable. For a service named `database` in the backend namespace, I'd run `nslookup database.backend.svc.cluster.local`. If this fails, the problem is with CoreDNS, not Pod-to-Pod connectivity.

2. **Inspect NetworkPolicies**: If DNS works, the next suspect is a `NetworkPolicy`. I would run `kubectl get networkpolicy -n <namespace>` in both the source and destination namespaces. A missing or overly restrictive policy is a common cause. For example, an egress policy on the source namespace might not allow traffic to the destination, or an Ingress policy on the destination namespace might not allow traffic from the source.

3. **Check the CNI plugin**: If there are no blocking `NetworkPolicies`, the issue could be with the CNI plugin itself (such as Calico, Cilium, or Flannel). This is less common but possible, especially if there have been recent upgrades or changes to the CNI configuration. I might check the logs of the CNI agent Pods running on the nodes."

Code/YAML example: An example of a restrictive `NetworkPolicy` that could cause this problem is as follows:

```
apiVersion: networking.k8s.io/v1
kind: NetworkPolicy
metadata:
  name: default-deny-all-ingress
  namespace: backend
spec:
  podSelector: {} # Selects all pods in the namespace
  policyTypes:
  - Ingress
  # This policy has no Ingress rules, so it blocks all incoming traffic
  # to all pods in the 'backend' namespace by default.
```

"If this policy were applied to the backend namespace, no Pods from the outside could communicate with it. To fix this, you'd need to add an explicit `Ingress` rule to allow the desired traffic, for instance, from Pods in the `frontend` namespace." Here is an example:

```
# A corrective Ingress rule
ingress:
- from:
  - namespaceSelector:
      matchLabels:
        name: frontend
```

Real-world example: "We once had a production outage where our frontend application couldn't reach user-service in the backend namespace right after a new security policy was rolled out. DNS was working, but any connection attempt would time out. I immediately checked the NetworkPolicies in the backend namespace and found that a new default-deny Ingress policy had been applied. The security team had forgotten to add a corresponding rule to allow ingress from the frontend namespace's Pods. We added the correct ingress rule, referencing the frontend namespace by its label, and connectivity was restored instantly. It was a valuable lesson in how critical explicit network rules are in a multi-tenant cluster."

To make the role of NetworkPolicies more concrete, here's a diagram showing how inter-namespace access is either blocked or permitted based on explicit policy rules:

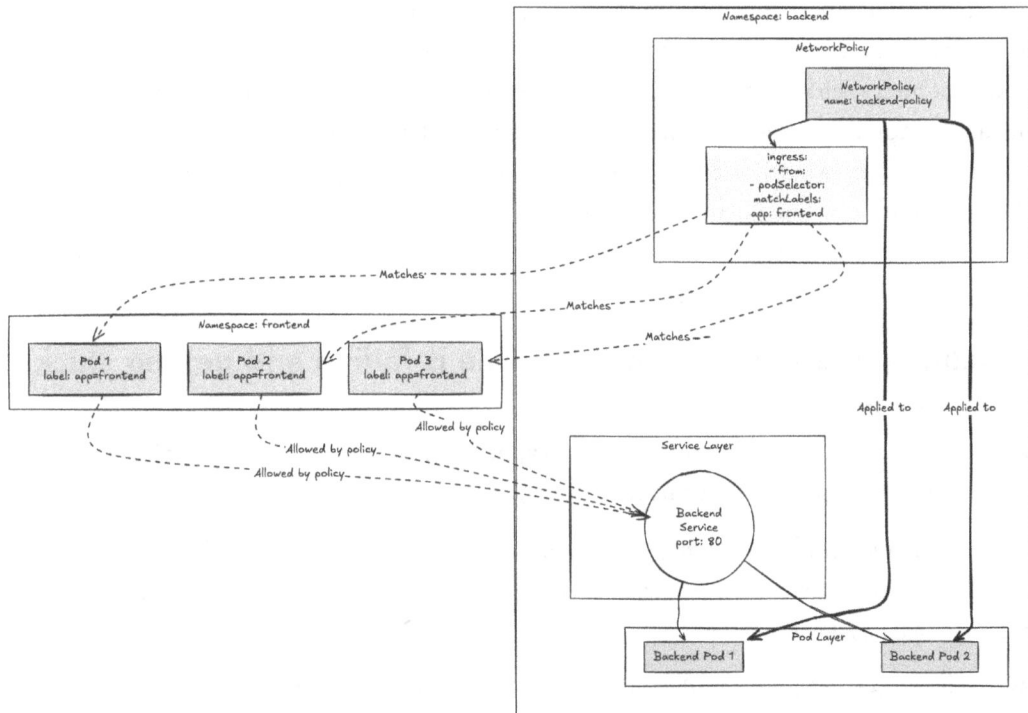

Figure 17.4 – How the policy grants access

This diagram illustrates how a restrictive NetworkPolicy in the backend namespace controls which Pods can communicate with backend services. By default, all ingress traffic is denied due to the default-deny-all-ingress policy. However, an explicit rule allows traffic only from Pods in the frontend namespace that match specific labels. The dashed lines represent intended or blocked communication paths, while solid arrows indicate allowed traffic as defined by the policy.

The service in the backend namespace selects backend Pods via a label selector, but communication from other namespaces succeeds only if the source Pods match the criteria defined in the policy's from clause. This visual reinforces the need for carefully scoped ingress rules when securing multi-namespace clusters.

With the core networking flows and inter-Pod policies covered, we're now ready to tackle more advanced scenarios: problems that often span layers, involve misaligned assumptions, or surface only at scale. Let's dive into the architectural challenges that truly test senior Kubernetes engineers.

Advanced and architectural problems

In this section, we move into the kinds of complex, architecture-level problems that separate experienced Kubernetes practitioners from true platform engineers. These questions aren't just about fixing a broken Pod; they test your grasp of how the control plane operates under pressure, how Kubernetes behaves at scale, and how subtle misconfigurations can ripple into cluster-wide instability. You'll be asked to think through rolling update failures, multi-node coordination issues, performance bottlenecks in etcd, and node state flapping. These scenarios require more than just command-line fluency—they demand a systems-thinking mindset and the ability to reason through distributed behavior under real-world constraints. Let's explore how to approach them with clarity and confidence.

A rolling update for our main service is failing and getting stuck. What are the potential causes?

This scenario is about deployment strategy and application health. The cluster is trying to perform a zero-downtime update, but it's not succeeding.

What the interviewer is really asking: Do you understand the mechanics of RollingUpdate? Can you connect the deployment configuration (maxSurge and maxUnavailable) with the application health (readinessProbe)?

Your strategy: "A stuck rolling update means that Kubernetes can't get the new Pods into a Ready state, or it can't terminate the old ones gracefully. My investigation would follow these steps:

1. **Check new Pod status**: "First, I'd look at the new Pods being created by the update. Are they stuck in Pending (a scheduling issue)? Are they in CrashLoopBackOff (an application issue)? I'd use kubectl describe on one of the new Pods to find out."

2. **Investigate the readiness probe**: "The most common culprit is a failing readiness probe. The deployment will not proceed with the update until the new pods are marked as Ready. If the new application version has a bug, a bad configuration, or can't connect to a backend, its readiness probe will fail. The deployment will wait indefinitely (or until progressDeadlineSeconds is exceeded) for the Pod to become ready. I'd check the application logs of the new Pods."

3. **Review deployment strategy**: "I'd look at the strategy section of the deployment manifest:

   - maxUnavailable: If this is set to 0, Kubernetes cannot take down any old Pods until a new one is ready. Combined with a failing readiness probe, this guarantees the deployment will get stuck.

   - maxSurge: If maxSurge is low and the cluster has limited resources, there might not be enough capacity to schedule the "surged" new Pods, causing them to get stuck in Pending.

4. **Check for resource quotas**: "The namespace might have a ResourceQuota that is being exceeded by the temporary increase in Pods and resources required by the rolling update. kubectl describe quota in the namespace would reveal this."

Real-world example: "We had a major deployment that got stuck at 75% complete. The deployment status showed it was waiting for the new Pods to become available. We checked the new Pods, and they were running, but not Ready. We looked at their logs and saw they were failing to connect to our main database. It turned out that the new version of the application required a new database password, which was stored in a secret. The deployment manifest had been updated, but the CI/CD pipeline had failed to apply the updated secret to the cluster. The new Pods were starting up with the old password, failing their health checks, and therefore never becoming ready. The rolling update was paused, exactly as designed, preventing a full-blown outage. We applied the new secret, the existing new Pods automatically picked it up, became Ready, and the deployment completed successfully."

To better understand how a rolling update can fail mid-process, here's a timeline diagram that walks through a common failure scenario:

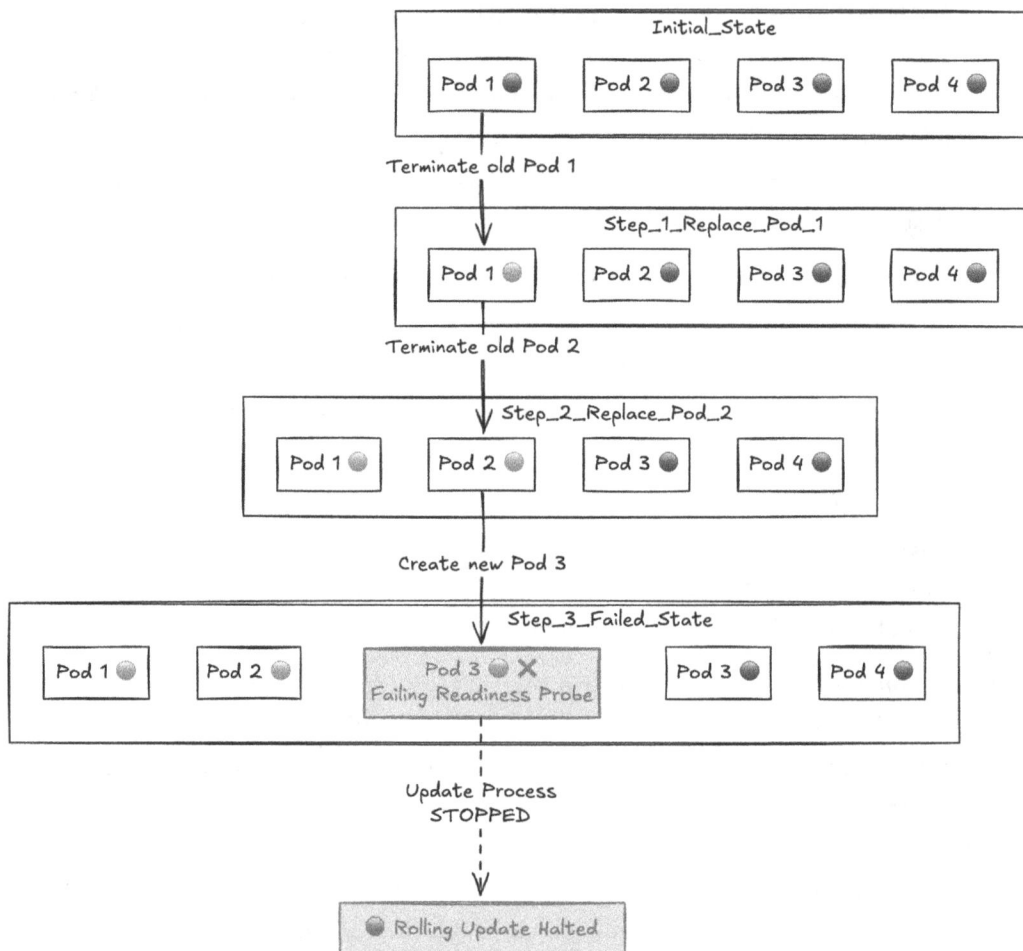

Figure 17.5 – A timeline diagram of a rolling update

This diagram illustrates the sequence of events in a rolling update and where it can get stuck. Initially, all Pods are healthy. As the update begins, older Pods are terminated one by one and replaced with new ones. However, when a newly created Pod (Pod 3) fails its readiness probe—often due to configuration issues or missing dependencies—the update process halts. Because Kubernetes requires the new Pod to be marked Ready before continuing, the failed readiness check prevents further progress. The diagram highlights how Kubernetes' rolling update strategy is designed to maintain service stability, but can also result in stalled deployments when readiness checks fail.

Now, let's shift from deployment flow to control plane scalability, specifically, how to keep etcd performant and reliable in large clusters with thousands of nodes.

> **Interview tip**
>
> **Question:** *During a rolling update, the deployment stalls and never completes. What is the most likely reason for this, and is it considered a failure or a safety feature?*
>
> **Answer:** Yes. This is a **safety feature**, designed to prevent a full-blown outage. The most common cause is that the new Pods created by the update are failing their readiness probe. The Deployment controller intentionally pauses the rollout because its rules require the new Pods to be in a Ready state before it terminates more of the old ones. This failure could be due to a bug, a missing ConfigMap or Secret, or an inability to connect to a backend, which you can diagnose by checking the logs of the new Pods.

Optimize etcd performance for a 5,000-node cluster

This question targets your senior-level knowledge of the control plane's heart: **etcd**.

What the interviewer is really asking: They're assessing your understanding of Kubernetes scalability, reliability, and the performance characteristics of its core data store. Do you know where the bottlenecks are in a massive cluster and how to mitigate them? This is about proactive, architectural thinking.

Your strategy: This question requires a multi-faceted answer that covers hardware, configuration, and monitoring.

"Optimizing etcd for a large-scale cluster is critical for the stability and performance of the entire control plane. My strategy would focus on three main areas—hardware, database maintenance, and client (API server) behavior:

- **Hardware is non-negotiable:** First, etcd is extremely sensitive to I/O latency. It *must* run on the lowest-latency storage available, which means local NVMe SSDs. Using slower magnetic disks or general-purpose network-attached storage is the single biggest mistake you can make. The latency for **Write-Ahead Log (WAL)** fsyncs must be consistently low, as every change in the cluster (a Pod starting, a deployment updating, etc.) is a transaction in etcd.

- **Compaction and defragmentation**: etcd keeps a history of all changes, which causes its database size to grow over time. This can slow down reads and eventually exhaust its storage space. To manage this, you need a robust compaction strategy. I would configure etcd for aggressive auto-compaction, perhaps every 5 minutes for a cluster of that size, based on revision history. Additionally, I would schedule periodic defragmentation to reclaim space from the compacted entries. This is a blocking operation, so it needs to be run on a rolling basis across the members during a low-traffic maintenance window.

- **Monitoring and metrics**: You can't optimize what you can't measure. I would set up detailed monitoring and alerting on key etcd metrics from Prometheus, specifically the following:

  - etcd_disk_wal_fsync_duration_seconds: Spikes in this metric are a leading indicator of I/O issues. For a healthy cluster, p99 should be <10ms.

  - etcd_mvcc_db_total_size_in_bytes: A rapidly growing database size signals that compaction isn't keeping up.

  - etcd_server_leader_changes_seen_total: A high rate of leader elections indicates network instability between etcd members.

- **API server caching**: Finally, I'd ensure the Kubernetes API servers are properly configured to cache objects. This reduces the read load on etcd, as many requests can be served from the API server's watch cache instead of hitting the database directly. Tuning the watch cache size is an important optimization for large, busy clusters."

Real-world example: "I was part of a team that scaled a cluster from 1,000 to over 4,000 nodes. As we grew, we noticed API server requests were becoming sluggish, and Pod startup times increased. Our monitoring showed that the p99 fsync duration for etcd was spiking into hundreds of milliseconds. We discovered that our cloud provider had placed the etcd volumes on general-purpose SSDs, which couldn't handle the write load. We planned a migration to dedicated I/O-optimized instances with local NVMe storage. After the migration, the p99 fsync duration dropped to under 10 milliseconds. We also implemented a Kubernetes CronJob to automatically run defragmentation on the etcd members one by one every weekend. These two changes dramatically improved the performance and reliability of the entire control plane, even as we continued to scale."

To visualize what a performant and resilient `etcd` setup looks like in a large-scale Kubernetes environment, here's an architectural diagram of a highly available `etcd` cluster:

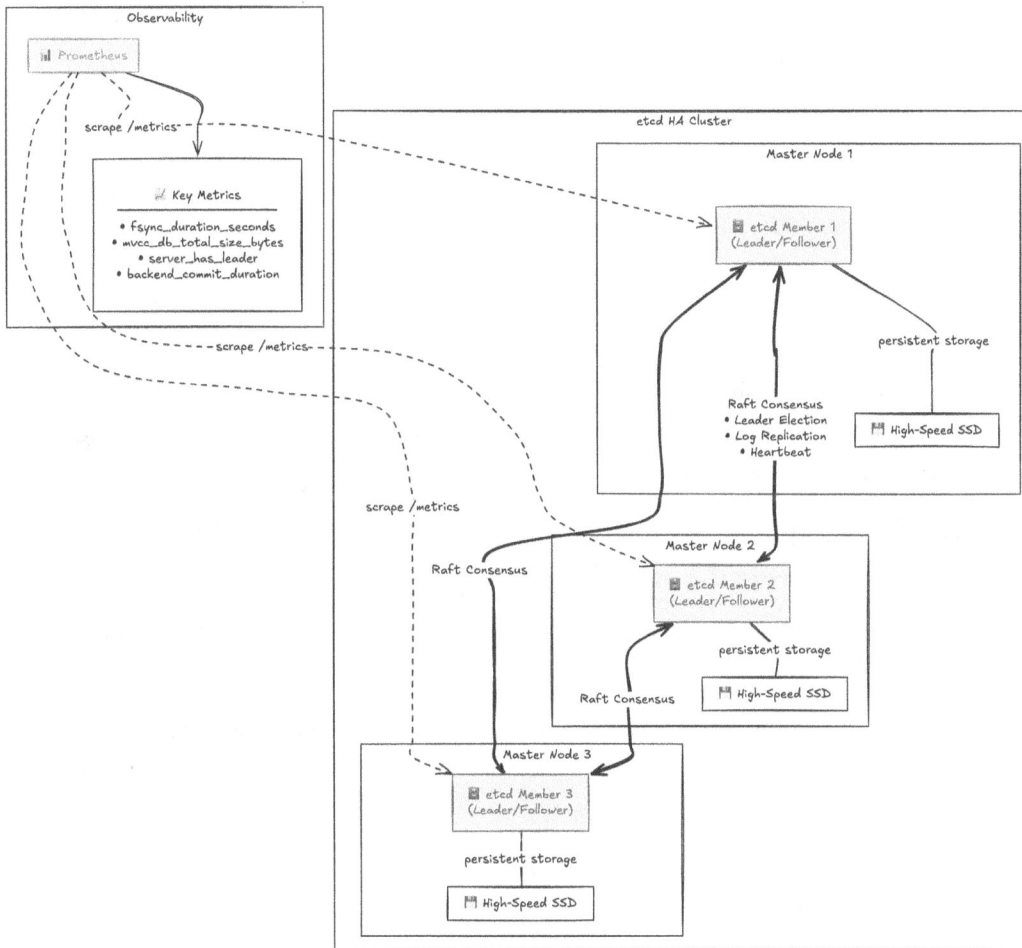

Figure 17.6 – An architectural diagram of a highly available etcd cluster

This diagram shows a three-node `etcd` cluster distributed across Kubernetes master nodes, each with high-speed SSD storage and full participation in Raft consensus operations. Each `etcd` instance can act as a leader or follower, with leader election, heartbeat, and log replication occurring between members. Prometheus scrapes metrics from each node to monitor critical health indicators such as write latency, database size, and election frequency. The diagram emphasizes the importance of local persistent storage, network stability between members, and continuous observability for detecting performance bottlenecks. Together, these design elements support the scale and reliability required for clusters with thousands of nodes.

> **Interview tip**
>
> **Question:** *When managing a large Kubernetes cluster, what is the single biggest hardware mistake that can degrade etcd performance, and what metric would you monitor to detect it?*
>
> **Answer:** The single biggest mistake is running `etcd` on slow storage such as magnetic disks or general-purpose network storage. `etcd` is extremely sensitive to I/O latency because every change in the cluster state is a transaction that must be synchronously written to its WAL. The key metric to monitor is `etcd_disk_wal_fsync_duration_seconds`. For a healthy cluster, the 99th percentile for this value should be under 10 milliseconds; spikes in this metric are a direct indicator of storage I/O issues.

With `etcd` performance stabilized, let's turn our attention to the nodes themselves—specifically, how to troubleshoot when a node repeatedly flips between `Ready` and `NotReady` states, signaling deeper issues in cluster health or infrastructure.

A node in the cluster is flapping between Ready and NotReady states. What's your troubleshooting process?

A flapping node is a serious issue that can cause cascading failures as Pods are repeatedly evicted and rescheduled.

What the interviewer is really asking: This probes your understanding of the node-to-control-plane relationship. Do you know how a node communicates its health? Can you diagnose system-level issues on the node itself, outside of Kubernetes?

Your strategy: "A flapping node means the kubelet on that node is failing to post its health status to the API server consistently. My process is to investigate both the node itself and its communication path:

1. **Check Kubelet logs**: My first step is to get onto the node itself. I'd check the kubelet's logs for errors. On most systems, this is done with `journalctl -u kubelet`. This often reveals the root cause directly, such as problems communicating with the container runtime or the API server.

2. **Check system resources**: A node under extreme resource pressure can cause the kubelet to become unresponsive. I'd check the following:

- **Memory**: Use `free -m`. Is swap being heavily used? Is the `oom-killer` active (`dmesg | grep -i "kill process"`)?
- **CPU**: Use `top` or `htop`. Is a runaway process consuming all the CPU, starving the kubelet?
- **Disk**: Use `df -h`. Is the root filesystem or `/var/lib/kubelet` full?
- **PIDs**: Use `sysctl kernel.pid_max` and `ps -eLf | wc -l`. Is the node running out of process IDs?

3. **Inspect PLEG health**: **PLEG** stands for **Pod Lifecycle Event Generator**. Its job is to keep the kubelet's view of Pods in sync with the container runtime. If PLEG is unhealthy, the kubelet can't report accurate Pod statuses. The kubelet logs will contain messages such as `PLEG is not healthy`. This often points to issues with the underlying container runtime (such as Docker or containerd).

4. **Check network connectivity**: Can the node reliably reach the API server? A simple `curl -k https://<api-server-ip>:<port>/healthz` from the node can test basic connectivity. Intermittent packet loss or firewall issues can cause the kubelet's heartbeats to be dropped, leading to a `NotReady` state.

Real-world example: "We had a node start flapping every few hours. Pods would get evicted, causing service disruptions. We logged into the node, and `top` showed memory and CPU were fine. However, checking the kubelet logs revealed a recurring message: `PLEG is not healthy`. Digging deeper, we found that the version of Docker running on that node had a known bug related to health checks on a high number of containers. This was causing the container runtime to become unresponsive, which in turn made PLEG unhealthy and caused the kubelet to miss its heartbeat. The fix was to drain the node, upgrade the Docker engine to a patched version, and bring it back into the cluster. The flapping stopped completely."

Mastering the art of troubleshooting is only half the battle. Identifying a root cause is critical, but your value as an engineer is multiplied by your ability to clearly and concisely communicate that problem, its impact, and its solution to your team, your leadership, and—most importantly for our purposes—your interviewer. A brilliant diagnosis delivered poorly can sound like a lucky guess. In the next section, we will shift our focus from the command line to the conversation, ensuring that when you find the problem, you can explain it in a way that builds confidence and demonstrates true expertise.

Technical communication mastery

Mastering the art of troubleshooting is only half the battle. Identifying a root cause is critical, but your value as an engineer is multiplied by your ability to clearly and concisely communicate that problem, its impact, and its solution to your team, your leadership, and—most importantly for our purposes—your interviewer. A brilliant diagnosis delivered poorly can sound like a lucky guess.

This section shifts our focus from the command line to the conversation. We will cover how to break down complex topics into simple, powerful explanations and how to frame your personal experiences as compelling stories that showcase your skills and cultural fit. When you can do both, you're not just answering questions; you're demonstrating true expertise and proving you're someone they want on their team.

How to communicate technical concepts effectively

The best engineers aren't just the ones who know the most; they're the ones who can make their knowledge accessible to others. In an interview, this means proving you truly understand a concept by explaining it simply.

The core technique: the Feynman method

Nobel Prize-winning physicist Richard Feynman believed that if you couldn't explain a concept in simple terms, you didn't understand it deeply enough. The Feynman technique is a powerful mental model for achieving this clarity. It consists of four steps:

1. **Choose a concept**: Pick a topic (e.g., Kubernetes Service).
2. **Teach it to a child**: Write down an explanation of the concept as if you were teaching it to a 12-year-old. Use simple language and avoid technical jargon.
3. **Identify gaps and simplify**: Review your explanation. Where did you stumble? Where did you have to use complex terms? This reveals the edges of your understanding. Go back to the source material to fill these gaps, then simplify your explanation further.
4. **Refine and use analogies**: Organize your simplified notes into a clear narrative. The secret weapon here is the *analogy*. Compare the complex technical concept to something familiar in the real world.

To see how the Feynman technique applies in a Kubernetes learning context, here's a visual walkthrough using the concept of a Kubernetes Service:

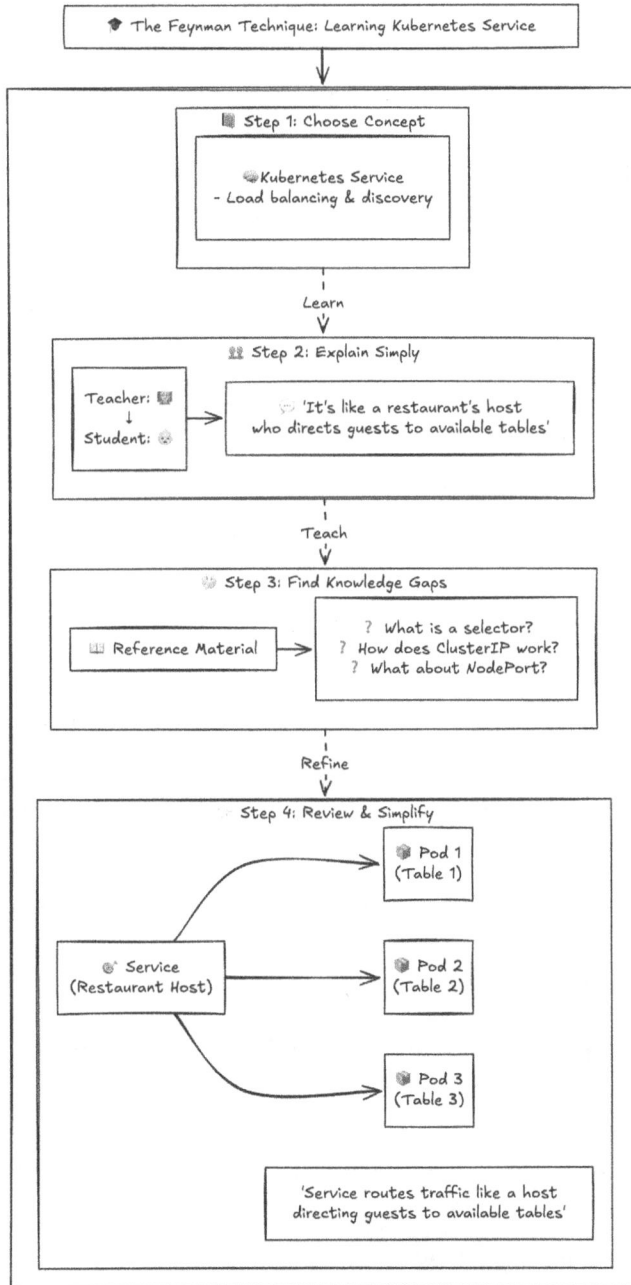

Figure 17.7 – Feynman technique

This diagram breaks down the four steps of the Feynman technique using a Kubernetes Service as the example concept. In *Step 1*, the learner chooses the concept—Kubernetes Service, focusing on load balancing and discovery. In *Step 2*, they simplify the idea using a relatable analogy: a restaurant host who directs guests to available tables, representing how a Service routes traffic to Pods. *Step 3* identifies knowledge gaps such as "What is a selector?" or "How does `ClusterIP` work?", prompting a return to reference material. Finally, in *Step 4*, the learner refines the explanation, incorporating the analogy and reinforcing clarity. The diagram shows how this method not only aids in understanding but also builds confidence in communicating complex ideas simply and effectively.

> **Interview tip**
>
> **Question**: *How would you answer "Tell me about your most challenging production outage" to demonstrate ownership and a blameless culture?*
>
> **Answer**: Using the STAR method, I would structure my answer to highlight systematic diagnosis and learning:
>
> - **(S) Situation**: "I was the on-call SRE for a checkout service when our primary database, a `StatefulSet`, became unresponsive at 2 AM, causing 503 errors."
>
> - **(T) Task**: "My goal was to restore service immediately to stop revenue loss and then identify the root cause to prevent a recurrence."
>
> - **(A) Action**: "I started a war room, diagnosed an OOM kill from kernel logs, and scaled up the `StatefulSet`'s memory to restore service in 15 minutes, all while communicating my actions."
>
> - **(R) Result**: "Service was restored quickly. In the blameless post-mortem I led, we found a memory leak, fixed it, and, more importantly, added a new proactive Prometheus alert to prevent similar outages.

Applying the Feynman technique in an interview

Let's apply this to a common, high-level interview question.

Can you explain what a Kubernetes Service is and why it's necessary?

What the interviewer is really asking: They're not just testing your textbook definition. They want to see whether you can articulate the *problem* that a Service solves. Do you understand the ephemeral nature of Pods? Can you explain the abstraction layer that a Service provides in a way that someone from the product team could understand?

Your strategy: Rather than opening with *"A Service is a Kubernetes object that...,"* start with the *why* (i.e., the problem the service solves) and use an analogy.

"Absolutely. The fundamental problem in Kubernetes is that Pods are unreliable individuals. They can crash, be rescheduled, or get scaled up and down, and every time a new Pod is created, it gets a new IP address. If you tried to have your application's frontend talk directly to a backend Pod's IP address, that connection would break the moment the backend Pod was replaced. It's like trying to call a friend who changes their phone number every five minutes. You'd never be able to reach them reliably.

This is the problem a Service solves. A Service acts like a permanent, stable phone number for a group of Pods. I like to use the analogy of a restaurant host:

- The Pods are the individual chefs in the kitchen. There might be one chef, or five if it's busy. They might change shifts (get replaced), but their job is to cook the food (run the application).
- The Service is the host at the front of the restaurant. The host has a single, well-known job, which is to take orders from customers and give them to an available chef.
- Customers (other applications) don't need to know which specific chef is working or how many there are. They just need to give their order to the host. The Service does the same thing: it takes incoming network traffic and automatically routes it to one of the healthy, ready Pods (chefs) behind it.

So, in short, a Service gives you a single, stable IP address and DNS name that load-balances traffic across a constantly changing group of Pods, making your application reliable and discoverable."

Behavioral and cultural fit: Applying the STAR method

Earlier in the chapter, we introduced the STAR method as the gold standard for structuring your experience. Now, let's apply it directly to the behavioral questions designed to uncover your soft skills, problem-solving approach, and how you handle pressure. Remember, the worst way to answer these questions is with a vague, generic statement. The best way is with a story.

Let's walk through common behavioral questions with STAR-based answers.

Tell me about your most challenging production outage.

What the interviewer is really asking: How do you perform under extreme pressure? Are you systematic in your troubleshooting? Do you take ownership? Do you learn from your mistakes (i.e., conduct a blameless post-mortem)?

Your strategy:

- **(S) Situation**: "In my previous role, I was the on-call engineer for a critical checkout service. At 2 AM on a Saturday, I received a `PagerDuty` alert that the service's API was returning 503 errors, and our primary database, a PostgreSQL instance running in a `StatefulSet`, was completely unresponsive."

- **(T) Task**: "My immediate goal was twofold: first, restore service to stop customer impact and revenue loss, and second, identify the root cause to ensure this wouldn't happen again."

- **(A) Action**: "I immediately started a *war room* chat and began my diagnosis. First, I checked the Pod status. The Postgres Pod was in a `CrashLoopBackOff` state. I ran `kubectl describe pod` and saw the last state had an exit code of 137, which I knew often indicates an OOM kill. I then checked the node's kernel logs using `dmesg` and confirmed that `oom-killer` had terminated the Postgres process. Looking at our monitoring dashboards, I saw a slow memory leak over the past 48 hours. To restore service immediately, I scaled up the `StatefulSet`'s memory request and limit in the manifest, applied it, and the Pod came up healthy. All the while, I was posting my findings and actions in the war room chat."

- **(R) Result**: "The service was fully restored within 15 minutes. In the following week, I led the postmortem. We identified that the memory leak was caused by an inefficient query. We optimized the query and deployed a fix. More importantly, I configured Prometheus with a new alert that would trigger if memory usage exceeded 80% for 30 minutes, giving the on-call engineer a chance to intervene *before* an outage occurred. The incident resulted in a more resilient system and better proactive monitoring."

Describe a time you had a disagreement with a colleague on a technical approach

What the interviewer is really asking: Are you a team player? Can you advocate for your ideas constructively? Can you disagree and commit? Are you driven by ego or by the best outcome for the project?

Your strategy:

- **(S) Situation**: "Our team was tasked with building a new internal logging pipeline. I advocated for using a standard stack of Fluentd for collection and Elasticsearch for storage. A senior engineer on the team strongly preferred a newer, lighter-weight solution called Loki."

- **(T) Task**: "My task was to ensure we chose the best tool for the long-term health of our platform, balancing performance, maintainability, and our team's existing skill set."

- **(A) Action**: "Instead of arguing based on opinion, I proposed we conduct a two-day **proof-of-concept (PoC)**. I set up a small-scale Fluentd/Elasticsearch pipeline, and my colleague set up the Loki pipeline. We defined objective criteria to measure: resource consumption, query latency, and configuration complexity. I presented my findings, highlighting that while Elasticsearch used more resources, its powerful query language was a better fit for our complex debugging needs. My colleague presented Loki's benefits, focusing on its efficiency and lower storage costs."

- **(R) Result**: "After reviewing the data, the team decided to go with Loki. Although it wasn't my initial proposal, I was happy with the data-driven decision. I was fully committed to the chosen path and helped build out the production Loki pipeline. The experience taught me the value of rapidly testing assumptions instead of debating them in the abstract."

Summary

Throughout this chapter, we have moved beyond simple command-line knowledge to build a holistic framework for succeeding in high-stakes Kubernetes interviews. The journey was twofold: mastering the *what* and the *how*.

First, we established systematic, repeatable frameworks for diagnosing the most common and challenging production issues. From a Pod stuck in Pending to a flapping node or a struggling etcd cluster, you now have a tiered mental model for troubleshooting. You've learned to start with kubectl describe for Pod-level issues, trace the network path from Ingress to Service to Pod for connectivity problems, and inspect system-level metrics for control plane instability. The goal was not to memorize error codes, but to build the diagnostic muscle memory of a seasoned SRE.

Second, and just as critically, we focused on communication. We introduced the STAR method as a powerful tool to structure your experience into compelling narratives. We then put it into practice, showing how to transform real-world outages, disagreements, and automation wins into stories that showcase your judgment and collaborative spirit. To complement this, we explored the Feynman technique as a method to deconstruct complex topics such as Kubernetes Services into simple, powerful analogies that demonstrate true understanding.

You have learned that a successful interview is a performance where technical depth and communication clarity are intertwined. You are now equipped not just to solve the problem, but to articulate the solution in a way that inspires confidence and proves your value. The final step is to see how these principles come to life in the real world.

Having built your arsenal of diagnostic frameworks and communication strategies, it's time to see them in action. The theoretical becomes tangible when viewed through the lens of experience. In the next chapter, we step away from the "how-to" and into the "what happened." We will hear directly from seasoned professionals who have navigated the same interviews you are preparing for, turning their hard-won lessons into your competitive advantage.

Unlock this book's exclusive benefits now

UNLOCK NOW

Scan this QR code or go to `https://packtpub.com/unlock`, then search for this book by name.

Note: Keep your purchase invoice ready before you start.

18

Interview Stories from Authors

Interviews for Kubernetes and DevOps roles often go beyond textbook questions and delve into real-world scenarios that test your problem-solving abilities, critical thinking, and adaptability.

In this chapter, we'll explore four real questions from DevOps interview experiences in which candidates encountered unusual, funny, and thought-provoking questions. These questions aren't just for entertainment; they highlight key areas of Kubernetes knowledge and provide smart strategies for handling challenging situations in interviews.

The authors have drawn from their extensive experience conducting and passing DevOps interviews. Whether you're preparing for your first Kubernetes-related interview or looking to sharpen your skills, these stories will offer valuable lessons and practical advice.

We will be covering the following four questions:

- How would you fit the entire internet into a single Kubernetes namespace?
- What would happen if you created an infinite number of Pods in Kubernetes?
- What's wrong with this Dockerfile?
- Your Kubernetes Pod keeps getting evicted. What do you do?

Let's tackle each one of them one by one.

How would you fit the entire internet into a single Kubernetes namespace?

This is one of the most unusual questions candidates might face. This question was asked in an interview in which Alex was participating as a candidate for the senior DevOps position. Let's see how you can use your Kubernetes fundamentals to handle it with composure. At first glance, this question might seem ridiculous. However, the interviewer often intends to see how well a candidate can break down a complex problem, understand resource limitations, and design scalable architectures within Kubernetes. It also tests the candidate's composure when faced with an unexpected question.

Possible incorrect answer

A less prepared candidate might panic and give an oversimplified answer, such as "That's not possible!," or try to joke their way out without providing an honest answer. While humor might occasionally work, failing to address the underlying technical concepts would show a lack of understanding. Responding with "It's too large for one namespace" without further elaboration shows limited knowledge of Kubernetes architecture.

Correct approach

A better response would involve a calm, structured approach:

1. **Clarify the question**: First, acknowledge the humor in the question, but then ask clarifying questions, such as the following:

    - "Are we discussing the internet's data, services, or infrastructure?"
    - "Is the focus on scaling limitations, namespace design, or Kubernetes resources?"

    This shows you're not rushing to an answer and instead want to understand the technical focus.

2. **Break down the problem**: You can then explain what a namespace is and how Kubernetes uses it:

    - "Kubernetes namespaces are used to partition resources within a cluster logically. Each namespace can host multiple services, deployments, and Pods, but they have limits based on the cluster's overall capacity."
    - Discuss limits such as memory, CPU, and the number of Pods a single namespace can manage effectively.

Next, relate this to Kubernetes scalability concepts:

- Explain that "While namespaces provide isolation within a Kubernetes cluster, Kubernetes itself imposes scaling limits."

- Detail how, rather than fitting everything into one namespace, "The internet's services would likely be distributed across multiple namespaces in a Kubernetes cluster for better management and resource allocation."

3. **Wrap up with scalability and microservices**: End with a discussion on how real-world scalable systems work. You could say something like, "In practice, even Kubernetes operates within physical limits. To scale a system such as the internet, you would likely rely on multiple clusters, distributed systems, and a microservices architecture."

The takeaway is that Kubernetes offers ways to manage resources effectively, but no single namespace could house an internet-sized workload without thoughtful partitioning across namespaces or clusters.

When preparing for interviews, be ready to break down even the most unusual questions. Interviewers often test your thought process, not necessarily looking for a definitive answer. Practice explaining basic Kubernetes concepts such as namespaces, resource limits, and scalability, and be comfortable asking clarifying questions to understand the interviewer's intention.

Building on the theme of handling hypotheticals confidently, here's another question that tests your understanding of Kubernetes resource limits and scheduling.

What would happen if you created an infinite number of Pods in Kubernetes?

Alex asked another tricky question in another interview for the tech lead position some time ago. This seemingly hypothetical question assesses a candidate's knowledge of Kubernetes resource management, scheduling, and scaling. The key to answering this question well is understanding the mechanics behind Kubernetes and its components.

Possible incorrect answer

The following are two possible wrong answers:

- "Kubernetes will crash if you create too many Pods."
- "It's impossible to create infinite Pods."

While technically not incorrect, these answers miss the opportunity to demonstrate more profound knowledge about how Kubernetes handles Pod creation, resource allocation, and autoscaling.

Correct approach

Here's how to structure a strong response:

1. Acknowledge the hypothetical nature of the question and say something like this:

    -   "Creating an infinite number of Pods isn't feasible due to the physical constraints of the cluster's resources, such as memory, CPU, and node availability."

    -   Clarify that "Kubernetes relies on the availability of resources to schedule and run Pods, and every Pod consumes some of these resources."

2. **Explain resource quotas and limits**, and dive into how Kubernetes controls resource consumption:

    -   "In practice, Kubernetes prevents resource exhaustion through quotas and limits. These limits define the maximum number of resources (e.g., CPU or memory) allocated to a namespace or a Pod."

    -   Explain how, if a Pod creation request exceeds the available resources, the Kubernetes scheduler cannot place the Pod on a node, resulting in the Pod staying in a pending state.

3. **Introduce cluster autoscaling**. Talk about scaling and how Kubernetes handles increasing workloads:

    -   "To manage growing workloads, Kubernetes uses the HPA, which scales Pods based on CPU/memory usage or custom metrics."

    -   Remember to clarify that even with autoscaling, there are still limits: "The Cluster Autoscaler can add nodes to a cluster, but only up to the limits of the available infrastructure."

4. **Highlight scheduler behavior**. Explain what happens when the scheduler is overwhelmed: "If you continuously attempt to create Pods beyond resource limits, Kubernetes may leave them in a Pending state. The Kubernetes scheduler will continuously try to allocate them, but will be constrained by available resources."

    Summarize by explaining the following aspects:

    -   "In a real-world scenario, trying to create infinite Pods would be prevented by Kubernetes limits, and any excess Pod requests would be left unscheduled."

    -   You could also discuss the impact on performance and stability by saying something like "Node exhaustion leading to evictions or degradation in cluster performance."

Interviewers want to see whether you can explain how Kubernetes handles scaling, resource management, and scheduling. Be familiar with the **HPA**, **Cluster Autoscaler**, **resource quotas**, and how the Kubernetes scheduler works to manage Pods. Practicing scenarios where resources are exhausted helps sharpen your troubleshooting skills and demonstrate practical knowledge. If you want to refresh your memory, return to *Part 2* (specifically *Chapters 3*, *4*, and *5*).

Switching gears slightly, interviewers may also test your practical skills beyond Kubernetes by examining your ability to optimize and debug Dockerfiles, which remain essential for building reliable containers.

What's wrong with this Dockerfile?

Viktor loves to ask this question in interviews, even though it's connected to Kubernetes at a high level and is a little bit outside the scope of this book. Let's review it. This question tests your attention to detail and understanding of writing optimized and efficient Dockerfiles, even when the file appears error-free. Interviewers want to see how well you can identify improvements and suggest best practices rather than simply pointing out obvious errors.

Possible incorrect answer

"There's nothing wrong with this Dockerfile; it looks fine." Although this might be factually true, it shows a lack of understanding of Dockerfile best practices and optimizations, which are critical in production Kubernetes environments.

Correct approach

Here's how to handle this:

1. **Start by reviewing the Dockerfile**: Explain that "Even if there are no errors, Dockerfiles can often be optimized for performance and security." Then, take time to review the file for areas of improvement, such as reducing image size, security vulnerabilities, and efficiency.

2. **Multi-stage builds**: One potential improvement could be to "Consider using multi-stage builds to reduce the final image size. This allows you to include only the necessary binaries in the final image while removing build-time dependencies."

3. **Highlight the importance of minimizing layers**: "Each instruction in a Dockerfile creates a new layer. By combining commands, reducing the number of layers can make the image smaller and more efficient."

4. **You might also mention the caching mechanism of containers**: "Optimize the order of instructions to use Docker's build cache. For example, placing instructions less likely to change (e.g., RUN apt-get update) earlier in the file allows Docker to cache these layers and avoid rebuilding them every time."

5. **Security best practices**: These are important, so consider recommending that "It's important to avoid running containers as root. A better practice would be to add a non-root user to the Dockerfile to run the application" and to "Regularly update base images and use minimal base images such as Alpine or distroless/scratch-based images to reduce the attack surface."

In Kubernetes-related interviews, be prepared to discuss Dockerfile best practices, even when no apparent errors are present. Focus on optimizations such as multi-stage builds, layer minimization, and security improvements. A strong understanding of these practices demonstrates that you can create production-ready container images.

Next, let's consider a troubleshooting scenario you're likely to encounter in real-world clusters and interviews alike: dealing with Pod evictions under resource pressure.

Your Kubernetes Pod keeps getting evicted. What do you do?

Alex and Viktor were asked this question in different ways, but the idea is simple—it tests your troubleshooting abilities, particularly in situations where resource limits are not immediately clear. Pod evictions happen when a node is under resource pressure, and the cluster cannot accommodate all running Pods. The interviewer is looking for your understanding of resource management, evictions, and how to respond to such scenarios effectively.

Possible incorrect answer

A typical incorrect response might focus solely on Pod restarts or overlook resource constraints. A candidate might say, "I'd check the Pod logs for errors or redeploy the Pod." While checking logs can be helpful, redeploying a Pod that has been evicted due to resource constraints doesn't address the root issue. The Pod will likely keep getting evicted if the underlying resource issue isn't resolved.

Correct approach

The correct approach involves methodical troubleshooting and paying attention to resource limits and node pressure:

1. **Check resource pressure:** Start by explaining that Pod evictions typically occur when a node experiences resource pressure, such as CPU or memory shortage. You can say something such as, "I would first check the node's resource usage using `kubectl describe nodes <node_name>` or monitor metrics through Prometheus/Grafana to see whether the node is under resource strain."

2. **Check Pod resource requests and limits:**

   - "The next step would be to inspect the resource requests and limits defined for the evicted Pod using `kubectl describe pods <pod_name>`."

   - "If the Pod requests too much memory or CPU, or the node is oversubscribed, I might lower the resource requests or assign the Pod to a less stressed node."

3. **Discuss common node conditions that lead to evictions:** "If the node is experiencing disk pressure or insufficient memory, this can trigger evictions. I would check the node's status conditions and event logs for any signs of resource depletion."

4. **Node autoscaler and quotas:** "If this is a persistent issue, I would look into adjusting resource quotas or enabling the Cluster Autoscaler to add nodes when resources are insufficient."

5. **Finish by summarizing:** "Pod evictions are often tied to resource management issues within the cluster. You can prevent frequent evictions by understanding node pressure and adjusting Pod resource settings."

Pod eviction is a common problem in Kubernetes (especially in significant and complex clusters), and handling it requires a good understanding of resource allocation. Be ready to explain how you would troubleshoot resource pressure, investigate node conditions, and adjust resource requests and limits. Understanding how the Cluster Autoscaler or Karpenter works can also demonstrate a more advanced resource management level in Kubernetes.

Summary

In this chapter, we explored some real-life interview stories that showed how tricky and unexpected Kubernetes-related DevOps questions can be. These stories weren't just for fun—they helped show the challenges you might face in an interview and how thinking carefully and staying calm can help you give great answers. Each story provided practical tips that will help you prepare for your interview. Even the strangest questions can have simple, logical answers if you know the core concepts.

As we close this book, it's important to remember that Kubernetes is a significant and sometimes complex tool. Still, with the proper preparation, you can feel confident in using it and discussing it in interviews. Interviews are not just about having the correct answer—they're about showing that you understand how things work and can solve problems, even under pressure. By learning from the experiences and advice you share, you're better equipped to do just that.

Kubernetes will keep growing in importance, and so will the demand for skilled professionals. Keep practicing, stay curious, and remember that every challenge is a chance to improve. With everything you've learned, you're on the right path to becoming a strong candidate in Kubernetes and DevOps.

‹packt›

packtpub.com

Subscribe to our online digital library for full access to over 7,000 books and videos, as well as industry leading tools to help you plan your personal development and advance your career. For more information, please visit our website.

Why subscribe?

- Spend less time learning and more time coding with practical eBooks and Videos from over 4,000 industry professionals
- Improve your learning with Skill Plans built especially for you
- Get a free eBook or video every month
- Fully searchable for easy access to vital information
- Copy and paste, print, and bookmark content

At www.packtpub.com, you can also read a collection of free technical articles, sign up for a range of free newsletters, and receive exclusive discounts and offers on Packt books and eBooks.

Other Books You May Enjoy

If you enjoyed this book, you may be interested in these other books by Packt:

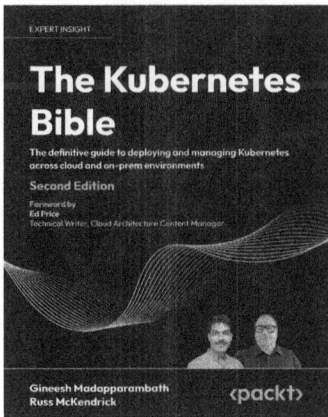

The Kubernetes Bible

Gineesh Madapparambath, Russ McKendrick

ISBN: 978-1-83546-824-1

- Secure your Kubernetes clusters with advanced techniques
- Implement scalable deployments and autoscaling strategies
- Design and learn to build production-grade containerized applications
- Manage Kubernetes effectively on major cloud platforms (GKE, EKS, AKS)
- Utilize advanced networking and service management practices
- Use Helm charts and Kubernetes Operators for robust security measures
- Optimize in-cluster traffic routing with advanced configurations
- Enhance security with techniques like Immutable ConfigMaps and RBAC

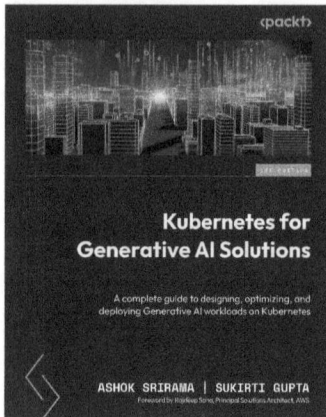

Kubernetes for Generative AI Solutions

Ashok Srirama, Sukirti Gupta

ISBN: 978-1-83620-992-8

- Explore GenAI deployment stack, agents, RAG, and model fine-tuning
- Implement HPA, VPA, and Karpenter for efficient autoscaling
- Optimize GPU usage with fractional allocation, MIG, and MPS setups
- Reduce cloud costs and monitor spending with Kubecost tools
- Secure GenAI workloads with RBAC, encryption, and service meshes
- Monitor system health and performance using Prometheus and Grafana
- Ensure high availability and disaster recovery for GenAI systems
- Automate GenAI pipelines for continuous integration and delivery

Packt is searching for authors like you

If you're interested in becoming an author for Packt, please visit authors.packt.com and apply today. We have worked with thousands of developers and tech professionals, just like you, to help them share their insight with the global tech community. You can make a general application, apply for a specific hot topic that we are recruiting an author for, or submit your own idea.

Share your thoughts

Now you've finished *Cracking the Kubernetes Interview*, we'd love to hear your thoughts! Scan the QR code below to go straight to the Amazon review page for this book and share your feedback or leave a review on the site that you purchased it from.

https://packt.link/r/1835460038

Your review is important to us and the tech community and will help us make sure we're delivering excellent quality content.

Index

www.ingramcontent.com/pod-product-compliance
Lightning Source LLC
Chambersburg PA
CBHW081216220326
41598CB00037B/6797